MODERN GROUP BOOK IV

Sensitivity Through
Encounter and Marathon

BOOKS BY DRS. KAPLAN AND SADOCK

Comprehensive Textbook of Psychiatry
Alfred M. Freedman and Harold I. Kaplan, Editors

Studies in Human Behavior
Alfred M. Freedman and Harold I. Kaplan, General Editors

Modern Synopsis of Comprehensive Textbook of Psychiatry
Harold I. Kaplan, Benjamin J. Sadock, and Alfred M. Freedman

Comprehensive Group Psychotherapy
Harold I. Kaplan and Benjamin J. Sadock, Editors

Modern Group Books
Harold I. Kaplan and Benjamin J. Sadock, Editors

HAROLD I. KAPLAN

Harold I. Kaplan received an undergraduate degree from Columbia University and an M.D. from the New York Medical College. He trained in psychiatry at the Kingsbridge Veterans Hospital and Mount Sinai Hospital in New York and became a Diplomate of the American Board of Psychiatry and Neurology in 1957; presently he is an Associate Examiner of the American Board. He began the practice and teaching of psychiatry and was certified in psychoanalytic medicine at the New York Medical College in 1954 where he became Professor of Psychiatry and Director of Psychiatric Training and Education in 1961. He is Attending Psychiatrist at Metropolitan Hospital Center, Flower and Fifth Avenue Hospitals and Bird S. Coler Hospital. He is the Principal Investigator of ten National Institute of Mental Health training programs, specializing in the areas of undergraduate and graduate psychiatric education as well as the training of women in medicine. He is the author of over seventy scientific papers and co-author and co-editor of the books listed on this page.

BENJAMIN J. SADOCK

Benjamin J. Sadock received his A.B. from Union College and his M.D. from New York Medical College. He trained at Bellevue Psychiatric Hospital. During his military service as an Air Force psychiatrist he was also on the faculty of Southwestern Medical School. Dr. Sadock became a Diplomate of the American Board of Psychiatry and Neurology in 1966 and is an Assistant Examiner for the American Board. Currently Associate Professor of Psychiatry and Director of the Division of Group Process at New York Medical College, Dr. Sadock directs the training program for group therapists and is Chief of Continuing Education in Psychiatry, Chief Psychiatric Consultant to the student health service and co-director of the Sexual Therapy Center. He is on staff of Flower and Fifth Avenue Hospitals, Metropolitan Hospital, and the New York State Psychiatric Institute. Dr. Sadock is active in numerous psychiatric organizations, an officer of the New York County District Branch of the American Psychiatric Association, a Fellow of the New York Academy of Medicine, and has written and lectured extensively in general psychiatry and group psychotherapy. He is co-editor with Dr. Harold I. Kaplan of *Comprehensive Group Psychotherapy* (1971) and co-author with Drs. Alfred M. Freedman and Harold I. Kaplan of *Modern Synopsis of Comprehensive Textbook of Psychiatry* (1972).

MODERN GROUP BOOK IV

Sensitivity Through Encounter and Marathon

Edited by

HAROLD I. KAPLAN, M.D.

Professor of Psychiatry and Director of Psychiatric Education,
New York Medical College, New York, New York

and

BENJAMIN J. SADOCK, M.D.

Associate Professor of Psychiatry and Director,
Division of Group Process, New York Medical College,
New York, New York

1972

E.P. DUTTON & CO., INC.
NEW YORK

Published simultaneously in Canada by Clarke, Irwin & Company Limited,
Toronto and Vancouver

SBN: 0-525-03973-2

The editors express their appreciation to the following persons, publishers and publications for permission to reprint portions of the works cited.

Aldine-Atherton, Inc. for "The Marathon Group," by G. R. Bach, reprinted from Hendrik M. Ruitenbeek, editor, *Group Therapy Today* (New York: Atherton Press, 1969); copyright © 1969 by Atherton Press. Reprinted by permission of the author and Aldine-Atherton, Inc.

Bruner/Mazel, Inc. for "The Use of Videotape in the Integrated Treatment of Individuals, Couples, Families, and Groups in Private Practice," by Milton M. Berger, M.D., reprinted from *Videotape Techniques in Psychiatric Training and Treatment*, Milton M. Berger, M.D., editor. Bruner/Mazel, Inc., New York, 1970.

Dr. Herbert Holt for the unpublished essay, "Existential Group Therapy: A Phenomenological Methodology for Psychiatry."

International Journal of Group Psychotherapy for "Sexual Acting Out in Groups," by the members of the Workshop in Group Psychoanalysis of New York: A. Wolf, R. Bross, S. Flowerman, J. Greene, A. Kadis, H. Leopold, N. Locke, I. Milburg, H. Mullan, S. Obers, and H. Rosenbaum. *International Journal of Group Psychotherapy*, Vol. 4, pp. 369-380, 1954.

for "Accelerated Interaction: A Time Limited Approach on the Brief Intensive Approach," by Frederick H. Stoller. *International Journal of Group Psychotherapy*, Vol. 18, pp. 220-235, 1968.

for "Group Therapy and the Small Group Field: An Encounter," by Morris Parloff. *International Journal of Group Psychotherapy*, Vol. 20, pp. 267-304, 1970.

International Universities Press for "Group Therapy with Alcoholics," by A. Stein, M.D. and Eugene Friedman, Ph.D., Chapter III of *Fields of Group Psychotherapy*, S. R. Slavson, editor. International Universities Press, 1956.

American Psychiatric Association for "Phoenix House: Therapeutic Communities for Drug Addicts," by M. S. Rosenthal and D. V. Biase, *Hospital and Community Psychiatry*, Vol. 20, p. 27, 1969.

W. W. Norton & Co., Inc., and the Hogarth Press Ltd. for an excerpt from *An Outline of Psycho-Analysis*, Volume XXIII of Standard Edition of Sigmund Freud, revised and edited by James Strachey. Copyright 1949 by W. W. Norton & Co., Inc., and copyright © 1969 by the Institute of Psychoanalysis and Alix Strachey.

The Williams & Wilkins Co. for an excerpt from "Group Therapy in Married Couples," by Helen Papanek, M.D., reprinted from *Comprehensive Group Psychotherapy*, Harold I. Kaplan and Benjamin J. Sadock, editors. Copyright © 1971 by The Williams & Wilkins Co.

for an excerpt from "Videotape Feedback in Group Setting," by F. Stoller. *Journal of Nervous and Mental Disorders*, Vol. 148, No. 4, pp. 457-466.

Seymour Lawrence/Delacorte Press for an excerpt from *Cat's Cradle* by Kurt Vonnegut, Jr. Copyright © 1963 by Kurt Vonnegut, Jr. A Seymour Lawrence Book/Delacorte Press. Reprinted by permission of the publisher.

Contents

Preface

The emergence of group psychotherapy within the past two decades constitutes one of the most significant and extraordinary developments in the field of psychiatry. Gradually during this period, but particularly within the past five years, group therapy has come to be chosen for the treatment of a widening range of patients with highly diverse problems. Concurrently, professionals and laymen alike see a growing interest in the relationship of group therapy to sociocultural and educational concepts, processes, and systems. Predictably, these theoretical developments are accompanied by the development of myriad therapeutic approaches which vary with respect not only to their underlying philosophy but also to the planning and conduct of treatment.

Psychotherapy is an art as well as a science. What is taught via the lecture hall or seminar room constitutes just one aspect of the teaching curriculum. Training in psychotherapy must also include clinical exercises performed under the supervision of an experienced clinician who acts as a model for the student. The editors' commitment to this project, and its concomitant goals, evolved from their extensive experience as both educators and clinicians. The editors' special interest in group psychotherapy as a treatment technique, and an awareness of the need for more intensive training in this discipline to ensure its continued growth and development, led to the establishment, at the New York Medical College, of the first medical-school-affiliated postgraduate certification program in group psychotherapy. In addition, they have participated in the organization of training programs in group therapy for workers in other mental health disciplines —psychology, psychiatric social work, and psychiatric nursing.

The stated goal of this series—to provide a survey of current theoretical and therapeutic trends in this field—carries with it the obligation to pursue an eclectic orientation and to present as comprehensive an account of events at every level of its development as is possible. The organization and orientation of this series attempts to provide a comprehensive survey of the theories, hypotheses, and therapeutic techniques which dominate contemporary group practice. There are no final answers, as yet, to the problems and issues which currently face group psychotherapy. But we may help to identify these problems and issues and place them in proper perspective.

This book is one of a series of paperback volumes based on *Comprehensive Group Psychotherapy,* which we previously edited. New articles have been written for each of these volumes and certain subjects have been updated or eliminated in an effort to reach a wider audience. Invitations to participate were extended to those workers who have made major and original contributions to the field of group psychotherapy and who are acknowledged experts in a particular area of theory and/or practice. Thus the preparation of this series afforded the editors a unique opportunity to engage in a stimulating interchange of ideas and to form many rewarding personal relationships. As a result, what would appear to have been an ardous undertaking has in fact been a most gratifying experience.

The editors have received dedicated and valuable help from many people to whom they wish to express their appreciation. For their secretarial and editorial help, we would like to thank Robert Gelfand, Sylvia Houzell, Mercedes Paul, Paulene Demarco, Louise Marshall, and in particular Lois Baken, who coordinated these efforts. Spe-cial thanks are extended to our publishers, E. P. Dutton, and to our outstanding editor, Robert Zenowich.

Finally, the editors wish to express their appreciation to Virginia Sadock, M.D., who acted in the capacity of assistant to the editors and assumed the multitudinous tasks of that office with grace and charm

HAROLD I. KAPLAN, M.D.

BENJAMIN J. SADOCK, M.D.

Introduction

The encounter movement is probably the fastest growing group technique in society today. Like group psychotherapy, which began in this country in the early 1900's, it is a distinctly American phenomenon. The expansion of the encounter movement can be attributed to two streams in American culture. Americans have always prized rugged individualism while simultaneously valuing collective attempts to solve common problems. This characteristic is reflected in the conventional therapy group, which is exceedingly tolerant of deviant behavior provided the individual patient attends to the common group goal of achieving mental health.

Conversely the American culture is now displaying the breakdown of what might be called society's natural groupings—the family and organized religion. The nuclear family has contracted; it no longer includes nearby grandparents and other relatives in close interactions. At the same time, religion has become fragmented and has lost, to a great extent, its relevance for a large segment of our society.

Man, a gregarious animal possessing a herd instinct, requires a new social network to gratify important needs that the culture no longer provides. Perhaps it is inevitable that the artificial small group has become the latest "natural" grouping; for both the therapy group and the encounter group recreate interactional proximity in a variety of ways. Like religion and families, however, the groups that have evolved to replace them take a variety of forms, each with its own standards, beliefs, mores, and culture.

Psychotherapy or Encounter?

The psychotherapy group and the encounter group may both meet on a regular basis, and have seven to nine members and a nominal leader. But they differ in a variety of ways—the quality of leadership, the personality functioning of the membership, and the goals of both leader and members.

The most important difference between the two is that, traditionally, the psychotherapy group is composed of individuals who are suffering from a variety of emotional problems. The leader of such a group should be a qualified mental health professional trained in group psychotherapy —a psychiatrist, psychologist, or psychiatric social worker. The goal of the group should be equally clear—correction or amelioration of personality problems.

The encounter group—a term used here to include the sensitivity training group, T-group, sensory awareness group, and similar groups—should be composed of people free of serious mental derangement. The encounter group does not offer therapy; rather, it offers instruction and education about one's own psychological processes and the processes inherent in group formation. As Gottschalk and his colleagues have pointed out, however, distinctions between the two types of groups have become blurred. Ideally, the encounter group participant should be reasonably well-integrated and possess sufficient mental health to learn from experience. He will be confronted with, among other things, behavioral characteristics that, although not pathological, may interfere to some extent with his interpersonal relaionships.

Because of these factors, referral to one experience or the other cannot be haphazard. The emotionally ill person should not be referred to an encounter group with the expectation that he will achieve relief from his suffering. Conversely, the healthy person should not be referred to a therapeutic group when his expectations are for instruction and education.

Among the recent innovations in encounter methods has been the introduction of a number of nonverbal techniques to stimulate the learning process. At the present time these techniques are so numerous that they defy description, and a careful distinction must be made between a technique and a gimmick. The techniques—or gimmicks—run the gamut, and may include one person falling backward into the arms of another group member or the leader to test his ability to trust, or having a member pound a pillow to express aggressive impulses of which he may or may not be aware, to having two members hand-wrestle in order to realize their competitive strivings. Applied indiscriminately, they are best called gimmicks; applied with discretion and with a particular purpose related to a particular set of circumstances, they can be called techniques.

The competent encounter group leader should have the requisite knowledge of the value of these individual dynamics. The line between psychotherapy and education is often a thin one. Training is of crucial importance. The untrained leader or one with only a superficial knowledge of psychodynamic and psychiatric diagnosis could precipitate an adverse psychological reaction to what otherwise might be a valuable educational experience.

History

The encounter movement, which began in the late 1940's, is an outgrowth of the group psychotherapy movement, which began around the turn of the century. Despite the differences between the two techniques and their different theoretical orientation, they share the same historical roots. Therefore an understanding of the evolution of group psychotherapy as a treatment modality is a prerequisite for the understanding of the current status of the encounter movement. This essential background material is provided in the chapter by Anthony, an overview of group psychotherapy's history. The chapter's contents extend well beyond the traditional chronological account of events. In it, the author synthesizes events to form a cohesive whole, describing and placing in proper perspective the innovative contributions of behavioral scientists to a variety of disciplines.

Many Techniques Available

In logical sequence is a chapter by Spotnitz, who provides a comparison of different types of group approaches. The very fact that so many group techniques are available to the clinician suggests that no one technique is superior to the others. Nevertheless, the determination that a particular method is suitable for a given person should be based on a comparative evaluation of the diverse methods available in terms of specific parameters. The leader must take into consideration the ideal goals he hopes to achieve for the participant; that is, the patient's optimal level of functioning consonant with his level of ego strength; his motivations for participation; and such practical considerations as his financial resources and current life situation. The leader can then compare the various group approaches in relation to the depth of personality exploration desired. Certain group psychoanalytic approaches are geared to produce significant personality changes in much the same way that individual psychoanalysis provides an opportunity for personality reconstruction. Other methods such as the behavioral or transactional group therapies place emphasis on symptom removal and do not stress the relationship of these symptoms to past events in the patient's life.

Treatment Selection

Some individuals may not be eligible for an encounter group at all and can best be placed in a treatment situation, either group or individual. To make such a determination, the leader must understand the essential differences between these modalities as well as their interfaces.

The specific techniques—such as sensitivity training, marathon, or encounter group—are in their infancy and do not, strictly speaking, fall within the purview of group psychotherapy. But despite fundamental conceptual differences, there are important similarities between these new methods and traditional group psychotherapy. These concepts are discussed in the chapter by Gottschalk and Davidson, who provide a comprehensive view of the field as it now exists. Specific techniques—their indications, applications, and potential hazards—are described in great depth.

Jacob Moreno is identified mainly with the technique of psychodrama, which he introduced into the United States in 1925. But he was also one of the European pioneers in group psychotherapy, who described his use of a variety of group approaches as early as 1910. The Theatre of Spontaneous Man, the vehicle for psychodrama, role-playing, and encounter, was first set up in Vienna. There Moreno encouraged the acting-out of problem situations to achieve a heightened awareness of conflict and its possible resolution. In his group work, the therapist (called the director) encourages the patient (called the subject) to express himself spontaneously by enacting a role from his past experience or his current life situation. Other members of the group (called the audience) may comment and so be of help; or they may see one of their own problems portrayed and so be helped. The chapter by Moreno describing his technique represents the most up-to-date exposition of

psychodrama as it exists. Actual case reports of psychodramatic sessions are included and provide vivid demonstrations of the method.

Marathon groups were developed by George Bach and Frederick Stoller whose original papers describing the technique are included in this volume. The marathon —also known as accelerated interaction— is a group meeting that lasts from 8 to 72 hours, although some sessions last for a week. The session is interrupted only for eating and sleeping. The leader works for the development of intimacy and the open expression of feelings. The time-extended group experience culminates in an intense feeling of excitement and elation. Most persons who have participated in such an experience report a subjective case of elation and of having received some benefit. But it should be noted that no adequate studies have been made about the factors that account for this subjective appraisal, and, most important, the long term results of such an experience have not been evaluated.

In the first of its series of Task Force Reports, which are geared to "the state of the art in a problem area of current concern to the psychiatric profession, to related disciplines and often to the public," the American Psychiatric Association (APA) dealt with the encounter movement. The report described what was already well-known about the quality of leadership—that many group leaders lack formal training or institutional backing, and that they "recruit participants by word of mouth or through written advertisement." The methods of the leaders vary widely, and they range from experienced clinicians to those who have undergone a "mystical conversion" as a result of an encounter group experience and who want others to share a similar one. Most ominously, the report noted that other group leaders were motivated by "personal needs for power, influence, sex, money or self-aggrandizement." One of the most up-to-date and authoritative summaries of these issues to be found is the paper by Parloff, who discusses the small-group field and its implication for society as a whole.

Summary

All psychological techniques are valuable when they are practiced appropriately. When practiced improperly or without adequate control, they are potentially dangerous. Without adequate standards there is no protection for the participants *or* the practitioner.

Sensitivity Through Encounter and Marathon

1

The History of Group Psychotherapy

E. James Anthony, M.D.

INTRODUCTION

History can be written in at least two distinctly different ways. The historian can choose to tell it as it really happened (*wie es geschehen ist*, in Ranke's famous phrase) or to reconstruct it in the context of present-day theory and practice. The first method has little dynamic value for the clinical historian, and there is no convincing reason why one should have to contemplate past ideas solely in terms of the *Zeitgeist* prevailing at the time. Moreover, it tends to place history firmly and disjunctively in the past, with little or no bearing on the present except as interest or illustration.

The second historical approach was first opened up by Nietzsche in his *Unseasonable Reflexions* and carried, as so much of his work did, psychoanalytic undertones. According to him, the reconstruction of the past should not be an end in itself but the means of relating the past to the present in a meaningful and operational way. This process could be understood as the historian's equivalent to the transference. This approach assumed that the historian could and should live contemporaneously in the two worlds of the past and the present. In fact, only by linking these two together dynamically could the historical past be made to have both relevance and value in the present. Sometimes surprisingly, the apparently demoded insights of the past could be refurbished for current use. The student of history frequently sees how the present unconsciously plagiarizes the past.

This dynamic viewpoint ensures that history becomes an indispensable handmaiden of on-going life rather than remaining monolithically isolated as a monument to the past. It allows what is now to transact with what was then, and it finds an equal place for both within the continuous historical process. In this crucial scientific dialogue between past and present, the present must take and keep the initiative. The present should in no way become a slave to the past in the manner of tradition; it must be free to make full use of the past for its own evolving purposes.

The essence of the dynamic historical method is to select the significant facts of history and arrange them within a temporal sequence. Inevitably, some manipulation is involved in this selection and arrangement, but there must be no distortion of the facts. The clinical historian must be ready to admit that, although he may have a bias in his arrangement of facts, he is still able to recognize other perspectives, even when they contradict his own thesis. Like the good therapist, he should be able to see in this multiplicity of incompatible perspectives not failure or foolishness but the very richness of life.

The never-ending discovery and rediscovery of past developments by present-day workers are the expression of a dialectic that will last as long as the particular discipline concerned remains viable and growing. On the other hand, the workers who disconnect themselves from the past not only miss out on the enrichment and self-revelation provided by the past but are also fated, if Freud and Santayana are right, to

1

repeat compulsively the past while deluding themselves that they are breaking new theoretical or technical ground. An attentive awareness of past modes of feeling, thinking, and doing—what Meinecke refers to as historicism—helps to safeguard against this proclivity.

It would be a naive conceit on the part of the historian to suppose that he can reduce the conglomerated past to a unified and linear development. In this discipline, as in all other disciplines, there is always an irreducible plurality of operating systems. It is, therefore, important to preserve a wide-angled viewpoint on all the global conspectuses that have existed within the historical evolution—whether actual, factual, mythological, or fantasied—granting to each the recognition of its particularity.

There is another reason for mapping out the topology of the historical field. By doing so, the worker can develop what Whitehead, in a different context, aptly termed graded envisagement. He can become aware of a system of kinship within the general population of ideas belonging to his discipline. For example, the group worker can begin to realize that the disparate concepts of Gestalt therapy and analytic group therapy not only have antecedents in common but are often in close theoretical relationship, separated only by semantic confusion. Since all these ideas fall more or less within the same family system, it is not altogether surprising that intellectual totems and taboos are set up, so that it seems to become something horrendous to mate what are apparently neighboring ideas. Many theorists, having swallowed their own intellectual totems, react to closely related ideas as if they were incestuous.

The ultimate lesson from history, therefore, is that for coherent, logical development in a discipline, one must constantly and consistently remember where he came from and where he is going. The past is conglomerate, complex, confabulatory, and conflictual, but it is incumbent on every worker to resolve these perplexities and complexities for himself and, by so doing, discover his own professional identity and ultimate purpose. Each group psychotherapist must become his own historian and

thread his way with open-mindedness and relative impartiality through the shoals of psychobiologically improbable, mythological, mystical, and paralogical ideas of the past and present, asking his own questions and seeking his own answers within the totality of what is known or imagined. He has to undertake this job for himself, since no one can do it for him.

The scientific mind that is brought up and nurtured on history obtains an equanimity and objectivity that becomes characteristic of the scientist in all his dealings. Bronowski, in describing how scientists communicate, has this to say:

They do not make wild claims, they do not cheat, they do not try to persuade at any cost, they appeal neither to prejudice nor to authority, they are often frank about their ignorance, their disputes are fairly decorous, they do not confuse what is being argued with race, politics, sex or age, and they listen patiently to the young and to the old who both know everything.

Patience, that essential scientific virtue, can come not only from listening to patients but also from listening to history.

GROUP PSYCHOLOGY

The beginning is always difficult, wrote Schopenhauer. This is true for birth, for writing history, and for history itself. Once, however, one recognizes that the beginning is never really the beginning and that there is always a prehistory antedating every start, the conflict of inertia can be solved. One can deal with group psychology and, by means of it, find his way imperceptibly, if the historical development holds true, into the field of group psychotherapy.

World War I proved to be a great impetus to the development of group psychology and World War II, to the development of group psychotherapy. This relationship to war cannot be regarded as entirely accidental. In war, individual man is forced into groups of all sizes and structures for reasons of survival. In war, he loses much of his identity and becomes better known for fighting, rationing, and security purposes as a number. The understanding and maintenance of group morale becomes a critical factor in the country's struggle for existence. In World War I, various group psychologists stepped forward to meet this pressing need.

A pioneer in this field, and one of the most scintillating intellects of his time, was Wilfred Trotter, a neurosurgeon who, in the middle of World War I, published a remarkable document on the herd instinct in peace and war. Whether there is such an organizing instinct in man has been much debated and is still in dispute, but Trotter developed the insight that it is both logical and biological for human groups to form if one regards the group as a continuation of the multicellular character of all higher organisms. The instinct to come together and develop multifunctional skills for the sake of individual and group survival would be in keeping with evolutionary trends. Later authors also pointed to needs for pairing and fighting as basic elements in group formation, but they gave psychodynamic reasons.

Le Bon and the Popular Mind

It was Le Bon who inadvertently gave the group a bad name to begin with, in 1920. He cannot be blamed for this, since he was careful to specify that his descriptions applied to large groups or crowds that are essentially unorganized or under the mysterious and irresistible influence of charismatic leadership. The capacity of a leader to sway a crowd in the direction of his own purpose—playing on its suggestibility, its exaggerated emotionalism, and its credulity—has never been as subtly portrayed as in Mark Antony's brilliant display of demagoguery in Shakespeare's *Julius Caesar*.

According to Le Bon, the person who joins a group, especially a large group, sacrifices something of his precious individuality. He becomes more suggestible and, therefore, more susceptible to the contagion of neighboring minds. Le Bon's description of the group mind has many of the characteristics of the child, the primitive, and the impulse-ridden psychopath. The group mind is illogical, intolerant, prejudiced, rigid, uninhibited, and submissive to any dominant force that exerts its authority.

If this were even partly true, it would follow that the group is more susceptible to therapeutic influence than the individual and, therefore, a better bet with regard to treatment. Freud, however, pointed out that this detrimental and depreciatory appraisal of the group mind reflects the contempt with which certain thinkers view the masses. This appraisal is certainly not very different from prejudices characteristic of the aristocratic elements of society at all times.

Other critics, such as Kraskovic, held the view that group enthusiasm would bring about the most splendid achievements. The question of who was right gave place, with further consideration, to the view that perhaps both could be right and that the group contained within itself the seeds of both success and failure.

McDougall and the Group Mind

In 1920, McDougall started out from this apparent contradiction and found a solution for it in the factor of organization. In his understanding, there are two psychologies of the group, the one dealing with an unorganized group and the other with a group that is organized.

McDougall's judgment of the unorganized group is as severe as Le Bon's. He, too, saw it as emotional, impulsive, violent, fickle, inconsistent, irresolute, suggestible, irresponsible, and at times almost like a wild beast. But this is not the whole story. A marked change occurs when the group is organized and task-oriented. The collective mental life is then raised to a higher level, and some of the psychological disadvantages of group formation are removed. In addition, the exaltation or intensification of emotion that takes place in every group member and that stirs each one to a degree that they seldom attained under any other conditions can now be used for great achievement.

The "primitive sympathetic response," which is somewhat similar to Le Bon's "contagion," can be harnessed for better purpose if five main organizational conditions are established: group continuity, a system of group relationships, the stimulus of intergroup rivalries, the development of traditions, and the differentiation and specialization of functions. A sixth condition that can be added to these five is the emergence of leadership, a phenomenon that later workers have tended to focus on, since it has special bearing on the therapist's role in group psychotherapy.

The problem for the group psychotherapist using McDougall's frame of reference is how to further the organization desirable for optimal collective life and at the same time make therapeutic use of the primitive sympathetic response that brings with it the mutative affective experience. Throughout the subsequent history of group psychotherapy, workers would be torn between the therapeutic potential of the group mind and the group emotion.

Freud and the Group Leader

In 1921, Freud first outlined a group psychology that was and still is meaningful to the group psychotherapist. One can only conjecture, with regret, what extraordinary developments could have occurred had he been able to follow up on his group psychology and do for group psychotherapy what he did for psychoanalysis. He himself did not feel that the two psychologies are as different as they seem on first glance. He felt that it does not make sense to consider the individual psychologically except in relation to other individuals, so that in a way all psychology is essentially group psychology, and group psychology is the original and older psychology. He was thus able to speak of a group of two, by which means he was able to link individual and group psychology together.

The repercussions of this viewpoint still haunt group psychotherapy. The question of treating the individual through the group or the group through the individual is a perennial one, and one might conclude, in agreement with Freud, that it is largely a pseudoquestion and that the therapist always does a bit of both.

Freud addressed himself to three problems. These are crucial not only for the understanding of group psychology but also for the practice of group psychotherapy: (1) What is a group? (2) How does the group come to exercise such a strong influence over the mental life of the individual? (3) What changes does the group bring about in the mental life of the individual?

Freud indicated that a collection of people is not a group but, given the proper conditions, can develop into a group. A major condition for this to happen is the development of leadership, but to what extent this is dispensable depends on the nature of the group and on the presence of strong group bonds. A leading idea can substitute for an actual leader, especially if it occasions the same strong feeling tones and identifications.

Morphologically, Freud distinguished between transient and permanent groups, homogeneous and heterogeneous ones, natural and artificial ones, and organized and unorganized ones, but his major differentiation was undoubtedly between leadered and leaderless groups.

All these distinctions are still of great importance to the field of group psychotherapy. Therapists are still wondering whether they do better with short-term groups than with long-term groups, whether heterogeneous groups are less therapeutic than homogeneous ones, and whether natural groups, such as families, start off with a stronger therapeutic advantage than artificial stranger groups.

It was Freud's opinion that the mechanism of identification is a basic one in group formations. The group members identify with the leader, whom they view as a father surrogate, and they identify with one another and relate to one another through their common tie to the leader.

A second important mechanism at work in the group is that of empathy, which enables the group members to experience their group life through one another.

By means of these two powerful mechanisms, the one leading to the other, the individual patients in the group are able to obtain an inward experience of another's mental life. Identification not only helps to further positive feeling within the group but also helps in limiting aggressiveness, since there is a general tendency to spare those with whom one is identified.

The psychological cement responsible for group ties is, according to Freud, a composite of cohering elements, such as imitation, identification, empathy, relatedness, sympathy, common purpose, mutual interests, and, more fundamentally, a recognition of something common that is incorporated and shared by all the membership. In its most concrete form, the cohesive element would be eating together; on a more psychological level, it would be taking in and sharing a leader. In the therapeutic group, the feeling of having similar problems, sharing the same therapist, and being together in the same group makes for unification. Some of the narcissism of the members is projected onto the group, so that it becomes something very special, and some of it is projected onto the leader, making him an ego ideal. Under conditions of charismatic leadership, the group may become, as it were, hypnotized, surrendering to the superior power of the leader. The members may then show a marked dependency and submissiveness, a set of circumstances frequently seen in psychotherapeutic groups.

Freud's perception of group formations as being cardinal to the life of the group was indeed an accurate one. To the extent that the members develop into a real group, there is less need for dominant leadership. The more leader-centered the group is, the more regressive does its organization tend to become. For group psychotherapists, the paradox has long been a familiar one. In the words of Lao-tse, the best leader is he who knows how to follow.

When a group with a strong leader loses its leadership, a dissolution of ties rapidly occurs, and, as a result, panic ensues. The members cease to relate to one another in an integrated way, cease to listen to orders, cease to have any concern except self-concern, and become susceptible to the sudden emergence of a gigantic and senseless dread that spreads through them like contagion. Later psychotherapists have substantiated Freud's original observation and have attempted to account for its occurrence. How Freud could develop so much insight into the workings of a group without systematic group experience or experience in a group psychotherapy group remains as much a mystery as how he acquired so much insight into intrapsychic matters

without undergoing a training analysis.

Having coped brilliantly with the questions that he himself raised, Freud confronted himself with still another perplexing problem: What brings the group together?

It has always been recognized that man is a social animal born into a group, living within a group, and usually dying supported by a group. In some religions, it is alleged that he rejoins the group in the afterlife. The instinct theorists, from Trotter on, have postulated some kind of herd instinct that makes the human animal, like other gregarious animals, feel incomplete when he is alone. There is also some sense of security that comes from being with individuals like one's self, the corollary being the sense of threat when associating with individuals unlike one's self.

Freud, although an instinct man, was inclined to reject the theory of a social instinct. For him, man is not a herd animal but a horde animal—that is, an individual brought together with other individuals into a group by a leader. The group is a revival of the primal horde conjectured by Darwin— the herd that is ruled over despotically by a powerful male. What brings the individual members together into the group is the leader, but this is essentially different from what brings the leader into the group. There were thus two basic psychologies within group psychology: the psychology of the individual members of the group and the psychology of the leader of the group. It is these two psychologies, operating in every group psychotherapy group, that makes group psychotherapy twice as complicated as individual psychotherapy.

Deeper forces that keep a group together concerns the erotic impulse, but Freud had less to say about these ties, chiefly because it could not have been possible for him to analyze them without the help of a therapeutic group. However, his hunch was that homosexual love was far more compatible with the maintenance of group ties than was heterosexual love. Both love and neurosis he saw as having a disintegrating effect on the group.

At this point, Freud made one of his most important pronouncements regarding group psychology and group psychotherapy. He pointed out that, where there is a powerful impetus to group formation, neurosis tends to diminish and eventually to disappear, and he felt that it is justifiable to turn this inverse relationship between neurosis and group formation to therapeutic account. He observed that well-organized groups are a powerful protection against the development of neurosis and that, when the individual is excluded from the group, he is compelled to replace group formations with neurotic formations. If Freud had followed up this lead to its logical conclusion, he would have created a complete system of group psychotherapy.

Why did Freud stop at that point? Curiously enough, he did the same thing with the natural group of the family as he did with the artificial stranger group. In his book *Totem and Taboo*, he set out three postulates that could have laid the foundation of systematic family theory and therapy: first, that there is a family psyche whose psychological processes correspond fairly closely to those of the individual; second, that there is a continuity of emotional life in the family psyche from one generation to the next; and third, that the mysterious transmission of attitudes and feelings through the generations is the result of unconscious understanding that makes the latent psychic life of one generation accessible to the succeeding one.

These three postulates could have become the cornerstone of a dynamic and developmental family psychopathology. They presumed a collective psychological life for the family, a process of intergenerational transmission of neurosis, and an unconscious understanding that assimilates neurotic disturbances and generates family pathology.

Why did he stop at these critical points? Who can tell? It is possible that his intense interest in individual intrapsychic conflicts—his own—superseded everything else.

Burrow and Group Analysis

Trigant Burrow gave the name group analysis to the type of behavior analysis first conducted in groups. Since this name led to a great deal of misunderstanding as to what he was doing, he dropped the term and spoke instead of phyloanalysis, which indicated that his interest was in man in his evolutionary status. Although he had a background of psychoanalytic knowledge and working in groups, he did not strongly affect the field of current group psychotherapy. Essentially, he does not belong to the history of group psychotherapy, but one might consider some of his ideas in the light of present-day knowledge. In the first place, he refused to polarize the therapeutic situation into a sick patient needing help on the one side and a well physician giving him help on the other hand. Burrow saw both as elements in a sick society, with both needing to understand the social aberration from which they were suffering. This abdication of the therapist from the leader's role has its current counterpart. In the second place, Burrow stressed the importance of the here-and-now and paid scant attention to genetic aspects. Third, his concern was not with words but with the visible somatic manifestations of stress as they are subjectively or objectively experienced.

What Burrow was searching for was some undiscovered factor within the sphere of man's behavior that belonged to the biophysical bedrock. This factor was observable, physiological, and concrete, with definite localization, and was most manifest in a group setting. To study it, he set up, with his associate, what almost amounted to prolonged sensitivity training groups conducted over many years. Within these groups, he made use of a series of laboratory exercises in an effort to make subjective man objectively appreciative of his own subjective processes. All this sounds as if he were a precursor of the National Training Laboratories at Bethel except for the fact that his frame of reference was radically different.

Since his terminology is often needlessly difficult, it may be helpful to quote a lucid discussion of his approach given in his book *The Social Basis of Consciousness:*

I was led to the idea of an analysis which should take place in a group of persons in which no one individual would hold an authoritative position in relation to the others except in the measure in which his thoughtfulness and intelligence automatically qualified him to act in a responsible capacity. My idea was that each participant would seek to discover the nature of the motivation to the customary expression of his thought and feeling as well as test for himself the nature of the motives to the reactions socially stimulated by him. At the same time he was to register and, in as far as possible, determine in turn the motive to whatever reserve or hesitation or distortion might occur in the spontaneous expression of himself and of others. There was not the slightest interest in hearing about the individual's ideas or opinions as such, or in knowing what he might at any time have thought, said or done. Such reminiscent preoccupations were neither here nor there. Nor was there any concern to know what he planned at some future time to do. *The effort was to reach the organism's immediate motivation in relation to the situation at hand.*

Here is a group in which spontaneity, immediacy, and process are at the heart of things. What Burrow tried to accomplish was a bridging of the gap between words and feelings and a recognition by all the group members that verbal expression is incorrigibly false. He discovered that people in groups exist in a general state of repression and that there is a covert covenant to present one's self in the most acceptable light.

Burrow's training labs discouraged self-consciousness and secrecy and were conducted, as far as possible, nonjudgmentally. The social image or what encounter theorists would call a mask came under close scrutiny in the group experiments. Behind the social image lie Freudian resistances, and behind these resistances lie the bedrock physiological factors continuous through the phylum. Once the group penetrates behind the artificial personality that the individual member created verbally for himself, he is able to function at a more preconscious level that gains expression in a quiet, self-possessed mood.

Burrow can be considered a pioneer of training groups, of the laboratory approach to social neurosis, and of recent work dealing with psychophysiological responses within the group. He progressed from psychoanalysis through group analysis to phylo-analysis, and somewhere along the line, perhaps because of his medical preconceptions, he appeared to take a wrong turn and ended up with an inflated evolutionary theory in which both the individual and the small group were totally lost.

Lewin and Field Theory

Strong primitive forces emanate from groups before they become domesticated by organization. But the controls are never complete, so the life of any group can be plotted in terms of both progressive and regressive outputs.

According to Kurt Lewin, conflict is inherent and inevitable in the group. As he put it, every group contains within it the seeds of its own destruction. In terms of his topological or field theory, each individual member of a group struggles for adequate life space in the way that animals struggle for territory, and it is inevitable that the needs of any particular member conflict in this respect with the needs of the group as a whole. The group situation always demands some sacrifice on the part of the individual member and some limitation on his space for free movement. The amount of conflict generated varies with the amount of restriction imposed by the group as compared with the amount of mutual support and involvement that it gives in exchange.

What the membership does with such group tension depends partly on the structure of the group and partly on its leadership. Two group prototypes in this respect can be described. In the one, the group is poorly organized, weakly integrated, and leaderless; as a result, tension is poorly distributed and tends to rise to disruptive levels. In the contrasting type, the group is well-organized, well-integrated, and well-led; the tension is more evenly distributed, and communications flow more smoothly. Here again, in quite a different conceptual framework, are the two types described by McDougall.

Almost all group behavior may be said to lie somewhere between the two extreme types described. In every group, there is a balance of cohesive and disruptive forces, and the level of tension depends on which factor is paramount. Under benign leadership, the tension within the group remains optimal, allowing for constructive group activity.

As a function of group structure, group leadership, and group interaction, every group develops an atmosphere characteristic of it. The leader may be potent in creating this atmosphere, but the atmosphere, in turn, may create the leader, so that leaders tend to emerge spontaneously from different group situations.

The members of the group also bring into the group with them the status that they habitually occupy and the roles that they normally play. Unless new roles are assigned to them in the group, they will attempt to affirm their usual roles and manipulate other group members into supporting such role activity.

The leadership role is perhaps the most complex of the different roles open to group members and may take different forms. The leader, for example, may be required to coordinate the group's activities, control its internal relationships, symbolize its unity and integration, take the blame for its failures, assume the place of the father in the lives of the members, act as arbitrator in their conflicts, display expertise on all matters, and serve as a model for appropriate attitudes and behavior. In addition to all this, he is expected to take full responsibility for the present and future life of the group, gaining praise for its successes and censure for its failures.

Lewin, despite his profound involvement in social issues and his dedication to action research, had neither the wish nor the capacity to contribute directly to group psychotherapy. He was too much of an experimentalist to be a therapist himself. However, his system of group dynamics and his ahistoric conception of group tensions have been incorporated into several systems, even those with a psychoanalytic structure. The here-and-now is prominent in the encounter groups, but it is also a feature of every group-oriented group where the developmental aspects of the individual are left in abeyance. The psychoanalytic concept of transference has the advantage of linking past and present into a coherent whole and is a more useful tool for the group psychotherapist. The delineation of the leadership role covers most of the functions assumed by the group psychotherapist but omits his representation within the unconscious minds of the group participants. Field theory may complement but never substitute for the more complex and analytic theories.

Bion and the Basic Assumptions

Once the group is civilized and organized, the more primitive elements are largely underground and tend to show themselves only in situations of panic, disrupting tension, and disorganization. The group, like the individual member, functions on both a latent level and a manifest level. Le Bon and McDougall visualized the latent forces as primitive to the point of psychopathy, whereas Bion sees them as psychotic. This latent layer is covered over by the organization that allows the group to become task-oriented. At this manifest level, the group gets to work and occupies itself in ways that are conscious, rational, constructive, and busy. And at this level it needs a leader who can drive the group and direct it. When, however, the group has nothing to do and no leader to lead it, the inner irrational feelings and fantasies become mobilized and rise to the surface, where their presence is felt by a marked increase in tension.

Like Freud, Bion poses some interesting questions and offers some even more interesting answers. He, too, asks why the group comes together in the first place and what keeps it together once it has formed. In addition, he wonders how it deals with its inner tensions, especially when it has been deprived of its leader, and in what way the members get in touch with one another.

At the overt level, the group members are brought together and held together by anything they they have to do together, and, when this is ended, they may disband. They may also continue to work together without a leader, but after a while, unless someone emerges to fulfill this function, the work they do begins to suffer. While they are engaged in legitimate work, the level of interaction rarely deepens. The members communicate mostly in verbal terms and dissipate their tensions in a number of social ways, so that the level of tension never gets to the point of disruption.

Below this overt level, the life of the group is entirely different and has little relationship to reality The group members come together and stay together because of strong basic needs. They want to find and keep a leader who will meet all their dependency needs, assist them in finding a sexual partner, and direct them into fight or flight when danger becomes threatening. The search for a leader, therefore, brings the group members together, and, once they find him, they cannot do without him. If rendered leaderless, they invent a leader in the shape of some predominant idea around which they can coalesce. A leaderless group, consequently, spends a large part of its time searching for a leader, and, depending on the state of the basic assumptions within the group, some kind of leader eventually emerges.

The student of history is intrigued by the fact that similar ideas keep recurring and are always treated as if they were something quite novel. It was once said that there are only seven basic story plots and that storytellers manipulate these with considerable skill to produce new stories for each new generation. The world of ideas may well be similarly impoverished, but theorists become so skillful at putting old ideas into new language that an exhilarating sense of progress is produced. Therefore, the two-group concept has dominated the history of group psychology from the very beginning and is an outcome of the manifest and latent, the conscious and unconscious postulates put forward by psychoanalysis. The two groups within the group perform different activities, have different needs, and speak essentially a different language, since the basic assumption group can communicate nonverbally, empathically, intuitively, and by contagion. Nevertheless, Bion has created, even if only in a limited form, a group psychology of the unconscious and, by linking this psychology with Kleinian metapsychology, has made it directly available to the group psychotherapist. Furthermore, Bion has raised the important question of how the manifest and latent groups interact. The manifest and latent layers of the mind, as described by psychoanalysis, are in continuous transaction, and one's personality is to a great extent determined by what happens at the interface. Although it may be confounding to extrapolate from the individual member to the group, there is no doubt that the personality of the group may also be a product of a similar interplay. The manifest group tries in all sorts of devious ways to manipulate the latent group, although it keeps an eye on its realistic aims and purposes. If the manifest group becomes disorganized in any way, there is the immediate danger that the basic assumptions will return from the unconscious and take control of the situation, leading to a rise in tension followed by the appearance of primitive drives and feelings.

On the basis of this model, Bion has been able to describe different types of group culture in which some of the basic assumptions are gratified and some frustrated. These cultures represent a transient ascendancy, so that a pairing state may be prominent on one occasion and a fight-flight state on another. This means that one can follow cultural variations over time in the same way as in Lewinian groups; the climate may undergo alteration with any change in leadership.

One can invent a group psychology and not follow it up by making it applicable to group psychotherapy. This happened with Freud and, to some extent, with Bion. He sees himself not as a group psychotherapist but rather as a group investigator.

Whitaker and Lieberman and Focal-Conflict Theory

Focal-conflict theory, thought up by Thomas French, attempts to explain the current behavior of a person as an expression of his method of solving currently experienced personality conflicts that originated very early in his life. The person is constantly resonating to these early focal conflicts. The original solutions and the original feelings are modified by the altered circumstances of later life. The conflicts and their attempted solutions are so much part of the person's way of life that he can hardly do without them, however much he may want to rid himself of them.

In the context of the group situation, Whitaker and Lieberman suggest that each member of the group is affected by some group-focal conflict, as a result of which he tends to behave in a particular stereotyped way. The group conflicts are a threat to the individual member, since they expose him to personal conflicts. The individual member sticks to his pathological solutions because they protect him from the anxiety stemming from unconscious conflicts, and the other group members may respond helpfully or unhelpfully to these lifelong solutions. As the group progresses, the hidden conflict begins to emerge both as a wish and as a fear, and the group may act to reduce the fear and maximize the wish-fulfillment.

This type of group psychology has an artificial ring about it. In the first place, it is an oversimplified adaptation of an individual psychological approach that itself has never gained much general acceptance because of its somewhat schematic nature. The propensity to use borrowed theories has certain pitfalls. As Freud was first to point out, a group does not occur simply by putting a number of people together. Why it comes together and why it stays together are integral parts of how it functions together. Focal-conflict theory has nothing to say about these parts; as a consequence, it lacks the appeal of the conceptual framework put forward by Freud and Bion.

Ezriel and the Common Group Tension

Ezriel, as a psychoanalyst working with groups, also became interested in the interaction between the manifest and latent levels of the group. In the place of Bion's basic assumptions, he postulated an underlying common group problem that gives rise to tension and is a common denominator of the dominant unconscious fantasies of all the group members. In addition, each member projects his unconscious fantasy-objects upon various other group members and then tries to manipulate them accordingly.

This theory is not so difficult to accept. The idea of a collective fantasy may sound Jungian, but then group psychotherapists and group psychologists are always skirting the Jungian unconscious without acknowledging it in any way. The manipulation of the group members in terms of the internal object society is simply an example of group transference and the tendency everyone has of manipulating transference figures.

The emphasis put on insight as an experience leading to change is generally in keeping with the psychoanalytic approach. Others have tended to depreciate the value of insight as an essential therapeutic factor and to accord the leading position to experience.

Foulkes and the Network

What happens in the other 22 or 23 hours of a patient's life when he is not engaged in a psychotherapeutic situation is becoming increasingly important, even to the psychotherapist. Community psychiatry attempts to follow the patient out of the clinic into his world to arrange helpful contacts for him outside of his hour. The more one considers the social orbit of a patient in the framework of the newer ecological approach, the more one becomes aware of the many pathogenic and therapeutic influences at work within it. The idea of a network—that is, the natural group in which the patient lives at the time of his illness and his treatment—was formulated by Foulkes as an adjunct to the fuller understanding of the group analytic situation that he refers to as the group matrix. The matrix and the network together can help to illuminate the understanding of illness as a social process. The matrix is the frame of reference for the interactional context of the group as expressed manifestly, symbolically, symptomatically, effectively, behaviorally, and verbally.

The dynamically interacting network of the patient has, according to Foulkes, a fundamental significance in the production of illness in the patient. And when a significant change occurs in a patient, particularly a change toward greater independence, the other members of the network become active. The network covers not only the nuclear but also the extended family group and can involve friends as well. (It is interesting, in this context, to note that Post found more psychiatric illness within the social orbit of psychiatric patients than one would expect from the distribution of psychiatric illness in the general population.)

The thesis put forward by Foulkes is that illness and related disturbances are due in part to psychopathological processes that involve a number of interacting persons. In the psychoneuroses this multipersonal network of interaction is of central significance, and change in any member of such a network is linked to corresponding changes in other members. Even the nature of individual symptoms may rest on this interdependence. Therefore, the emotional disturbance can no longer be regarded in a vacuum, limited to one individual personality; it is always a function of relationships involving many people. The disturbance is an expression of a disturbed equilibrium in a total field of interaction. The patient is more or less unaware of this fact and may expect changes in himself without concomitant changes in the rest of the network. But it is impossible to change the patient without changing his network. There are, therefore, two important crises in the patient's life. The first period of disequilibrium occurs in the network with the onset of the original disturbance, and the second period of disequilibrium takes place at the cessation of the emotional disturbance. There may be a final re-equilibrium after an enforced readjustment of roles in the various members of the network.

The concept of the network certainly extends the understanding of the group, since each participant enters the group as a representative of his more or less sick network. No doubt the psychotherapist enlarges the scope of his understanding through these twin concepts, but it is difficult to say to what extent the psychotherapy itself gains from this extended viewpoint. Like the researcher, the therapist can easily get bogged down when his variables are multiplied beyond necessity. The psychoanalyst achieves his goal by focusing intensively on the intrapsychic processes. He can widen his focus to include nonverbal behavior. But once he brings in extra-analytic factors, not only does his field of therapy become contaminated, but he may lose his way within the multiplicity of influences at work. Whether the matrix-plus-network perspective is too wide for focused and intensive therapy remains to be investigated.

Moreno and Acting Out

The end of man, said Goethe, lies not in thought but in action, and Moreno has always been action-oriented. This action includes acting, drama, catharsis, spontaneity, creativity. Moreno is essentially an actor who became a therapist, and the role he has set for himself in therapeutic life is to help produce Everyman's drama. He has taken the Shakespearean lines to heart:

All the world's a stage,
And all the men and women merely players.

And he has made use of Aristotle's proposition that the task of tragedy is to produce, through the exercise of fear and pity, a liberation from such emotions; the audience is purged and absolved from the necessity of expressing these emotions in their own lives. Moreno extends this theory. According to him, the playwright, the actor, and the spectators all undergo catharsis.

Moreno coined the term acting out more than 40 years ago, and, oddly enough, it is one of the few things that psychoanalysts have borrowed from him. Psychoanalysts and psychoanalytic group therapists are not generally dramatic men and are not given to dramatizing the emotional struggles going on within their patients. They are more voyeuristic than exhibitionistic, whereas the reverse may be true of the psychodramatist. Furthermore, the individual psychoanalyst and the group analyst are apparently satisfied to reconstruct the conflictual situation presented to them by their patients verbally without making it a flesh-and-blood reality involving all the senses. This objectification, however, is apparently necessary to Moreno's way of doing things; he has to be shown in addition to being told.

The patient, depending on his personality, may derive a certain satisfaction from acting out rather than simply verbalizing his conflicts. For Moreno, acting out represents a great therapeutic maneuver; for the analyst, it is resistance.

The patient is said to gain insight from doing, but catharsis has a tendency to interfere with the acquisition of insight, and the outpouring of emotion may be the patient's only benefit. By training the patient through behavior therapy, the therapist attempts to alter fixed patterns of behavior.

The dramatic enactment of problems may be carried out through psychodrama, in which the patient relives an actual situation or acts out a situation posed by the director, who knows the patient's special problem; through sociodrama, in which the patient is confronted with some concrete social problem that characterizes the society to which he belongs; and through role-playing, in which the patient assumes the role of another person, thus allowing him to try out new types of behavior and new forms of communication in a relatively nonthreatening situation.

The theatre of spontaneous man is a brilliant idea, and it certainly deserves a place in the history and practice of group psychotherapy. But whether all the complex resistances that make up modern civilized man can be dissolved by means of a simple dramatic device is open to question. Is it indeed acting, or is it really acting out in the psychoanalytic sense?

The dramatic approach has spawned a large number of dramatic games that are used to warm up a patient in the initial phase of therapy. These exercises have been incorporated into training groups and other modern departures from classical therapy. In fact, Moreno has claimed with some truth to have pioneered the development of encounter groups, Gestalt therapy, transactional analysis, behavior therapy, and joy workshops. He feels that, together with Buber, he has been responsible for the existential encounter—the real, concrete, complete experience involving both physical and psychic contact with a convergence of emotional, social, and cosmic factors. He feels that psychodrama is the essence of encounter, since it entails the experience of identity and total reciprocity.

Moreno is a creative, dramatic, spontaneous, and charismatic man whose quasi-religious, dithyrambic style of writing makes him sound at times like a latter-day Nietzsche. His sociometry is a genuine contribution to group psychology and has been widely used by the scientifically oriented who spurn the other side of Moreno, his psychodrama. To many group psychotherapists, he represents a detrimental influence that has split the group world in two, seducing many a group therapist from the careful and patient practice of classical group psychotherapy and leading him into wildly exciting, highly controversial, short-cut methods of treatment.

GROUP PSYCHOTHERAPY

Pioneer Efforts

In 1907, Pratt described what he called a class method of treating tuberculosis in the homes of the poor, and a year later he discussed his results. It was known then, as it is known now, that tuberculous patients are prone to be difficult people and to have emotional problems. Since tuberculous patients, like psychotics, are often herded together and are treated with fear and rejection by the general populace, it seemed appropriate to use group techniques. After Pratt's original efforts, other psychologically oriented physicians have tried to do the same thing.

The psychiatrists in mental hospitals were stimulated by the possibilities of this new technique. Lazell in 1921 and Marsh in 1931 instituted the group method with psychotics.

All these early practices were psychologically naive, and they made little or no use of group dynamics. The instructor lectured to a group of patients on their illness, and sometimes these lectures were broadcast through the hospital by means of loudspeakers. In 1940 Snowden actually gave a course of lectures in which he described the causes of different mental illnesses and then had the patients discuss the lecture in the context of their own illness.

The methods began to grow in sophistication. In 1941 Low and in 1946 Klapman put aside the lecture format and began to use the group as a group.

Burrow. Parallel to these developments in general psychiatry, certain psychoanalysts became interested in group treatment and the possible application of psychoanalysis to it. Trigant Burrow was psychoanalytically minded, but what he did could not really be called group psychotherapy. However, Burrow did note that many of the characteristics of a psychoanalysis could be found in the group. The patients were able to verbalize actual fantasies and family conflicts and even to manifest defense and transference mechanisms—a discovery that has been replicated many times since. Freud had hinted at the same things earlier. Today, it is accepted that groups do have many of the psychological qualities of the individual, although therapists are now as much interested in the differences as in the similarities in the two approaches.

Burrow treated patients in groups because he felt that a patient is less resistant to the treatment process in a group than in individual therapy. Within the setting of the group, the patient becomes aware that he shares many things with others, good things as well as abnormalities. He is no longer alone, his problems are no longer unique, he no longer feels the need for isolation and secrecy, and he is increasingly appreciative of the group support. Burrow felt that, whereas Freud was treating the individual, he was dealing with the human race, but both were using psychoanalytic methods and insights. But Freud put the major emphasis on the past; Burrow stressed the present and eschewed personal reminiscences.

Wender. Wender was probably the first to conduct psychoanalytically oriented groups, and he did so in a hospital setting. In 1936 he combined the group method with individual interviews and made the discovery—also replicated by many others—

that patients involved in group psychotherapy move much more freely and more productively than in the individual situation. However, like the general psychiatrists, he took a didactic line and started each group session with a lecture on the dynamics of behavior and the significance of dreams. Wender, like Burrow, also found that transference relationships develop within the group in relation to both the therapist and other patients. He further found that patients in groups appear to be better motivated than patients in individual psychotherapy.

Wender's work represented a fairly straightforward application of early psychoanalytic theory within a group setting. His observations that the groups themselves did helpful things to patients, apart from lowering their resistances and increasing their spontaneity, were almost incidental to the fact that he was applying his knowledge of psychoanalysis. But psychoanalysts at that time were not well-read in group dynamics (they are not so well-read in group dynamics today), so the significance of the group by itself and in itself did not get any profound consideration.

Schilder. During the same decade of the 1930's, Paul Schilder began to work psychotherapeutically with groups. From every point of view, Schilder was an extraordinary person. With his encyclopedic mind and his tremendous scientific drive, he was the one person who might have become the Freud of group psychotherapy, had he given it his whole attention. He also possessed the flexibility of the genuine scientist, in that he was not bound by any dogmatic adherence to rules. Not only was he a first-class theoretician, but he was well-grounded in the theories of others. He was not only interested in individual patients but deeply interested in their various conglomerates in society; he was interested not only in adults but also in children. His range of interests was extremely wide. As a psychiatrist, a psychoanalyst, and a phenomenologist, he could draw on physiology, neurology, and general psychiatry to serve his purpose as an investigator. His influence on Rapaport and through Rapaport on psychoanalysis was appreciable. Rapaport referred to him as an unsystematic genius who sowed scientific seeds without any thought of the harvest that others might be able to reap.

Schilder, like Burrow, began his group interest with the body, more specifically with the body image. It was Schilder's conviction that the system of ideologies a patient develops around his body and the self associated with his body plays a major part in his psychopathology. Any injury to the body, no matter how slight, has an effect on the patient's body image, on the ideology that goes with it, and on his way of life. The exploration of ideologies is especially attuned to the group situation. The patient shares with others the basic tenets that govern his life and faces the criticism that they provoke. The group discussion often starts on an intellectual level but gradually becomes more personal and emotional. When others are able to identify with the particular ideology, the patient professing it is better able to work through it.

One rather surprising fact regarding Schilder as a group psychotherapist is his willingness to reveal his own ideology and to justify it before the group. He was, therefore, very much a member of the group in a way that therapists before him were not.

In response to a direct question, Freud once remarked that he was not a good psychoanalyst because he was too interested in finding out original facts about the patient and tying these facts to his developing theories. The same is probably true of Schilder. His encyclopedic mind ranged over so many interests in such depth that he may have experienced some difficulty in dealing with the everyday problems of everyday patients in a way that was immediately meaningful to them. He was, perhaps, a little too cognitive to be therapeutic and too theoretical to be practical.

The technique of analyzing ideologies has not really caught on in group psychotherapy, although most group psychotherapists from time to time have to deal with the ideologies put forward by their patients. But therapists are more inclined to treat these ideologies as resistances than as illuminating psychological material to be investigated in their own right.

World War II Efforts

The major impact of emigrating psychoanalysts from Germany and Austria on American psychiatry and psychotherapy has only recently begun to subside. In Britain, the effect was less marked, chiefly because psychoanalysis never managed to get a strong foothold into academic medical circles.

In Britain as in America, psychoanalysts were drafted into the Army, and they eventually congregated at centers for the treatment of psychiatric casualties. The main center in Britain was at Northfield, and Northfield's main claim to fame was that it provided a setting for the application of analytic ideas to groups and communities.

The Northfield experiment gathered together a group of analysts or analysts in the making—Freudian, Kleinian, and Adlerian. The roll call included Anthony, Bierer, Bion, Bridger, Foulkes, Main, and Rickman—all of whom later made contributions to group psychotherapy. The first phase of the Northfield experiment was sparked by Bion and Rickman. In a revolutionary way, they attempted to cut Army red tape and treat a whole ward of soldiers almost as if they were civilian patients with rights and responsibilities of their own. Ward discipline was maintained through free discussion with the soldier patients. Not surprisingly, this revolution was brought to a sudden end, but the two venturesome analysts, so far away from their private offices and couches, had made their point and had facilitated the development of the second phase at Northfield.

During this second phase, Foulkes, who at the start of the war in civilian practice had been undertaking analytic group psychotherapy, introduced his method into Northfield. In so doing, he established a milieu that was highly propitious to group psychotherapy. At the time, Foulkes looked beyond the group to the community as a whole, regarding the group instrument as a crucial one for dealing with the individual patient's network of relationships within the community.

The Northfield experiment was the training ground for group theorists, group activists, and group practitioners. There, both group psychotherapy and community psychotherapy received the vital stimulus and momentum that carried them through the unsettled postwar years. The author has described Northfield's significance this way:

To some, it presented an unrivaled opportunity to apply their analytic knowledge to a challenging new field, while for others, it carried the hope that this new method of exploring the human mind might add significant chapters to psychopathology. In many respects, it had something about it of the Vienna of early psychoanalysis, when almost everyone was a contributor of some sort because almost everything was so new. We talked, then as now, about field theory, leaderless groups, group dynamics, group tensions, the analytic approach, etc., but already group styles were beginning to separate out, and one could detect growing differences between the group-analytic groups, the Bion-type groups, Adlerian groups and Tavistock-type groups. With the dissolution of Northfield after the war, each went his own way and more or less lost contact with the others. The war had been the great harmonizer and integrator; with peace came rivalry, dissension and disruption. I do think, however, even though some of us may be reluctant to admit it, that we learned a great deal from one another in those early, encapsulated days and that, perhaps, more cross-fertilization took place than subsequent published acknowledgments admit.

Something of the same quality was noted by Main:

It was a time of freshness, activity and high morale but it would be wrong to suppose that there were no strains at Northfield. We were, after all, like any other group. There was quarreling and dissension on theory, and, as well as friendship, personal malice and rivalry, not less than in any other fiercely active organization

The first Northfield Experiment fathered by Rickman and carried out by Bion produced some ideas about groups which have had their own developmental life ever since. Foulkes' work with groups had precedence, but it was of a different order and went in a different direction. The two developments were each legitimate, novel, brilliant; but because they concerned the newly entered area of group work the excitement and vehemence of argument tended to set them up as rival systems and for dissensions to take on personal forms.

What is apparent from these comments is that engagement in group work carries with it no immunity from group dissension and strife. In fact, at times group therapists seem to bring their group skills strategically into the polemical battle with them.

It is also apparent that the dialectics of controversy had a marked creative influence on British group psychotherapy. One seems to need the impact of thesis and antithesis to spark off new levels of theory and practice.

A third conclusion is that theorists who are loved and admired within their immediate circle but are treated outside with criticism and even hostility often appear to thrive on such a situation. Freud was a striking example, and so today is Moreno.

Foulkes and the Group Analytic Approach

Foulkes has always been an innovator, and at no time during his long career has he ceased to make original observations and contributions. As Main remarked of him:

Anyone can be a pioneer for a short time by accident, but it takes the patience and doggedness of a Foulkes to make the most of a chance setting and to become an innovator: to study, criticize, check, correct, gain colleagues, undertake experiments, erect, criticize and refine theory and grow bodies of ideas for further examination.

Foulkes was, as Main remarked, at the center of all the group treatment at Northfield,

interested, puzzled, inspiring, enjoying his work and infectiously formulating ideas about the nature of group process.

The author, as a close collaborator of Foulkes, feels that the puzzlement was the most creative thing about Foulkes. Many leading group theorists present a clear, concise, positivistic, and optimistic statement of their theoretical ideas, almost as if the ideas were all cut and dried and ready to be served out, shaped forever. With Foulkes, on the other hand, one always felt a groping toward some profound insight that was never immediately manifest but always several fathoms below in the depths. This habit of groping was sometimes mystifying, often nebulous, and almost always exasperatingly slow for those in search of immediate answers, however glib these might be. One soon learned, however, either in a dyadic or group relationship with him, that behind chiaroscuro was a subtle and steady mind at work. A personal comment from a group member, Abercrombie, is perhaps the nearest one can get to this style, which is so hard to describe, so difficult to imitate, and so effective, not only in theory but also in therapy.

It is extraordinarily difficult to communicate to one who has never been there the subtle, rich and profound experiences of being in a group conducted by Dr. Foulkes. Superficially, the group has no obvious structure or palpable texture; it may seem formless, embedded in an intangible, floating vagueness. At Dr. Foulkes' treatment of the group, or rather, one should say, his participation in it, he is in fact highly disciplined, dictated by a sure perception of strong and rigorous, but changing, patterns of relationships. What may seem to the other group participants a serene, withdrawn passivity is one manifestation of his intense involvement and of his sensitive and steely mastery of technique.

With Foulkes, more than anyone else in the field, one can say that the style is the man, and the man is his theory, so that there is a completeness about him that comes through when one is sitting with him in a therapeutic group.

His contribution on the group matrix and its ambient social network furnish the practitioner with a triple perspective on the individual patient, on the group, and on the interpersonal environment from which the group members come. The intrapsychic, the intragroup, and the intranetwork provide a comprehensive frame of reference to bolster the confidence of any beginning group psychotherapist. Technically, the advantages for the therapist are considerable. The approach enables him, as Foulkes says, to apply a figure-ground orientation to events, to locate the configuration of disturbances in all their variety within the group, and to envisage each member in a more intensive and extensive way.

The group analytic psychotherapist sees the group analytic situation rather the way the psychoanalyst perceives the psychoanalytic situation. The therapist establishes and maintains the arrangements, the setting, the fees, and the total culture in a dynamic way as essential elements for the initiation of the therapeutic process. The therapist is passive in the sense that he puts himself at the service of the group and follows it wherever it goes; but on the other side, he actively analyzes defenses and resistances. His accepting attitude embraces all communication, from both the here-and-now and the there-and-then. The atmosphere generated is one of perpetual attentiveness, tolerance, and patience. With Foulkes, as a co-therapist in the group, one gets the feeling that he is always waiting for something to happen but is in no way discomforted when nothing happens. There is no pressure on the patients to perform for his benefit, as there sometimes is with other group therapists. Occasionally, reading the protocols given by certain authors, one is left with the impression that the members are putting on a show to keep the therapist happy and interested and totally absorbed with them.

As a psychoanalyst, he inevitably focused on the transference situation—between the members and the therapist, between the members themselves, and between the members and the group as a whole. This array of reference has excited many group psychoanalysts, but the group analytic psychotherapist observes it as one aspect of the total phenomena occurring in a group. He often works through it and with it but not in the genetic sense of the psychoanalyst.

The influence of Kurt Lewin and his group dynamics is also obvious in the conduct of analytic group psychotherapy, although Foulkes himself has concentrated on the interpersonal rather than on the group as a whole. The field and its boundaries are well-delineated, and the incidents at the interface between group and outside are easy to detect. Within the field, the temporal perspective is very much on what is happening now in the field and within the individual life space of each member. The network is an important extension of the concept of life space. The current life situation and the current life network remind the therapist that the patient is only the top of the iceberg and that, to know him fully, one has to know him, as Freud once said, both from the inside and from the outside.

The intrapsychic life of the patient takes

second place to his life as a group member. In this permissive, neutral, nondirective situation, it is not surprising that a fully formed transference neurosis can often be clearly recognized in the group and, to some extent, analyzed. But the group analytic psychotherapist realizes that the transference does not develop in pure form and cannot be worked through in quite the same detail as in psychoanalysis. Some group analysts, such as Durkin, feel that the fundamental character of the transference neurosis is not affected by the group context and that it can be effectively analyzed for the purpose of achieving structural change in the personality of the patient. Durkin is fairly convinced that a systematic analysis of the resistance inherent in the defensive transferences can be carried out, that infantile conflicts can be resolved, and that working through does occur in group therapy.

The group analytic approach also takes note of the patient's development in his early family setting as it reappears in the transference.

Very little work has been done on the development of the ego's capacity to create and to maintain a group relationship. A conceptual model that is also developmental could be very useful in group psychotherapy. There is an implicit assumption in psychosexual development that a person passes from a one-body to a two-body to a three-body and finally to a multibody situation, using Rickman's terminology. In the theoretical development proposed by Talcott Parsons, these external groups are internalized in terms of the role played by the individual members. Susan Isaacs also described early group developments in nursery school children, pointing out that group relationships at this stage of life are evanescent and vivid and that hostility is often the factor that draws the children together, either in attacking or in defending their rights and areas.

Foulkes and Anthony have described in detail the construction of the group situation, the material arrangements for conducting a group, the natural history of group development, and the phenomenology associated with the group situation, such as resonance, mirroring, chain phenomena—all indicating the reactivity of the members to one another.

Bion and the Leaderless Group

Bion is tentative about describing himself as a group psychotherapist, as are many analysts on both sides of the Atlantic. Perhaps such work is beneath their dignity, or they do not wish to be labeled unorthodox, but one is left with the conclusion that there is something peculiar about working therapeutically with more than one patient at a time. Bion admits to little more than that he had an experience of trying to persuade a number of patients to make the study of their tensions a group task. It is, perhaps, permissible for a psychoanalyst to be interested in group psychology, since Freud had that interest, but group psychotherapy is not for analysts, and it is true that Freud never attempted to practice it.

The best way to describe what Bion does in a therapeutic group is to use his own words:

At the appointed time members of the group begin to arrive; individuals engage each other in conversation for a short time, and then when a certain number has collected, a silence falls on the group. After a while desultory conversation breaks out again, and then another silence falls. It becomes clear to me that I am, in some sense, the focus of attention in the group. Furthermore, I am aware of feeling uneasily that I am expected to do something. At this point I confide my anxieties to the group, remarking that, however mistaken my attitude might be, I feel just this. I soon find that my confidence is not very well received. Indeed, there is some indignation that I should express such feelings without seeming to appreciate that the group is entitled to expect something from me. I do not dispute this but content myself with pointing out that clearly the group cannot be getting from me what they feel they are entitled to expect. I wonder what these expectations are and what has aroused them.

The effect of this type of group management is almost predictable. The group comes with the high expectation that they will be treated, and the therapist does nothing about it at all. He simply wants to discuss their expectations. The group does not like what he does with them, and they see his behavior as provocative and deliberately disappointing. They feel that he is perverse, that he could behave differently if he wanted to, that he has chosen to behave in this peculiar way out of spite.

Bion then points out that it must be hard for the group to admit that this could be his way of taking groups, that perhaps he should be allowed to take them in his own way, and that there is no reason why he should take groups in the way expected by the patients.

The group members, of course, know that he is a very clever and well-known clinician, so that he cannot be doing what he does for want of knowledge or technique. They are inclined to interpret his attitude as artificially naive and egotistical.

It becomes clear after a while that—because of Bion's tentative, evasive, and noncommittal attitude and behavior—the group cannot stop themselves from being preoccupied with him. Eventually, they can stand it no longer, and one of the members begins to take over and repair the iatrogenic damage. This deputy leader wonders why Bion cannot give a straightforward explanation of his behavior. Bion can only apologize and state that he, too, feels that his explanation that he is in the group to study group tensions is really inadequate, but he confesses that he is unable to throw any light on the matter. The group seems determined to find out what *his* motives are for coming to the group, not what their own motives are. The group situation seems about to break down because of the inability of the group to tolerate the therapist's behavior, and a movement gets under way to exclude the therapist from the group or, if exclusion is not possible, to ignore his presence.

Eventually, a member speaks up on behalf of the therapist, only to state that the therapist must have some good reason for taking the line he does. This statement relaxes the tension in the group immediately, and a more friendly attitude toward the therapist becomes apparent.

A lesson is slowly emerging in the group, and this lesson is pointed out to them—namely, that it is difficult for an individual member to convey meanings to the group that are different from the meanings the group wishes to entertain. This lesson annoys the group, but they are then informed that they have every right to be annoyed. Nobody ever explained to them what it means to be in a group in which Bion is present, and nobody ever explained to Bion what it is like to be in a group in which all these individual members are present.

The only disagreeable member of the group at this point is the therapist, and he points out that he thinks his interpretations are disturbing the group. A crisis is now reached. Certain members may well have discovered that membership in a group run by Bion happens to be an experience that they do not wish to have. The group has to face the fact that some of the members may want to leave.

Bion then tells the group that he considers the emotional forces underlying this situation to be very powerful. He is, he says, merely one member of a group possessing some degree of specialized knowledge. Although he is no different from any other member of the group, they are quite unable to face the emotional tensions in the group without believing that the therapist is some sort of god who is fully responsible for all that takes place. When the group turns resentfully and somewhat anxiously to another member, Bion sees them as looking to this other member to be leader but without any real conviction that he could be the leader.

The conversation dies down. For most members the experience is becoming painful and boring, so a fresh thought occurs to Bion, and he passes it on to the group. He tells them that they seem determined to have a leader and, moreover, a leader with certain characteristics that are not easy to describe. Why should they have any leader at all?

Both Foulkes and Bion seem on superficial inspection to be like corks floating on the sea of group turmoil, never sinking under the fury, and apparently drifting aimlessly at the mercy of the group. As the Bion and Abercrombie accounts illustrate, this impression is highly illusional. Both Foulkes and Bion, while seeming to follow the group, are subtly leading it to a resolution of its tensions and other problems.

Slavson and Analytic Group Psychotherapy

Slavson, although not a qualified psychoanalyst, stays close to the psychoanalytic model. He refers to his method as analytic group psychotherapy, which contrasts in more than name with the title used by Foulkes of group analytic psychotherapy. With Slavson, the prime emphasis is on the analytic; with Foulkes, the emphasis is on the group. This is not to say that Slavson is not aware of the group process, but he has battled constantly and vigorously for the autonomy of the individual patient in the group. Each patient, he insists, must remain a detached entity in whom intrapsychic changes must occur.

In the therapeutic group, according to Slavson, it is each patient for himself, and the therapist should, therefore, concentrate on the individual rather than on the group as a whole. Slavson recognizes that the individual members affect one another in a variety of ways, including sibling and identification transferences and mutual empathies that make for a collective experience based on the integration of the individual member into the group. The group tends to catalyze the dynamics of the individual patient, accelerating regression, weakening defenses, and at least transiently impairing individuation.

Slavson differentiates between transference and what he calls the basic solidity of the therapeutic relation—what psychoanalysts refer to as the therapeutic alliance. He recognizes that the transference is modified both quantitatively and qualitatively in the group, where he perceives levels of transference.

Slavson has been prolific in his group writing, and his influence on American group psychotherapy has been enormous. He has instigated its development as a profession, its recognition as a therapeutic discipline, and its acceptance as an area of worthwhile research by behavioral scientists. He has also appointed himself as a watchdog who can be depended on to bark at strangers and bite the wild men who haunt the fringes of group psychotherapy. Because of him, group psychotherapy in the United States operated for many years as a branch of applied psychoanalysis, which had two effects: This arrangement was a powerful impetus to the development of group psychotherapy; at the same time, the arrangement set limitations to the further growth of group therapy as a form of treatment in its own right. Slavson has introduced a number of terms and phrases, some of which have become incorporated into general use. Because of his didactic skills, this tentative branch of therapeutics can now be codified into textbooks. As a theoretician, he is more categorical than creative, and there is a positiveness about his position that the state of the art hardly merits.

Perhaps his greatest contribution has been the development of group therapy with children—in its play form with preschoolers and in its activity form with those in the latency phase. The psychological treatment of children in any form poses a number of technical problems, largely because children at different stages of development are almost different species. They think differently, feel differently, and act differently. These differences necessitate treating them differently, which is what Slavson set out to do. Perhaps because he was not a developmental psychologist, his conclusions about what children could or could not do and could or could not understand were essentially faulty. As a consequence, his group work with children, although novel and interesting, is lacking in a rich developmental background. Nevertheless, his expectation that children prefer to act out rather than speak out is confirmed by his protocols. His patients do abreact physically in groups. The group analytic approach to children makes no such assumption. As a result, the patients undergo conversational catharsis, which goes to show that children in therapy have a habit of living up or living down to the expectations of the therapist. What the analytic group and group analytic approaches have both established beyond question is that group psychotherapy can be applied naturally to children. As Slavson says:

Group experience holds limitless growth possibilities for children.

This is true not because children are limited in their understanding but because children, like adults, can learn to make use of people according to their therapeutic needs.

Today, the activity-interview method sounds a little old-fashioned in the light of modern ego psychology. For Slavson, the child is a function-mechanism whose psychological development results not from thought but from action, not from knowledge and ideas but pragmatically through experience and association. Because the child is immature and cognitively deficient, he must be treated through action and by action, using controls and affectionate guidance rather than interpretations. To child psychoanalysts, this type of release and ego-strengthening therapy rings a familiar bell. For a long time the child was considered unanalyzable because he was allegedly unable to free-associate, develop transference, handle deep-going tensions, or work through resistances. Today, an interpretative form of psychoanalysis can be carried out with quite young children. Likewise, today interpretative forms of group analytic psychotherapy can be carried out with quite young children, and acting out is treated as a defense in children, as it is in adults. In fact, what Socrates described as the remedy of sweet words is effective with all human beings at all stages of life, since words specifically separate them absolutely from the dumb brutes.

There is much argument in the literature as to who began group psychotherapy and where. Various claims have been made involving different therapists and different countries. But the group idea was really part of a *Zeitgeist*, as a result of which there was a gradual convergence of ideas that characteristically led to the plethora of approaches that usually antedate the evolution of any unified theory. Slavson felt that, unlike many other techniques in psychiatry that had their beginnings in Europe, group psychotherapy originated in the United States—and quite understandably so, since American culture is essentially a free group culture. It is probably truer to say that the United States is a place where things catch on because there is more freedom for them to develop. And this is as true for an individual therapy such as psychoanalysis as it is for group psychotherapy.

Wolf and Psychoanalytic Group Psychotherapy

In the two decades of the 1930's and 1940's, several psychoanalysts began to carry out therapeutic work with groups based on the psychoanalytic model. They followed the free-associative technique and attempted some degree of psychoanalysis with each patient. Schilder and Wender were two of these psychoanalysts, and Weininger was another. Weininger's method was essentially different in that he confined the entire treatment session to one patient, with the others in the group playing the part of spectators. The psychoanalytic approach came to fruition in the hands of Alexander Wolf, who began to develop psychoanalysis in groups in the first place to offset the burden imposed on many patients by the cost of individual psychoanalysis.

For Wolf, the group situation is not essentially unfavorable to the type of psychic work carried out in ordinary psychoanalysis, such as the uncovering of infantile amnesia, the interpretation of transference, the analysis of dreams, and genetic reconstruction. He assumes that the patient's unconscious is as accessible in the group situation as it is in the individual psychoanalytic one and is explorable by identical techniques. The group situation is thus conceived of as a set of interlocking psychoanalytic situations.

Whereas Slavson has continued to believe that transference cannot be as intense in groups as in individual treatment and that interpretations in groups cannot penetrate into areas of personality as deeply as in psychoanalysis, Wolf believes that the group situation often allows for deeper analytic exploration than is possible in individual psychoanalysis. The reason he gives is that the group ego, with which each member gradually comes to identify himself, offers the necessary support for more radical probing. The tolerance for anxiety, which is the limiting factor in all psychological analysis, is upgraded by the group. Not only is each member a source of support for other members, but he is also an ancillary therapist in his own right—capable, after a certain amount of group experience, of a well-high professional analysis of the material.

One of the most debatable practices inculcated by Wolf has been his attempt to direct the course of treatment in a series of preconceived stages. Since Freud's early suggestion that the period of treatment be portioned off, like a game of chess, into an opening gambit, a middle phase, and an end game, various therapists have attempted to distinguish a natural historical development in the course of therapy. Group therapists have also succumbed to this evolutionary exercise, and some have built up elaborate stratified models of therapeutic development. A few, like Wolf, have gone even further and have tried to impose a dynamically logical sequence leading to a programming of therapeutic tasks for the group.

In view of these psychoanalytic and quasi-analytic approaches to group psychotherapy, one can only wonder what course Freud himself would have taken had he followed through from group psychology to group psychotherapy. No doubt, his preoccupation with group leadership would have led him to concentrate particularly on the functions of the group therapist and on the relationship between the therapist and the group membership. Although well-aware of the individual mechanisms of identification operating within the group, his closely argued discussion of Le Bon and McDougall would have led him eventually to the concept of the group functioning as a whole.

Whether Freud would have created a group dynamics out of the workings of the nuclear Oedipus complex seems less easy to conceive. However, Foulkes has pointed out that the Sophoclean tragedy could without distortion be considered in group terms, as the hero and the chorus interact in the working out of the plot. The same inescapable emotional tie unites all the people on the stage; at any one time, some are active, and some are passive, and at moments of high tension the conflicting tendencies in the group also find their spokesmen, who voice feelings common to all. The group's defensive mechanisms, operating to preserve an ignorance of its own wishes and projecting them instead onto some individual scapegoat, are very much like the driving demand of the chorus that the hero fulfill its group expectations. The scapegoat is frequently the conductor, who is called on to know the things that the group does not as yet dare to know. The re-enactment of the drama of a conflict under the guidance of the conductor can lead to a re-evaluation and re-integration of feelings, which finally make the presence of the conductor unnecessary.

Freud might have accepted this transposition. He would most certainly have reached the conclusion that any event in a group must be regarded as something that potentially involves the group as a whole and that, like the Oedipus complex in the individual patient, can express itself in a wide variety of configurations. The therapist's task is to examine this matrix and locate—to use the language of Foulkes—the crucial disturbance. It is hardly likely that Freud would have been content to make a simple extrapolation from the psychoanalysis of the individual patient to the psychoanalysis of the group without considering the nature of the transformation involved. He was too aware that something fairly radical took place when what he termed the group of two was extended to encompass a much larger number of persons. He was a group psychologist on his way to becoming a group psychotherapist but was deflected by pressing intrapsychic considerations.

It was left to others to follow his lead, and group psychotherapy has undoubtedly profited from the fact that a number of dedicated people have made it their life work to carry on where Freud left off and to pursue the path to its logical conclusion. Every discipline must be explored to its very edge of non-sense and beyond, so that practitioners can learn from recountable experience where the impossible lies. It is fairly certain that Freud himself would have soon recognized that the group is not the most suitable place to analyze a transference neurosis, and he would then have focused on group formations as the nub of therapy in the group situation. (It is one of the historian's prerogatives to speak for the dead, who can no longer speak for themselves!)

Powdermaker and Frank and the Eclectic Approach

By 1953, the literature on group psychotherapy was already voluminous, although the body of established knowledge was still small. There was a wide range of group practice from simple exhortation to profound psychoanalysis. The gamut, according to Slavson, ran from

the authoritarian approach of Low, the confessional-inspirational method of Pratt and his followers, the didactic technique of Klapman, the aesthetic activation of Altschuler, the drama forms of Moreno, the social-educational method of Bierer, and the quasi-analytical approach of Wender and Foulkes, to the psychoanalytic method of Schilder.

Therefore, Powdermaker and Frank thought it necessary to carry out some studies on how group psychotherapy works. To observe and study the therapeutic process, however, they had to decide on some form of group psychotherapy. Their choice fell on the analytic for two reasons: They thought that it would be of greater help to their patients, and they thought that the analytic approach offered considerable promise of adding to the understanding of group dynamics in relation to therapy. The next question was: What choice of analytic? Here they decided on an eclectic compromise that tries to draw from the best of everyone while eschewing their faults.

Their eclectic treatment is of importance in the history of group psychotherapy because it induced a large number of therapists to practice it. Even today, many American group psychotherapists continue to use the method without being aware of its origins. This composite technique is best summarized by Powdermaker and Frank themselves:

Our approach to group therapy with neurotic patients had points in common with that of Foulkes, Ackerman, Slavson, and Wolf, and we were influenced in our thinking by Schilder's analytic concept and Trigant Burrow's emphasis on the study of group interaction. We were stimulated by Bion's descriptions of the group process but avoided his exclusive attention to it. Although our groups were not social groups as were Bierer's, the leadership was completely informal. We differed from Schilder in not using questionnaires and set tasks, and from Wender, Klapman, and Lazell in that in no case did the psychiatrist in charge give case histories or systematic presentation of psychiatric concepts. We encouraged interaction among the patients. We helped them to examine their attitudes and behavior toward one another (*process*) as well as the personal material which they presented (*content*).

The striking and unique thing about this venture is that it was simultaneously engaged in treating the patient and studying the process. This dual approach is, unfortunately, unusual in the history of group psychotherapy. The attitude toward research, nevertheless, was essentially clinical, and the patient's needs were always put before the investigation. Both the individual patient and the group were brought under scrutiny, although the examination of process was organismic rather than elementaristic. Their method was to single out and describe patterns of change involving individual patients, the group, and the therapist, and these descriptions were termed situation analyses based on running accounts.

An illustration of a situation analysis will help to clarify the way in which significant developments within a session can be delineated and stored for later examination in relation to previous and subsequent sessions. The example given is abstracted from a first meeting and demonstrates the rallying of the group after a typical sticky beginning.

Doctor	Nonsupportive, passive, silent.
Group	Patients seemed to know they should be discussing personal matters; afraid to reveal themselves to others; talked on impersonal subjects. Tension rose.
Central patient	X, dominating member; repeatedly tried to get focus of attention.
Situation preceding rally	Group talked on impersonal subjects.
Precipitating event	Doctor intervened: "Have you any idea of the trend of the discussion?" Tension rose sharply. X, after trying in vain to question others, introduced rallying topic.

Event   Rally round topic: feelings about psychoanalysis and resistance to therapy.

Effects   Intimate discussion of illness. Relief of tension.

On several occasions over the next seven sessions, the crucial role of the therapist in precipitating a rally was nicely brought out. He precipitated a rally mainly by indicating to the group, in an uncritical way, that he was aware of their difficulty and that he was not at all anxious or uncomfortable about it.

If more such careful investigations had been carried out over the last two decades, the history of group psychotherapy as a branch of scientific medicine would be completely different, and therapists would be less confused by the confusions and the wild uncertainties that pervade the field today. Of even greater interest: The follow-up evaluation was included in the study and underscored the advantage of constantly monitoring work in this way. It cannot be emphasized too strongly that the lack of such basic procedures is a serious handicap. True, evaluation of therapy is a major methodological problem, but even tentative efforts in this direction are better than none and would certainly help to maintain a vigilant self-critical posture, without which therapists are at the mercy of every passing therapeutic whimsy.

If good or even acceptable evaluative techniques had been available, the Powdermaker and Frank investigation would have been a great and epoch-making one instead of simply an interesting and unusual attempt. For example, changes were assessed somewhat loosely in terms of symptoms, social adjustments, and characteristic responses to such stimuli as the Rorschach test. Such assessments were good enough for the time but would demand more rigorous application today.

From a conceptual point of view, the study was curiously barren, as if the authors were frozen in their methodology and unable to go beyond the observed facts. In their defense, however, it should be emphasized that, at the present time, group psychotherapy stands more in need of facts than of concepts, and there is much need for another such detailed study.

New Developments

The term "new" has a serious limitation when it is applied to a rapidly growing field in which anything new soon changes into something old. However, the beginnings of group psychotherapy are still near enough to have the term "new" simply denote something not there from the start. There are new developments by the pioneers Moreno, Slavson, Foulkes, Bion, Bierer, Dreikurs, and others who are still with us and still actively developing; and there are new developments by those who have invaded the field within the last two decades.

Moreno, although practicing a particular form of group treatment that is different from classical group psychotherapy in the way it is set up and structured, has generated a number of important theoretical concepts that have become part of group psychotherapy and are acknowledged by both analytic and nonanalytic schools. He has claimed, with some justification, to have fathered many of the new movements, such as encounter groups, training groups, and existential approaches. His warming up procedures have been incorporated into laboratory exercises used by most of the new methods, and his sociometric tests have been widely employed, not only by sociologists and social psychologists but also by group therapists desirous of sampling group characteristics during the on-going life of the group.

Within recent times, a cascade of experimental approaches has inundated the group arena, so that the more conventional procedures have been transiently swamped by fresh waves of novel and largely untried techniques to which the public has oriented itself because of the novelty, the implicit seductiveness, and the promise of quick change. Often there is a pursuit of the unusual for its own sake on the part of the therapist and a craving for new experiences in human relatedness on the part of the patients. It is difficult to say whether the bewildering situation today in the field of group psychotherapy reflects the primitive phase of its development or the disturbing nature of the world. Perhaps both.

If anxiety was the menace to our patients 20 years and more ago, alienation has emerged as the imperative concern now. The multiple and miasmic urgencies of life today have brought about an impatience with slower historical procedures, and immediate existence in all its calamitous ramifications has become the focus of therapeutic concern. Anything outside the here-and-now is poorly tolerated by the driven inhibitants of this nuclear age. The situation—first postulated by Trigant Burrow many years ago, when he saw therapists and patients in the same predicament—has been incorporated into the existential group movement.

The group therapist is no longer the most psychologically knowledgeable member of the group, the recognized and revered expert in theory and practice; instead, he stands out only by virtue of being the most honest, the most sincere, the most authentic, and the most accepting, both in his commitment to life and to the group. In fulfilling this role, he is obliged to be as open and as honest about himself as he expects the group members to be about themselves. He is offered no special privileges, no diplomatic immunity, no special status. He is a human being among other human beings, a patient among other patients—but perhaps a little more aware of what is implied than are the others in the group.

The development has been a fascinating one. Although it was Freud who first talked of the leaderless group and the deep anxieties that this situation aroused, it was Bion who put these theoretical ideas to the clinical test and examined the panic that ensued at the deepest levels. The group analytic approach, on the other hand, keeps the therapist in the background but sees him as indispensable to the therapeutic life of the group; he does not have to prove his indispensability by defaulting. Today, in some circles, the therapist has become the model of the good patient. He lays on the table not only all his countertransference cards but also his self-recognized human failings, so that he can no longer claim differentiation from his fellow members because of his mental health or superior clinical insights. He is no longer an alarming model of conventional normality. As a consequence, the group can get closer to one another without guilt or shame, since there is apparently no conscience figure to watch over them like the eye of God.

This godlessness has been much exploited by encounter groups. Under the highly emotional impact deliberately fostered by such settings, an exhilarating sense of freedom from prohibitions and inhibitions is rapidly generated. To the uncritical and naive observer, the internal censors seem to have been eradicated or at least put to sleep. Unfortunately, the vacation from conscience is more apparent than real and more short-lasting than claimed. The return to conventional circumstances soon reactivates the dormant conscience and may even intensify its more punitive and primitive qualities. Fenichel wrote that the superego is soluble in alcohol; it is also soluble—as Le Bon, McDougall, and Freud pointed out—in the ecstasies occasioned by close group interaction, but there is always a hang-over when reality once again asserts itself. This is, in fact, the oldest lesson in psychotherapy: The internal structures of the mind were not built in a day and cannot be reconstituted over a weekend.

American vs. European Group Psychotherapy

Psychotherapy, like other social institutions, is extraordinarily sensitive to cultural influences. The organizational competence of American group psychotherapists has fast brought about a professionalization of group psychotherapy in the United States. What is gained by annual and regional meetings, with their opportunity for scientific interchange, is to some extent lost by the conforming influences of the Establishment. It is here that the experimentalists have a necessary role to play. Every movement is both embarrassed and vivified by its lunatic fringe; heresy, as St. Augustine once pointed out, can be both a threat and a stimulus to progress. The recent rash of experimental approaches has led to some understandable alarm in established circles but also to a surprising willingness to consider these approaches as potential contributions awaiting the test of time and experience. Although American group psychotherapy at times gives the impression of originating from committee work, there are enough unpsychotic and unpsychopathic experimentalists in the field to ensure a measure of vitality to the group movement. What is not acceptable and what can be incorporated into the body of knowledge must engage in a running battle if the field is to advance.

The criterion for acceptance has been laid down in somewhat categorical fashion by Slavson. According to him, all sound psychotherapies have five elements in common: relation or transference, catharsis, insight or ego-strengthening or both, reality-testing, and sublimation. In an acceptable technique, at least the first three of these five criteria should be present. These canons are too much in some respects and insufficient in others. The criteria refer to group psychotherapy solely as a treatment and not as a scientific practice, so that blatantly nonscientific techniques could find acceptance. Many of these nonscientific techniques, especially the cathartic variety, are put forward in Messianic fashion, advertised with Madison Avenue skills, and practiced with a complete absence of discrimination. Their proponents seem singularly blind to all shortcomings and tend to respond to the enthusiasm of their patients rather than to the considered criticisms of their colleagues.

The situation in Europe, especially in Britain, is somewhat different, with the disequilibrium on the other side. There is a striking absence of professional government. The field is small, the practitioners are few, and the handful of theoreticians wend their own lonely ways far from the clamor of conventions. They behave, in all respects, like gifted amateurs, seeking an internal consistency in their systems and failing to respond to outside comment. By American standards, the approach in Britain is less dramatic, less positive, more ambiguous, and given to understatement. There is something peculiarly reticent about the procedures employed, reflective of the culture as a whole. Here, for example, is a comment by Foulkes and Anthony:

The group-analytic approach is complex but not spectacular. It lays stress on under-emphasis and sees merit in the minimum. It recognizes the importance of the conductor's role, but it prevails on him to function as much as possible behind the scenes in the background.

The absence of affirmation sometimes verges on the negative side, so that the technique may seem, to Americans at least, eccentrically unforthcoming. There is a defaulting tendency on the part of British group therapists that can mislead not only their colleagues but also their patients.

CONCLUSIONS

For a scientific purpose, a system of group psychotherapy should demonstrate certain characteristics: It should be impartable to students by the ordinary routines of training, including training therapy, and impartable to colleagues who do not wish to join an esoteric cult to complete their understanding; it should provide a therapeutic model that helps to explain the process of therapy and the process of change; it should carry out periodic research evaluations on the efficacy of its treatment; it should be flexible enough to develop and alter under the impetus of further knowledge and practice; its proponents should remain eternally vigilant with respect to the tightening grip of dogma and fully aware of the limitations as well as the assets of their particular treatment model; and, finally, the system should provide an economic, elegant, and powerfully explanatory theoretical framework linking together group psychology and group psychotherapy in an indivisible whole. There should be special regard paid not only to the individual patient's status and behavior in the current group but also to him as a member of many human groups from infancy on. Group psychology must become developmental if group psychotherapy is to develop further.

These unseasonable reflections may not be altogether in keeping with the contemporary mood, and the bias is often unashamedly blatant. But they do try, in Nietzsche's terms, to bring the past into a living contact with the present for the ultimate good of both. The past looks much better viewed in the context of the present, and the present gains enormously in the logic of its position when it is placed in the perspective of time. From such beginnings, each practitioner must improvise a serviceable history for himself.

REFERENCES

Abercrombie, M. L. J. Group Analysis International Panel and Correspondence, *2:* 145, 1970.

Ackerman, N. W. Some general principles in the use of group psychotherapy. In *Current Therapies in Personality Disorders*, p. 279, B. Glueck, editor. Grune & Stratton, New York, 1946.

Anthony, E. J. Reflections on twenty-five years of group psychotherapy. Int. J. Group Psychother., *18:* 277, 1968.

Bierer, J. *Therapeutic Social Clubs*. H. K. Lewis, London, 1948.

Bion, W. R. *Experiences in Groups*. Tavistock Publications, London, 1961.

Burrow, T. *The Social Basis of Consciousness*. Harcourt, Brace & World, New York, 1927.

Ezriel, H. A psycho-analytic approach to group treatment. Brit. J. Med. Psychol., *23:* 59, 1950.

Foulkes, S. H. *Introduction to Group-Analytic Psychotherapy*. William Heinemann, London, 1948.

Foulkes, S. H. *Therapeutic Group Analysis*. International Universities Press, New York, 1965.

Foulkes, S. H., and Anthony, E. J. *Group Psychotherapy, the Psychoanalytic Approach*. Penguin Books, London, 1957.

Freud, S. *Group Psychology and the Analysis of the Ego*. Hogarth Press, London, 1953.

Klapman, J. W. *Group Psychotherapy: Theory and Practice*. Grune & Stratton, New York, 1946.

Lazell, E. W. The group treatment of dementia praecox. Psychoanal. Rev., *8:* 168, 1921.

Le Bon. *The Crowd*. E. Benn, London, 1952.

Lewin, K. *Field Theory in Social Science*. Harper & Brothers, New York, 1951.

Main, T. F. GAIPAC Meeting, London, August 1969. Group Analysis International Panel and Correspondence, *2:* 133, 1970.

Moreno, J. L. *Who Shall Survive?* Beacon House, New York, 1953.

Mullan, H., and Rosenbaum, M. *Group Psychotherapy*. Free Press of Glencoe, New York, 1962.

Powdermaker, F., and Frank, J. D. *Group Psychotherapy*. Harvard University Press, Cambridge, 1953.

Pratt, J. H. The principles of class treatment and their application to various chronic diseases. Hosp. Soc. Serv., *6:* 401, 1922.

Schilder, P. The analysis of ideologies as a psychotherapeutic method, especially in group treatment. Amer. J. Psychiat., *93:* 601, 1936.

Slavson, S. R. *Analytic Group Psychotherapy*. Columbia University Press, New York, 1950.

Slavson, S. R. *A Textbook in Analytic Group Psychotherapy*. International Universities Press, New York, 1964.

Wender, L. Group psychotherapy: a study of its application. Psychiat. Quart., *14:* 708, 1940.

Whitaker, D. S., and Lieberman, M. A. *Psychotherapy through the Group Process*. Atherton Press, New York, 1964.

Wolf, A., and Schwartz, E. K. *Psychoanalysis in Groups*. Grune & Stratton, New York, 1962.

2

Comparison of Different Types
of Group Psychotherapy

Hyman Spotnitz, M.D., Med.Sc.D.

INTRODUCTION

The practice of group psychotherapy is based on the finding that mental illness and mental dysfunctioning can be ameliorated through the psychological effects of several persons upon one another. The fact that improvement in mental functioning tends to alleviate and may eventually cure mental illness has inspired countless efforts to exploit the healing force of the group to meet the therapeutic needs of a widening range of patients—people with highly diverse problems seeking treatment at all phases of the life cycle. Concurrently, the commitment of virtually all schools of psychotherapy to group practice and its elaboration in their respective conceptual frameworks have encouraged the parallel development of a wide array of group psychotherapeutic approaches. These approaches have developed so rapidly and have been described so idiosyncratically by some of their proponents that the literature gives the impression that there are as many different ways of treating groups as there are group psychotherapists.

That impression is also generated by the therapist's use of himself as a professional instrument. In psychological treatment, personal influence cannot be discounted. Each practitioner is a unique personality. His style of conducting a group cannot be duplicated by another therapist, however similar their professional qualifications, treatment philosophies, and clinical skills may be.

Nevertheless, group psychotherapy as a scientific discipline owes its development to the systematic application of validated discoveries about the therapeutic needs of people with psychological problems and to carefully formulated specifics about the planning and conducting of their treatment, the selection and grouping of patients, and related considerations. These specifics are indices to the built-in limitations and potential values of group psychotherapy and thus offer a means of comparing its different forms.

This chapter serves two purposes: (1) It helps the student penetrate barriers of theory and language that separate the different systems of group psychotherapy and distinguish their actual differences from their common factors. (2) It suggests general guidelines for determining the specific effectiveness of one or another approach for a given patient. No attempt is made to discuss or even mention all the group methods that have been reported, but this comparison does encompass those methods that dominate contemporary practice.

DEFINITION OF GROUP PSYCHOTHERAPY

The presence of three or more persons in the same place at the same time is essential to qualify a procedure as group psychotherapy. The triadic formations covered by the term include one patient working with

27

two therapists as well as a pair of patients, often a married couple, working with one therapist. Another essential factor in group psychotherapy is that they meet for the express purpose of influencing one another, directly or indirectly, by psychological means. Still another requirement is that this reciprocal influence be therapeutic to the participants—in no wise harmful to any of them—and help them improve their functioning as human beings.

Defined loosely in terms of those core requirements, group psychotherapy is a procedure in which three or more persons assemble at an appointed time and place for a definite period to beneficially influence their mental health and functioning by psychological means.

The main value of that broad designation is that it serves the purpose of this chapter, specifying only the factors that distinguish all forms of group psychotherapy and accommodating the innumerable diverse factors associated with its practice—factors related to the participants and their joint activities. Among the major differences are the subjects of the treatment, the composition of the group, the therapist's general orientation and specific strategies, the goals of the treatment, and the nature of the results achieved. Experimentation with these variables, which has recently increased, accounts for the kaleidoscopic character of contemporary group psychotherapy.

Descriptive terms frequently used in the literature convey some of the most obvious differences. Groups are dichotomized as large and small, inpatient and outpatient, long-term and short-term, continuous and time-limited, open and closed. Groups based on specific criteria for membership are referred to as structured; those whose composition follows no plan are blanket groups. The dichotomy of heterogeneous and homogeneous also relates to composition.

The labeling of the established procedures is haphazard. The name may be derived from any one of the group's properties or dimensions, such as its size, membership, field of application, duration, or operational principles. The theroretical framework in which the group is conducted may or may not be indicated. For example, "family therapy" is a label attached to groups whose only shared characteristic is that they are composed of members of the same family. More adequately identified are groups whose names derive from two or more variables, such as "psychodramatic family therapy" and "activity group therapy for latency-age boys." In striking contrast are the catchy names attached to tangential variants referred to as personal growth groups, the human potential movement, etc. A strong element of salesmanship pervades such christenings as "nude marathons," "basic encounters," and "group grope."

VARIATIONS IN PRACTICE
Size

The number of participants ranges from one patient with two or more therapists, as already indicated, to one hundred or more group members. There is no fixed boundary between large and small groups, but those referred to as small or face-to-face usually contain no fewer than four patients and no more than ten. Some practitioners regard six, seven, or eight patients as the ideal number. Small groups prevail today. Even though depth of treatment is primarily a function of the therapist's technique, it is not possible to work effectively for characterological change in groups that are too large for member-to-member interaction.

Groups larger than 12 and with an upper limit of 20 or 30 patients are sometimes designated as intermediate groups. They provide a suitable format for lectures and the discussion of common problems. In larger formations, therapy necessarily merges into educational, morale-building, or social activity. Large therapy groups, usually conducted in institutional or community settings, are more or less limited to the repressive-inspirational approach. Such groups are often organized to work on a specific problem—for example, alcoholism or obesity. Some are known as self-help groups because they operate without a professional leader. In many cities, Recovery, a self-directed group of psychiatric patients discharged from institutions, conducts a supportive program known as will training.

Composition

Although groups composed of patients of the same age or sex are sometimes referred to as homogeneous, that term is more strictly applied to those in the same diagnostic category or presenting the same problem. Persons suffering from different forms of psychoneurosis or from the same psychoneurotic condition, such as hysteria or phobia, may constitute a group. Similarly, the group identified as homogeneous may be made up of homosexuals, drug addicts, or patients with the same psychosomatic condition. In medical group therapy, those with a particular organic illness, such as cardiac disease, are treated together.

The majority of groups treated in private practice are heterogeneous, selection being based on the principle of mixing rather than matching personality types. This practice, begun as a matter of expediency, has been reinforced by the finding that the balancing of persons with diversely structured personalities facilitates the development of therapeutic interchanges, provided their socioeconomic backgrounds are reasonably compatible. Thus, different diagnostic categories are represented in heterogeneous groups, among them psychoneuroses, personality disorders, the milder psychosomatic complaints, borderline conditions, and some prepsychotic and postpsychotic states.

Therapists who conduct heterogeneous groups try to exclude persons who would not benefit from the shared treatment experience or who might be a disruptive influence on others, but there are no generally accepted criteria for exclusion on the basis of psychiatric classification. Whereas some authorities, notably Slavson, exercise extreme care in selection and advocate the exclusion of patients in specific diagnostic categories from group treatment, others pay scant attention to diagnosis. For example, Berne stated that almost any patient, if properly prepared, can be assigned to a group. He advocated the policy of picking candidates at random or in order of application, on the assumption that such selection favors heterogeneity.

Some practitioners, the author among them, rather than ignoring the diagnostic factor, regard it as an inadequate source of information on how patients will behave in the group setting. Therefore, these therapists try to ascertain the types of defenses that each candidate activates in interpersonal situations. The assessment of current impulses and defenses is one aspect of achieving a balancing of personality types, which facilitates the functioning of the group as a unit. The blending of placid and excitable persons with some who tend to arouse excitement and others who check it is sought by therapists who conduct group treatment as a primarily emotional experience.

Some differences in individual modes of conducting groups are dictated by the personal characteristics of their members. Their age, sex, and one or another particular about their life status are often reflected in the labels attached to their groups.

Age. Therapy groups are conducted for people in all age categories. Groups for adults often include the middle-aged as well as young adults, but the age span is narrower in those groups conducted for children, adolescents, and elderly people. Children treated together are generally at the same developmental level.

Sex. Private practitioners customarily treat men and women together. However, participation in some groups is limited to members of the same sex.

Kinship. Some therapy groups are composed of strangers, others of persons in real-life relationships. Outstanding among the natural groups are those consisting of members of one family. Some practitioners of family therapy treat several families together; the creation of an artificial group through the fusion of natural groups has also been reported in the treatment of married couples. Relatives of patients with similar conditions—for example, parents of severely disturbed children or the spouses of alcoholics—participate in groups organized to deal with the management of these patients. Friends and neighbors as well as family members are assembled in social network therapy, a brief series of meetings organized to deal with a crisis situation in the life of a schizophrenic person; the tribal support of his natural group is solicited as a possible alternative to his hospitalization.

Socioeconomic Affiliations. People who work together may be assembled for a specific therapeutic purpose, such as sensitivity training. Although these groups are usually characterized as group work for normals, some are so conducted as to be relatively indistinguishable from conventional therapy groups. Sensitivity training is also carried on under the auspices of social organizations and churches.

Professional Status. A prime example of groups constituted on the basis of professional identity are those conducted under the aegis of training in psychotherapy. To an increasing extent, group training in the behavioral sciences is oriented to therapeutic goals.

General Orientation and Approach

Most group therapists adhere to a theoretically grounded approach, the labeling of which reflects, implicitly or explicitly, their *modus operandi* and treatment philosophy. To identify a practitioner as an analytic group therapist, as a psychodramatist, or as a behavior therapist, for example, is to give important clues to how he views and addresses himself to his patients' problems. However, some therapists rather consistently apply the procedures consonant with their own school of therapy while others operate more empirically—a difference conveyed by the terms "strict methodology" and "fluid methodology."

The majority of therapists who conduct outpatient groups practice analytic group psychotherapy. The therapist who operates according to psychoanalytic principles, as adapted for the shared treatment experience, and applies the working concepts of transference and resistance remains a relatively unobtrusive figure in the group, intervening primarily to interpret behavior. Within that frame, three somewhat different approaches have developed: Some therapists

treat the individual *in* the group; others treat him *through* or *by* the group; and still others take an intermediate position, treating the individual as much as possible through the group as an entity and focusing on him separately to the extent necessary to resolve specific problems. Parloff has referred to these positions, overlapping in some respects, as intrapersonalist, integralist, and transactionalist or interpersonalist. The intrapersonalists place the least emphasis, and the integralists the most emphasis, on the role of group processes. The interpersonalists or transactionalists try to extract maximal therapeutic leverage from group processes in order to facilitate concurrent characterological change.

The theoretical divergences are reflected in the labeling of the analytic approaches. Therapists referred to as intrapersonalists have established such designations as "group psychoanalysis" and "psychoanalysis in groups" for their procedures; "psychoanalysis" has been abjured by other therapists. For example, Whitaker and Lieberman identify their system as "psychotherapy through the group process," and Foulkes introduced the terms "group-analytic psychotherapy" and "therapeutic group analysis."

Specific Strategies

Among therapists operating in the same general frame of reference as well as among those of different persuasions, much variability in therapeutic strategies and personal functioning in the treatment sessions is reported.

Probably the most obvious difference is the way therapists relate to patient-members of the group. Personal styles of conducting treatment range from authoritarian through didactic, blank screen (where the predominant attitude is passivity), and permissive to leaderless. The term "leaderless" may denote the therapist's physical absence from some or all treatment sessions or his attitude of scientific detachment, an attitude maintained by some research-oriented practitioners. But in the present context, "leaderless" refers to the disclaimer of more responsibility for the operation of the group than that assumed by the patients—an attitude characterized by Mullan in 1955 as status denial. Leaderlessness in that sense usually implies a high degree of personal involvement, the communication of information about the therapist's real-life identity, values, and immediate emotional reactions— all expressed in behavior as well as in words in some of the new approaches.

Diversity in professional backgrounds among practitioners of group psychotherapy helps to account for the wide spectrum of strategies and attitudes reported. Rather than adhering to the traditional view of their role as one of healing sick people, some therapists implement other assumptions about the problems of their group members. Practitioners, physicians among them, who depart from the medical model to an appreciable extent find it more congenial to view the therapy group as a social system and relate to its members in terms of sociological, philosophical, or theological systems of thought. The specific problems presented by patients are often regarded as social tensions, dynamic pressures, and the like. Surveying this variegated picture, Lieberman, Lakin, and Whitaker stated:

Therapeutic strategies range from those in which the therapist possesses a total encompassing charisma and, much like a guru, acts as the interpreter of reality and the center of emotional cathexis, to those in which the therapist acts as conductor or a social engineer.

Little is known about the therapeutic implications of these departures from the more or less established role of parent surrogate.

Sessions without the Therapist. The majority of practitioners maintain the policy of conducting all sessions of a group. Others incorporate meetings without the therapist in the treatment process. This practice was introduced by Wolf and Schwartz, who refer to these regularly scheduled gatherings as alternate sessions.

Use of Co-Therapists. Most groups are conducted by a single therapist, but current reports suggest an appreciable increase in the number treated by two or more. The practice of dual therapy was probably introduced for training purposes, with the second therapist serving primarily as a recorder and observer while his more experienced colleague actually conducted the group. However, many co-therapy teams today are composed of a male and a female therapist who share this responsibility.

Co-therapy is a controversial practice. Authors who question its value argue that it compounds countertransference phenomena, that it tends to contaminate the transference reactions of patients, and that their treatment is also interfered with because competitive strivings and even serious differences between the team members develop more or less inevitably. Exponents of co-therapy claim that the family constellation is replicated with the presence of mother and father transference objects, thus facilitating the progress of specific categories of patients. Exponents also point out practical considerations, such as the fact that one therapist can conduct the group in the absence of the other.

Since 1957, when Spitz and Kopp investigated the wide range of methods employed in co-therapy, including the treatment of one patient by as many as ten therapists, many additional variations have been reported.

Group Stimulus Situations

In any type of group psychotherapy, the stimulus situation is fundamentally different from that in the one-to-one treatment relationship. In individual analytic therapy, for example, the patient is stimulated mostly through verbal communication and auditory feedback, from his own words and the interventions of the analyst. The group setting adds to these the important factor of visual stimulation and visual feedback.

In the verbal group therapies, the therapist may limit himself to intellectual communication, which is generally effective in dealing with emotional problems that originated in the oedipal stage of development. Patients whose problems are associated with pre-oedipal (preverbal) stages are usually more responsive to emotional and symbolic communications.

Group therapists have traditionally limited themselves to auditory and visual modes of influence. The major exceptions are found in psychodrama and in the play and activity group therapies for children, in which feedback from action is a significant source of stimulation. The plethora of group methods recently introduced, some under the aegis of therapy and others characterized as growth experiences, relegate auditory and visual stimulation to a less important role. These new methods operate primarily through bodily sensations, including tactile and kinesthetic. Participants are encouraged to touch one another and to engage in other forms of physical contact—sexual or aggressive or both. Even taste and smell sensations may be stimulated.

Much experimentation is going on at the present time to determine whether such stimulation is necessary or desirable in psychotherapy. In the author's experience, physical contact and tactile stimulation do not contribute to significant personality change. In some instances, they preclude successful treatment.

HISTORY OF CLASSIFICATION

Various sorting racks have been devised to accommodate the multitude of practices designated as group psychotherapy and to elucidate their significant similarities and differences. But few schemata in this field have escaped the fate of rapid obsolescence. No generally accepted classification exists today.

Early attempts to classify the group methods reflected the initial need to know the different ways psychotherapy can be conducted in the group setting. Descriptive classifications are characteristic in an early developmental period, but, after one knows how to do it, answers are needed to the questions "For whom?" and "What does it accomplish?" Successive classifications have moved somewhat closer to supplying answers to those questions, although these classifications are still hampered by the clinical-impressionistic nature of the reports on treatment and the consequent difficulties of conducting evaluative research. The classifications discussed below in chronological sequence were made over a period of 25 years, and they illustrate how different investigators have attempted to rise above the level of descriptiveness in an immature field of practice.

1943

Giles Thomas, following Merrill Moore's simple differentiation of the individual psychotherapies, discerned two major categories of group psychotherapy—the repressive-inspirational and the analytic—"with various degrees of combination of the two." Accordingly, he arrayed the methods reported by the early 1940's along an axis, with Schilder at one end and Alcoholics Anonymous at the other end (see Figure 1). In the accompanying review, Thomas stated

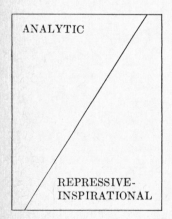

ANALYTIC

REPRESSIVE-
INSPIRATIONAL

Schilder

Wender
Lazell

Chappell
Marsh

Pratt, Rhoades, Buck, Harris, Hadden, Snowden
Schroeder
Altshuler

Alcoholics Anonymous

Figure 1. The first and best-known descriptive classification of the methods of group psychotherapy, by Giles W. Thomas. (From *Psychosomatic Medicine.*)

that good results had been claimed in a "large proportion of the patients treated (more than half)" but that it was not possible to compare them.

Thomas's survey, published in the journal *Psychosomatic Medicine*, was introduced by the following editorial note:

This is a new field, and the review covers extremely heterogeneous material: therapeutic procedures based completely on rough empiricisms like Alcoholics Anonymous, together with therapeutic efforts like Schilder's carefully analyzed and planned experiments and the experimentation of psychodrama based on definition of psychodynamic observations and concepts. The critical reader may receive the impression that this field is not yet ripe for this type of descriptive reviewing and needs above all a critical evaluation of the methods employed and the results reported. However, the Editors feel that this review gives, if not a complete, a rather broad descriptive view of the various attempts of group therapy and might stimulate interest in the obvious possibilities of this type of treatment.

That statement, expressive of the customary reaction of practitioners trained in the principles of scientific reporting on treatment, is of more than historical interest. The classification that provoked this reservation has attracted much attention over the years; Thomas's schema is still used and is regarded as one of the most helpful descriptions of the group approaches. Moreover, the above-quoted comment, published in 1943, has not, regrettably, lost its pertinence. Similar views have been expressed, particularly by those engaged in evaluative research in the field. For example, Goldstein, Heller, and Sechrest observed in 1966 that

group psychotherapy literature as a whole has remained at the earliest and most primitive level of observation and inquiry. . . . The plateau of descriptiveness which the current group psychotherapy literature represents must be built on, developed, and elaborated.

1945

J. L. Moreno formulated a table of eight polar categories and three points of reference to accommodate all the group approaches. He suggested that the methods be categorized as follows:

Subject of Therapy

(1) Constitution of the group (amorphous or structured on the basis of diagnosis); (2) Locus of treatment (natural life setting or special clinical situation); (3) Aim of treatment (causal or symptomatic);

Agent of Therapy

(4) Source or transfer of influence (therapist-centered or group-centered); (5) Form of influence (spontaneous and freely experienced or rehearsed and prepared);

Medium of Therapy

(6) Mode of influence (lecture or verbal, dramatic, or other actional mode); (7) Type of medium (conserved, mechanical, unspontaneous, or creative); (8) Origin of medium (face-to-face or presented from a distance, as from radio or television).

Actual distribution of the group methods under this comprehensive plan was not reported.

1957

Raymond J. Corsini, making a distinction between methods per se and the different ways each is applied, identified more than 25 methods by name. He distributed them under the headings of directive and nondirective to indicate the degree of control exercised by the therapist. The directive therapist was described as setting limits on the group members, the nondirective as setting limits on himself; the crucial factor was considered to be the

latitude permitted for decision making, especially in regard to interpretations.

Under his main headings, Corsini arranged the group methods under four subheadings: verbal-deep, verbal-superficial, actional-deep, and actional-superficial:

Directive

Verbal-Deep: (1) *Multiple therapy* (Dreikurs, Adlerian school)—one patient meeting with two therapists; (2) *Analytic therapy* (the circular-discussional approach common to the analytic schools, the main difference in its use being in the nature of the interpretations provided); (3) *Co-therapist methods: Behind-the-back technique;* (4) *Projective methods* (circular discussion of the spontaneously produced drawings of members);

Verbal-Superficial: (5) *Will training* (A. A. Low) in large and self-directed groups; (6) *Adlerian group counseling;* (7) *Lecture methods* (Pratt's class method, the repressive-inspirational procedures employing music or other attention-getting devices, repetition lectures, and procedures utilizing visual aids); (8) *Case histories* with discussion initiated by the therapist (Wender); (9) *Anonymous participation* (answering of questions written on unsigned slips of paper); (10) *Group bibliotherapy* (including J. W. Klapman's textbook-mediated therapy); (11) *Mechanical group therapy* (short recorded messages over a loudspeaker system);

Actional-Deep: (12) *Psychodrama* and related procedures introduced by Moreno;

Actional-Superficial: (13) *Dramatics* (theatrical productions by hospitalized patients); (14) *Puppets* (used for psychotherapeutic purposes in mental hospitals); (15) *Acting-out techniques* (as introduced by Ernst Simmel for release of repressed hostilities); (16) *ABC* (alphabet writing and other simple tasks performed cooperatively by patients using a blackboard);

Nondirective

Verbal-Deep: (17) *Client-centered method* (Carl Rogers); (18) *Leaderless therapy* (Bion-Rickman's research-oriented method, in which the therapist may engage himself verbally but assumes no special responsibility); (19) *Round-table psychotherapy* (introduced by McCann and Almada, in which the therapist is inactive while a small panel of patients sits around a table and many more constitute an audience);

Verbal-Superficial: (20) *Social-club therapy* (Joshua Bierer); (21) *Alcoholics Anonymous;*

Actional-Deep: (22) *Psychodramatic group therapy* (an adaptation of psychodrama with the group meeting in a circle);

Actional-Superficial: (23) *Activity group therapy* (Slavson); (24) *Music therapy;* and (25) *Auroratone* (abstract color films synchronized with music).

Corsini's classification, which affords a panoramic view of the practice of group therapy in the 1950's, illustrates the rapid rate of attrition in group methods. Many of the methods he listed have virtually disappeared from the current literature. The schema, moreover, does not distinguish between small and large groups. But the chief drawback of Corsini's classification lies in its failure to indicate the specific values and limitations of each method listed, the types of patients for which it is effective, and what it can accomplish.

1959

Although the classification proposed by J. W. Klapman in the second edition of his textbook on group psychotherapy has similarly outlived its usefulness, it represents the first attempt to categorize methods of group therapy on the basis of their suitability for patients. Decrying a preponderance of emphasis on any one approach as well as the waning status of approaches that he regarded as most appropriate for severely regressed patients, Klapman formulated a gradient classification presenting criteria and indices for

any given patient at any given time at any given level of aberrant psychic functioning.

He suggested that patients entering treatment in groups structured for the most disturbed patient population should be "upped" in due time to groups permitting a greater degree of autonomy. Consonant with those views, he described three degrees of disorganization observed in adult patients and matched these personality states with the optimally applicable group methods.

Patients in minimally disorganized states, encompassing most of the patients who qualify for treatment on an outpatient basis, were designated as patients of choice for analytic group therapy, psychodrama, and client-centered group therapy. Klapman listed about a dozen approaches as optimally applicable in moderately disturbed states. Among these approaches were a hierarchy of didactic procedures oriented to an improvement in intellectual functioning in groups small enough to permit two-way communication. For his third category—severely and relatively severely disorganized personality states—he recommended a score of methods oriented to different levels of ego functioning, from calisthenics and other physical activity to textbook-mediated therapy. The majority of the approaches described by

Klapman have fallen into disfavor, and his idea that the therapist is perforce limited to the lecture methods when treating psychotic patients has not been sustained. Nevertheless, the schema itself is notable in a period dominated by method-oriented classifications.

The classification by Frank and Powdermaker, also presented in 1959, has been more widely used. It suggests that the group treatment procedures, though marked by a considerable degree of overlap, fall into five general categories:

Didactic Groups, with guided discussions based on lectures by the therapist directed toward the promotion of intellectual insight and also allowing emotional interaction, used primarily with hospitalized psychotic patients;

Therapeutic Social Clubs, conducted especially for promoting skills in social participation among patients discharged from hospitals, and organized along parliamentary lines with the therapist intentionally maintaining an unobtrusive role;

Repressive-Inspirational Groups, designed chiefly to arouse positive group emotions and build morale through strong group identifications, in which the therapist gives inspirational talks and conducts relaxation exercises or group singing, and the patients may present testimonials or recitations;

Psychodrama;

Free-Interaction Groups, encompassing the various forms of group psychotherapy conducted by psychoanalytically oriented therapists and also group-centered psychotherapy, which promote an atmosphere conducive to the free verbalization of feelings and to the exposure and correction of immature attitudes.

1964

In a schema elucidating differences in depth of small-group approaches, S. R. Slavson distinguished group psychotherapy from group counseling and guidance, reserving the first term for procedures aiming at significant intrapsychic change in subjects with real pathology. By contrast, counseling and guidance, identified as different levels of psychonursing, are concerned with ego functioning and offer assistance with immediate and specific reality problems. Counseling is viewed as the most superficial and time-limited method, designed to clarify a course of action; guidance deals with emotional impediments to carrying through action by providing support and clarification without, however, tracing the blockages back to their source. Four major types of group therapy are discerned: activity group therapy for children, analytic for adults, para-analytic—a therapy of less depth for adolescents, the elderly, and specific diagnostic categories of adults, among them schizophrenic and borderline patients—and directive.

Slavson's classification illustrates one of the terminological confusions in the field, that generated by different conceptions of group counseling. Nonmedical therapists, in particular, tend to use the term group counseling interchangeably with group psychotherapy or regard it as a more intensive procedure than group guidance.

1965

Instead of compartmentalizing the systems of group treatment, some classifiers have represented them as constituting a continuum. Max Rosenbaum, for example, discerns a succession of interrelated methods, ranging from repressive-inspirational to regressive-reconstructive, which reflect the two extremes in the extent of personality change worked for. Between them he places the supportive and reparative therapies, the latter being oriented to the building up of weak defenses. A directive-didactic category, including behavior therapy in groups, is differentiated from nondirective methods, such as the group version of client-centered psychotherapy, psychodrama, therapeutic social clubs, and analytic group therapy.

1968

Howard A. Blatner's chart (see Figure 2) shows further progress toward specificity. It has a dual significance. Proposed as an aid in the selection of the type of group experience that will meet the patient's therapeutic

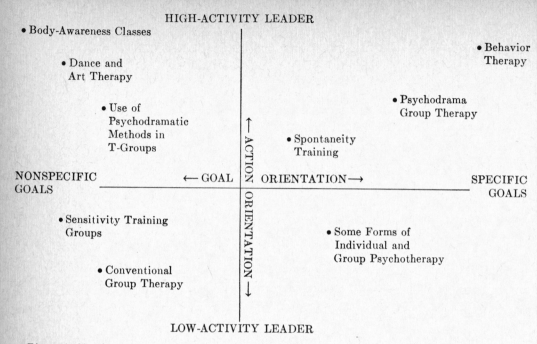

Figure 2. Classification of group procedures in relation to goal orientation and action orientation, by Howard A. Blatner. (From *Voices.*)

needs most efficiently, this schema appears to be the first to focus on the group approaches that were introduced during the 1960's. Moreover, methods are differentiated in terms of factors that were not mentioned in earlier classifications—the amount of structured activity imposed on group members by the therapist and the degree of specificity of the goals on which they agree. Of interest in this context is Eric Berne's suggestion in 1966 that therapies in which the practitioner's goals are limited or diffuse be identified as "soft," while those geared to more far-reaching, clearly defined goals and to achieving these goals expeditiously be identified as "hard" therapies.

A comparison of Figures 1 and 2, reproduced from clinical reports that span a period of 25 years, highlights the on-going shift from method-oriented to goal-oriented classifications. The comparison also suggests that group psychotherapy has been developing from an assortment of more or less similar instruments for doing psychotherapy in a general sense into an armamentarium of different instruments fashioned to achieve highly specific objectives.

SIGNIFICANCE OF GOALS

In the absence of scientific findings on the comparative values and limitations of the different types of group therapy, recommendations for treatment are usually based on clinical judgment and experience. By and large, the personal predilection, theoretical allegiance, training, and expertise of the practitioner whom the patient happens to consult determine the type of group experience he undergoes. Happenstance in selection, understandable as it is in this still primitive stage of development of group psychotherapy, is undesirable. It may deprive the patient of the type of treatment experience that would be most efficacious for him; it may also expose him to a distinctly harmful treatment experience. Rapid expansion of the group psychotherapeutic armamentarium increases the responsibility of the practitioner for discriminative selection of the instrument to be applied in each case.

Specificity in treatment will eventually be facilitated by objective evaluations of the results achieved through the different approaches. Without such evidence, however, the most reliable guide to specificity is a comparison of the stated treatment goals and results reported by the proponents of each procedure. The theories applied are of some significance because they indicate how the therapist attempts to influence the group through his behavior. But primary consideration needs to be given to what is sought, anticipated, and achieved through the use of the procedure. In short, the preferred method for a patient can best be determined by investigating the respective goals and results achieved through the alternatives available.

With increasing effectiveness in the matching of methods to patients, such data will probably be included in classifications of the group treatment approaches. At the present time, the facts have to be extracted from the professional literature—a laborious and not very rewarding task, owing to the unscientific nature of much of the reporting. Differentiations are vague; the range of applicability of some methods may not be defined; follow-ups are exceptional, claims in some instances being based exclusively on behavioral change in the treatment sessions.

Like individual psychotherapy, group psychotherapy has only one *raison d'être*—to benefit the individual. Although that justification may seem too elementary to mention, the prolonged preoccupation with methodology has tended to obscure it. *How* the patient is treated in the group setting has received much more attention than the precise benefits the therapist was striving to accomplish through his procedure. Nevertheless, distinct differences in the goals reported are readily discernible.

Distinctions are made in psychotherapy between *attainable* goals and *ideal* goals. An attainable or practical goal is commonly viewed as one that helps the patient achieve the optimal level of functioning consonant with his financial resources and material circumstances, his motivations when he enters treatment, and his ego capacities. It is generally recognized that such goals represent a modification of what theoretically constitutes the ideal objective of psychotherapy—personality maturation. What this notion implies offers a desirable criterion for a comparative evaluation of the goals reported.

Personality Maturation

Undoubtedly, the most ambitious goal that is pursued in psychotherapy is that of arresting an illness, repairing its ravages, and helping the patient outgrow his emotional immaturities so that he may realize his potential in life performance and happiness. Such an outcome, although more far-reaching than symptomatic relief or social recovery, does not necessarily mean that he has been relieved of all his problems or that he will not encounter new ones in the future. That outcome does signify, however, that he has the ability to feel, think, and behave appropriately in all normal situations and to meet the impact of extraordinarily traumatic experiences with considerable resiliency. Emotional versatility is an important measure of recovery because the seriously disturbed patient entering treatment tends to be bogged down in the essentially gross feelings of the young child. In the process of refining them and acquiring more discriminatory feelings, the patient eventually commands the hierarchy of feelings that characterize emotional evolution. The author therefore conceptualizes such curative change as the emergence of the emotionally mature personality.

Personality maturation is considered to be the natural outcome of biological and psychological growth in a succession of reasonably favorable internal and external environments. Highly specific reactions to disruptions of these growth processes at different developmental levels constitute the spectrum of functional disorders to which the psychotherapist addresses himself. The earlier the processes were thrown out of gear, the more damaging the impact on the organism. Disruptions of the maturational sequences that unfold during the first year of life are associated with psychosis. Other disruptions during the pre-oedipal period (the first two years) are associated with the impulse disorders, character disorders, severe obsessive-compulsive illness, and some psychosomatic disturbances. Vicissitudes encountered at later maturational levels are linked with psychoneurosis and the relatively minor disturbances experienced by the normal person in emotionally stressful circumstances.

In a person suffering from a deep-seated disorder, the psychotherapist usually recognizes two types of interferences with further personality growth: fixations and maladaptations. Both types are associated with the failure to meet maturational needs. Fixations result from exposure to situations of undue frustration or gratification or both. Maladaptations are perceived as the persistence of certain repetitive behaviors, patterned in these deficiency states, that drain off psychic energy into circuitous processes. These defensive maneuvers may interfere with the meeting of needs that are subsequently experienced. The psychological ingredients that would satisfy the later needs are usually available but cannot be assimilated because of the deviant patterns formed to compensate for the original deficiencies.

Patients succeed in liberating themselves from the compulsive operation of the maladaptive patterns when they are helped to engage in defense-freeing exercises and to re-experience the original fixations. They also require, concomitantly and subsequently, experiences that contribute to further growth.

Treatment oriented to the goal of personality maturation entails three essentially different dynamic operations. In this discussion, these dynamic operations are referred to as discrete steps and are focused on in the order in which each operation dominates the psychotherapeutic process, but they are overlapping concerns.

Step 1. In the treatment situation, reactivate and deal with the forces that prevent the patient from meeting his maturational needs. This step is what the psychoanalytically trained therapist refers to as controlling the development of transference. The interfering forces are aroused, analyzed, and influenced in terms of dealing with transference resistance.

Step 2. Help the patient meet his own maturational needs. This step is, in a sense, a tactical operation, engaged in to help the patient give up the maladaptive behavior. During the treatment, he experiences many psychological needs, such as a need for some immediate gratification, but in principle these needs are not met. The therapist extends aid only for meeting those needs that hamper emotional growth.

Step 3. Help the patient give up the maladaptive behavior without endangering the degree of personality maturation that he has achieved. In technical terms, this step is referred to as the working through of transference resistance.

Case History

John, 35 years old, was frequently referred to by the co-members of his group as "the great protector." He talked repeatedly in the sessions about disagreements with his wife concerning her disciplining of their 10-year-old son. John's tendency to rush to the little boy's defense whenever he was reproved for misbehaving and his refusal to associate himself with his wife's disciplinary measures gave rise to much friction in the family.

In the treatment sessions, John characteristically came to the defense of a young man whenever he was criticized by another member, a middle-aged woman. John made no effort to investigate the merits of the criticism. Objections to this behavior were voiced by several members of the group.

In the process of dealing with this maladaptation, the group came to recognize it as a component of John's infantile personality. His early years had been marked by emotional deprivation. After his parents' divorce, when John was two, he never saw his father. John eventually disclosed that he felt like a little boy. The pattern of "the great protector" appeared to represent an indirect attempt to call attention to his own need to be taken care of. The other group members responded to this understanding by helping him with his current problems with his wife. A progress report on his home life was often demanded of him in sessions when he did not volunteer such information.

As a group member, John functioned more and more appropriately as his need for help was satisfied. He tried to understand the communications of the other patients and to be helpful to all of them.

The resolution of the pattern of automatically jumping to the defense of the young man in the group was followed by a gradual but observable change in John's behavior with his family. He began cooperating with his wife in the upbringing of their son. John informed the group that he felt like a husband as well as a father.

In this case, the group therapist worked primarily on Steps 1 and 3. He conducted the treatment in such a way as to maintain a transference climate, addressed himself to the obstacles to cooperative functioning in the treatment sessions—illustrated by John's little-boy feelings—and helped the patient work through these interfering forces in the context of innumerable treatment situations. Step 2, on the other hand, was performed mostly by the group members themselves. His feelings of being understood and cared for by his co-patients, for example, helped him significantly in outgrowing the "great protector" pattern.

Emotional Feeding

As a matter of principle, the majority of analytic therapists who conduct individual treatment to produce significant personality change do not help the patient meet his maturational needs. They assume that the understanding they provide through their interpretations will suffice to free him to meet them himself through the emotional nourishment inherent in ordinary social situations. In the shared treatment experience, on the other hand, patients spontaneously "feed" one another, session after session, with feelings that satisfy different kinds of psychological needs.

Much of this emotional feeding is of little or no significance for personality growth; it provides momentary gratification without influencing the obstacles to change. But in addition to nutriments that create spells of excitement and dilute feelings of depression and alienation without helping to induce corrective change and the more conventional verbal communications of support or reassurance—all viewed by the author as meeting gratification needs—patients also pick up from one another specific feelings that stimulate growth processes. One of the special values of group psychotherapy lies in the contribution of patient interaction to the reciprocal meeting of maturational needs.

TYPES OF GROUP THERAPY

A classification of the various group procedures in terms of the type of problems they deal with and their relative effectiveness in clearing up these problems is not yet possible for reasons that have already been mentioned, notably the lack of specificity in the practice of group psychotherapy and discrepancies in the standards of reporting in the field. At the present juncture, however, these procedures can be differentiated roughly on the basis of the operational principles applied. The extent to which the practitioners employing each procedure deliberately address themselves to the three operations entailed in resolving the forces that have blocked personality maturation serves as the principal criterion in the assessment of each type of group therapy discussed.

Taking a phenomenological stance, the author has attempted to picture the field of contemporary practice and has, therefore, included in his sampling, along with the major established approaches, some that are innovative and unvalidated and whose status as psychotherapy is moot. Clinical concepts and techniques are delineated when deemed necessary to clarify their relation to the manifest goals of the treatment or the composition of the group or to facilitate the evaluation of the claims made.

Goals, it should be borne in mind, do not necessarily convey the therapeutic power residing in a method. In the course of the method's development, the results achieved most consistently come to be identified as its objectives. Goals are thus an expression of therapeutic outcome most efficaciously secured through past applications rather than a final pronouncement on therapeutic action. Hitherto untapped values may emerge in the future with somewhat different applications. As already mentioned, however, the goals currently enunciated and information on the extent to which these goals are attained provide the most reliable evidence available on the suitability of a procedure for a given patient and the predictable outcome of the case, assuming that the therapist is reasonably proficient.

The procedures surveyed below cover the spectrum of contemporary practice. The sequence in which they are discussed does not accurately reflect the order in which they were introduced; psychodrama, for example, antedates the cluster of analytic approaches that are reviewed first. Procedures with relatively similar goals are viewed in succession. The progression is from long-term to short-term, with approaches of the most recent vintage completing the series.

The author's impressions are based primarily on information provided by practitioners adhering to the procedure under review. Their assumptions, clinical practices, observations, and claims have been gathered from the literature. Personal communications from patients were another source of information. The claims advanced for each procedure were assessed on the basis of the data available.

Analytic Group Psychotherapy (Freudian)

It was pointed out earlier that therapists whose procedures are derived from individual psychoanalytic therapy differ substantially in the extent to which they integrate group processes into their conceptual framework as well as in their modifications of the parent techniques. In general, however, they conduct treatment on a long-term basis to produce significant characterological change in persons who are highly motivated to achieve such change. The treatment is conducted in a transference climate; transference and resistance phenomena are analyzed and, in some cases, worked through; the group equivalent of free association is employed; dreams are interpreted. Great reliance is placed on the acquisition of insight. Rapid change is not looked for, and the therapist does not necessarily apply himself to help the patient improve his interpersonal functioning.

Careful attention is given to the selection and grouping of patients, but criteria for admission vary. Patients with psychoneurotic conditions, character disorders, and other disturbances of the oedipal type are widely regarded as the most likely candidates. Practitioners who conduct analytic groups on an ambulatory basis usually exclude patients with more severe disorders or limit the number of such patients in composing a group. For instance, Wolf reported in 1968 that for psychoanalysis in groups he accepts persons with borderline and mild psychotic conditions and specifically excludes paranoid and hypermanic patients, those who hallucinate, severe stutterers, the seriously psychopathic, alcoholics, mental retardates, and patients with some types of cardiac disorder.

Some analytic group therapists structure treatment to include regular sessions without the therapist. Wolf claims that these alternate sessions promote

more spontaneous interactivity as well as more inappropriate responses and impulsivity.

This practice is predicated on the assumption that the group members will not seriously misbehave in the therapist's absence. Other therapists, including the author, challenge the assumption and believe that alternate sessions are undesirable for groups with acting-out or potentially psychotic patients. But such meetings may conceivably be recommended for the promotion of spontaneity in rigid and overcontrolled patients.

The goals of this method are defined in terms of psychosexual maturation. The therapist addresses himself to resolving the emotional forces that thwart maturation and focuses on the working through of maladaptive behavior (Steps 1 and 3).

Cautious assessment of ego strength and tolerance for regression is important before exposing a person with a severe disturbance to this regressive-reconstructive approach. The more deep-seated his problems, the more retrograde movement he has to engage in, and the more difficult it becomes to influence him effectively by interpretive interventions. Problems rooted in the preverbal period are more responsive to emotional and symbolic communications. Moreover, it is difficult to work on these problems without stimulating regressive tendencies that threaten the degree of adjustment to reality that the patient has achieved.

Consistent and confirmed techniques for the individual treatment of pre-oedipal patients have been reported, but the development of such approaches for group treatment oriented to meaningful change has not been claimed. Analytic therapists who accept severely disturbed persons in their groups do so within the framework of combined treatment.

Analytic Group Psychotherapy (Neo-Freudian)

Therapists who adhere to the theoretical constructs of the cultural and interpersonal schools of psychoanalysis differ notably from those who implement Freudian principles in their interpretations and formulation of goals.

Adler School (Individual Psychology). Adlerian therapists, notes Dreikurs, view their group members as social beings whose behavior is purposive and directed to social survival and self-realization. Although the group members have not learned to live together as equals, their life styles are based on self-set goals, and they do only what they intend to do. Frequently, they are unaware of these goals and intentions. Another principle of Adlerian psychology is the unity of the personality, which is viewed as an intertwining of dynamic, somatic, psychological, and social processes. Interpreting the phenomena observed in the group sessions, particularly the social aspects of the patients' problems, the therapist strives to bring them into awareness.

Psychotherapy is conducted primarily as an educational process in which emotional experience reinforces intellectual learning. Insight is not viewed as a prerequisite for change. Patients are encouraged to improve, recognize, and correct value systems that militate against desirable social functioning. An atmosphere of social equality and mutual helpfulness is created to counteract fears, anxieties, and emotional isolation. Intrapsychic dynamics are explored, and understanding is communicated, but more emphasis is placed on social reorientation and the counteracting of fears.

Changes in attitudes toward life are reported to express themselves in the alleviation of symptoms, improved functioning, and a sense of general well-being. Changes in the patient's early recollections are characteristic.

The goals are to increase the patient's self-respect and self-confidence—to remove feelings of inferiority—and to enhance his faith in his own worth and ability to grow. Character traits and ego functioning of the mature personality are described, but precisely how these improvements are brought about is not clear from the data available. The therapist concentrates on correcting maladaptive behavior (Step 3). The goals as conceptualized do not encompass the identification and meeting of the maturational needs that preserve the illness. Unless feelings of inferiority are permitted full expression in the process of removing them, the risk of producing fresh repressions is courted. In that case, improvement may be temporary, and psychosomatic problems may ensue.

Horneyan School. The therapist, notes Rose, assumes that a unifying process goes on in the group that can be turned in a healthy direction and used to work through neurotic blocks to growth. Sensitive to group atmosphere, the therapist distinguishes between cohesiveness that serves merely to relieve basic anxiety (feelings of weakness and isolation from the real self and the feeling that others are hostile) and cohesiveness that develops when the patients get to feel that belonging to the group is a healthful experience. Conflict and the emergence of anxiety are encouraged, but the anxiety is not permitted to become so intense that patients withdraw from the group.

The democratic values of the group help to liberate strivings toward cooperative mutuality, but, when corrective processes fail to operate, the therapist may intervene on any one of three levels, focusing on the group atmosphere, on interpersonal behavior, or on intrapsychic mechanisms. Through their interpersonal reactions, the group members repeatedly demonstrate the multidimensional and self-perpetuating nature of their individual neurotic patterns. The therapist permits these patterns and their consequences to be experienced for the purpose of encouraging new modes of behavior (Step 1).

Emphasis is placed on the here-and-now. Childhood memories are used as a vehicle for the expression of immediate feelings, and neurotic reactions are seen in terms of present character structure. The idiosyncratic defensive patterns of the patient are identified not in terms of repetition-compulsion or transference reactions but in terms of abnormal character structure, originating in childhood disturbances that led to a distorted concept of the self and the world (Step 3). Interpretations elucidate discrepancies between the idealized image of the self (the ideal self) and the real self.

The goal of the treatment, in Horney's term, is self-realization. The therapist works for significant and enduring character change, a restructuring of the personality. Self-realization is correlated with the capacity to feel free and independent and possession of a unified personality, a sense of inner-directedness, and a recognition of one's responsibilities and limitations.

The group therapeutic process is aimed at producing the mature personality. The therapist arouses and deals with transference resistance (identified as patient-patient and patient-therapist relationships) and works to remove maladaptations. The meeting of maturational needs is not described.

Sullivanian School (Interpersonal Psychiatry). The therapist who operates in the framework of Harry Stack Sullivan's interpersonal theory, notes Goldman, conducts himself in the group as a representative of constructive culture. He engages in interpersonal transactions with the patients to correct their distorted perceptions and socially ineffectual behavior, and he communicates attitudes of acceptance and respect. He focuses on feelings, particularly anxiety and loneliness, rather than on unconscious memories. Maladaptive behavior, the motivation for which is explained in terms of avoidance of anxiety and the search for security, is explored in historical perspective. Much attention is given to nonverbal behavior. Transference phenomena are regarded as one among various types of personalized childhood fantasies that are carried over into the immediate situation (parataxes); these fantasies are elucidated as an aid in correcting misperceptions and modifying present behavior. Acceptance of the therapist's interpretation

of a patient's defense maneuver is facilitated by identical reactions of other group members (consensual validation), which helps each member to become aware of his behavior and to analyze it.

The therapist, as an expert in human relations, attends primarily to problems raised by the patients. In the final phase of treatment, he summarizes what has gone on in the therapy and suggests ways of improving future functioning.

The goal of treatment is to help the patient become a well-integrated and socially effective person who tends to see things as others in his culture see them and who behaves in ways they approve of.

This operational approach focuses strongly on the elimination of maladaptations (Step 3). The development of transference is not controlled because the therapist presents himself as a real person. The degree of personality maturation achieved through understanding of the patient's history and interpersonal relations and through correction of his misperceptions is not made clear.

Since the full expression of feelings and the meeting of maturational needs do not appear to figure in the therapeutic process, the improvement achieved may be superficial in nature. Later somatic illness is a possibility.

Psychotherapy through the Group Process

The model of treatment developed by Whitaker and Lieberman is illustrative of systems of group therapy that supplement concepts of individual therapy with the findings of group dynamicists. The therapist views the movements of the group as successive attempts at the resolution of unconscious conflict. The immediate behavior of the members represents a compromise between conflicting motives—disturbing and reactive—and the quality of the group climate is determined by whether the solutions worked out are restrictive or enabling.

The group members are described as homogeneous in terms of vulnerability of defensive structure and heterogeneous in their areas of conflict and ways of dealing with conflict. Candidates evaluated as highly vulnerable, including the acutely psychotic and some neurotics, are not accepted. The consistently silent patient is thought to obtain only limited benefit from the therapeutic process. The group is regarded as the major vehicle of treatment, and patients are not seen routinely on an individual basis.

As the successive group conflicts elicit habitual maladaptive behavior and attitudes originating in the patient's interpersonal relationships, the therapist focuses on modifying those maladaptations and facilitating new learning. Individual patterns that are irrelevant to the focal conflict are not investigated. The contribution to changes in behavior made by reality-testing in a climate of safety is emphasized.

The therapeutic experience itself is regarded as the core factor. Insight and catharsis may occur, but they are not regarded as significant mechanisms. The promotion of permanent change is not claimed; it is pointed out that behavioral change in the group sessions does not automatically carry over into life.

The goal of the therapist is to promote the growth of the patient. He tries to achieve growth by working on maladaptation patterns (Step 3).

Referring to the maladaptive behavior patterns that the patient brings into the group, Whitaker and Lieberman state that "some may yield, others may not." A corrective emotional experience is offered, but the therapist disclaims responsibility for resolving the patient's fundamental problems as they become manifest in the group conflict. The observation that changes in behavior may not carry over into the life situation suggests that the transference is not deep enough or that the maladaptations are not worked through sufficiently.

The inactivity of the therapist may largely be accounted for by the primacy of his interest in studying group dynamics. Whitaker and Lieberman, like Bion and others, have made important contributions to the study of group processes by withholding their influence and permitting the group to go where it wants to go. As research-oriented therapists shift their attention from group processes per se to the investigation of how these

processes can be exploited to facilitate personality growth, they will probably function as more active therapeutic agents.

Existential-Experiential Approaches

These unstandardized and vaguely differentiated procedures, reported by psychoanalytically trained therapists, appear to represent a multifaceted protest against the traditional concern with childhood experience and ego psychology. Existentialists commit themselves to here-and-now interaction with their patients. Experientialists stress the primacy of experience and relatedness over understanding. Some practitioners identify themselves as both existentialists and experientialists.

Among those whose theoretical framework reflects the teachings of existential philosophy, Hora describes existential psychotherapy as a process of cognitive unfoldment and as one in which the practitioner "lives" psychotherapy instead of trying to "do" it. Rather than interpreting, evaluating, and judging, he opens himself up to existential encounter and clarifies what he understands.

The existential groups, designed for study as well as treatment, are composed of from eight to ten persons in diverse diagnostic categories. They are viewed as suffering from disturbed modes - of - being - in - the - world. Their emotional and somatic problems are attributed to preoccupations with the need to confirm one's being. Since their capacity to communicate meaningfully is restricted, they experience frequently recurring conflicts and a sense of isolation.

Revealing themselves at the start as inauthentic people who are concerned with releasing tensions, existential group members move through phases of self-discovery and growing understanding, of being burdened by their defensive strivings and of giving them up, of learning to accept their own anxiousness, and of ultimately discovering themselves as being authentically in the world. On the road to authenticity, they achieve truthfulness in expression, develop mutual regard and respect for the integrity and freedom of one another, and become more perceptive and creative in their thinking.

Group communications focus on the immediate experience. The past may be revealed through proper elucidation of the present, but this revelation is not regarded as significant. Unconscious motivation is not explored. Emphasis is placed on helping the patient achieve harmony with life.

Some existential group therapists apply the working concepts and techniques of analytic psychotherapy, despite their philosophic divergences. Others reject the operational concepts of transference, countertransference, and resistance.

Experimental therapists stress the feeling experiences of the patient. They view sickness as dynamic pressure rather than as disease, and they view health as continuous personal growth, which expands the capacity to choose. The therapist works actively to augment this capacity, using his total person and striving through his preconscious and unconscious responses to stimulate reparative forces working within the patient. The transference relationship, the function of which is to permit the development of responsiveness and counterresponsiveness, is eventually replaced by a nontransference or existential relationship. As Malone et al. state:

> The intrapersonal experiences of both therapist and patient function as reciprocals primarily through nonverbal communication.

Goals are formulated by existential therapists in terms of liberating cognitive and creative potentialities, self-discovery, and deepening understanding. They appear to be working for personality maturation and, in the results claimed, come close to describing it. Experientialists aim for characterological and other growth changes, the breaking up of repetition-compulsions, and the release of the patient from impassed living. Other goals of the experiential therapist are to promote congruence between the patient's intrapsychic realities and his manifest attitudes and behavior and to help him expand his feeling repertoire. Little attention is directed to alleviating symptoms or to improving the patient's social adjustment.

When diagnostic inquiry is bypassed and treatment is based on the therapist's advance assumptions of what his patients need, some patients may be exposed to a group experience that will not meet their specific therapeutic needs and that may, indeed, be harmful. This problem, though by no means limited to practitioners of existential psychotherapy, is well illustrated in their reports. The nature, origin, and history of each patient's disturbance are not investigated; instead, it is assumed that he will benefit from communing, interpreting, valuing, being spoken to truthfully, and the like. But, truthfulness in expression, for instance, is not likely to improve the interpersonal functioning of the person who is insensitive to the feelings of others. It is necessary at times to withhold information of a sensitive nature from group members who tend to be destructively truthful with one another. Suicidal reactions have been reported in patients who were informed by co-patients that they were latent schizophrenics or latent homosexuals. Full and conscious participation in the process of existence is not desirable for those persons in whom it arouses intolerable impulses and anxieties.

These are a few illustrations of the neglect or damage that a patient may sustain when his problem is viewed through the prism of the therapist's blanket assumptions rather than being studied. Such assumptions, whether or not they are derived from a philosophical system of thought, are not applicable to all patients and may interfere with the meeting of their particular therapeutic needs.

An exclusive focus on immediate experiencing (here-and-now) prevents the full mobilization of regressive states and makes it impossible to deal with the patient's primitive maturational needs. Controlled regression is essential for the resolution of patterns of maladaptation that originated in early-life situations.

Transactional Group Psychotherapy

Eric Berne, who introduced this approach, has referred to it as (1) a "happy remedy" for the unsuitability of psychoanalysis for conditions other than the transference neuroses, (2) an effective procedure in a transference neurosis when psychoanalysis, the treatment of choice, is not available, and (3) an appropriate forerunner of other procedures, being more general than any of them and overlapping with analytic and existential therapies at late stages.

Initially the transactional therapist focuses on loosening up resistances—the troublesome games the patient plays in the group sessions. After the patient becomes symptom-free, resistances may be analyzed, but the uncovering of the cause of his problems and of unconscious material is not stressed. It is hypothesized that the patient, by learning to control his free energy, becomes capable of shifting his authentic self from one ego state to another by an act of will. External stimuli are first relied on to accomplish such shifts, but, as treatment progresses, they are made more and more autonomously. Authenticity in social behavior is stressed.

The transactional group therapist accepts patients in many diagnostic categories. They are picked at random, with a view to forming as heterogeneous a group as possible. Rapid improvement and results as stable as those achieved through other approaches are claimed—especially in borderline cases, for which the treatment seems to be designed. Patients are reported to express confidence in the method. It is also claimed that the transactional approach is easily learned.

The goal of the treatment is to cure the patient—for example, as Berne states, to "transform schizophrenics into nonschizophrenics"—and all techniques at the therapist's disposal are used to effect a cure as expeditiously as possible.

The transactional group therapist appears to work for personality maturation, primarily by addressing himself to Step 3. The significance of Steps 1 and 2 is impossible to determine, but the use of techniques for facilitating deep transference is not described. The gratification needs of the patient are identified but not distinguished from maturational needs.

The playful character of the presentations reported may obscure the development of serious relationships. The crucial question is whether, in the course of the clever games they engage in, the patients and the therapist come to develop real feelings for one another. These feelings are indispensable for the maturation of the pre-oedipal personality.

Adaptational Approach

Broadly representative of much group treatment conducted on a supportive level in outpatient as well as institutional settings is the practical approach detailed by Johnson. Patients are helped to overcome uncomfortable and distressing manifestations of emotional illness through understanding of the anxieties they develop in group situations as a defense and protection against the dangers of close relationships. They are also helped to "practice new methods of adaptation," initially in the group sessions and later in their regular social relationships. The therapist does not attempt to remove deep-seated conflicts or to change the basic personality.

Neurotic and psychotic adults are treated in separate groups; a major criterion in the selection of the members of a group is the patient's ability to tolerate anxiety. Children, adolescents, juvenile delinquents, and geriatric patients are among the other subjects with whom this group-oriented model is employed.

The group therapist is an authority figure. He maintains control in the sessions, by active measures when necessary. He refrains from doing individual therapy in the group. He stimulates mutual analysis of the maladaptive behavior observed and encourages the ventilation and recognition of hostility. In the process of clearing away hostility, he serves as the group's scapegoat but does not attempt to work through the hostility completely. The precipitation of psychotic behavior in the group sessions is carefully avoided.

Goals, concretely formulated in advance, vary with the type of patients treated but are in all cases moderate: to improve reality-testing, promote socialization, foster awareness of how feelings are related to anxiety and behavior, and motivate patients for additional psychotherapy on a group or individual basis. The therapist strives to provide a learning-relearning experience that enables the group members to perceive the similarities between their maladaptive behavior in the treatment sessions and their habitual behavior with their life associates.

These general goals are applied in a restrictive manner in groups of psychotic patients. In long-term therapy, psychotics are permitted to become more dependent on one another and on the therapist. Specific goals for a group of psychotically ill patients are the strengthening of defenses, provision of support and dependency, and increase in repression.

This supportive approach is illustrative of the traditional group therapy programs at many mental hospitals, although the practitioners do not invariably lead their groups in an authoritarian and directive manner. Reports indicate that many of these groups are too large to permit much patient-to-patient interplay.

Undeniably, such groups perform a practical function, enabling the patient to achieve more comfortable control of his feelings and behavior. His adjustment to his present environment is improved, and his symptoms may be temporarily alleviated.

An attempt may be made to control transference and deal with common transference resistances. Maladaptive defenses are recognized, and some maturational needs are inadvertently met. Common bonds of interest develop, and feelings of isolation are reduced by the socializing effects of the group sessions.

But the results achieved are not usually self-sustaining. There is no assurance that the postpsychotic patient will not fall apart again after the group experience ends. Since the working through—emotional *unlearning* —of his deep-seated patterns of maladaptation is not attempted, he is likely to revert to them in stressful circumstances. By and large, therefore, the changes effected cannot be equated with personality growth to maturation.

Psychodrama

This multifaceted procedure, introduced in 1925, has been employed in a variety of settings with children, adolescents, and adults. The use of this approach in marital counseling is also reported.

As formulated by J. L. Moreno in the context of his theories of role behavior and group structure, psychodrama requires a large staff and an elaborate format for the directed acting out of problems, but modified versions are employed by practitioners applying other theories, including psychoanalytic concepts. Some elements or techniques of psychodrama, such as role-playing, enter into the contemporary crop of procedures, which also borrow from Moreno's terminology. Moreno and Kipper characterize psychodrama as an elaborate form of encounter, the scientific exploration of the truth by dramatic methods, and the depth therapy of the group.

The acting out of immediately pressing problems or past situations is based on the principles of therapeutic interaction, spontaneity, catharsis, and reality-testing. Five instruments are described: the group (as audience and participants), the patient-protagonist, the stage, auxiliary egos (other group or staff members playing assigned roles), and the director (the therapist). Numerous techniques are employed, some of them to stimulate spontaneity of body and in action.

Psychodrama is reported to benefit persons with psychological and social problems and related somatic disturbances. Among the problems specified are psychomotor disturbances, such as tics, stuttering, and bedwetting; marital maladjustments; and inhibitions in self-expression. Psychodrama is employed with hospitalized schizophrenic patients.

The goals of the psychodramatist are to help people express themselves with greater ease, to structure internal and external experiences, and to bring forth their thoughts and feelings in structured form. An unstated goal appears to be the stimulation of spontaneity and creativity.

Some reports on this procedure suggest that emotional growth does occur, but the goals to which it is addressed do not encompass the notion of producing the mature personality. No distinction is made between gratifying a patient and helping him to mature. Dramatic experience and encounter are therapeutic only in the sense of providing some needed gratification. The psychological needs of the patient in a regressed condition are not met.

In describing the structuring of a psychodrama, Moreno and Kipper point out that

by forcing the protagonists to stick to actualities, he [the director] warms them up to present the facts directly and to express their actual experiences.

The failure to permit random behavior in the treatment setting may serve to foreclose the full development and integration of the personality. The capacity to use one's own initiative freely is an important attribute of the emotionally mature individual. Procedures that force the patient to comply with specific instructions and that do not provide him with opportunities to express himself freely or to develop awareness of the pressure of self-demand are essentially driving rather than growth therapies.

Group-Centered Psychotherapy

This short-term procedure, introduced by followers of Carl Rogers, corresponds to the client-centered method of individual counseling and is widely applied in a variety of educational, social, and industrial settings. Initially, this nondirective and nonclinical approach was employed with maladjusted and neurotic children, adolescents, and adults, but its use with more disturbed patients, including chronic schizophrenics, has recently been reported.

Little attention is paid to diagnosis. It is hypothesized that the same psychotherapeutic principles apply to normal, neurotic, and psychotic persons. However, hostile or aggressive persons are excluded from these groups on the grounds that they might threaten the climate of safety and acceptance that the therapist strives to maintain.

The group members are not viewed as objects of treatment but as potentially adequate and responsible persons who became maladjusted by excluding significant experiences from awareness and by failing to value and integrate all aspects of the self. The therapist assumes that unconditional positive regard, communicated to the members genuinely and sensitively, will enable them to deal constructively with their problems.

Reconstruction of the perceptual field of the group member or client is regarded as the therapeutic task. His mind is not directed into particular channels, nor is he provided with interpretations. Assuming the client's own frame of reference and paraphrasing the content of his communications, the therapist clarifies the feelings expressed and consistently conveys acceptance, empathic understanding, and respect (Step 2). Transference attitudes are not distinguished from other affect-laden expressions. No attempt is made to uncover or explain the conflicts that underlie problematic behavior.

The goals sought through this procedure are to help the group member achieve a more realistic perception of himself and to enhance his self-esteem, capacity for self-direction, openness to experience, and ability to cope with stressful situations. Significant changes in personality, in attitudes about the self and others, and in behavior are claimed.

Rogerian postulates on personality organization resemble those of the Sullivanian school of psychiatry, notes Glad. The practitioner of group-centered psychotherapy—in his nonjudgmental concern with the phenomenological world of the client, his commitment to direct person-to-person encounter, and his open reflection of the feelings and attitudes he is experiencing and may verbalize when they persist—functions in a manner similar to that of the existential therapist.

People who are exposed to this approach secure a great deal of emotional release. The climate maintained in the group is particularly appealing to persons who were subjected to discipline and domination early in life and who greatly resented it. It also appeals to those who crave freedom from certain immediate personalities. The authoritarian personality is not likely to benefit from the experience, but it has been recommended for persons who have democratic attitudes and some ability to maintain understanding relationships with others.

Some degree of personality change can be achieved through this approach. The communication of understanding and acceptance serves to meet maturational and other psychological needs and leads to functional improvements. However, the treatment is directed to relatively limited goals. It does not provide the long-term psychological ingredients that are essential for emotional maturation of the individual with deep-seated problems.

Since patients are not diagnosed and are accepted on the assumption that their problems are psychological, there is some risk of mistreatment.

Behavioral Group Psychotherapy

Behavior therapy in groups encompasses a broad range of short-term procedures that are grounded in the premise that acts are more potent than thoughts and words for influencing human responses. The desensitization and assertive-training procedures focused on here were reported by Lazarus.

Group desensitization treatment, first applied to phobic patients, is now employed in a wide range of disorders, such as sexual impotence, frigidity, and, in a modified form, chronic anxiety. Psychotic patients are specifically excluded.

Various conditioning and anxiety-eliminating techniques based on modern learning theories are applied in homogeneous groups. These techniques are flexibly combined with didactic discussions and with techniques borrowed from other schools of psychotherapy, whose explanations are, however, rejected. Therapy is mainly in, not by, the group, primarily through patient-to-therapist communication. Results are evaluated in terms of the number of maladaptive habits that have been eliminated.

The therapist's attitudes in the desensitization group are didactic, sympathetic, and nonjudgmental. But in the assertive-training group he functions by and large as a participant-observer. Training in self-assertiveness implements the hypothesis that failure to assert oneself is in most cases a manifestation of anxiety. It is assumed that frankness in verbalization and the spontaneous expression of basic feelings will improve the patient's interpersonal functioning.

The group conducted for this purpose is small, carefully composed, and homogeneous, and the course of treatment usually covers from 15 to 20 sessions. The therapist opens the first meeting with an address on the art of relaxation, and preliminary training in relaxation follows. In later sessions, when productive interchanges are not going on among the group members, the therapist usually lectures. The techniques he employs may include open discussion, role-playing, modeling, behavior rehearsals, and psychodrama. A whole session is occasionally devoted to the needs of one member.

The goal of the desensitization procedure is primarily symptomatic improvement. By changing habits deemed to be undesirable, the therapist also endeavors to eliminate suffering and to increase the patient's capacity for productive work and pleasurable interpersonal relationships. It is claimed that the rate and extent of improvement achieved are superior to those produced through other procedures. Secondary benefits reported include changes in personality and self-concept, increased self-esteem, and the development of friendships among the group members.

The goals of assertive training are the acquisition of adaptive responses and the extinction of maladaptive responses. Quantitative measurement of the results achieved is more difficult in assertive training than in the desensitization procedure, but behavioral improvement in nearly all the participants is claimed. The majority of patients report that the improved modes of behavior are transferred to life situations and that they are able to develop more satisfying and enduring relationships with their associates.

The behavioral therapist exerts pressure on patients to change specific patterns of behavior. He secures improvements in functioning by extirpating maladaptations. The psychopathological forces in which these overt patterns are rooted are not investigated or dealt with.

Verbalization is permitted, but the therapist does not work for the expression of all impulses. The question thus arises: What is done with impulses that are not put into words? A person who is put under pressure to behave in ways not consistent with his impulses to action may find self-damaging ways of expressing those impulses. In patients who are not properly selected for these procedures, psychosomatic problems may develop, notably in those who have strong tendencies to repress and suppress their impulses. Patients with impulse disorders are more likely to respond favorably to this punitive approach, but they may later require treatment for a neurotic condition.

Some investigators report that personality *is* dealt with in behavior therapy. The crucial issue is whether the therapist does so sufficiently to prevent some part of the personality from becoming inhibited and repressed.

The value of this approach is that it is short-term and rapidly achieves demonstrable results. Reports do not delineate the possible long-term costs of the short-term improvement.

Gestalt Therapy

The experiential group approach developed from Gestalt psychology by Frederick Perls and his associates revolves around a flexible set of rules and games. These techniques are designed, according to Levitsky and Perls, to help the members of the group assimilate emotional and other psychological experiences with the active coping attitudes that characterize healthful feelings. They are influenced to stay with feelings they have a strong urge to dispel. Much attention is paid to physiological manifestations.

Rules are introduced as a way to unify thoughts with feelings, to heighten awareness, and to facilitate maturation. Communication in the present tense is encouraged; the past is not dealt with, other than to delineate present personality structure. The games, proposed by the therapist to meet individual or group needs, represent a commentary on social behavior and stress the polarity of vital functioning. For example, a need for withdrawal from contact is respected, but the patient may be asked to withdraw in fantasy to a place or situation where he feels secure, to describe it with feelings, and then to return to the group. The use of an awareness continuum is designed to guide the participants away from explanations and speculations to the bedrock of their experiences. Some games have a definite interpretive element, but their primary function is to move patients from the "why" to the "what" and "how" of experience.

The goals of the Gestalt therapist are to promote feelings, to prevent their avoidance, and to help the participants function in a more integrated way. It is claimed that group members become more self-confident and that the group experience increases their capacity for autonomous functioning.

The Gestalt procedure is focused exclusively on maladaptive behavior, and the therapist deals with it primarily by trying to knock out inappropriate patterns. No attempt is made to work them through or to meet the maturational needs that uphold them. The practitioner deliberately refrains from arousing old personality problems. Temporary improvements in feelings are effected by meeting present functional needs. Constructive modification of the current personality structure is sacrificed for short-term benefits.

This form of group therapy may benefit a patient who suffers from low drive. The stimulus of the situation will increase his drive intensity. But exposure of a high-drive patient to this procedure is contraindicated. The experience may traumatize him and provoke suicidal behavior.

Bio-Energetic Group Therapy

Alexander Lowen's procedure involves the body in the psychotherapeutic process and apparently does so more directly and more fully than other approaches that entail body activity and physical contact between participants. Lowen refers to the procedure as a double-barreled approach that provides insight more convincingly than the use of words alone. Personality change is not regarded as valid until it is paralleled by improvements in the form, motility, and functioning of the body.

The variety of techniques employed include simple breathing exercises to facilitate the expression of feelings, manual manipulation to soften chronically spastic areas of the body, embracing, and other types of physical contact expressive of acceptance, reassurance, and support. The participants are taught simple ways of easing tensions. Bodily expression is analyzed and interpreted as a reflection of mental functioning. Verbal interchange goes on primarily in the context of these activities. Therapeutic strategies include encouragement of the venting of negative feelings before expressions of affection.

It is reported that the participants develop a feeling of unity and a respect for the body and the uniqueness of others and are directed to new sources of health and pleasure. Hysterical episodes, precipitated by intense emotional experiences, have been brought under control through bodily contact and physical expressions of reassurance.

The goal of bio-energetic group therapy is to facilitate personality change and unification through activation of healing forces on the deepest and most powerful level.

This method is oriented to personality integration, which is certainly an aspect of emotional maturity. The therapist deals primarily with maladaptations. Maturational needs may be met indirectly.

The chief beneficiary would appear to be the person whose mental and physical functioning are not harmoniously coordinated. Another value is the rapidity of the improvements achieved, which is encouraging to patients. Discouragement may follow later if they have serious problems.

The procedure runs the risk of being a repressive form of treatment. The encouragement given to one form of activity may lead to the suppression or repression of other forms. The mobilization of more psychological energy than a patient can discharge appropriately, leading to impulse acting out or even psychotic behavior, is another possibility.

Marathon Group Therapy

George Bach, who was associated with Frederick Stoller in the development of this procedure during the 1960's, refers to it as a psychological pressure cooker in which genuine emotions emerge as phony steam boils away. He also calls it a

practicum in authentic communication, based on freedom from social fears conventionally associated with transparency.

Group pressure is exploited to generate psychological intimacy as quickly as possible. Stoller refers to the approach as accelerated interaction.

Concentrating therapy into a single experience of a day or two, often over a weekend, the marathon is an outstanding example of the continuous, time-extended format. Both clinical and nonclinical settings are used. Some practitioners conduct marathons in their homes and press their wives into service as co-therapists. Follow-up sessions may be held. Some psychotherapists report the use of the marathon as a supplementary rather than a basic procedure.

Patients are selected on the basis of interest in self-actualization and in undergoing an intensive experience. Usually strangers are assembled, but specialized marathons for marital couples and other natural groups are reported. The participants may or may not be undergoing conventional psychotherapy.

The therapist actively sets the tone and pace for intimate encounter by any means at his disposal, including rejection of professional status and assumption of the patient role to engage in the mutual exploration of feelings. The orientation is ahistorical; the participants are encouraged to own up to and share their immediate feelings and to try out new ways of being in the group.

The goals, as stated by Bach, are to produce a change in orientation and to find new and more creative ways of dealing with old problems. Rapid changes in behavior are reported. It is claimed that the participants become more interested and involved with others, more honest, and less defensive. Behavioral breakthroughs have occurred, but their permanence is admittedly unknown.

The marathon is structured to arouse emotions quickly, thus generating instant intimacy among the participants. The therapist addresses himself primarily to patterns of maladaptive behavior. The procedure is calculated to overpower such patterns by exposing the assemblage to a new experience that has an intense emotional impact. The assumption that the overpowering of defenses can be therapeutic in the long run has yet to be confirmed, notes Yalom. Pending such confirmation, the procedure should be identified as an experiment in group process rather than as a psychotherapeutic method.

Lengthy and fatiguing experiences of this nature are contraindicated for patients with psychosomatic conditions, for those who are in a prepsychotic or postpsychotic state, for people with a strong suicidal disposition, and for those whose marriages are unstable.

Disclosures made to the author by participants in weekend marathons reveal their variable effects. First, some of the values reported: Commitment to the treatment offers the hope of an immediately helpful experience, and some who have undergone it have referred to it as both enjoyable and educational—enjoyable because it dispelled feelings of loneliness and because they derived some gratification from the instant intimacy with strangers; educational because the experience helped them become aware very quickly of their own interpersonal problems. The stimulus of the situation and the exposure to a battery of emotions aroused intense emotions in them. One consequence was that innate tendencies that are usually held in check were uncovered in a matter of hours. The participants were thus able to discover what attracted or disgusted them and whether they had suicidal tendencies, harbored murderous wishes, were easily seducible, etc. One woman characterized the marathon as a dramatic introduction to individual and group psychology.

Other informants have supplemented published reports of social and psychological damage sustained in one-shot marathons or encounters. The uninhibited communications that the marathons encourage often lead to impulsive behavior. To be sexually seductive or to permit oneself to be seduced without regard for the consequences is all too often regarded as operating in the spirit of the occasion.

On returning home after a marathon, a man who had committed himself in treatment to preserving a shaky marriage told his wife that he had felt pressure from several female participants to engage in sexual intercourse during the weekend. He was puzzled to observe how enraged his wife became. Another crisis in their relationship had to be dealt with in his long-term psychotherapy.

A woman whose promiscuous behavior in the past had caused her much unhappiness participated in a marathon, where she met a married man who complained that he had never enjoyed sexual intercourse. She responded forthwith to the challenge. Because their intimacy during the weekend proved to be mutually gratifying, they ended up by having an affair. The man obtained a divorce but refused to marry his new sexual partner on the grounds that they were socially incompatible. Thus, her impulsive behavior, besides causing her fresh unhappiness, led to the dissolution of the marriage of two other persons. In other cases, guilt over the sexual stimulation of the situation has precipitated psychotic episodes.

Self-destructive tendencies of which a person has no awareness can be unleashed in an emotional experience that is highly concentrated in time and pervaded by a built-in sense of intimacy. A man, after discussing his business affairs during a marathon, was stimulated to act on the advice of other participants and commit himself to a foolhardy investment. A few days later, given the opportunity to explore his motives and weigh the risks involved, he changed his mind. In the process of marshaling the pros and cons of the new venture, he recognized that his mounting emotional involvement in the weekend events had significantly dulled his judgment. A state of manic excitement had propelled him into a decision that a person of his astuteness would not otherwise have made.

Sensitivity Training (T-Groups)

A product of the laboratory training movement associated with the National Training Laboratory at Bethel, Maine, programs for sensitivity training in groups have burgeoned in recent years, thrusting themselves into a variety of community, educational, and industrial settings for many different purposes. The members of these relatively unstructured groups participate as learners and use their on-going interpersonal transactions as data in the learning process. As the use of the group setting for experiential learning has expanded and as group leaders or trainers have tended increasingly to concentrate on affective blocks to learning, the boundaries between training and therapy have become more and more diffuse. Gottschalk and Pattison have delineated many overlapping areas. Moreover, sensitivity training itself is a far from standardized procedure. Garwood has pointed out that what occurs in the T-groups

varies with their composition and *most especially with the trainer* [her emphasis].

T-groups are generally short-term, time-limited experiences, concentrated into a week or two, with the participants meeting several hours a day in a special setting. Sometimes the group begins during a weekend in a special setting and then continues in a series of meetings conducted in the participants' own community. Originally the group format was used for the first-hand study of group processes, but the early focus has broadened to encompass the study of the participants' conscious and preconscious behavior and their interpersonal functioning. Some T-group leaders encourage the reporting of dreams and fantasies. The number of techniques employed has increased; some T-group leaders employ nonverbal techniques, including body-contact activities. Role-playing may be engaged in for the purpose of increasing self-awareness.

By and large, the leaders of T-groups state that they are not conducting psychotherapy but are trying to promote personal growth or provide positive and creative emotional experiences for the participants in order to make them more effective in their work and other life activities.

The goals of sensitivity training programs, as formulated by Gottschalk and Pattison, are the heightening of interpersonal coping skills, the sharpening of interpersonal perceptions, and the imbuing of life experience with authenticity and greater self-awareness.

Sensitivity training in groups is of value for developing leadership skills and helping people become more perceptive of their own feelings and the feelings of others, provided they are well-defended and not unduly suggestible personalities. But such training is not universally beneficial, and a substantial number of cases of serious psychological damage caused by these experiences have been described in the literature. Reports call attention to two limitations in these programs: (1) No criteria for evaluating personality strengths are applied in the selection of the trainees. (2) Sensitivity training is mandatory in many organizations.

Kuehn and Crinella recommend the systematic exclusion of four types of persons: psychotics, characterological neurotics, persons with hysterical personality traits, and those who are in a crisis situation. These authors suggest that the usefulness of the procedure depends on the maturity, experience, and expertise of the T-group leader, his knowledge of diagnosis and treatment, and the availability of professional consultation, particularly when psychiatric first aid is required.

Encounter Groups

Thirteen years after J. L. Moreno referred to encounter as a meeting on the most intensive level of communication, his wife and associate, Zereka T. Moreno, remarked in 1969, "Everybody under many flags, is doing what we started." In the interim, a philosophical concept that had permeated relatively few systems of psychotherapy became an umbrella term sheltering a variety of innovative methods, which some mental health professionals refer to as the encounter movement. Firm differentiations among these methods, some of which have already been discussed, are not yet possible. Hence, some labels are used synonymously—for example, T-group and encounter group. As a rudimentary distinction, Yalom points out:

Generally encounter groups have no institutional backing, are far more unstructured, are more often led by untrained leaders, may rely more on physical contact and nonverbal exercises, and generally emphasize an experience, or getting "turned on," rather than change per se.

Encounter as a psychotherapeutic procedure encompasses the investigation of immediate emotions in a dramatically direct manner. In contrast to the long-established approach of establishing a relationship before beginning to work on a problem, encounter therapy relies on the efficacy of blunt honesty. Total reciprocity in the revelation of feelings is worked for through a variety of verbal and action techniques. Many diverse constructs are applied. Candidates for the experience are accepted without screening.

Development of the ability to be honest and open and to express warmth freely is among the values reported. It is also claimed that buried feelings are worked through. The limitations of the procedure are the lack of appropriate safeguards for people with serious disturbances and the stigma placed on emotional unresponsiveness.

The goals of encounter therapy are formulated in terms of personal growth—to promote physical and mental awareness of self and others and of social realities.

Various explanations have been advanced for the proliferation of encounter groups. It has been attributed to the overpopularization of group psychotherapy and to widespread cravings for self-discovery and intimacy among the psychologically sophisticated. Encounter groups also serve to counteract a pervasive sense of estrangement, alienation, and loss of personal identity, produced by the accelerating tempo of technological and sociological change.

In the phenomenal development of the encounter movement, the author also discerns evidence of public dissatisfaction with the practical dictates of the established psychotherapeutic approaches and their doubtful results in severe psychiatric conditions. The length and cost of traditional treatment have stimulated a search for short cuts and guaranteed results—preferably through a less rigorous treatment experience than that oriented to personality maturation.

More specifically, encounter groups may evince a reaction to the limitations of the classical psychoanalytic method. Modifications of the orthodox psychoanalytic situation reach their extreme in the encounter groups. Instead of the dyad, for example, the groups engage as many as 20 persons. There are many variations in the number of group leaders and participants and in their modes of functioning. However, the initially directive and nonrevealing posture of the analyst and the cooperative, self-revealing attitude of the analysand are definitely renounced for mutuality in interchange. The careful control of regression, to permit the arousal and gradual working through of emotional blockages, is abdicated for more

dramatic breakthroughs and occasional peak experiences through direct onslaughts on the defense system. Instead of being limited to verbal communication, the encounter groups sanction nonverbal communication, including physical contact. Diverse activities and modes of communication are studied for their possible therapeutic effects.

Whether such experiences are harmful or helpful depends on the immediate emotional state of the participant. He is exposed to a great deal of stimulation. If he needs it and can assimilate it, the encounter will have a positive impact. If he does not need such excitement or cannot tolerate it in the heady dosages offered, the encounter is, from a therapeutic standpoint, a waste of time and the participant runs the risk of incurring damaging effects.

In general, these experiences appear to be more gratifying than therapeutic or educational. In the participant who is undergoing conventional psychotherapy, they may increase his resistance to working consistently to resolve his problems. Desires to take the easy way out are stimulated.

CURRENT STRENGTHS AND WEAKNESSES

The scientific importance of a psychotherapeutic procedure is determined by the type of problem it is addressed to and its effectiveness in clearing up that problem. As already indicated, there is a pressing need for a serious evaluation of group procedures in these terms, but outcome research has not yielded this information and is not likely to do so for some time.

One of the major shortcomings highlighted by a study of the professional literature is the lack of distinction between the group approaches that are designed to provide the patient with the type of experience he needs to become healthy and mature and those group approaches that are addressed to needs that have an immediate gratification value. Every procedure needs to be evaluated from this standpoint: Does it primarily offer a gratifying experience or one that will help the patient mature?

When this elementary distinction is made,

it becomes evident that what is really new about the procedural innovations that have become the object of controversy are the forms of gratification they provide. Feeling better in the present is often equated with characterological growth. But the success or failure of these experiences depends on their ability to produce long-range results.

Reports on the majority of the procedures reviewed suggest that contemporary practice is more involved in shoring up the personality at the premorbid level of adjustment and in teaching adaptive patterns of behavior than in working for self-sustaining change at a higher level. The procedures that are addressed to significant gains require an undue expenditure of time and effort to clear up the more serious of the oedipal-type conditions, and they fail rather consistently to clear up pre-oedipal problems. In fact, some of the approaches addressed to ambitious goals are not generally applied to patients with severe forms of mental illness. No procedure has demonstrated superiority in cases of this nature.

A moot issue among analytic group therapists is whether to adhere to the operational principles of individual psychoanalytic therapy or to extract as much therapeutic leverage as possible from group process. Many of these practitioners express their personal preference for one theoretical approach or the other, but their clinical reports do not demonstrate that better results can be secured from the approach they prefer.

The large majority of group therapists address themselves primarily to maladaptive interpersonal behavior. In one way or another, they help the patient to recognize it and to master better patterns of behavior. The acquisition of new action patterns, however, does not liberate the patient from the compulsive grip of the old patterns. Unless these patterns are freed of their emotional charge—unless they are emotionally unlearned through the solution of the underlying problem—the patient will continue to revert to them.

Each group procedure is based on a different assumption of the patient's therapeutic needs. To cite a few examples: The analytic group psychotherapist assumes that the way to help the patient is to reawaken the fundamental problem or conflict in the treatment situation and to focus on early as well as present growth needs. Practitioners who reject the historical approach assume that all the patient requires is to learn to express himself more honestly, or to coordinate his present psychic and physical functioning, to develop more awareness of his feelings, to learn to stay with what he feels, to relate authentically to others, or to have powerful and concentrated emotional experience that will unmask his defenses, etc. The behavioral therapist assumes that change entails desensitization of the patient. The T-group leader assumes that the members of his group need to increase their sensitivity to feelings.

The assumptions on which the present approaches are based often diverge to the point of contradiction, but what each strives to accomplish is a potential contribution to emotional maturity. When the treatment achieves its objective, the patient has acquired some attributes of the mature personality.

APPROACHES TO SPECIFICITY

Group psychotherapy has definitely emerged from the period when its acceptance as an effective mode of treatment was in doubt. The question, "Can it help a patient improve?" has been answered in the affirmative. However, the results obtained through its indiscriminate use have aroused much dissatisfaction. Clinical experience has amply demonstrated that the efficiency of the group psychotherapeutic process hinges on the degree of specificity achieved in relating the procedure applied to the patient's condition. Little is accomplished through haphazard use of the group setting; patients do not secure appreciable benefits simply because they are treated together. Desirable change is a function of helping each group member deal with his particular problems. Consequently, there has been a concerted effort in recent years to secure more specific results. In the process of transforming what was all too often regarded as a panacea into a precise instrument, clinicians discovered that it could be refined to produce different results.

Group psychotherapy thus appears to be thrusting toward the development of a larger number of dissimilar procedures that will influence patients in different ways. This trend is very desirable. If the group psychotherapist is committed to help people become effectively functioning individuals, whatever their problems and stage of life, many different procedures are required. But the crucial issue is not the number of approaches at his disposal, but which approach is the best to use in each situation and for each purpose.

Clinical Experimentation

The 1960's ushered in a period of great therapeutic creativity. Along with efforts to increase the effectiveness of the established approaches and to make them less interminable, there was much experimental activity, which is continuing into the present decade. The fact that some of this activity has been misrepresented to the public as psychotherapy has stimulated negative attitudes toward experimentation per se.

Psychotherapy by its very nature requires experimentation, which was vital to the development of psychological treatment and is the key to further progress. However, the practice of psychotherapy does not readily lend itself to objective evaluation. The treatment process entails confidential relationships, subjective and objective assessment by the same person, and freedom to experiment as and when necessary to achieve an immediate objective. This state of affairs makes it difficult to determine at times whether one is engaging in responsible psychotherapy or in irresponsible experimentation. Evidence of the latter occasionally comes to the fore, and efforts are being made to lay a foundation for responsible experimentation.

General Guidelines. Two basic principles of clinical experimentation that the author recommends relate to mutuality and the selection of appropriate subjects.

1. In responsible experimentation, the patient is diagnosed, and his specific problem is carefully studied. On the basis of the diagnosis and with the goals in mind, a plan is formulated for working with him. The patient is then informed what the therapist is striving to accomplish and what results can be expected. The patient is not exposed to an experimental procedure unless he consents to it; his wishes in the matter are respected. It is also made clear to the patient that, if the attempt to help him does not yield the desired results, the therapist will at least explain to him why the failure occurred. This principle is applicable in group as well as in individual treatment.

2. The patients with whom it is most appropriate to experiment are those who do not respond to the established approaches. These approaches are effective in dealing with most of the conditions associated with oedipal development and with run-of-the-mill problems for which people solicit professional help; hence, little is gained from experimenting in such cases. The subjects with whom experimentation is justifiable and most likely to be scientifically rewarding are those with more severe disturbances.

Experimentation with Schizophrenia. The main challenge in the field of psychotherapy lies in the development of more effective approaches to the pre-oedipal disorders, especially schizophrenia. Despite the fact that many cases of schizophrenia appear to have more than one cause, the disorder invariably testifies to basic defects in the maturation of the personality. The author regards this condition as psychologically reversible in principle. In his experience, the schizophrenic patient does not respond on a long-range basis to individual or group psychotherapeutic experiences that are primarily gratifying. Quite the contrary. Such experiences tend to produce psychotic episodes —which is one reason why many therapists conducting treatment on an outpatient basis are reluctant to treat the schizophrenic patient. If the procedure employed does not contribute to the reversal of the illness, it is likely to have more gratification than maturational value. The response of the schizophrenic patient is, in a sense, the ultimate test of the procedure's effectiveness in dealing with fundamental personality problems. Since relatively few group therapists work with schizophrenic patients on other than a supportive level, the scientific importance of experimentation of the nature just suggested is obvious.

Schizophrenic patients do not respond to a purely neutral approach. They need an emotionally responsive therapist, one who can tolerate the patient's emotions and feed them back to him in a controlled, goal-oriented manner.

The schizophrenic patient's individual treatment was once thought to call for two or more analysts. If the first analyst was a man, the patient was usually transferred at some stage of their relationship to a woman, and vice versa. But even with a change in analysts, emotionally responsive though they might be, they could not, in the dyad, meet the schizophrenic's special need to experience different feelings simultaneously. The multiple charge of member-to-member verbal interchanges in the group setting makes an important contribution to the meeting of this maturational need. More difficult to meet in the shared treatment experience is the schizophrenic's high-urgency need for the adequate release of aggressive energy; his co-patients are not happy to hear how much he hates them.

Combined Treatment

Present evidence suggests that what will be most effective in the treatment of pre-oedipal disorders is a highly specific combination of individual and group treatment based on psychoanalytic principles, understanding of personality development, and incorporation of meritorious techniques of various schools of practice. To resolve pre-oedipal conditions through the exclusive instrumentality of group psychotherapy would be exceedingly difficult; in the group setting the therapist does not have as exquisite control of all stimuli, including his own responses, as he has in the one-to-one relationship. The patient's group therapeutic experience usually follows a period of individual treatment, during which he works on his bipersonal problems; but in some instances, generally when there are special transference difficulties, the patient begins treatment in a group. Properly timed, the shared treatment experience is particularly valuable for the

severely disturbed person who is totally unable to benefit from group association, such as the postpsychotic college student who told the author:

I've never known how to tolerate, feel close to, feel comfortable with, find myself accepted by, feel non-self-conscious in groups and group activity with my peers.

Supplementary Treatment

Although the new short-term procedures are not corrective per se, their specific values can be exploited when they coincide with maturational needs that are uncovered in patients undergoing long-term psychotherapy. For instance, a person who suddenly experiences a great hunger for human companionship may benefit from an encounter-group experience. For one who is totally divorced from his feelings, the T-group or marathon may serve as a springboard for their arousal and expression.

The use of these supplementary measures is likely to increase, but the practitioner who recommends them to patients needs to recognize the possibly psychonoxious effects of the experience on a person who demonstrates a strong need to withdraw from people. The advance safeguard, of course, is study of the patient's current functioning and understanding of why he says he needs additional stimulation to feel more deeply or to make his life more interesting and exciting. The patient's reaction to his initial venture in instant intimacy also needs to be investigated. If the experience does not lead to emotional withdrawal, loss of identity, sense of alienation, or similar signs of severe regression, and if the patient wishes to repeat the venture in accelerated emotional education, it will probably stimulate further improvement.

CONCLUSION

The introduction of community psychiatry is greatly enhancing the reliance on group psychotherapy as the most available approach for producing the socially effective individual. To meet this additional responsibility, the present armamentarium of emotional-impact instruments needs to be substantially refined and scanned closely for their specific therapeutic and antitherapeutic effects. Dissatisfaction with all psychotherapeutic procedures will continue until they achieve significant results more rapidly. New ideas for group formation will probably emerge in this era of therapeutic creativity, and they need to be studied, not rejected out of hand. No one knows all the answers today. A demonstrably superior approach may emerge for dealing with the enormous range of psychologically reversible disease states and states of dis-ease to which human beings are prone throughout the life cycle. This superior method is conceivable, but it is not on the horizon today. At present, the key to fulfilling the promise that group psychotherapy has held out to the public is more precise wielding of the instruments it has forged.

REFERENCES

Bach, G. The marathon group: intensive practice of intimate interaction. In *Group Therapy Today*, p. 301, H. M. Ruitenbeek, editor. Atherton Press, New York, 1969.

Berne, E. *Principles of Group Treatment*. Oxford University Press, New York, 1966.

Blatner, H. A. Patient selection in group therapy. *Voices, 4:* No. 3, 90, 1968.

Corsini, R. J. *Methods of Group Psychotherapy.* McGraw-Hill, New York, 1957.

Dreikurs, R. Group psychotherapy from the point of view of Adlerian psychology. In *Group Therapy Today*, p. 37, H. M. Ruitenbeek, editor, Atherton Press, New York, 1969.

Foulkes, S. H. *Therapeutic Group Analysis.* International Universities Press, New York, 1965.

Foulkes, S. H., and Anthony, E. J. *Group Psychotherapy: The Psychoanalytic Approach*, ed. 2. Penguin Books, Baltimore, 1965.

Frank, J. D., and Powdermaker, F. B. Group psychotherapy. In *American Handbook of Psychiatry*, vol. 2, p. 1362, S. Arieti, editor, Basic Books, New York, 1959.

Garwood, D. S. The significance and dynamics of sensitivity training programs. Int. J. Group Psychother., *17:* 457, 1967.

Glad, D. D. *Operational Values in Psychotherapy.* Oxford University Press, New York, 1959.

Goldman, G. D. Some applications of Harry Stack Sullivan's theories to group psychotherapy. In *Group Therapy Today.* p. 58, H. M. Ruitenbeek, editor. Atherton Press, New York, 1969.

Goldstein, A. P., Heller, K., and Sechrest, L. B. *Psychotherapy and the Psychology of Behavior Change*. John Wiley, New York, 1966.

Gottschalk, L. A., and Pattison, E. M. Psychiatric perspectives on T-groups and the laboratory movement: an overview. Amer. J. Psychiat., *126:* 823, 1969.

Hobbs, N. Group-centered psychotherapy. In *Client-Centered Therapy*, p. 278, C. R. Rogers, editor. Houghton-Mifflin, Boston, 1951.

Hora, T. Existential therapy and group psychotherapy. In *Basic Approaches to Group Psychotherapy and Group Counseling*, p. 109, G. M. Gazda, editor. Charles C Thomas, Springfield, Ill., 1968.

Johnson, J. A. *Group Therapy: A Practical Approach*. McGraw-Hill, New York, 1963.

Klapman, J. W. *Group Psychotherapy: Theory and Practice,* ed. 2. Grune & Stratton, New York, 1959.

Kuehn, J. L., and Crinella, F. M. Sensitivity training: interpersonal "overkill" and other problems. Amer. J. Psychiat., *126:* 840, 1969.

Lazarus, A. A. Behavior therapy in groups. In *Basic Approaches to Group Psychotherapy and Group Counseling*, p. 149, G. M. Gazda, editor. Charles C Thomas, Springfield, Ill., 1968.

Levitsky, A., and Perls, F. The rules and games of Gestalt therapy. In *Group Therapy Today*, p. 221, H. M. Ruitenbeek, editor. Atherton Press, New York, 1969.

Lieberman, M. A., Lakin, M., and Whitaker, D. S. Problems and potential of psychoanalytic and group-dynamic theories for group psychotherapy. Int. J. Group Psychother., *19:* 131, 1969.

Lowen, A. Bio-energetic group therapy. In *Group Therapy Today*, p. 279, H. M. Ruitenbeek, editor. Atherton Press, New York, 1969.

Malone, T. P., Whitaker, W. C., Warentkin, J., and Feder, R. Rational and nonrational psychotherapy. Amer. J. Psychother., *15:* 212, 1961.

Moreno, J. L. Scientific foundations of group psychotherapy. In *Group Psychotherapy and Group Function*. p. 242, M. Rosenbaum and M. Berger, editors. Basic Books, New York, 1963.

Moreno, J. L., and Kipper, D. A. Group psychodrama and community-centered counseling. In *Basic Approaches to Group Psychotherapy and Group Counseling*, p. 27, G. M. Gazda, editor. Charles C Thomas, Springfield, Ill., 1968.

Moreno, Z. T. Moreneans, the heretics of yesterday are the orthodoxy of today. Group Psychother., *22:* 1, 1969.

Mullan, H. Status denial in group psychoanalysis. In *Group Psychotherapy and Group Function*, p. 591, M. Rosenbaum and M. Berger, editors. Basic Books, New York, 1963.

Parloff, M. B. Analytic group psychotherapy. In *Modern Psychoanalysis*, p. 492, J. Marmor, editor. Basic Books, New York, 1968.

Rose, S. Horney concepts in group psychotherapy.

In *Group Therapy Today*, p. 49, H. M. Ruiten-beek, editor. Atherton Press, New York, 1969.

Rosenbaum, M. Group psychotherapy and psychodrama. In *Handbook of Clinical Psychology*, p. 1254, B. B. Wolman, editor. McGraw-Hill, New York, 1965.

Rueveni, U., and Speck, R. V. Using encounter group techniques in the treatment of the social network of the schizophrenic. Int. J. Group Psychother., *19:* 495, 1969.

Slavson, S. R. *A Textbook in Analytic Group Psychotherapy*. International Universities Press, New York, 1964.

Spitz, H. H., and Kopp, S. B. Multiple psychotherapy. In *Group Psychotherapy and Group Function*, p. 391, M. Rosenbaum and M. Berger, editors. Basic Books, New York, 1963.

Spotnitz, H. The borderline schizophrenic in group psychotherapy. Int. J. Group Psychother., *7:* 155, 1957.

Spotnitz, H. *The Couch and the Circle: A Story of Group Psychotherapy*. Alfred A. Knopf, New York, 1961.

Spotnitz, H. *Modern Psychoanalysis of the Schizophrenic Patient*. Grune & Stratton, New York, 1969.

Stoller, F. H. Accelerated interaction: a time-limited approach based on the brief, intensive group. Int. J. Group Psychother., *18:* 220, 1968.

Thomas, G. W. Group psychotherapy: review of the present literature. Psychosom. Med., *5:* 166, 1943.

Whitaker, D. S., and Lieberman, M. A. *Psychotherapy through the Group Process*. Atherton Press, New York, 1964.

Wolf, A. Psychoanalysis in groups. In *Basic Approaches to Group Psychotherapy and Group Counseling*, p. 80, G. M. Gazda, editor. Charles C Thomas, Springfield, Ill., 1968.

Yalom, I. *The Theory and Practice of Group Psychotherapy*. Basic Books, New York, 1970.

3

Sensitivity Groups, Encounter Groups, Training Groups, Marathon Groups, and the Laboratory Movement

Louis A. Gottschalk, M.D. and Robert S. Davidson, Ph.D.

INTRODUCTION

Some of the most pervasive problems experienced by members of our society are boredom, fear of intimacy, fear of self-disclosure, lack of commitment, loneliness, and alienation. Students complain of a wide gap separating them emotionally and intellectually from their parents, their teachers, other adults, and each other. Some people are puzzled about the apparent meaninglessness of existence. If they are unable to find ready answers in organized religion, they struggle to find earthly reasons besides earning a livelihood, existing, reproducing, achieving. Many of those who try to comfort themselves by allegiance to traditional religious explanations of the meaning or purpose of existence are dissatisfied and are working toward having their religious organization more involved in secular matters and more helpful in guiding their lives. In a society that has distinguished itself by the invention of new psychoactive drugs that can influence man's emotions and thought, many persons are seeking to control the neurochemical environment of their brain and, hence, the oppressive anxiety and depression of their subjective experience by overusing tranquilizers, sedatives, antidepressants, and even psychotomimetic pharmacological agents. Those who cannot afford to purchase these chemicals or who are uninformed about their effects and availability fall back on that age-old pacifier, alcohol, and hide periodically from themselves, their memories, or their impulses by escape-drinking. People in great industrial organizations worry about fragmentation of goals and expend their efforts on how to improve management decision-making, labor-management relationships, and mutual collaboration.

In this contemporary scene, there has come to fruition the growing conviction that many of these discontents of civilization can be favorably influenced through various techniques involving small groups.

HISTORY

During the 1920's, social scientists began to study natural groups in society, with the conviction that the solution to social problems could be facilitated by the study of social interaction and normal social groupings. This conviction was translated into social work practice with groups and social welfare projects. Likewise, within the mental health framework a variety of group approaches were developed, including the group discussion method of the 1920's, culminating in the 1930's with the formation of the group psychotherapy movement.

In the 1930's a spurt in the development of an intellectual climate was conducive to the widespread application of principles of social psychology. The fervor of the decade was reflected in the progressive era in the classroom, the church, and psychoanalysis. The goal of society was no less than the uplifting of the entire society. The "war of democracy" and its aftermath of economic depression created a universal need for help and stirred the cultural consciousness of many professions. It was the era of the social gospel dedicated to the reformation and salvation of not just the individual but society. It was the era of psychoanalytic optimism that the soft voice of reason might free man from the tyranny of his emotions and consequent problems of society.

In this sociocultural arena, Kurt Lewin developed his now famous field theory and began to implement action research as an approach to social change. Lewin, his early collaborators, and his students constituted an academic and community test force that, on the one hand, led to the development of small-group sociology as an academic discipline and, on the other hand, laid the groundwork for the laboratory movement as a community enterprise.

The direct development of the training laboratory came from the collaboration of three men: Leland Bradford, Ronald Lippitt, and Kenneth Benne. All three had an educational background in psychology, experience in working with community educational projects, and involvement in numerous national projects dealing with major social problems related to human relations. They had been exposed to and influenced by J. L. Moreno's methods of psychodrama and had experimented with various role-playing procedures in community educational projects directed toward effecting social change.

The seminal ideas of the laboratory movement were developed in Bethel, Maine, during a conference at the Gould Academy. There, a procedure was developed for training people from communities in the process of democratic group formation. The new method was to be a laboratory for self-examination of group process. Between 1949 and 1955, each summer at Bethel, a variety of experiments were tried with different methods of refining the laboratory group method. Two rather different methods began to emerge. In those early years, the mornings at Bethel were spent in training groups (T-groups), which were relatively unstructured, small, heterogeneous groups of people who focused on an analysis of their immediate interactions. The afternoons were spent in action groups (A-groups) composed of persons from the same organization, who focused on structured group-task exercises, including planning for action back home. However, the action groups rapidly changed into training groups unless strenuous effort was made to keep the action groups task-oriented. The basic dichotomy between a personal, subjective orientation and an external-task, group-work orientation has remained the crucial issue in the training laboratory movement.

Since 1955 the training laboratory movement has developed in such diverse directions that it is difficult to trace a single pattern. Training laboratories, often with great autonomy, were established in other parts of the United States. This development has resulted in submovements that often have disparate goals and methods. In the past 15 years, the movement has become multipurpose and multimethod. The major branches of this diversification can be noted briefly.

The laboratory movement in education has been one of the major institutional bases for the method, even though only a minority of schools of education participate widely in group training laboratories for their students. This movement aims at enhancing the educational enterprise beyond cognitive learning to include socioemotional learning. Human relations training in the classroom exemplifies this tradition.

The laboratory movement in business and industry has been the most firmly established institutional base. The concern here is for the improved function of administrative leadership and the more humane and effective function of work groups. This training movement has focused both on the sensitization of leaders to their impact on their work team and on task-oriented learning experiences for teams of persons who work together (Argyris, 1962).

The training movement in social action was the initial concern of the founders of the movement, but community social action groups seem to have been uneven in their development. Only in the late 1960's was this concern again receiving attention in the laboratory literature. However, instead of the early interest in helping natural community groups to function in a more democratic fashion, the current concern focuses on laboratory consultation to community agencies.

The training movement as a therapeutic method for normal persons found expression in the early T-groups and has steadily gained in popularity and prestige. This part of the movement was totally influenced by the upsurge of interest in humanistic and existential psychology. It has also been the source of origin of many variants, such as marathon groups, sensitivity groups, encounter groups, and personal growth laboratories.

Finally, the training movement has continued to provide impetus for the scientific study of group dynamics, group process, leadership functions, decision-making, and conflict resolutions. However, the early pioneers in the laboratory movement with research orientations from the fields of psychology and sociology have, for the most part, departed from the scene and have transferred their research to the more scientific arena of their respective disciplines, leaving the laboratory movement as a predominantly clinical and applied discipline.

As one surveys the literature of the laboratory movement, especially the small monographs published by the National Training Laboratories (NTL), a definite trend is discernible. In the 1940's the movement expressed a concern for a method of teaching American communities techniques for participatory democracy. Group process and task-oriented group function dominated the scene. In the 1950's, the concern shifted to individual growth, self-knowledge, actualization, and maturation. Indeed, the movement shifted in emphasis from an educative to a therapeutic goal. Subse-

quently, the rather distinctive differences between training and therapy became more and more blurred.

DEFINITIONS

In 1962, Weschler et al. stated:

> Today it is difficult to talk about what sensitivity training or psychotherapy is and should be. Nor is it necessary to draw a clear-cut distinction between them.

Nevertheless, some definitions may serve as guideposts.

Training Laboratory

A training laboratory is an educational procedure that aims to create a situation in which the participants, through their own initiative and control but with access to new knowledge and skilled professional leadership, can appraise their old behavior patterns and attitudes and look at new ones. A laboratory recommends a temporary removal of the participants from their usual living and working environment, where attempts to re-evaluate attitudes or to experiment with new behavior patterns might involve risks and possible punishment. It provides a temporary artificial supportive culture (hence the designation "laboratory") in which the participants may safely confront the possible inadequacy of their old attitudes and behavior patterns and experiment with and practice new ones until they are confident in their ability to use them.

The assumption of the laboratory method is that skills in human interactions are best learned through events in which the learners themselves are involved. The training activities, therefore, are social experiences in which the trainees take part and then reflect on their patterns of participation. Essentially, the laboratory scene provides an occasion for experimental learning.

Sensitivity Training

Sensitivity training is any of a set of experiences, including but not restricted to the training group, attempting to help each participant recognize and face, in himself and in others, many levels of functioning (including emotions, attitudes, values, and intellect), evaluate his behavior in light of the responses it elicits from himself and others at these various levels, and integrate these levels into a more effective and perceptive self.

Training Group

T-group, the most common format for sensitivity training, is a relatively unstructured group in which individuals participate as learners. The basic data for learning come from the participants themselves and from their immediate experiences within the group as they interact with each other in the effort to create from their own resources a productive and meaningful group. The experience is designed to provide a maximal opportunity for the participants to expose and analyze personal behavior and group performance, to learn how others respond to their behavior, and to learn effective personal and group functioning.

Marathon Group

This term is used to describe a sensitivity training group that meets continuously for periods of time ranging from 12 to 36 hours. The purpose of this technique is to heighten the impact of sensitivity training by not interrupting the interactions being generated within the group. Members leave the room only for absolutely necessary reasons. Marathons have been used in weekend laboratories, where the total amount of time available is short, and in longer-term laboratories as a device to move the group to a greater depth of involvement and group interaction. Proponents of such groups report heightened emotionality, a greater expression of negative feelings, and a decrease in defensive role-playing because of fatigue and nearly constant pressure to be more open.

A variation on the marathon is the weekend encounter group, whose sessions are three or four hours in length but occur several times during each day and evening of the weekend, with time out for eating, exercise, and sleep. In such a group there are usually many opportunities for formal and informal pairings, triads, and quartets. These small groups plus the varied activities allow for normal social relationships. Many trainers believe that, rather than detracting from the pressure-cooker formula of the marathon, these more informal groups allow less-threatening relationships to develop. These relationships are then deepened during the formal sessions. The theory is that the participants develop more trust during their informal encounters and therefore relax their guard because of lessened fear rather than heightened external pressure.

Trainer

The trainer is the experienced educator within a sensitivity training group who serves as a resource to the group. Since the primary social learning data for the participants come from their own involvement with each other and with the group, the role of the sensitivity training group trainer is different from that of the usual role of an educator. He cannot assume the role of the expert, controlling and directing the group, without making the group dependent on him, thereby undercutting the experience of group responsibility and participation that is supposed to be the primary source of learning data. The trainer, therefore, is supposed to serve as a facilitator, helping the group to make its own decisions and to use its own resources. He does this by calling the attention of the group from time to time to the behavior being exhibited and the relationships emerging in the group and by helping the group to clarify its own goals and procedures. The trainer focuses primarily on here-and-now events and relationships that have been experienced within the life of the group.

LABORATORY TRAINING

Three different group activities are subsumed under laboratory training: (1) the sensitivity, personal encounter, or training group; (2) the task-oriented group involving structured group exercises aimed at teaching group function skills; and (3) intervention laboratories that are established for functional work groups in the community or industry. All three types of group activities may overlap or may be conducted separately.

T-Groups vs. Traditional Group Therapy

The sensitivity or T-group has received the most publicity, yet in itself it is the least innovative and may prove to be the least significant of the three group activities. The overlap between T-groups and group therapy is considerable, and at times they are indistinguishable. The problem is compounded by the fact that T-group leaders vary so much among themselves that one cannot really describe a model or typical T-group. One can only describe typical differences between T-groups and group therapy. In the early days, the distinctions between the two kinds of groups seemed fairly clear. But both the T-group and group psychotherapy have been changing over the past 20 years. Now one can cite examples of therapy groups that follow the T-group pattern and vice versa.

Participants. Traditionally, the T-group is designed for normal people with good ego defenses and good ego-coping skills who can readily learn from experience. The group therapy participant, on the other hand, is selected because he has deficient ego skills and an inability to learn from immediate experience.

Although T-groups may be made up of nonrelated persons, much of the T-group method has been concerned with groups of people who work together. Group therapy, in contrast, has traditionally been conducted with persons who have no extra-group relations.

Although T-groups and their variants are used as therapy groups for normals, therapy groups are also used for nonpatients, such as wives of alcoholics and parents of neurotic children. The distinction between education, training, and therapy becomes blurred, as does the distinction between patients and nonpatients.

T-group literature has long debated the merits of working with related vs. unrelated members. The issue seems to be resolving itself in terms of goals. T-groups aimed at personal growth are likely to be composed of unrelated members; T-groups aimed at work-group intervention are likely to be carefully composed of persons with interlocking work or community relationships. The same can be said of therapy groups. The traditional advantages of working in therapy with persons who have no relationship with each other are well-known. However, the recent development of family therapy has stressed the importance of working with people who are intimately related to each other. Similar emphasis has been made in therapeutic work with groups of married couples, in extended family therapy, and in social network therapy.

Goals. The T-group seeks to heighten interpersonal coping skills, sharpen interpersonal perception, and increase self-awareness and the authenticity of life experience. In group therapy, these goals may be seen as prerequisite learning that will enable the patient to work out his emotional problems.

But some T-group trainers disdain group process or group growth, for they see their goal as solely personal change. On the other hand, many group therapists see individual change as accomplished only through effective group process. Hence their therapeutic effort is directed at maximizing group process. In this instance, the T-group and the therapy group have reversed the traditional stances of both fields.

Leadership. In the T-group, the trainer or leader is seen as an expediter or catalyst who may become fairly assimilated into the group—at least in theory. In group therapy the leader is traditionally a therapist who not only catalyzes group process but also has a responsibility for making the group experience a therapeutic experience for each patient. The therapist can never fully shed his role, even if he attempts to do so.

But some T-group trainers see the leadership function as indispensable for effective T-group function—some of them acting in very authoritarian or autocratic roles that give little control to the T-group participants. Other trainers work toward total assimilation and actually give up leadership role and function. Likewise, in group therapy, therapists maintain various degrees of leadership, ranging from those who do individual therapy with a patient while the group watches to those therapists who deal only with group process and never with individual patients. Yet other therapists of existential persuasion move toward assimilation into their therapy groups, with virtually total abnegation of the therapeutic role. In addition, there have been a number of recent experiments with alternate sessions of therapy groups where the therapist is not present and even experiments with leaderless therapeutic groups.

Duration of the Group Activity. The T-group experience is short-term. Typically, T-groups meet for several hours daily for two weeks. On occasion, the experience has been lengthened to a month or more; in the other direction, there has been experimentation with one or two continuous group sessions—marathon-type experiences. The therapy group typically meets for one to two hours over a long period of time, even four or five years in extreme instances.

There has been increasing emphasis in the laboratory movement on follow-up work. Recent articles have suggested that the first T-group experience is only 20 per cent of the task, to be followed by many months of subsequent meetings with the group membership. On the other hand, some therapy groups are now being conducted on a short-time basis, such as crisis intervention groups, diagnostic intake groups, and marathon therapy groups.

Content of Discussion. The T-group has been seen primarily as an arena for the elaboration, analysis, and discussion of conscious thought and feeling, interpersonal interaction, and here-and-now issues. The therapy group has been concerned with the genetic there-and-then, the intrapersonal, the preconscious, fantasy, and dreams. The T-group focuses on "how we function in this group"; the therapy group focuses on "using that group to see how I function."

T-group emphasis on the conscious here-and-now has remained a major focus, but many trainers have expanded the repertoire of the T-group to the exploration of dreams, fantasy, and primary intrapersonal experiences as relevant to the major focus of the T-group. On the other hand, much of family therapy and group therapy has moved to a here-and-now focus and to an exploration of the interpersonal, with a de-emphasis of the genetic there-and-then and purely intrapersonal experience.

Other Facets of the Laboratory Movement

The laboratory movement has initiated and supported research on group dynamics, group leadership, and participant function that has contributed significantly to the general body of group theory. These data and related research techniques have not yet been substantially incorporated into the body of psychiatric theory; they may prove more germane than T-groups in the areas of group therapy, family therapy, and community psychiatry.

The laboratory movement has introduced a number of innovative techniques that may have therapeutic applicability. Examples include leaderless groups, group action techniques, role-playing, and psychodramatic methods. In addition, the emphasis on group process dynamics has had a direct and continuing influence on the group dynamics approach in group psychotherapy.

The development of structured laboratory exercises for task or action groups has considerable importance for community psychiatry. Very often the community mental health worker is called on to provide consultation to work groups in the community. Since the T-group is best known, there has been a trend toward turning group consultation in the community into pure T-group sensitivity exercises. Such exercises may be neither asked for, contracted for, nor relevant to the immediate tasks that face the community group. Group consultation is just beginning to be developed as a skill in community mental health work, and here the interests of the community mental health movement not only overlap but are at times identical with the group consultation concerns of the laboratory movement.

The laboratory movement innovations in the area of organizational intervention are also of direct relevance to community psychiatry. The corollary interest in mental health has been the milieu therapy movement. In mental health, the concerns have been more diagnostic than interventional. In fact, Schiff has pointed out that mental health professionals are notoriously untrained and unskilled for administrative intervention. Yet the concern for increasing-the humaneness of social systems is remarkably similar to that of the laboratory movement. Recently Klein, Peck, Scheidlinger, and others have begun to develop some preliminary models of small-group interaction as basic for community mental health work and community intervention. Already a number of community mental health centers are using consultants from the laboratory movement to plan and implement community intervention programs.

The laboratory movement techniques, especially the T-group method, have been applied or modified for the training of mental health professionals. A number of university departments of psychiatry now provide some type of training group experience for their psychiatric residents, other professionals, and staff. In addition, many community mental health centers are introducing training group experiences for in-service training of staff, including indigenous workers and nonprofessionals.

A number of derivative methods of group therapy have been generated by the laboratory movement. Such methods in some areas have been sensationalized, have become fads, or have challenged therapeutic concepts. In any case, such methods merit careful professional presentation, investigation, and evaluation. An example is the attempt to appraise seriously the marathon group movement, described by Stoller.

Since the laboratory movement encompasses many types of people involved in powerful human-change activities, clinical consultation is needed. This is not to say that untoward reactions will necessarily reflect faulty procedures. It does suggest, however, that the mental health professions may provide a real contribution to the laboratory movement by collaboration in responsible laboratory exercises. Also, clinical consultants may assist in anticipating and preventing untoward reactions. Finally, with the present variability in the laboratory movement, clinicians will encounter problems in which clinical care follows the onset of unfortunate experiences.

GOALS AND PURPOSES

Sensitivity training may range in goals between two extremes: (1) the mainly *agency-oriented* or *task-oriented* training, so structured as to enlighten the participants concerning more effective communication, problem-solving methods, and leadership patterns, primarily for the purpose of better influencing the environment, particularly other people; (2) the *communion-oriented* training, so structured as to give participants a variety of experiences, often nonverbal, which put each participant in touch with inhibited sensory and emotional facets of his personality, not for purposes of influencing people but for purposes of improving his capacity to be closer to others.

There is a wide range of task-oriented and communion-oriented sensitivity training groups and facilitators. Paradoxically, an apparently task-oriented group may develop a great sense of communion, and an apparently communion-oriented group may be completely sacrificed to the demands of the task, depending on the agenda of the participants and the leadership styles of the group facilitators.

Theoretically, a group of sales people being trained by the laboratory method to deliver the most effective sales pitch and to develop the best closing methods might be thought of as receiving sensitivity training in that the participants are being consciously sensitized as to how they come across as persuaders. They are being taught more effective communication; they are being made aware of the nuances of both their own and their customers' lexical, vocal, and kinesic means of communication. The primary goal of this awareness training is the control and change of other human beings, generally, of course, without intent to harm. Yet an important side effect of this training may be the development of communion and a feeling of union among the participants without any conscious planning on the part of the trainer.

At the opposite end of the continuum is the primarily sensory-experiential group, such as one practicing Esalen massage, in which either a one-to-one or a many-to-one sensory-emotional union is intended during a thorough and loving-encounter massage given or experienced by participants in the nude. In such an encounter the less cognitive material introduced (except for how-to explanations) the better. Here the communion of feeling between the masseur and the person being massaged and the internal experience of each are the goals of the sensitivity training.

Common to both types of groups, regardless of the amount of cognitive and sensory input, is the laboratory or experiential method—learning by doing, practicing, trying different ways of relating to other human beings, getting immediate feedback. Somewhere on the continuum toward the task-oriented side of center are the East-Coast-style T-groups as practiced originally by the National Training Laboratories—more agency, less communion. Toward the communion side of the continuum are the West-Coast-style T-groups as presented, for example, by the Institute of Industrial Relations at the University of California, Los Angeles (UCLA), and as increasingly practiced by NTL. Personal growth labs, ordinary marathons, encounter groups, and nude marathons theoretically fall more toward the communion end of the continuum.

The nude marathon is an example of the communion type of group experience; it is not intended as an orgy. The spirit of such an encounter group depends somewhat on the participants and a great deal on the motivation and agenda of the facilitator. The experience of being literally uncovered before one's peers may be a constructive emotional experience, an initially embarrassing and later satisfying self-revelation leading to self-acceptance of one's body, an antidote to repression, a deeply moving sharing of fears and anxieties, a motivation to care more for the body, an esthetic delight, or a sexually stimulating event. In short, it may mean different things to different people. Since the nude marathon is not, when ethically facilitated, primarily agency-oriented, the participants are likely to perceive each other not as sexual objects but as human beings with whom to experience mutual feelings, evaluations, and sensations as uncovered, natural people. Whether being in the nude aids the process of communion is not known. Proponents assert that it increases acceptance of one's body and that this acceptance is enhanced by open discussion and by sharing nonsexual ways of observing and experiencing another unclothed person.

The earliest NTL groups (basic skills training groups) were given considerable didactic material, particularly in group dynamics. But within several years a definite separation developed between the T-groups, whose subject matter became the interpersonal relations of the participants, and the A-groups, whose subject matter included skill in leadership, understanding group process, conflict management, and other agency-oriented functions. Since 1956 a movement in the NTL has tried to reintegrate the T-groups and A-groups within the laboratory. However, the clinical influence—that is, the interest in individual transactions—has been so strong on the West Coast that T-groups in that section of the country are hardly distinguishable from encounter groups. Sensitivity training as practiced at UCLA, for instance, is intended much more for the total growth of the individual—with his search for personal indentity, his ability to be open and authentic, his manner of giving and receiving love and affection—than for his intellectual understanding of group process and human relations problems.

Even so, it is interesting to note the differences that appear in the stated goals of sensitivity training groups conducted by the Institute of Industrial Relations at UCLA and those of marathon encounter groups. Some of the UCLA goals are stated very much in agency terms, such as:

to increase the *effectiveness* of our relations with others we need to know... what we do that is *useful* ... you may get a more accurate image of yourself as an *instrument* of interpersonal relations ... learn how to help groups *function* more *effectively*.

NTL literature, as in Bradford et al., also lists five objectives for participants of T-groups that are slanted toward task or agency orientation: (1) increased sensitivity to emotional reactions in one's self and in others; (2) better ability to understand the consequences of one's reactions; (3) better understanding and development of personal values and goals that are in line with democratic relationships; (4) development of cognitive concepts that can be used to link personal values to actions; and (5) better ways of integrating intentions and actions. Other goals in NTL members' writings include learning to diagnose individual, group, and organizational behavior; gaining self-insight; understanding the actions of people in groups; and learning what conditions facilitate or inhibit group functioning.

In contrast, the communion-oriented goals of encounter groups, as Gazda describes them, provide experiences for: (1) leveling with other members as equals; (2) developing trust and intimacy; (3) taking responsibility for one's own actions—realizing that one can make choices; (4) feeling free to express honest aggression explicitly and to share affection, loneliness, fear, and joy; (5) exploring new ways of being one's self and of discovering one's potential; (6) developing fully by facing up to crises, taking risks, and dropping protective roles.

Thus, the goals of sensitivity training run the gamut from better-performing beings to more social beings. In actuality, the training process, so long as it encourages authentic interaction in the here-and-now, is almost bound to increase communion regardless of the stated objectives (see Figure 1).

Many organizations—whether private businesses, school systems, the government, churches, or charitable institutions—encourage their personnel to take sensitivity training in the hope that they will function more effectively in the performance of their roles, and agency function. Although better functioning may be a result of the training for some participants, follow-up studies of T-groups show more communion-type changes, such as increased openness, flexibility, and interest in people. Both the personal learning and the organizational change that come from the T-group experience may be largely the result of increased self-acceptance and of lessened defensiveness in the participants.

TECHNIQUES

Regardless of its type, an experiential group devoted primarily to the actualization of the participants uses certain fundamental attitudes and processes to help its members grow.

The Facilitator

The facilitator or trainer is probably the single most influential factor in the group. But in a well-functioning sensitivity training group, it is difficult to distinguish

Cognitive and Perceptual				*Sensory and Emotional*	
AGENCY					**COMMUNION**
Salesmanship training	Early NTL T-groups	Conflict management labs	More recent NTL T-groups	Experiential encounter groups and marathons	Esalen massage
Supervisory training		Leadership training labs	UCLA T-groups, church, and YMCA groups		

Figure 1. Sensitivity training goals cover a wide range, from agency-oriented to communion-oriented.

the facilitator from any other member. He interacts as an actual member of the group, although he has the additional responsibilities of seeing that the other members are supported or confronted when necessary and that the group process continues to offer the members opportunities for growth. He sets the example for emotional expressiveness by his spontaneous affective and intellectual behavior toward the other participants. This means that he cannot remain in an aloof role. Nor does he behave primarily as a teacher who gives didactic inputs. It is his own openness, his daring to reveal his own feelings and to confront others about theirs, his staying in the here-and-now that sets the tone for the group and encourages the participants to drop their stereotyped social roles.

Rather than enunciating rules for the group, at least at first, he illustrates through his own actions. Later on, if he were to formulate some principle that furthers the group process, he might announce the one major rule: no physical violence. And then he might add a few suggestions such as: (1) Express your feelings and actions in the here-and-now. (2) Talk directly *to* people in the group and not *about* them to the group. (3) Try to be specific about your feelings and perceptions and do not generalize; statements such as "Most people feel this way" and "All men are like that" are out. (4) Instead of asking the question "Why?" ask for feelings. "Why" makes people rationalize. (5) Try to make "I" statements in which you express your feelings and perceptions. These are much more effective than interpretations of your feelings and keep defensiveness from developing in others by blaming them with "you" statements. Example: "I'm furious with you!" rather than "You're too dumb to fight your way out of a paper bag!"

Intervention

Interventions unfreeze the attitudes and definitions of people toward themselves and others that block and inhibit their natural growth. In general, as Tate notes, there are two main types of intervention in the group: contrasting and substituting.

Contrasting interventions are usually verbal; substituting interventions are usually nonverbal. Contrasting interventions are cognitive; substituting interventions are experiential. Contrasting interventions involve a verbal comparison by a group member or the facilitator between what is actually happening in the group and what another member perceives is happening. Substituting interventions involve introducing experiences for group members from which they may grow. Contrasting interventions help a group member to understand so that he can improve his behavior. Substituting interventions may improve his behavior but not his understanding; what are substituted are experiences he has missed, usually in his early life, or has had infrequently in his development. Substituting interventions provide the participant with new information about himself. Contrasting interventions, on the other hand, usually provide no new information but help the participant become better at discriminating the veracity of information he possesses.

An example of contrasting intervention: A facilitator points out that, although a group member has just announced that he is happy, he still looks depressed. The group and the member then explore this incongruity together.

An example of substituting intervention: A facilitator leaves his seat and sits beside a group member who needs support.

Stimulation

Development is possible for everyone in four main areas of experience: cognition or thinking, perception, affect or emotion, and sensation or physical feeling at the sensory level. In this culture, thinking and perception are highly valued, and affect and sensation gain limited value, so sensitivity training groups, particularly encounter groups, are likely to encourage the experience of physical and emotional expression. Cognition and perception are typically agency-oriented, but affect and sensation are primarily associated with communion. To an agency-dominated person, emphasis on affect and sensation seem disruptive and threatening—something outside the realm of his control.

Some people are almost completely out of touch with their gentler feelings of affection or sadness, and others are not even aware of stronger affects, such as anger or elation. Most people are shy about the expression of certain feelings.

The facilitator can use some exercises or devices to stimulate experience in each of the four areas mentioned. But the greatest influence for change is the democratic and accepting attitude of the facilitator and the group rather than any gimmick or device. The exercises are intended only as boosters to launch the group or individual into the orbit of an experience. There are literally hundreds of experiential stimulators. Only a representative few are discussed below.

Cognition Stimulation. One of the simplest of the diagrams that explain the purpose of sensitivity training is the Johari Window, so-called because it is the brain-child of Joseph Luft (Jo) and Harrington Ingham (Hari).

The diagram (see Figure 2) indicates that one's public self is that part known both to oneself and to others; that the hidden self, representing what one does not divulge, is known to oneself but not to others; that the blind self is a part known to others but not to oneself (for example, how one looks or sounds to others); and that one's undeveloped potential is unknown both to others and to oneself. In sensitivity training, the participants attempt to expand their public selves by purposely taking the risk of revealing some of their hidden selves. There is also the hope that, through honest feedback from others in the group, each participant's blind self will become smaller. The dotted lines in the diagram represent

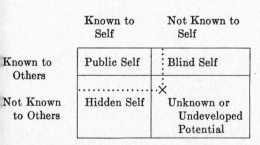

	Known to Self	Not Known to Self
Known to Others	Public Self	Blind Self
Not Known to Others	Hidden Self	Unknown or Undeveloped Potential

Figure 2. The Johari Window is used to explain the purpose of sensitivity training in cognitive terms.

the new boundaries of the public self as a result of group interaction. In the process, a small part of the undeveloped potential, represented in the diagram at ✕, will become available to each group member. When group participants ask the facilitator for some intellectual structuring of the encounter process, this diagram is helpful.

Sometimes simple explanations of interpersonal exchanges can become meaningful when put in terms of the Parent, Adult, and Child of Berne's transactional analysis, as explained by Harris. By encouraging a group member to question the values and assumptions of the critical or ignoring Parent and the overly rebellious, indulged, or adjusted Child, the facilitator can often make astoundingly good sense for that group member out of an apparently complicated interpersonal or intrapersonal situation.

Other cognitive inputs by the facilitator may include requesting group members to reveal their hidden agenda and discuss various other aspects of group dynamics. The introduction of cognitive inputs is probably best reserved until such inputs can be used to clarify an immediate group experience. If presented without reference to group experiences, they have little meaning.

Perception Stimulation. One of the best devices to enlarge one's perception is role-playing, which can be done in a number of ways. One can, for example, follow Shapiro's theory of a number of subselves in the individual—reminiscent of Federn's 1943 concept of multiple ego states in every person—and encourage a member who is having an intrapersonal conflict to role-play it by himself (the facilitator acting as coach), using several chairs to represent the selves in conflict and moving from one chair to another as he speaks extemporaneously for each subself. Gestalt therapy methods also fit this category of perceptual expansion. Role-training is a psychodramatic technique in which, with the help of other group members, one can play out a conflicted relationship, ask others to play the same scene—handling it as they perceive it— and then try out some of the suggested solutions.

In recent years videotape has allowed

participants to see as well as hear themselves in social action. Wherever this device is used, it reveals its great value for self-revelation.

A favorite device for perceptual enlightenment is the group-on-group technique. This consists in having one half of the T-group observe the other half of the group in interaction. Each person in the observing group chooses a partner to watch in the interacting group. Group A, the first half of the T-group to interact, works together for 20 to 30 minutes while being observed by Group B. Then Group B feeds back information to Group A about what Group B observed about both individual and group behavior and process. After that, each member of Group A joins his observer from Group B for five minutes, and the observer feeds back to the Group A member whatever he can of his (A's) behavior, i.e., A's blind self. Then Group B, the other half of the T-group, interacts while Group A observes, and the feedback process is reversed. This technique is generally most effective early in the life of the group.

Having each member of the group draw a picture of the group with crayons on large pieces of paper is a technique for opening up a great deal of interpersonal perception. The group members may be represented symbolically or actually. The participants, working simultaneously, are given about 20 minutes to draw the group and then each speaks in turn, showing his drawing and telling how he perceives each member and why he represented each as he did.

Affect Stimulation. The general verbal techniques used by the facilitator to stimulate affect are to keep asking participants for feelings rather than thoughts and to serve as a model by showing his own feelings. An attitude of unconditional acceptance and the practice of active listening for feelings as well as for content encourage the expression of affect.

If a member starts to cry, a sympathetic participant may shut off the crying member's feelings too quickly by moving in right away with the Kleenex or a physically comforting gesture. It is often better to let the weeping person experience his sadness in depth before making the comforting gesture.

Finney has developed a verbal method of breaking through the ideational shield into affective states. In this method, which Finney calls "say it again," the facilitator sits in front of a group member, takes his hands, and asks him how he feels. As the member begins to talk, the facilitator makes him repeat emotional phrases by telling him, "Say it again," sometimes feeding him what he intuitively senses would be appropriate phrases, which the group member may feel free to repeat or reject. By having the group member talk constantly on a feeling level, the facilitator frequently breaches the barrier to affect, and much emotion pours out.

Somewhat similar is a technique derived from Janov, in which the group member is encouraged to imagine himself as a child and to call his daddy or mommy for help. Frequently, much repressed feeling comes out under such circumstances.

Both the facilitator and the group members are expected to feel free to move around in the group and to show affection and empathy either physically or verbally. They should feel free to care physically for each other by touching, taking a person's hand, putting their arms around him. All these physical methods of communicating are of the substitution type and, as such, increase access to or expression of a group member's blocked-out or limited experiential data.

A device that aids in releasing anger is pillow-beating or mattress-pounding. By encouraging a group member who is evidently repressing his rage to beat up a hated introject in the form of a pillow, much relief may accrue to him, especially when he acts with the blessings of the group.

By such nonverbal expression, a group member is often able to bypass inhibitions that have hindered his perception of his emotional self from an early age. The affect that emerges is often painful at first, but the relief is worth the effort.

Sensation Stimulation. Gestalt therapy has particularly emphasized getting in touch with the senses in order to function fully as a person. Perls has a famous dictum:

You must lose your mind to come to your senses.

The child in each person can be revived joyously if he allows himself to re-experience childlike modes of relating. Perls, Hefferline, and Goodman have developed special exercises to revive the senses of taste, touch, smell, sight, and sound. Encounter groups have taken these and similar experiential exercises into their repertoire of antirepression devices. In one exercise to help revive the sensation of taste, the group members eat a silent meal together, concentrating on the food, its taste, and its texture. Smelling various substances while blindfolded or paying attention to the smells of the earth, grass, flowers, and trees may make group members feel more alive again by re-establishing their union with nature, a union often repressed from childhood.

An artist may make a great contribution to the experience of a group by pointing out different designs, shadings, colors, and textures in the environment or by sitting in a group and drawing his impressions of members, their poses, and their interactions and then discussing his perceptions with the group. Group members often benefit from being encouraged to look at each other, to consider carefully which side of another person's face seems more dominant, to examine the texture of someone's skin.

With eyes closed, the group members may listen to music of different sorts; or they may go out into the woods in the quiet of an early morning, with each one sitting by himself for half an hour, listening to the sounds of nature, and tuning in on his own feelings. After this solitary experience, the group members come together again and share.

Touching, of course, is one of the most potent of all contacts—one of the first experienced by infants. It is rare that a touch fails to elicit a response from a group member. A simple but effective exercise in touch stimulation consists of one person's standing behind another and, at a signal from the person in front (a partly raised arm, for example), touching that person with both hands on the head. This action is repeated three times. The person doing the touching tries to imagine a flow of energy from him through his hands and into the person in front of him. When several people take turns touching another this way, great differences become apparent to the person being touched, and he usually feels that he knows each toucher much better from this contact. If this exercise is tried, (1) the person being touched must keep his eyes closed; (2) the person touching must do nothing but touch (he must not, for example, give a massage); (3) the touching must be done completely in silence; and (4) it must be done unhurriedly.

Another simple exercise in learning about another person through touch is to sit or stand in front of him, place your palms flat against his in a patty-cake gesture, and then move your hands together with his in any way that suits the mutual feeling of the partners. Sometimes this exercise results in aggressive pushing in a power play, sometimes in a delicate hand-dance, sometimes in a joking, funny, or hilarious encounter. As with other nonverbal exercises, this one is done without talking.

A great deal of the kinesthetic sense may be experienced in the pushing, wrestling, hand-wrestling, bio-energetic exercises of Lowen and by lifting and rocking group members or passing them around in the inside of a tight circle formed by the group. A well-known version of this last technique is described by Schutz as roll and rock. In this exercise, the facilitator or group having decided that a member needs a special kind of affection, the group forms a tight circle with the subject inside. Standing with eyes closed, he is rolled around in a circular motion from one person to another in the group while he relaxes against the tight circle, trusting the group to support him. After a short period of this rolling, the group members gently help the subject lie down in the center of the circle. Then they carefully pick him up and, holding him at their chest height, rock him slowly back and forth about a dozen times. They then lower him gently to the floor and either leave him there with his eyes closed for several minutes until he has completely absorbed the experience or sit beside him, all continuing to touch him until he gradually rejoins them from his reverie. The whole exercise, usually an emotionally moving experience for all participants, is completely nonverbal.

Nonverbal Techniques for Special Situations

Some nonverbal exercises are peculiarly helpful for group members who need to experience and fulfill directly, more than to talk about, some deeply personal need.

The Outsider. He seems to stay aloof from the group, he does not join in, he does not respond to encouragement by the group to participate. Particularly—but not necessarily—if he himself admits to feeling left out, the following exercise can be explained to him, and the group can then carry it out without words.

The group forms a very tight circle, with arms locked around each other. The outsider is placed physically outside of the circle and is told that he must break through to the center in any way he chooses, except that he may not physically hurt anyone. The group cohesiveness ensures his having to work hard to achieve his getting in.

The Nontruster. Like the roll-and-rock exercise described above, several simple experiences may become turning points in the nontruster's group life. In one, the subject, eyes closed, stands 18 inches or more in front of someone strong enough to support him. Facing away from this partner, at a signal or when he and his partner are ready, he falls backward into the arms of his catcher, who must, of course, not let him down. After several instances of giving himself in this vulnerable way to another person, the nontruster is much more likely to allow himself to be vulnerable in other ways with the group.

Another exercise that develops trust is the blind walk, in which one person, eyes closed, is led by his partner through a house, outside into the garden, up and down steps, and so forth. The nontruster completely relies on his partner not to let him trip or hurt himself. This exercise is particularly helpful for people who are anxious about being dependent or submissive.

The Timid Person. A humorous and noisy exercise to use when someone in the group speaks timidly or seems unable to show aggression or self-assertion is the karate-chop experience. In this exercise, the facilitator or an assertive group member stands facing the timid person, and the two pretend to be karate antagonists, making fake karate chops and kicks at each other, without touching but yelling the karate "Hai!" as loudly as possible with each chop. The group vocally encourages the timid one to yell more loudly, to be "vicious," and to let go. The usual result of such an exercise is increased acceptance by the timid person of his aggressiveness.

General Group Inhibition or Warm-up. A series of two- to four-minute non-verbal exercises help in warming up a cold group. The following are a few suggestions:

1. The group members choose partners. One rolls up in a ball on the floor, and his partner unravels him while he resists strongly. Then the partners reverse roles.

2. One partner plays dead and takes on the waxy flexibility of the catatonic. The other partner places him in different positions, finally putting him in an appropriate rest-in-peace position.

3. Partners, lying on their stomachs and facing each other, arm-wrestle while making great grunts and groans of anguish.

4. Partners sit on the floor back to back, arms engaged, and try to "talk" with their backs.

5. Partners sit facing each other, eyes closed, and explore each other's hands, arms, faces, necks. Or they "talk" with their hands.

6. Partners lie with heads on each other's shoulders, bodies at 180 degrees to each other, eyes closed, listening to music while each has a fantasy about the other. When the music stops, they share their fantasies, first with each other and then with the group.

After each of these exercises, the partners talk to each other about their experiences. During the exercise itself, however, no words are said, although appropriate sounds are permissible.

Sociometric Feedback. The following problem is posed to the group:

All of you have been together on a ship that has just sunk. You [point to one member] have just found a small life raft capable of holding three other people. Ahead is an island on which you can live fairly comfortably; but, because it is out of the shipping lanes, you will have to be there at least six months. What three other people in this group will you ask to join you on the raft, row to the island, and live there together? What do you expect of them during that six-month period? [Build in your own questions.]

Each person in the group announces his choices and talks about his decision with the group. Often someone is left out by everyone else. This can be turned into a growth experience for the person left out as he discusses his feelings and gets honest feedback from the group about why he was avoided. The difficulties and style of choosing companions with whom to live become sources of confrontation and feedback.

Group Cohesiveness and Humor. This exercise is a delightful version of the island fantasy, particularly after the group has become fairly cohesive and needs a release from tension. The group members lie on the floor in a close circle, with their heads as the axis in the center, bodies extending out, eyes closed. They are asked to have a fantasy about their life together on a lush tropical island, where food, water, and weather are no problems. Once someone starts the fantasy, each person spontaneously adds whatever occurs to him. The project usually becomes a warm, affectionate, sometimes moving, often hilarious experience of joy, humor, and closeness. The facilitator may bring the exercise to a close by some appropriate fantasy, such as the group's being picked up by a passing ship. Very often no one wants to leave the island.

TECHNICAL AND POLICY ISSUES

Are there conflicting goals in sensitivity training? In trying to conceptualize the wide range of practices subsumed under the name of sensitivity training and to evaluate the meaning of research on the T-group process one may find the terms "agency" and "communion" helpful. Bakan used these terms

to characterize two fundamental modalities in the existence of living forms, *agency* for the existence of an organism as an individual, and *communion* for the participation of the individual in some larger organism of which the individual is a part.

Agency is manifested by protecting, asserting, and expanding the self; by remaining separate and alone; by mastery, control, and affecting people and things; by repression of innovative and spontaneous thought and emotion except in the service of mastery; by the accumulation of wealth and possessions; by achievement of status and power. In our society one's place in the pecking order is determined by how successfully he functions in the realm of achievement. Western culture is a monument to the success of the agency use of human energy. The purpose of agency is to relieve one's existential anxiety by keeping busy controlling the environment.

Communion, on the other hand, is manifested by the experience of openness and nondefensiveness; by joining with others; by contact—physical, intellectual, emotional; by removal or lack of repression, especially inhibition of feelings. The purpose of communion is to experience intimacy with some other living thing.

Sensitivity training was developed originally to help people function more effectively as team members in task groups either in businesses or in institutions, to help them understand and control group processes, and to help them become aware of their impact on other people. The learning was intended to be task-oriented, to achieve a goal. However, an important by-product of the earliest T-groups was the experience of communion, an experience so satisfying that participants began to resent the introduction of agency-oriented theoretical verbal inputs. So other groups, A-groups, were set up for the purpose of teaching specific task-oriented interpersonal skills.

The need for communion evidenced by the early sensitivity training group participants was to become a *Zeitgeist*. It is still a growing spirit in this country and in the world, an antiagency movement participated in by hippies, students, and drug-users of all descriptions as well as staid and well-function-ing adults. The encounter group, the experi-ential group, the group that is more communion-oriented than agency-oriented answers the need of the middle-class to miti-gate agency with communion and sometimes to discard agency almost completely. Growth centers such as Esalen and Kairos in Cali-fornia and Aureon Institute in the East are mainly supported by middle-class seekers of communion. Rock festivals such as Wood-stock and Newport allow the younger genera-tion to participate in communion. It is inter-esting to note that the earlier sources of communion—the church, fraternal organiza-tions, and the family—have lost some of their ascendancy as means of providing col-laborative experiences. Many churches have now incorporated sensitivity training in an effort to regain their original communion function.

The main value of sensitivity training, regardless of its justification through the rationale of its task-oriented function, may quite possibly be that it allows participants to experience communion. Thus, in consider-ing research that would support sensitivity training as worth its salt from an agency viewpoint, one should not be too surprised to find that (1) most facilitators of sensitivity training groups are not enthusiastic research people, preferring instead to participate in the experience itself, and (2) a good deal of research ends up with findings of commun-ion-oriented functions. For example, the sensitivity-trained people show increased openness, flexibility, and ease in interper-sonal relationships, although they may not show a concomitant increase in such agency functions as influencing people, interest in achieving, and completing a task. The ques-tion, "How valuable is sensitivity training?" depends on the philosophical value system of the questioner. To an agency-oriented questioner or researcher, the T-group must result in more effective functioning, in an agency sense, before he will consider it valuable. To the communion-oriented ques-tioner—and there are fewer of these in American culture—the T-group should re-sult in more contact, more participation, more love for one's fellow man. Except in some almost completely nonverbal encounter groups, sensitivity training groups blend agency and communion, with a steadily growing surge toward communion.

Exploitation

If the intensive group experience is essen-tially a leaderless group, how can the group handle skillful participants who are covertly exploitative? An ethic is often promulgated in a training group that the members can be trusted and that there need not be a leader. There is no certainty that a group-appointed leader has any way of checking and correct-ing deep-seated neurotic conflicts or blind spots or of refraining from forcing his own private value judgments or orientations on the other group members. If enough of the members in a group are honest, not corrupt, and altruistic, they can check the exploita-tive and sociopathic participant in his at-tempt to take over the group and have them do his bidding. But groups that invite people to join them in practicing hostile and aggres-sive behavior with one another may attract persons who, in everyday life, specialize and excel in these kinds of human behavior. There is no way of guaranteeing that the milder or more inhibited member who hopes to learn how to become more assertive by joining such a group will not be completely squelched or encouraged to behave in a socially destructive manner, not only in the group but outside the group.

Sociopaths

How can a training group handle socio-paths, especially if they predominate in the group? There is no evidence that intensive group experiences change the moral or ethi-cal behavior of a person. Groups that are constituted principally of socially destructive or sociopathic people are likely to behave collectively like their participants. The mass effect of such a group on an individual par-ticipant who has a sense of group belonging-ness or social responsibility will be a disrup-tive one.

Group Attention

Does the squeaky wheel tend to get the attention in training groups? Outspoken, socially proficient people tend to fare best in intensive group experiences, for there are social rewards for articulate and persuasive verbal communication. The reticent member is generally encouraged to speak up, to assert himself, to open up. An increase in group pressure is brought to bear on silent members. This approach sometimes has a salutary effect. An alert group leader or group participants who seriously feel concern for nonsqueaky people bring out such members, often in a sympathetic and reassuring way, but this happy eventuality cannot be guaranteed.

Leadership

Do persons who win leadership roles in training and action groups really constitute the best leaders? This question opens a whole bag of questions about leadership, its functions, its goals, and its purposes. Probably people who win leadership roles in intensive group experiences and maintain such leadership roles win them by acclaim or by consensus; otherwise, they are not tolerated for a prolonged time in an on-going group process. Such persons may not necessarily be the best leaders for the group that has permitted them the experience of taking a leadership role or for groups outside the specific group experience in which they have just participated. Obviously, leadership has many different functions and goals. Strong leadership may be exerted by someone who is not actively participating in the group, as, for example, by someone who has written a drama or a novel or an essay that has major and long-continuing effects on individual and group behavior. Moreover, leadership may be manifested in many ways other than by articulate verbal interaction—for example, by public self-defeating behavior, suicide, standing on a high building and threatening to jump, walking nude down the street, robbing a bank. The roles and functions of leadership need more careful study and explication before one can authoritatively and readily answer the question raised above.

Sociopathic Leadership. What about ensuring against sociopathic leadership? This is a problem! There is no clearly identifiable professional or institutional base for the recruitment, training, and practice of laboratory practitioners. Trainers are recruited from a variety of disciplines, backgrounds, and experiences. Their training is varied. Their practice is extremely variable. Within the laboratory movement this variability is perceived both as a strength and as a weakness—but it does present problems. Without an identifiable discipline, there are no norms for performance, no explicit forms for evaluation. Instead, shifting social sanctions support or undermine the context of training laboratory practice. The lack of disciplinary identity also presents problems in terms of clinical issues. The laboratory movement has yet to acquire a professional status. The issues confronting professionalization are complex, for the movement does not have a relatively uniform ideological base, nor are its goals confined to a narrow range of clinical or organizational concerns. Consequently, the laboratory movement has continued to develop apart from more structured and institutionalized concerns of university departments, well-delineated research fields, and the clinical professions. Schools of education and schools of business administration represent the major sources of institutional and professional support.

Strong Leadership. If one is a participant in a group with a strong, professionally trained leader, how does one distinguish the group process from group therapy? As noted earlier, the boundaries between the training group and the traditional therapy group are becoming blurred. This blurring of distinctions can have some serious consequences for some group participants. In contrast to most psychotherapies in which a patient asks to be changed in some respect—to be relieved of distressing symptoms or what he regards as personality or behavioral deficiencies—the training group participant does not regularly frame his goals in such terms. Rather, he wants to learn about groups, his behavior in groups, and how to improve his functioning in groups. When the training group is under way, many training group participants find that they are being induced to change in ways they did not anticipate. They find that the trainer and various group members are calling on them to stop certain ways of behaving, talking, thinking, and feeling, and that different ways of behaving are being prescribed. The pressure of the group and trainer may not necessarily be in the same direction. Or the trainer's silence may mistakenly be taken as a sanction, endorsement, or recommendation for behavioral change made by one participant with regard to another. Some of the T-group participants may become seriously upset under such pressure to alter their identity, especially when they do not recognize this identity as a problem or difficulty and when they have not even thought of trying to modify some aspects of their identity.

Countertransference. How about clearing adverse countertransference or seriously biased value judgments from trainers or facilitators? There is at present no professionally organized way of doing so. Indeed, more and more responsible professionals agree that some program of training is needed to minimize arbitrary, narrowly judgmental, personal value orientations of the group leader. Gottschalk and Pattison have stated:

An ethic is often promulgated in a T-group that the group should be trusted and can be trusted. There is an implication, moreover, that the trainers in a T-group have not only the sanction and blessing but the stamp of approval of the National Training Laboratories [or some other sponsoring organization] as wise, experienced teachers of group dynamics, counselors, and emotionally well-adjusted individuals.

Unfortunately, just as the distortions of the group members enter into the group processes, the unresolved emotional conflicts and the private value judgments of the T-group trainers may obtrude themselves into the group process. These colorful contributions to the group activities need not in themselves be a cause for concern, for such is life. But a participant in the T-group has the idea, somehow, that the group-appointed trainer, as any other group-appointed leader, has some way of checking and correcting deep-seated neurotic conflicts or blind spots or refraining from enforcing his own private value judgments or orientations, unless invited to do so, on the other group members. But there is apparently as yet no satisfactory system for such check-outs for trainers. Few have ever had a personal psychoanalysis, so that this avenue is not available for repeatedly exploring pathological countertransference reactions or other neurotically determined attitudes or behavior.

Each trainer goes through [one or] several T-groups himself. This procedure may select conceivably the more extroverted, self-confident, and socially proficient individuals but guarantees nothing about the trainer's emotional and intellectual acumen with respect to recognizing and preventing the development of disruptive emotional breakdowns in T-group members or his ability to examine such developments critically and discover his role in permitting or inciting them to occur.

Trainers for the most part are free to hold any theoretical orientation they choose. The influence of theoretical orientation on trainer behavior and the relative merits of different theoretical orientations are largely empirical questions that will require considerable research and time to resolve. It is therefore useless to debate such issues here.*

Authenticity

Regardless of the type or caliber of leadership and intensive group experience, what is authenticity with respect to personality? A key goal of all laboratory training has been called authenticity in interpersonal relations. This term signifies a relationship that enables each person to feel free to be himself and communicate openly with himself and others. Authentic, in this sense, refers to conscious or readily accessible emotions and thoughts and not to those that are unconscious and, hence, not easily available to awareness. Thus, a person could be encouraged to be more open and express some usually withheld hostility. This change could be labeled as becoming more authentic from the viewpoint of laboratory training, but underlying this hostility might be discovered, possibly through psychoanalytic therapy, more valid emotional love and yearning for others but anxiety over revealing it. The hostile emotion would then be a defensive emotion—the psychological mechanism of turning into the opposite. Though authentic, in the sense of being part of the individual's personality facade or character armor, the hostility would not typify the deeper, basic emotional need of the person.

Authenticity relates in part to what one is really like behind one's facade. One's facade, however, is also very much a part of oneself, and many people fail to realize that this

* From *The American Journal of Psychiatry*, volume 126, pages 823–839, 1969. © 1969, the American Psychiatric Association.

facade was socially acquired and need not, in every respect, be ready for the rubbish heap. Characteristic ways of relating to one another may be socially useful and reflect conventional ways that human beings, in Western culture, relate to and communicate with one another. Many of these traits can be so inflexible and ritualized that the more spontaneous, emotion-laden, or healthy impulsive aspects of a person are never permitted to appear. On the other hand, indiscriminate, sensual, aggressive, disorganized, and chaotic thinking or other kinds of expressive behavior are not necessarily more authentic.

Defenses

Why call one's facade necessarily defensive? One's characteristic way of relating to people does, indeed, sometimes result from previous painful experiences with other human beings and, hence, reflects guardedness, fear of closeness or intimacy, fear of being spontaneous, and so forth. The problem is that many people in everyday life may well reinforce one's guardedness and self-protective behavior. It is, in the writers' opinion, a serious error for therapists and trainers involved in intensive group experiences to blithely assume that the world, and hence all the groups in which one may be involved, is populated with friendly, loving, protective, sympathetic, altruistic people. Persons who are learning about how they function in groups need not go through the painful rediscovery that some people in groups are ready and poised to hurt them, possibly because that is the only way such hostile people know how to relate to people, possibly because they feel the best defense is a good offense. Many group leaders, extrapolating from psychoanalytic psychiatry, believe that psychological mechanisms and adaptive behavior can routinely be regarded as defensive and must be dismantled. Such was never done indiscriminately in psychoanalytic practice, and there are no advantages in proceeding in such a fashion outside the psychoanalytic process.

Intimacy

With strangers, what are the limits, if any, of intimacy? Is opening one's innermost feelings to strangers more authentic, more healthy, more characteristic of adjustment? Many of the sensitivity and encounter group and marathon group programs developing in the United States, which is relatively affluent and where most people can meet such physical needs as shelter and food, now emphasize the need to overcome what is perceived as a remaining psychosocial deficiency of existence, namely, loneliness and alienation. These programs emphasize that everyone's existence will automatically become more meaningful if stranger-anxiety is immediately and continuously dispelled and if everyone becomes completely intimate with anyone encountered. One is almost in the position of a devil's advocate if he asks whether there are limits to the notion that everyone should be equally intimate with everyone else and whether preference for limiting intimacy to a few others and for situations of privacy is necessarily deviant. These issues need to be explored during the group process.

CLINICAL ASPECTS

UCLA T-Group

The format of the UCLA T-group experience for business and professional people consists of two weekends at the university conference center on the shore of a lake. Between the weekends there are five weekly meetings consisting of dinner followed by a three-and-a-half-hour T-group session. On each of the weekends, about 100 participants arrive at the conference center before five o'clock Friday afternoon. They register and then relax at the self-service, unofficial bar. Nearly all the participants are strangers to each other.

After dinner comes the first session, a short orientation to the laboratory. Schedules are handed out, facilitators are introduced, and the goals of the laboratory are briefly stated.

After this brief introduction, the T-groups of 15 or 16 persons each go off to their meeting rooms, which are living rooms or bedrooms in motel-type cottages. Chairs and sofas are always arranged in a circle so that everyone can communicate with the whole group. The facilitator usually passes out stiff five-inch by eight-inch cards on which the participants print their first names. They set the cards in front of them on the floor or a coffee table. Facilitator styles vary, but often at this point the leader makes a short introduction, in which he states that the group will be largely unstructured, with no set agenda.

He usually states or implies that the participants will probably learn more from discussing the relationships and process within the group itself (here-and-now data) than from discussing outside activities (there-and-then data). He then defaults as leader, leaving the participants to their own devices as to how to become a group.

Each participant uses his own strategies in this process of group formation and, as time goes on, becomes aware of his own feelings and the feelings of others, partly by being encouraged to attend to his own inner processes and partly by feedback from other group members. He becomes aware of the problem of communication, of how little he and others actually listen with involvement, of how much they misinterpret. He also becomes aware of the real differences in the needs of members, their goals, and their ways of approaching problems.

Feedback and confrontation with other group members give a person an increased awareness of his own impact on others. The trainer often models feedback by giving members his own genuine reaction to their behavior, particularly in terms of his feelings.

The first session ends after two hours when the participants return to the bar, go to their rooms, relax in the village, or whatever.

During the next day, there are morning, afternoon, and evening sessions, with a two-hour break after lunch for informal walks, sports, meetings, rest, and relaxation. From time to time, as the facilitator deems it appropriate, he may introduce nonverbal exercises as interventions, but the main process is verbal interaction. As the weekend progresses, the interaction moves perceptibly from superficial role relationships—with the emphasis on cognitive, generalized, there-and-then topics—to genuine openness and the expression of emotion shared by group members with each other in here-and-now interaction. The first weekend concludes after the Sunday morning session and lunch.

During the next five weeks, each small group meets separately for dinner and a three-hour session (exclusive of dinner) with its facilitator and continues its work of learning less-defensive relationships from its own experience. The culmination of the course comes on the final weekend, which is structured like the first but has a very different feeling because of the greatly increased depth of openness and affection among the participants. The sensitivity training officially ends after the final Sunday morning sessions, although many groups continue to meet informally for some time, and some even engage their facilitator for a while.

NTL groups often meet for continuous periods of one or two full weeks rather than being spaced over a period of two weekends with an intervening five weeks of dinner meetings, as is the custom at UCLA.

Theory Sessions

Experience in the group precedes the introduction of theory. This is a basic principle of laboratory training. Yet raw experience without intellectual understanding may not produce learning that is useful and that can be taken from the laboratory to a person's outside life. In an NTL sensitivity training group, theory sessions are set up at varying intervals, and information is given on such topics as group members, problem-solving in groups, and styles of presenting oneself to others.

UCLA groups often truncate or skip theory sessions. But neither the T-group nor the theory session is complete without the other, according to NTL belief.

Focused Exercises

Exercises that highlight some specific behavior are sometimes introduced into the T-group. In standard sensitivity training, these exercises are likely to be carried out verbally and to consist of practice in various ways of communicating (one-way vs. two-way), leading groups, role-playing, role training, managing conflict, observing others, and observing group process. In the less cognitively structured encounter groups, the facilitator is likely to introduce at appropriate times many nonverbal exercises to stimulate and work through sensations and feelings of participants. In any case, after such an exercise, the group members are usually asked to share their experiences, whether they joined in actively or passively.

Informal Contacts

Some of the most valuable happenings associated with the laboratory method are the frequent informal contacts between different members and facilitators outside the scheduled sessions. During these informal meetings, much back-home information is shared, thus contributing to the data bank of shared knowledge between members through which they find more feelings and interests in common. The bonds of friendship established informally enhance the authenticity developing in the T-group. Late evening bull sessions between participants are considered of great value.

RESEARCH

Outcome Research

Evaluation of the effects of any change agent is difficult, as exemplified by the fact that many books and papers are written on how to do psychotherapy but relatively few on the evaluation of its effects. The relative paucity of good research into the outcome of psychotherapy has been occasioned by problems of research design, the setting up of adequate controls, and lack of interest of many psychotherapists in such research. On the other hand, evaluative research of the effects of psychoactive pharmacological agents is much more common and well-developed, probably because the use of such therapeutic agents involves the participation of the medical profession and the possibility of malpractice suits against either the physician who prescribes such drugs or the pharmaceutical company that manufactures and develops them. Pressure to pursue evaluative research into the effects of training groups is minimal because no profession monopolizes the administration of such procedures, because of the unresolved question of whether such techniques constitute education more than therapy, and because the majority of encounter group facilitators and trainers prefer to avoid doing such research. In fact, most of these practitioners scorn the up-tight investigator who seeks objective evidence of

change; instead, they readily accept the testimonials of growing numbers of people who have attended such groups.

Research into the effectiveness of T-groups involves all the ramifications and problems of psychotherapy research. Many factors are known to influence behavioral and attitudinal changes in psychotherapy research. First of all, the goals of psychotherapy itself are important. These goals differ considerably with different psychotherapy programs. For example, the psychotherapeutic program that has as its major aim an increase in the emotions experienced by an obsessive-compulsive patient will, obviously, require assessment procedures or measures different from those used for the psychotherapeutic program that aims to decrease a person's emotions or his capacity for emotional arousal. A psychotherapeutic program that seeks a change in a complex character trait requires an evaluative measure different from that needed by the psychotherapeutic procedure that aims to help a person over an immediate crisis reaction. So, in considering the evaluative research with various kinds of training groups, one must attempt to enumerate the goals of such group activities.

The therapist's personality, it has been well established, may influence the outcome of treatment. The effects of the psychotherapist's personality on the outcome of treatment has been studied most thoroughly and for many years by such psychoanalysts as Orr and more recently by such nondirective or client-centered therapists as Truax and Carkhuff, Bergin, and Shlien and Zimring. These studies indicate that the attitude and personality of the therapist does influence the immediate and often subsequent course of psychotherapy and that some psychotherapists regularly achieve patient improvement and others achieve patient worsening. Even in five-minute interviews, where standardized instructions for eliciting speech from the subjects are read and where the interviewer is silent during this time and maintains an unreactive facial expression, a content analysis of the subject's verbal behavior has shown significantly greater amounts of anxiety and hostility with some interviewers than with others (Gottschalk and Gleser, 1969).

Apart from the personality of the therapist or the patient, the therapeutic agent, whether psychoactive drug or psychological procedure, can be influenced by a person's mental set about the expected effect. For example, in a double-blind study, Gottschalk et al. (1968) noted that the written statements that subjects could expect to feel more peppy and energetic after ingesting a pill resulted in significant increases in achievement strivings, as measured by a content analysis procedure, whether or not the subjects received a placebo, 100 mg. of secobarbital, or 10 mg. of dextroamphetamine. The effects of the dextroamphetamine and the induced mental set were additive and resulted in greater achievement-striving scores when the drug and mental set were given together than when introduced separately.

Furthermore, psychopharmacological research on the effects of psychoactive drugs shows solid evidence that the socioeconomic class of patients can influence the effects of any one psychoactive pharmacological agent. For instance, Rickels et al. found that placebo responses are poorer and psychoactive drug responses are better in middle-class, neurotic, general practice patients; the reverse is true for lower-class, neurotic, psychiatric clinic patients. Higher-class patients, in response to tranquilizers and sedatives, complain more about drowsiness than do lower-class patients, who complain more about stimulation and autonomic nervous system side effects. If such factors are known to influence the outcome in instances where the therapeutic agent (a drug) is standardizable, certainly these same factors may be involved in outcome research of training groups, where it is impossible to standardize the therapeutic agent.

Improved Group Functioning. Process-centered groups have as one of their major goals the training of participants to experience and to recognize group dynamics and their own contribution to group dynamics. A test of such training is its practical application in improving the work of task-oriented groups at home. Campbell and Dunnette, after reviewing the literature in this area, concluded that there is only inconclusive evidence that T-group training has positive utility for organizational functioning. Stock, in her review, suggested that people from different kinds of organizations with different kinds of motivations and with different kinds of training group experiences learn different things in such groups and, hence, carry back to their organizations different potentials for attitudinal change. Thus, the final effect on the back-home group is likely to be varied.

Better Socialization and Interpersonal Relations. A number of reports claim to show that experience in T-groups and encounter groups produces increased skills in communication, independence, flexibility, self-awareness, and sensitivity to the feelings of others. Not only are these changes observed in the group, but they are apparently maintained in the back-home setting. Comparisons of persons who have completed a group experience and those who have not tend to show that the experimental subjects show two to three times as many interpersonal changes as do the control subjects. According to Bunker, for example, about 33 per cent of the 229 group members he studied tended to show increases in openness, receptivity, tolerance of differences, operational skills in interpersonal relationships, and understanding of self and others; only 15 to 20 per cent of the 125 persons in the control group showed such changes. An even higher percentage of favorable change in group participants—64 per cent—was reported by Boyd and Elliss.

Burke and Bennis studied the impact of the human relations laboratory on changes in the perception of self and other group members. Using a group semantic differential, they found that perception of the self and the ideal self converged and that the way people saw themselves and the way they were seen by others became more similar over a period of time.

Despite the evidence in favor of positive effects from T-group training, a number of problems exist in such studies. One of the difficulties is that the amount of change reported appears to vary with the source of the judgments. The trainee's opinion of the effectiveness of his behavioral change tends to be far more optimistic than that of observers. For example, Miles reported that, of 34 high school principals who had participated in NTL programs, 82 per cent indicated improved functioning subsequent to their training. Ratings by their back-home colleagues, however, indicated that only 30 per cent had changed. Taylor also found that the participants' own responses were more enthusiastic than those of their associates. Campbell and Dunnette, in summarizing the evidence for change, state that about 30 to 40 per cent of the trained persons they surveyed were reported to exhibit some kind of perceptible change.

The interpretation of data submitted by judges is difficult because peers tend to assign less change to colleagues who complete a group training experience than to either their superiors or their subordinates. Compounding the serious problem of judge bias is the fact that these studies were based solely on opinions obtained at the conclusion of the training period. There was no pretraining baseline.

Enhanced Sense of Well-Being. A number of encounter group leaders view the major function of the group as simply providing an intense emotional experience. This view shifts the criterion for assessing success to the internal subjective state of the participant. If one assumes that reactions to the encounter group are to be treated as private events, such as civic appreciation or recreational enjoyment, then reports of success may be assumed to have face validity. The participant may take whatever he chooses or is capable of choosing from the experience provided.

That most participants retrospectively report global satisfaction with their group experience is indicated by the survey findings of three investigators. The most careful study was that conducted by Rogers, who obtained responses to his questionnaires from 82 per cent (481) of the clients who had participated in groups he had led. Three-fourths reported that the group had been a helpful, positive experience; 30 per cent stated that the experience had been "constructive," and another 45 per cent described it as a "deep, meaningful, positive experience." An additional 19 per cent checked that it had been "more helpful than unhelpful."

About the same degree of participant satisfaction, 78 per cent, is implied by Bach,

whose 1968 analysis is based on reports by 612 participants. A 1967 report by Bach is more enthusiastic; there he reported that 90 per cent of 400 marathon group members evaluated their 24- to 48-hour group encounters as "one of the most significant meaningful experiences of their lives."

Mintz obtained follow-up reports from her group participants and found that, of 93 who evaluated their experiences immediately after the termination of the marathon group, 66 per cent reported they had profited greatly and 30 per cent reported they had profited moderately. In a sample of 80 who evaluated their marathon group experience after at least three months, 46 per cent said they had profited greatly and 41 per cent said they had profited moderately. A further analysis revealed that the rate of declining enthusiasm appeared to be differentially related to whether the participant was himself a psychotherapist. Although 70 per cent of the nontherapists reported immediately after group termination that they had greatly profited, only 34 per cent reported after three months or more that they were greatly helped. On the other hand, psychotherapists tended to maintain their enthusiasm or even increase it—62 per cent reported in the immediate response that they had profited greatly, and 67 per cent reported improvement in the follow-up response.

Most of the clients who choose to respond to the inquiries of their former group leaders report that they gained something from the experience. Neither Bach nor Mintz provides information regarding the number of eligible respondents who failed to reply to these questionnaires, and they do not attempt to compare the characteristics of the responders and the nonresponders.

Besides the issue of response bias, three other methodological problems limit the value of these studies: (1) No control groups aid in assessing the impact of technique, leader personality and style, level of leader training, length of meeting time, and other such obvious variables. (2) Measures were taken only after the group had disbanded, not prior to the group experience, which increased the opportunity for rater bias. (3) The measures used are global rather than specific, making it impossible to determine the specific nature of the change experience in terms of interpersonal sensitivity, empathy, objectivity, and other such presumed goals of the encounter groups.

A person who is already quite effective in groups when he first comes to a T-group may show no change. Is he to be counted as a failure? Also, when evaluations rely on self-.reports, the results are contaminated by attitudes and response sets that may have little to do with what has been learned.

When investigators attempt to identify specific rather than general changes induced by encounter-type groups—such as changes in self-concept, changes in inner or outer directedness, and changes in attitude and personality—the findings are less positive. Stock found that persons who reported the greatest degree of change in their self-percepts were also those who had become much less sure of what kinds of people they are. Kassarjian attempted to determine whether sensitivity training influenced participants to become more other-directed, as is claimed by some, or more inner-directed, as claimed by others. He failed to find any reliable directional shifts in ten groups of participants compared on measures taken before and after training. Kassarjian concluded that social character may not be one of the variables affected by such training. Other studies reveal that students who were exposed to a program of sensitivity training showed no significant change in such standard personality measures as the California Psychological Inventory, Minnesota Multiphasic Personality Inventory F-scale, and the Cattell 16-Personality-Factor Questionnaire.

The paucity of standardized scales makes it difficult to assess the attitude and personality changes that may be fostered in encounter groups. Of the attitude scales employed, only the Fundamental Interpersonal Relations Orientation-Behavior appeared to give positive results, as reported by Smith and by Schutz and Allen.

In summary, participants in encounter groups report favorable reactions and are frequently described by others as showing improved interpersonal skills. But the evidence is meager that such participants undergo significant attitude changes or personality changes, and the evidence that group training improves group or organizational efficiency is not persuasive. What is clearest is that these groups provide an intensive affective experience for many participants. In this sense, the groups may be described as potent. As is the case with all potent, agents, they may be helpful when properly administered in small doses and noxious when excessive or inappropriate doses are given.

Other Kinds of Research

Besides outcome research, other kinds of research in the area of laboratory movement are being pursued by a few investigators. For example, Cooper has studied the influence of the trainer on participant change in T-groups. He reports that, when the trainer is seen as attractive, participants identify with him and become more like him in attitude and behavior. Also, when the trainer is seen as self-congruent (genuine, direct, honest, sincere), participants change in ways that foster their own congruence.

In a review and critique of the research on trainer effects, Cooper found a number of limitations: (1) The findings are based mostly on small samples. (2) Most of the studies rely for their measurements on participant perception of behavior and not on direct observation of changes in behavior by unbiased observers. (3) There is lack of agreement and clarity about what constitutes the research focus; hence, widely varying measuring instruments are used. (4) Little attempt is made to establish a causal relation between specific trainer behavior and observed group or individual changes.

Marathon therapists claim that the maintenance of psychological defense systems, which inhibit the expression of emotions unacceptable in most ordinary social contexts, are more likely to break down in the longer, uninterrupted time period of the marathon group than in the traditional therapy group. This has been referred to as the too-tired-to-be-polite phenomenon. A recent process study by Myerhoff, Jacobs, and Stoller compared emotionality in marathon and traditional psychotherapy groups. The therapist was the same for both groups.

A generally higher rate of occurrence and variability in the expression of negative feelings was found in marathon groups.

EVALUATION

Assets of the T-Group Method

The T-group provides a vehicle for teaching the importance of interpersonal relations in natural group functioning. The T-group teaches through experience rather than through didactic description. An analogy might be made with the teaching of arithmetic. The teacher can do a problem on the blackboard, but the student does not learn the arithmetical maneuver until he has actually solved a number of similar problems for himself.

The T-group provides a means of sharpening perceptual skills—of recognizing interpersonal perceptual distortions, learning how to check out interpersonal perceptions, and learning how to correct interpersonal perceptions. A corollary is the learning of one's own functioning in a group—seeing the role one plays vis-à-vis others, how one distorts the presentation of self to others, and how to obtain corrective feedback.

The T-group teaches people how they communicate with others, the variety of modes of interpersonal communication, and how to increase the effectiveness of communication while decreasing the noise in the communication system.

The T-group provides a degree of experiencing isolation, similar to the isolation of psychotherapy, that may enable participants to test out different modes of interaction and broaden their repertoire of human relations skills.

The T-group and related laboratory exercises have provided theory and method for effective intervention in organizations. This intervention may range from natural community groups (churches) to community action groups (urban renewal), service organizations (YMCA), and business and industry (Shell, Esso, Bell Telephone).

The human relations emphasis in the T-group and laboratory method provides a technique for nurturing human growth that may be incorporated into the educational structure to counterbalance many of the dehumanizing elements of American culture, particularly the mechanistic elements in the American school system.

The laboratory movement has given impetus and support to the scientific study of group function, leadership, and function of different types of groups, which have received little emphasis in the clinical professions. The T-group provides a natural laboratory.

The T-group and laboratory movement, less tied to professional conventions, have introduced many innovations in group interaction that may have clinical applicability: brief therapy groups, intensive group experiences, use of nonverbal interaction methods, refined use of group process analysis, and increased effectiveness of task groups.

Liabilities of the T-Group Method

For the most part, the major problems that have arisen in the use of the laboratory method have not escaped the attention of leaders of the movement. In some exemplary instances, careful measures have been taken to deal with these problems. In other instances, such problems have been almost totally ignored.

Incompetent Leaders. Leaders have various degrees of competence, with few reliable norms for performance and with no professional peer group to whom they must answer. Thus, leaders may be incompetent—either accomplishing little or allowing unnecessary and destructive group activity.

Responsibility is not clearly defined. This lack of responsibility may range from a sense of no concern as to where a group ends up in its interaction to a failure to respond to members who are undergoing undue stress or personal decompensation.

The T-group has sometimes not been provided with appropriate leadership to teach or guide a group into optimal effective function. There is a common notion in T-group theory that the group can be trusted to provide a just guideline for appropriate interpersonal attitudes and behavior. But a group of people can be tyrannical and destructive, just as it can be beneficent and supportive. Carl Jung opposed group therapy because he felt it placed people at the mercy of others. The same objection is raised by such right-wing groups as the John Birch Society, who perceive group methods as ways to rob a person of his autonomy.

Shifting Focus. Among recent innovations in T-groups has been the introduction of various nonverbal techniques for increasing self-awareness. These techniques include various role-playing maneuvers, various types of body-contact-exploration maneuvers, and such action techniques as wrestling and lifting members. This trend raises a number of theoretical, technical, and ethical issues beyond the scope of this discussion. The one point to be made here is the shift of focus. These techniques, or some of them, may have a definite value. However, the focus has shifted from interpersonal learning and group process learning to individual learning. That shift in itself is not questionable. But if personal issues become the chief focus, then the original goal for T-group method as a democratic group process educational experience has been lost. The proponents of these new T-group techniques have reverted to the origins of group methods, when individuals were treated *in* a group, not *by* and *with* a group. The distinctiveness of group process and group method is largely discarded. Much may be learned through these innovative group techniques— but at the expense of what can be learned about how groups function. Some trainers have not recognized that they cannot have it both ways.

Time Limits. The question of time-limited experience has received inadequate attention. It is assumed that the T-group members all learn at the same rate, that the length of T-groups is a relatively minor variable in learning, and that preparation for learning and reinforcement of learning are relatively secondary to the immediate T-group experience. But the evidence from psychotherapy and education indicates that there are notable individual differences in cognitive and emotional learning. Some effort has been made to address this issue in the training literature, but generally no attempt has been made to define learning goals that can be accomplished in time-limited interaction and learning goals that require longer-term spaced reinforcement. The most careful experimental work in this regard has been done in terms of time-limited psychotherapy and brief therapy. It is surprising that this matter has not been a subject of more T-group research. Apparently, the time limits used for T-groups have been those of convenience and propitiousness rather than those proved to reach the learning goals sought.

Lack of Carry-Over. The T-group may provide a forum for more honest confrontation of self and others, but it may also be a hit-and-run game. For example, one may talk quite freely to a stranger on an airplane but be totally incapable of confiding in one's relatives. The T-group may foster a sense of pseudoauthenticity and pseudoreality—a sense that this is really living while the rest of life is phony. The reality of the situation may be that the T-group participant can afford to act in ways that ignore reality because he does not have to live with the consequences of his behavior. Some people return to national sensitivity groups year after year because they feel, "Here I can really be myself." They are, in fact, unable to be themselves. Or they may be inappropriately capable of sharing intimate details of their psychological life in a group of people but not able to do so when they should with someone close to them.

The T-group may foster a sense of new-found patterns of relationship that may be inappropriate to a participant's real-life circumstances. For example, T-group participants may return to their organization with new ways of being—only to find that the new self is not accepted by the old work group. The result may be ostracism or, more likely, a quick extinguishment of the new T-group self through involvement in everyday life and work that provides negative reinforcement of the new learning. The laboratory movement has sought to circumvent this problem by training people from an entire work group. But that solution does not adequately address the problems of differentiating a special group behavior from everyday group behavior. For example, if a patient talked to all his friends as he talks to his therapist, he would soon run out of friends.

Yet the T-group member may assume that T-group behavior should become the norm for interpersonal relations with everyone within his ken.

A premium may be placed on total participation, on experiencing, without self-analysis or reflection. The result may be an exhilarating experience but not a learning experience. A crass way of putting it is, "All id and no ego." One need not go that far, but an example will suffice. In several group process teaching laboratories, mental health professionals who had been in prior sensitivity and encounter groups participated. They reported that they had learned about themselves in their previous group experiences but that they had acquired little if any knowledge about how groups actually function. Nor had they acquired any usable knowledge about how they might effectively work with groups. The group laboratory should aim not only at acquiring understanding of the self but also at learning how to use the knowledge and experience in the group.

The T-group experience has often been conducted with a work group, disregarding the fact that this group must continue to work together after their T-group experience. The group is asked to participate as if their real-life work-role relationships did not exist. The result may be both nonlearning and disaster. For example, in one professional work team that participated in a T-group experience, the members were instructed to tell each other how they really felt about each other. The members told off their chief in the T-group. The result was total disruption of the effectiveness of that work team thereafter.

More important is the issue of goals. In this instance, the trainer ignored the goal of helping the professional team work together and share appropriate perceptions and feelings. Instead, "experiencing" and "honesty" became the catchwords for an exercise in the group denial of reality. At stake is the question of how to increase the effectiveness of a team that works together and has real, ongoing, and intimate relationships that may be influenced by revelations made in the T-group.

The above example points up another area of confusion. The professional team entered the T-group with a contract that asked for help in making the work group more effective. The trainer had his own personal contract, which dealt only with change in individual members, and he ignored the contract to help the team. A contract to help a team may not necessarily result in helpful changes for individual team members; and helping individual team members to change may not necessarily be helpful to team function.

The T-group has often been conducted with little concern for how the learning in the T-group setting is to be transferred to the on-the-job setting. Trainers may assume that the transfer of learning will occur automatically, that attention to transfer issues may interfere with the group process, or that the T-group experience is intrinsically valuable and that transfer of learning to the job or community is, in a sense, irrelevant. Pattison (1965) has reviewed research data which suggested that in-group behavior change in psychotherapy groups is often *not* accompanied by change in behavior outside the group. The same has been observed for T-groups. Until recently, much of laboratory training focused on the T-group experience alone and ignored the fact that little transfer of learning was occurring. Nor were provisions made for changing the T-group procedure to accomplish transfer of learning. More recently, structured programs for subsequent follow-up training experiences have sought to remedy this problem.

Deleterious Effects. The assessment of T-group results has failed to consider seriously the deleterious effects of group participation. The lessons learned long ago by psychoanalysts about the detrimental effects of adverse countertransference reactions and the rationale for the preparatory psychoanalysis of the student psychoanalyst before he undertakes a psychoanalysis under supervision have often been ignored by nonpsychoanalytic psychotherapists. Most outcome studies have been limited to investigating conditions of no change or degrees of improvement. In fact, there has been a subtle but pervasive notion that psychotherapy is purely a beneficial maneuver—at least in the hands of competent practitioners.

The recurring discovery of negative therapeutic effects occasioned by the therapist has been noted by such authors as Shlien and Zimring, Truax and Carkhuff, and Orr. The detection and recognition of such effects is a thorny research problem that admits of no easy solution. An enthusiastic partisan tone within the T-group movement fosters the concept that a T-group experience would be good for anybody and always profitable. The result may be a deluding distortion of participants' responses and a deceptive oversell.

Adequate participant selection criteria may be lacking. Persons who cannot tolerate or learn from intensive interpersonal relations may be involved in such groups. At best, these persons emerge untouched and unmoved; at worst, they decompensate.

There is no reason to assume that a small group will automatically develop into a structure supportive of increased selfhood. Yet some trainers covertly assume that T-groups will always proceed in benevolent fashion. In fact, some T-groups tyrannize their members—as do some therapy groups. In their eagerness to develop autonomous, democratic groups, some trainers overlook this fact. If the goal is to develop effective democratic groups, more attention must be paid to training groups in how to achieve that goal, rather than merely letting them flounder in dubious self-discovery.

The T-group has often ignored the necessity and utility of ego defenses. Exposure and frankness, attack and vulnerability may become premium values. Often, little attention is paid to the necessity for support and nurturance. Human foibles, inadequacies, and the normal range of variation in life style may be given short shrift. Some leaders have even theorized on the value of some type of total exposure. This trend ignores individual differences in the capacity to tolerate stress and frustration. Rather than adjust its expectations to the needs, capacities, and interests of each person, the group may use, as its covert norm, the self-reliant man who can take anything the group dishes out.

The T-group may foster a concept that anything goes, regardless of consequences. Instead of creating interpersonal awareness, it may foster personal narcissism. If a person can say anything he wishes, he may come to assume that just because he feels like expressing himself is justification enough to do so. This attitude may preclude effective communication, for he then ignores the other person's receptivity and the effect of his message on the other person. Communication may be seen not as an interpersonal event but merely as the opportunity to express oneself. The principle of optimal communication is ignored, and the principle of total communication is favored.

Summary

To summarize the assets and liabilities of the T-group method, one may state that the T-group presents a powerful means of involving people in human behavioral analysis. The method provides possibilities for a highly significant contribution to the humane quality of existence in Western culture and its various work and community components. The training laboratory has potential as a powerful instrument. Its liabilities lie in the area of utilization, as with any powerful instrument. Without adequate training, supervision, and guidelines, a powerful instrument may be destructive, just as a valuable drug may have undesirable effects if used unwisely or in incorrect doses. The liabilities described are not intrinsic deficits; rather, they are deficits of training, experience, clarity, and precision of goals. They can be avoided. Leaders within the laboratory movement are addressing themselves to the task.

Of more concern are the peripheral and derivative products of the laboratory movement—groups that have picked up bits and pieces of the laboratory movement but without the democratic concerns of the originators, without the clinical experience of the early leaders, without the informal communicative guidelines that tend to keep professionals within a self-corrective framework, and without the continuous inquiring, self-critical, self-evaluative, and research perspective.

Despite the enthusiasm that the laboratory movement has fostered, its practitioners have not fully realized how powerful are the tools they have developed. Therefore, their enthusiasm may not yet be tempered by respect and concern that these tools be rightly used.

OUTSIDE CRITICISM

Sensitivity Training as Brainwashing

Certain right-wing conservatives, particularly members of the John Birch Society, have viciously attacked sensitivity training as a form of Communist brainwashing, as Dieckmann reports. But brainwashing is the use of educational procedures, including some principles of psychology and psychiatry, to interfere with normal, healthy interpersonal relationships, particularly at the individual level, for the purpose of physically and ideologically manipulating the recipients. Sensitivity training, on the other hand, is the use of educational procedures, including some principles of psychology and psychiatry, to develop open, accepting, and spontaneous interpersonal relationships, particularly at the individual level, for the purpose of helping people to understand both individual and group behavior, thereby freeing them from being manipulated or manipulating without their knowledge, and to experience warm personal relationships with other people.

The purpose of brainwashing is indoctrination, leading to the acceptance of a closed system of values. The purpose of sensitivity training is the development of awareness and acceptance of the feelings of oneself and others and the acceptance of responsibility for one's own acts, leading to clearer, independent thinking and realistic behavior. With sensitivity training, a person develops a better understanding of group dynamics and individual motivation.

Both brainwashing and sensitivity training are usually carried out in small groups of ten to 16 people.

Brainwashing Techniques. The Communists used brainwashing during the Korean War. They divided American prisoners into small groups, each headed by a personable social scientist who announced that all the Communists wanted was the physical cooperation of the Americans—that is, they wanted the Americans to listen to the truth as the Communists saw it and to participate in discussions. For their cooperation, those being indoctrinated would be given good food, shelter, clothing, and medical care, and they would not have to work.

During the first six months, virtually no indoctrination took place. The prisoners referred to this as the dog-eat-dog period. They learned to reject any kind of authority, and each man was for himself. The individual and not the team or group became important. About half of the deaths of prisoners took place during this period from what psychiatrists later referred to as give-up-itis, a kind of individual depression-withdrawal, culminating in death.

After the first six months, the Communists began a formal education period, which they carried out seven days a week, every waking hour, for the next two years. The curriculum consisted of a discussion of the evils of capitalism, the number of American heroes who were wealthy, social injustices in the United States, and so forth—all of course, from the Communist point of view. The lectures were delivered to large groups of prisoners and lasted four to five hours. During the lectures the prisoners were compelled to stand up, so that they could not sleep, and were allowed no coffee or cigarettes. After the lectures, groups of ten to 12 men discussed the lectures in any way they wanted, with the guidance of a Communist instructor who lived with them in their barracks as a presumably friendly, cooperative, patient helper. Each prisoner had to participate in this discussion by putting into his own words what the lecture was about. He did not have to agree with the speaker. Group pressure was brought to bear on recalcitrant nondiscussant prisoners, since the group could not eat until every member had participated.

There were also more interesting activities, all centering around Communist propaganda, such as guest lectures, little theatre groups, movies, athletic programs, and arts and crafts instruction. Prisoners were rewarded for attending these activities by being allowed to participate in sports and by being given cigarettes, candy, and currency.

Two additional attitude-changing devices were brought to bear on the prisoners: informing on fellow prisoners and self-criticism.

American informers were encouraged by being publicly given material goods of some sort and by receiving extra status and approval from the Communists. What did they inform about? Simply any misdeed or anti-social acts or attitudes (in terms of Communist objectives) expressed by their fellow prisoners. The rationale was this: The anti-social prisoner needs to be helped. Therefore, do not inform out of hostility but only out of concern for your buddy. It is your social responsibility to inform the Communist leaders of disaffection in your group.

Since the person informed on was not punished but was only admonished kindly, he realized that he was not physically endangered by the informing. But he also realized that someone in his group, he knew not whom, had revealed him to the Communists. Three consequences of the informing resulted: (1) Each prisoner developed a lack of trust in his buddies. (2) Since no one was really punished, the act of informing was undertaken without guilt, and, the rewards to the selfish nature of the informer being considerable, he could thus regard informing as positive. (3) The prisoners started withdrawing psychologically from each other. Each American insulated himself in his own inner solitary-confinement cell, unable to communicate meaningfully with others. Nevertheless, a yearning for communication does not die easily. So the Communists set up a limited negative form of self-revelatory catharsis for the prisoners, which consisted of having the prisoners sit in a small group and admit their faults. They participated in this group activity because it kept their captors from nagging them and, in fact, brought their approval and also because it was virtually the only meaningful group belonging that was permitted. Since no one helped relieve the guilt and embarrassment of the prisoners as they revealed their less-acceptable impulses and acts, paranoid thinking eventually came to be a symptom of the men in these groups, even to the point of their believing that other prisoners could read their minds. It is this self-criticism aspect of brainwashing groups that the right-wing critics refer to as sensitivity training.

As a further refinement of attitude control, the Communists allowed only depressing and negativistic mail from friends and relatives to reach the American prisoners and withheld all the positive, loving, and encouraging letters. As a result, the prisoners stopped even thinking about their families and were thus cut off from their last source of emotional support.

Two main outcomes of this brainwashing were (1) the loss of the American prisoner's belief in his value as a human being worthy of dignity and respect and concomitantly his feeling that he was expendable for the good of some class survival and (2) a rampant form of the disease of give-up-itis. The general characteristics of survivors of this program were quietness, lack of exuberance, no interest in bull sessions, and lack of guilt when freely exploiting other people.

Brainwashing vs. Sensitivity Training. About the only similarities shared by sensitivity training and brainwashing are the use of small groups led by social scientists and a type of group pressure brought to bear on members. In the case of T-groups and encounter groups, however, the group pressure is to drop artificial roles and unwarranted covering-up mechanisms that interfere with collaborative group processes. Early in the sensitivity training, the group often express negative feelings, including criticisms of other members. This is a natural phenomenon of these groups. Many people believe that less is risked by someone who exposes negative feelings toward himself or others, for negative feelings are likely to draw negative feelings in return. But if warmth or affection toward others is expressed, a person who is uneasy about human warmth or love does not know what response to expect, and so he experiences more anxiety. Defensiveness and lack of trust are the most natural ways to experience interpersonal relationships in their early stages. Negative feelings, when accepted without undue rancor, usually give way to positive feelings. In the case of brainwashing, empathy and acceptance are almost totally discouraged. Instead, an attitude of each man for himself and his own best interests is systematically promoted.

The sense of group belongingness in brainwashing is experienced only in the self-criticism sessions. But group cohesiveness in sensitivity training is developed through empathy, identification, sharing of such emotions as joy and humor, life values, ethics, frustrations, longings, ideals, goals, and caring about the development of both one-self and the group. Instead of encouraging the formation of a group of self-serving, isolated, critical, informing individuals, as brainwashing does, sensitivity training attempts to weld the individual and group needs so that neither individual nor group is harmed by what each needs to develop fully. In sensitivity training, the greater the growth of the individual, the more valuable he is to the group; and the greater the growth of the group in awareness, acceptance, and caring, the more valuable the group becomes to the individual.

In sensitivity training there are no rewards for criticism in the sense of tearing down the feelings of oneself or others. Encouragement is given to people's taking risks in revealing personal feelings regarding other group members for the purpose of giving honest feedback and cutting through inappropriate covering-up defenses. For example, it is expected that people's styles of relating with others will become known to the members of the group. If a group member's style is repressive to other members of the group or to group growth, someone confronts him with this information. Such a confrontation may seem at first to be very negative, may cause feelings of anger, rejection, and hurt, and may result in a temporary strengthening of the defense mechanisms of the recipient of the feedback. But this reaction in itself is not harmful. Growth or change of any kind is often accompanied by risk and usually by pain. The child learning to walk falls down many times; learning to talk, he is often misunderstood and sometimes ridiculed; learning to master tools, he hurts himself; learning to ride a bicycle, he takes many tumbles; playing contact sports, he may be bruised or break a bone. So in interpersonal relations, learning new ways of growth entails psychological hurt. Dropping unnecessary self-protection defense mechanisms may seem to leave one vulnerable, and hostile bullies may appear to take advantage of the vulnerable person. Sensitivity training does not pretend to be an affair of sweetness and light; there can be pain along with the growth.

The main real difference between brainwashing and sensitivity training lies in their purposes. Brainwashing is an agency-oriented method to bring people into a completely dependent and selfish relationship with the ideological leaders while breaking down kinship among peers so that the individuals composing the group can be manipulated at the leader's will. Sensitivity training is a communion-oriented method that encourages responsibility for one's own actions, a spirit of inquiry among group members, a sense of empathy and identity among peers, a spirit of collaboration with each other and with the leader, a strong sense of belongingness and participation. The result of brainwashing is distrust, defensiveness, isolation, and lack of empathy. The result of sensitivity training is increased trust, openness, a sense of belonging, and empathy.

In hearing the arguments of ultraconservatives against sensitivity training, one is impressed, particularly by the Birchers, with their inability to conceive of the communion aspects—the sharing and belongingness—of the process. They perceive the process almost entirely as being agency-oriented and against the individual. Sensitivity training has become a vehicle for the right-wingers on which to project their own repressive, agency-oriented processes. The very tactics they use in attacking sensitivity training are those employed in the Communist process of brainwashing American prisoners—propagandizing, pointing out the occasional failures of sensitivity training as being typical of the results, denying the value of peer group relationships, attacking the democratic process of sensitivity training with the same smear and negative-instance tactics with which the Communists attack United States democracy and capitalism, and insisting that their concepts of God and the United States are the only true ways that one can believe, as the Communists set up their god of Communism as the only truth.

Sensitivity Training in the Schools

In some sections of the country, the ultraconservative elements have strongly attacked what they call sensitivity training in the public schools. In almost every instance, this term has referred to some informative discussion group, most often about the feelings of students concerning various aspects of the subject matter they are studying, sometimes sex. It would be a rare event, indeed, to find a real sensitivity training session for students. Nor would such training be particularly appropriate, except in special group counseling sessions. Discussions that begin at a topic level—for instance, a school group discussion of drug use and abuse—may turn into T-groups, but they would usually be appropriately handled by a counselor.

There has been a growing movement to involve teachers in sensitivity training. This is a healthy movement if teachers, by participating in T-groups, become more aware of their feelings, their roles, their impact on others. Ultraconservatives get upset when they think that teachers who have had T-group or encounter group experience will try to set up groups of their own in their classrooms and invade the privacy of the students (actually, the parents may sometimes be worried about being discussed), inflicting possible emotional trauma if any student should reveal more than was socially acceptable by community standards. The authors do not know how much of this T-grouping goes on in schools outside of group counseling or even if it would do any particular damage unless handled clumsily by a teacher.

What is of concern is the growing tendency of relatively few ultraconservatives to put great pressure on boards of education and school administrators to cut out of their curricula any innovative procedures involving dialogue within groups of students, especially if the dialogue or discussion allows freedom of expression of the students' personal feelings and fantasies. All such group discussions are now labeled sensitivity training by ultraconservatives and then, by their cloudy thinking and heavy-handed implication, become dangerous brainwashings, group criticism, self-criticism, and invasion of the privacy of the individual.

Glasser found his discussion methods so maligned by Birchers that he has publicly announced he does not do sensitivity training. A sex education course in the Anaheim, California, public schools that was touted as a model for the country was recently reduced to a pale shadow of itself by an ultraconservative group's repeated rabble-rousing attacks on the board of education and superintendent of schools. The leader of the group, a former Marine officer, revealed to a Los Angeles newspaper the power tactics his group used in destroying the board of education; the article contained chilling overtones of Hitlerian methods. In many communities the ultraconservatives have set up this straw man: Innovative discussion group = sensitivity training = brainwashing = Pavlovian conditioning = Communist plot. Therefore, to protect our God, our country, and our children, we must drive this menace of sensitivity training out of our schools and attack it wherever it appears and in whatever guise.

In general, the public is too little informed about sensitivity training to be able to combat right-wing charges that it is being brainwashed. More important, the public does not know that most of the student discussion groups are more-effective educational aids and *not* sensitivity training. These discussion groups are more effective than former didactic teaching methods because they involve the empathy and emotions of students and, therefore, make subject matter personally meaningful to them.

Richard Jones has presented a passionate case for educating the whole child, allowing him to experience himself in a feeling and imaginative sense as well as enlarging his fund of factual knowledge and increasing his cognitive ability. Repeatedly, Jones makes the point that, in solving problems and in posing problems, children and adults need to be able to express their emotions, share them, and use them; one way to help children learn to control and therefore use emotion is to bring it into discussion in the classroom.

Jones's idea of constructing knowledge, as opposed to attaining it by absorbing cognitive material or even by solving problems posed by someone else,

presumes freedom and skill in the sharing and use of controlled emotion and imagery.

Therefore, emotional skills as well as cognitive skills need to be taught. Jones points out that, as humans, people are always imagining and that at times· they are helpless and feel alone while doing this. If they are experiencing all three states— imagining while they are helpless and alone—then they are anxious. It is this anxiety that interferes with learning. Yet American culture tends to set up the conditions for the state of anxiety—children are taught embarrassment for feelings and are guarded against imagination. Since repression is part of the cultural mores, opposition of the ultraconservative type can be expected wherever these mores of repression are threatened. Yet without feelings and imagination, children cannot become personally involved in the subject matter, and it will be only superficially learned.

To summarize the main points: (1) School discussion groups that enlist the use of children's personal feelings and imagination with cognitive material are logically valid because the groups involve an integrated, meaningful learning experience. (2) The expression of feeling needs to be controlled sufficiently so that it can be used constructively to deepen the learning process. Feeling can be controlled through learning about it, experiencing it, expressing it, and then constructing new percepts with it. Such control can be gained through peer group interaction about cognitive material. (3) Such discussion groups are not actually sensitivity training. (4) Whatever these discussion methods are called, they are intended to educate the whole person intellectually and emotionally. (5) Attacks by ultraconservatives on integrated learning methods, usually group discussions, whether launched under the guise of attacking sensitivity training or for some other reason, must be met by informed adults with clear thinking and knowledge of the dynamics of learning rather than by fear, confusion, and withdrawal from the barrage of name-calling.

The agency aspect of the learning process —problem-solving, achieving status, grades, knowledge—must be tempered by the communion aspect—joining feeling and imagination with cognition, experiencing and sharing passion and emotion.

REFERENCES

Argyris, C. *Interpersonal Competence and Organizational Behavior*. Richard C. Irwin, Homewood, Ill., 1962.

Artiss, K. L., and Schiff, S. B. Education for practice in the therapeutic community. Curr. Psychiat. Ther., *8:* 233, 1968.

Astrachan, B. M., Harrow, M., Becker, R. E., Schwartz, A. H., and Miller, J. C. The unled patient group as a therapeutic tool. Int. J. Group Psychother., *17:* 178, 1967.

Bach, G. R. Marathon group dynamics. II. Dimensions of helpfulness: therapeutic aggression. Psychol. Rep., *20:* 1147, 1967.

Bach, G. R. Discussion. Int. J. Group Psychother., *18:* 244, 1968.

Bakan, D. *The Duality of Human Existence*. Rand McNally, Chicago, 1966.

Batchelder, R. L., and Hardy, J. M. *Using Sensitivity Training and the Laboratory Method*. Association Press, New York, 1968.

Beckhard, R., editor. *Conferences for Learning, Planning and Action*, National Training Laboratories Selected Reading Series, vol. 6. National Training Laboratories and National Education Association, Washington, D. C., 1962.

Benne, K. D. History of the T-group in the laboratory setting. In *T-Group Theory and Laboratory Method: Innovation in Re-education*, pp. 80–135, L. P. Bradford, J. R. Gibb, and K. D. Benne, editors. John Wiley, New York, 1964.

Bergin, A. E. An empirical analysis of therapeutic issues. In *Counseling and Psychotherapy: An Overview*, p. 175, D. Arbuckle, editor. McGraw-Hill, New York, 1967.

Berne, E. *The Structure and Dynamics of Organizations and Groups*. J. B. Lippincott, New York, 1963.

Berzon, B., and Solomon, L. N. The self-directed therapeutic group: three studies. J. Counsel. Psychol., *13:* 221, 1966.

Biderman, A. D., and Zimmer, H., editors. *The Manipulation of Human Behavior*. John Wiley, New York, 1961.

Block, H. S. An open-ended crisis-oriented group for the poor who are sick. Arch. Gen. Psychiat. (Chicago), *18:* 178, 1968.

Boyd, J. B., and Elliss, J. D. *Findings of Research into Senior Management Seminars*. Hydro-Electric Power Commission of Ontario, Toronto, 1962.

Bradford, L. P., editor. *Group Development*, National Training Laboratories Selected Reading Series, vols. 1–4. National Training Laboratories and National Education Association, Washington, D. C., 1961.

Bradford, L. P. Biography of an institution. J. Appl. Behav. Sci., *3:* 127, 1967.

Bradford, L. P., Gibb, J. R., and Benne, K. D., editors. *T-Group Theory and Laboratory Method: Innovation in Re-education*. John Wiley, New York, 1964.

Bredesen, K. N. Small group work—the need for some guidelines. Amer. J. Psychiat., *126:* 876, 1969.

Bunker, D. R. Individual application of laboratory training. J. Appl. Behav. Sci., *1:* 131, 1965.

Burke, R. L., and Bennis, W. G. Changes in perception of self and others during human relations training. Hum. Rel., *2:* 165, 1961.

Cadden, J. J., Flach, F. F., Blakeslee, S., and Charlton, R., Jr. Growth in medical students through group process. Amer. J. Psychiat., *126:* 862, 1969.

Campbell, J. P., and Dunnette, M. D. Effectiveness of T-group experiences in managerial training and development. Psychol. Bull., *70:* 73, 1968.

Cooper, C. L. The influence of the trainer on participant change in T-groups. Hum. Rel., *22:* 515, 1969.

Crenshaw, R. How sensitive is sensitivity training? Amer. J. Psychiat., *126:* 868, 1969.

Davies, J. C. *Neighborhood Groups and Urban Renewal.* Columbia University Press, New York, 1966.

Dieckmann, E., Jr. Sensitivity training: the network of patriotic letter writers, Pasadena, California. Amer. Mercury, 1967.

Durkin, H. E. *The Group in Depth.* International Universities Press, New York, 1964.

Edelson, M. *Ego Psychology, Group Dynamics and the Therapeutic Community.* Grune & Stratton, New York, 1964.

Emmons, S. Anaheim controversy: sex education —new direction emerging. Los Angeles Times, Los Angeles, March 29, 1970.

Fairweather, G. W. *Social Psychology in Treating Mental Illness: An Experimental Approach.* John Wiley, New York, 1964.

Federn, P. Psychoanalysis of psychosis, part I. Psychiat. Quart., *17:* 3, 1943.

Gazda, G. M., editor. *Innovations to Group Psychotherapy.* Charles C Thomas, Springfield, Ill., 1968.

Glasser, W. The "Sensitivity Letter," Bulletin No. 15. Educational Training Center, Los Angeles, 1969.

Glasser, W. *Schools Without Failure.* Harper and Row, New York, 1969.

Gottschalk, L. A. Psychoanalytic notes on T-groups at the Human Relations Laboratory, Bethel, Maine. Compr. Psychiat., *7:* 472, 1966.

Gottschalk, L. A. Some problems in the evaluation of psychoactive drugs, with and without psychotherapy, in the treatment of non-psychotic personality disorders. In *Psychopharmacology: A Review of Progress, 1957–67*, pp. 255–269, D. N. Efron, J. O. Cole, J. Levine, and J. R. Wittenborn, editors. Public Health Service Publication No. 1836, United States Government Printing Office, Washington, D. C., 1968.

Gottschalk, L. A., and Auerbach, A. H. Goals and problems in psychotherapy research. In *Methods of Research in Psychotherapy*, pp. 3–9, L. A. Gottschalk and A. H. Auerbach, editors. Appleton-Century-Crofts, New York, 1966.

Gottschalk, L. A., and Gleser, G. C. *The Measurement of Psychological States through the Content Analysis of Verbal Behavior.* University of California Press, Berkeley, 1969.

Gottschalk, L. A., Gleser, G. C., and Stone, W. N. Studies of psychoactive drug effects on non-psychiatric patients. In *Psychopharmacology of the Normal Human*, pp. 162–188, W. Evans and N. Kline, editors. Charles C Thomas, Springfield, Ill., 1968.

Gottschalk, L. A., and Pattison, E. M. Psychiatric perspectives on T-groups and the laboratory movement. Amer. J. Psychiat., *126:* 823, 1969.

Hare, A. P. *Handbook of Small Group Research.* Free Press of Glencoe, New York, 1962.

Harris, T. *I'm OK—You're OK: A Practical Guide to Transactional Analysis.* Harper and Row, New York, 1969.

Janov, A. *The Primal Scream. Primal Therapy: The Cure for Neurosis.* G. P. Putnam, New York, 1970.

Jones, M. *Beyond the Therapeutic Community: Social Learning and Social Psychiatry.* Yale University Press, New Haven, 1968.

Jones, R. M. *Fantasy and Feeling in Education.* New York University Press, New York, 1968.

Kaplan, S. R. Therapy groups and training groups: similarities and differences. Int. J. Group Psychother., *17:* 473, 1967.

Kassarjian, H. H. Social character and sensitivity training. J. Appl. Behav. Sci., *1:* 433, 1965.

Kernan, J. P. Laboratory human relations training: its effects on the "personality" of supervisory engineers. Dissert. Abstr., *25:* 665, 1964.

Klein, D. C. *Community Dynamics and Mental Health.* John Wiley, New York, 1968.

Klein, W. H., LeShan, E. J., and Furman, S. S. *Promoting Mental Health of Older People through Group Methods.* Mental Health Materials Center, New York, 1964.

Kuehn, J. L., and Crinella, F. M. Sensitivity training—interpersonal "overkill" and other problems. Amer. J. Psychiat., *126:* 840, 1969.

Lakin, M. Some ethical issues in sensitivity training. Amer. Psychol., *24:* 923, 1969.

Lippitt, R. L. *Training in Community Relations.* Harper and Row, New York, 1949.

Lorr, M., and McNair, D. M. Methods relating to evaluation of therapeutic outcome. In *Methods of Research in Psychotherapy*, p. 573, L. A. Gottschalk and A. H. Auerbach, editors. Appleton-Century-Crofts, New York, 1966.

Lowen, A. *The Betrayal of the Body*. Macmillan, New York, 1967.

Luft, J. *Of Human Interaction*. National Press Books, Palo Alto, Calif., 1970.

Malamud, D. I., and Machover, S. *Toward Self-Understanding: Group Techniques in Self-Confrontation*. Charles C Thomas, Springfield, Ill., 1965.

Mann, R. D. *Interpersonal Styles and Group Development: An Analysis of the Member-Leader Relationship*. John Wiley, New York, 1967.

Massarik, F. *Explorations in Human Relations Training and Research. A Sensitivity Training Impact Model: Some First (and Second) Thoughts on the Evaluation of Sensitivity Training*, No. 3. National Training Laboratories and National Education Association, Washington, D. C., 1965.

Mayer, W. E. Why did so many GI captives cave in? U. S. News World Rep., *40:* 56, 1956.

Mayo, C., and Klein, D. C. Group dynamics as a basic process of community psychiatry. In *Handbook of Community Psychiatry and Community Mental Health*, pp. 47–64, L. Bellak, editor. Grune & Stratton, New York, 1964.

McGrath, J. E., and Altman, I. *Small Group Research: A Synthesis and Critique of the Field*. Holt, Rinehart, & Winston, New York, 1966.

Miles, M. B. Changes during and following laboratory training: a clinical-experimental study. J. Appl. Behav. Sci., *1:* 215, 1965.

Mintz, E. E. Marathon groups: a preliminary evaluation. J. Contemp. Psychother., *1:* 91, 1969.

Moreno, J. L. The Viennese origins of the encounter movement, paving the way for existentialism, group psychotherapy, and psychodrama. Group Psychother., *22:* 7, 1970.

Myerhoff, H. L., Jacobs, A., and Stoller, F. Emotionality in marathon and traditional psychotherapy groups. Psychother. Theory Res. Pract., *7:* 33, 1970.

Orr, D. Transference and countertransference: a historical survey. J. Amer. Psychoanal. Assoc., *2:* 621, 1954.

Otto, H. *Guide to Developing Your Potential*. Charles Scribner, New York, 1967.

Parloff, M. B. Group therapy and the small group field: an encounter. Int. J. Group Psychother., *20:* 267, 1970.

Pattison, E. M. Evaluation studies of group psychotherapy. Int. J. Group Psychother., *15:* 382, 1965.

Pattison, E. M. *A Brief History of the American Group Psychotherapy Association: The First Twenty-Five Years: 1943–1968*. American Group Psychotherapy Association, New York, 1969.

Pattison, E. M., Courlas, P. G., Patti, R., Mann, B., and Mullen, D. Diagnostic-therapeutic intake class for wives of alcoholics. Quart. J. Stud. Alcohol, *26:* 605, 1965.

Peck, H. B. The small group: core of the community mental health center. Commun. Ment. Health J., *4:* 191, 1968.

Peck, H. B., and Kaplan, S. Crisis theory and therapeutic change in small groups: some implications for community mental health programs. Int. J. Group Psychother., *16:* 135, 1966.

Perls, F. S., Hefferline, R. E., and Goodman, P. *Gestalt Therapy*. Dell, New York, 1965.

Phillips, M. *Small Social Groups in England*. Methuen, London, 1965.

Redlich, F. C., and Astrachan, B. Group dynamics training. Amer. J. Psychiat., *125:* 1501, 1969.

Rickels, K., and Downing, R. W. Drug- and placebo-manifest anxiety, clinical improvement, and side reactions. Arch. Gen. Psychiat. (Chicago), *16:* 369, 1967.

Rickels, K., Gordon, P. E., Mecklenburg, R., Sablosky, L., Whalen, E. M., and Dion, H. Iprindole in neurotic depressed general practice patients: a controlled study. Psychosomatics, *9:* 208, 1968.

Rickels, K., Jenkins, B. W., Zamostien, B., Raab, E., and Kanther, M. Pharmacotherapy in neurotic depression: differential population responses. J. Nerv. Ment. Dis., *145:* 475, 1967.

Rickels, K., Ward, C. H., and Schut, L. Different populations, different drug responses. Amer. J. Med. Sci., *247:* 328, 1964.

Rogers, C. R. The process of the basic encounter group. In *Challenges of Humanistic Psychology*, p. 261, J. F. G. Bugetal, editor. McGraw-Hill, New York, 1967.

Rosenbaum, M., and Berger, M., editors. *Group Psychotherapy and Group Function*. Basic Books, New York, 1963.

Scheidlinger, S. Therapeutic group approaches in community mental health. Soc. Work, *13:* 87, 1968.

Scheidlinger, S. Innovative group approaches. In *Progress in Community Mental Health*, pp. 123–136, L. Bellak and H. H. Barten, editors. Grune & Stratton, New York, 1969.

Schein, E. H., and Bennis, W. G. *Personal and Organizational Change through Group Methods: The Laboratory Approach*. John Wiley, New York, 1965.

Schiff, S. B. Continuing education for professional personnel. In *The Practice of Community Mental Health*, p. 571, G. Grunebaum, editor. Little, Brown, Boston, 1969.

Schutz, W. *Joy*. Grove Press, New York, 1967.

Schutz, W., and Allen, V. L. The effects of a T-group laboratory on interpersonal behavior. J. Appl. Behav. Sci., *2:* 265, 1966.

Shapiro, S. B. Some aspects of a theory of interpersonal contracts. Psychol. Rep., *22:* 171, 1968.

Shlien, J. M., and Zimring, F. M. Research directives and methods in client-centered therapy.

In *Methods of Research in Psychotherapy* p. 424, L. A. Gottschalk and A. H. Auerbach, editors. Appleton-Century-Crofts, New York, 1966.

Silver, A. W. Interrelating group-dynamic, therapeutic, and psychodynamic concepts. Int. J. Group Psychother., *17:* 139, 1967.

Smith, P. B. Attitude changes associated with training in human relations. Brit. J. Soc. Clin. Psychol., *3:* 104, 1964.

Sprott, W. J. H. *Human Groups.* Penguin Books, Baltimore, 1958.

Stock, D. A. Survey of research on T-groups. In *T-group Theory and Laboratory Method: Innovation in Re-education*, p. 395, L. P. Bradford, J. R. Gibb, and K. D. Benne, editors. John Wiley, New York, 1964.

Stoller, F. H. Accelerated interaction: a time-limited approach based on the brief, intensive group. Int. J. Group Psychother., *18:* 220, 1968.

Tannenbaum, R., Weschler, I. R., and Massarik, F. *Leadership and Organization: A Behavioral Science Approach.* McGraw-Hill, New York, 1961.

Tate, G. *Strategy of Therapy: Toward the Engineering of Social Growth.* Springer-Verlag, New York, 1967.

Taylor, F. C. Effects of laboratory training upon persons and their work groups. In *Research on the Impact of Using Different Laboratory Methods for Interpersonal and Organizational Change*, p. 115, S. S. Zalkind, chairman. American Psychological Association, Washington, D. C., 1967.

Truax, C. B., and Carkhuff, R. R. *Toward Effective Counseling and Psychotherapy: Training and Practice.* Aldine Publishing, Chicago, 1967.

University of California at Los Angeles. *Extension Bulletin.* Fall, 1970.

Weschler, I. R., Massarik, F., and Tannenbaum, R. The self in process: a sensitivity training emphasis. In *Issues in Human Relations Training*, National Training Laboratories Selected Reading Series, vol. 5, p. 33, I. R. Weschler, editor. National Training Laboratories and National Education Association, Washington, D. C., 1962.

West, L. J. United States Air Force prisoners of the Chinese Communists. In *Methods of Forceful Indoctrination: Observations and Interviews*, p. 270. Group for the Advancement of Psychiatry, New York, 1957.

Whitaker, D. S., and Lieberman, M. A. *Psychotherapy through the Group Process.* Atherton Press, New York, 1964.

Whitehorn, J. C., and Betz, B. J. A comparison of psychotherapeutic relationships between physicians and schizophrenic patients. Amer. J. Psychiat., *113:* 901, 1957.

4

Psychodrama

J. L. Moreno, M.D.

HISTORY

Psychodrama represents a major turning point away from the treatment of the individual in isolation and toward the treatment of the individual in groups, from treatment by verbal methods and toward treatment by action methods.

As theories, psychodrama and psychoanalysis have diametrically opposite origins. This incident illustrates the point: The author met Sigmund Freud for the first time in 1912, while working at the Psychiatric Clinic in the University of Vienna. Dr. Freud ended one of his lectures with his analysis of a telepathic dream. As the students filed out of the lecture hall, he asked the author what he was doing.

"Well, Dr. Freud, I start where you leave off. You meet people in the artificial setting of your office. I meet them on the street and in their homes, in their natural surroundings. You analyze their dreams. I try to give them the courage to dream again. I teach people how to play God."

Dr. Freud looked at the author as if puzzled.

Two years later, in 1914, two antitheses to psychoanalysis emerged in Vienna. The first was group psychotherapy, which emphasizes the group rather than the individual. The author coined the terms group therapy and group psychotherapy to underscore the point

that the procedure concerns itself first of all with therapy of the group and not merely with sociological or psychological analysis. The second antithesis to psychoanalysis was psychodrama, which emphasizes the act rather than the word.

Between 1922 and 1925 the *Stegreiftheater* (Theatre of Spontaneity), located near the Vienna Opera, became a gathering place for malcontents and psychological rebels. From that theatre and from the author's book *Das Stegreiftheater*, published in 1923, came the inspiration for the use of play technique and role-training methods that many psychoanalysts and educators have gradually assimilated into their own work.

PSYCHODRAMA AND UNIVERSALS

The objective of psychodrama was, from its inception, to construct a therapeutic setting that uses life as a model, to integrate into the setting all the modalities of living— beginning with the universals of time, space, reality, and the cosmos—and moving down to all the details and nuances of life.

Time

From the point of view of therapeutic procedures, to what extent does time enter into and function in psychotherapeutic settings? Man lives in time—past, present, and future. He may suffer from a pathology related to each dimension of time. The problem is how to integrate all three dimensions into signifi-

The author wishes to acknowledge the influence of L. J. Bischof's *Interpreting Personality Theories* upon this section on Psychodrama.

cant therapeutic operations. It is not sufficient that they figure as abstract references; they must be made alive within treatment modalities. The psychological aspects of time must reappear *in toto*.

The Past. In orthodox Freudian psychoanalysis, time is emphasized in terms of the past. Freud, an exponent of genetic psychology and psychobiology, found going back and trying to find the causes of things of particular interest. Often, the further back he went, the more he thought he would find something worthwhile as a cause. And soon psychoanalysts began to go further and further back—into the womb and, if possible, even beyond that—until they got tired of this futile search and began to come back.

The Present. However important the past is as a dimension of time, it is a one-sided position, which neglects and distorts the total influence that time has upon the psyche. Time has other important phases, one of which is the present, the here-and-now. In 1914 the author began to emphasize the dynamics of the present and all its immediate personal, social, and cultural implications from the viewpoint of the therapeutic process as it takes place in connection with patients in patient groups—the encounter.

The encounter is a telic phenomenon. The fundamental process of tele is reciprocity—reciprocity of attraction, rejection, excitation, inhibition, indifference, distortion.

The Future. Until recently, the future has also been neglected as a dimension of therapeutic time. Yet it is an important aspect of living, for people certainly live a good part of their lives with an eye on the future rather than on the past. For example, since early this morning you may have been concerned with being on time to meet someone.

It is one thing to consider the expectancies of future happenings and another thing to simulate them, to construct techniques that enable one to live in the future, to act as if the future is on hand, right here. With therapeutic future techniques, one can act out a situation that he expects to happen tomorrow, a meeting with a new friend or an appointment with a prospective employer. He tries to simulate the morrow as concretely as

possible so as to predict it or to be better prepared for it.

Many patients suffer from an employment neurosis or an unemployment neurosis. They are anxious about getting a job or about having an interview with a boss to ask for higher wages. In psychodrama, the therapist rehearses such a patient a week in advance for what may happen; it is a sort of rehearsal for life. This rehearsal-for-life technique is also effective with patients concerned over affairs of the heart—whether it be a prospective marriage, a divorce, or a new baby. The problem is how to integrate these expectancies and concerns of the patient into the therapeutic operation as actualities so as to be of value for both client and therapist.

Space

Space, too, has been almost entirely neglected as a part of the therapeutic process. If you go into a psychoanalyst's office, you find an abstract bed, a couch, but the rest of the office space is not related to the therapeutic process. The patient is language-centered and the therapist is centered to listen. If you go into an office in which one of the current varieties of psychotherapy is practiced, you may find only a chair. The space in which the patient experiences his traumata has no place in that setting.

The idea of a psychotherapy of space has been pioneered by psychodrama, which is action-centered and which comprehensively tries to integrate all the dimensions of living into itself. When a patient steps into the therapeutic space, the therapist insists on a description of the space in which the ensuing scene is to be portrayed—its horizontal and vertical dimensions, the objects in it, and the distance and relationship of the objects to one another. The configuration of space warms up the protagonist to be and to act himself in an environment modeled after that in which he lives.

Here is an illustration of an actual case:

The patient, Jack, is a teen-age boy.
Jack: Doctor, I'm afraid to go home tonight.
Therapist: Why, what happened?
Jack: Well, this afternoon my mother and father had an argument, and my father hit my

mother and made her fall down the stairway. I saw her there, at the bottom of the stairs, and became so furious at my father that I hit him. But then I got scared, took my bag of clothes, and ran away. Here I am, and I don't dare go home.

Therapist: Jack, where is the stairway? And where is your mother? (Jack moves about on the stage, points out the location of the stairway, places it in relationship to the windows and the wall, shows his mother's position at the base of the stairway, points out the corridor, the front door, the bedrooms, the living room, moving around in the space in which he has experienced this episode, structuring it before the eyes of the group. At this point the therapist uses a future technique.)

Therapist: Jack, go home now. But instead of really going to Brooklyn, where you live, you are going home right here in this room. Let's say you will be home about an hour from now. Set up all the spatial configurations as closely as possible. Who is home when you arrive, and where are they located in space?

Jack (physically constructing the spatial arrangements): Well, first of all, I come in at the front door, here, into the living room. I expect my father to be over there, in his chair in the corner of the room, angry. My mother is in the bedroom upstairs, crying.

(Jack proceeds to set up the rest of the space—the ceiling, doors, windows, relationship to other rooms in the house, the garden, all the things that he feels to be significant. He warms up more and more and gets increasingly involved in the situation. Soon he begins to see pictures on the walls; he notices that his mother wears a certain dress, father smokes a cigar. In other words, the configurations of the space itself become a parameter for a therapeutic setting.)

Reality

Reality has undergone quite a change in the last 30 or 40 years. As psychiatry takes place more and more in the community, rather than in hospitals, reality begins to attain new meanings. The trend is very much along the lines of confrontation and concretization.

Infra Reality. The reality in a psychoanalyst's office, from the point of view of therapy, is a sort of reduced reality, an infra reality. The contact between doctor and patient is not a genuine dialogue but is more of an interview, a research situation, or a projection test. Whatever is happening to the patient—for example, a suicidal idea or a plan to run away—is not a phase of direct actualization and confrontation but remains on the level of imagining, thinking, feeling. To an extent, this is also true of the reality in the office of the patient-centered, existential, or interview therapist.

Actual Reality. The next step is the reality of life itself, of the everyday lives of all people, how they live in their own homes, in their businesses, and in their relationships to all the people who affect their lives—their husbands, wives, children, employers, teachers, clergymen—and to the world at large.

The manner in which they live in reality, their relationships with the significant people in their lives, may be defective or inadequate, and they may wish to change, to attempt new ways of living. But change can be both threatening and extremely difficult, to such an extent that they stay in their familiar ruts rather than risk a calamity they cannot handle. Thus, a therapeutic situation is needed in which reality can be simulated so that people can learn to develop new techniques of living without risking serious consequences or disaster, as they might if they first tried the techniques in life itself.

Surplus Reality. Surplus reality represents the intangible dimensions of intrapsychic and extrapsychic life, the invisible dimensions in the reality of living that are not fully experienced or expressed. The therapist uses certain operations and instruments to bring out these dimensions in therapeutic settings.

Role Reversal. One of the most popular surplus-reality techniques in psychodrama is that of role reversal. If a husband and wife fight in the reality of daily life, each remains in his own role, in his own life situation. The perceptions, expectations, fears, and disappointments of each remain unchanged. And even if both parties come to some point of agreement, they still maintain the same relative status: The husband remains the husband, the wife remains the wife. But in role reversal the wife takes the part of the husband, and the husband takes the part of the wife. Not only must they do this nominally, but each one must try to feel his way into the thinking, feeling, and behavior patterns of the other.

This technique is particularly useful in situations that are provoked by stress. Take a specific case:

It is eight o'clock in the morning. The husband, who is employed as the head of a sales office, comes down the stairs and rushes into the kitchen.

Bob: Mary, what's the matter with you, are you crazy? Why didn't you wake me up? It's already eight o'clock, and you know I have to be in my office by 8:15!

Mary (beginning to cry): But I'm just fixing your eggs. I knocked on your door three times, and you didn't wake up! Why do you have to yell at me? I'm doing the best I can. What's the matter with you?

(She bursts into tears, and he has a temper tantrum. This is the critical moment for role reversal. At this point the therapist steps in.)

Therapist: Now, Bob, you take the part of Mary, and Mary, you take the part of Bob.

(Bob, in the role of his wife, stands over the stove trying to fix the eggs and crying bitterly because Mary, in the role of the husband, is such a sadist. She is now the one who has the temper tantrum, who comes rushing down the stairs into the kitchen, shouting.)

Mary: You damn fool! What's the matter with you, are you crazy?

It is not always easy to establish identity with one's own self at a certain time in one's life, to recapture one's own feelings and behavior in a crucial episode—as a child or adolescent, for instance—but it is at least plausible. How then can one establish identity with another person, as one is requested to do in role reversal? It is possible, especially with two people who have lived a long time in intimate ensembles, such as husbands and wives, mothers and children, fathers and sons, sisters and brothers, or very close friends.

Auxiliary Ego. One of the basic instruments in constructing a patient's psychodramatic world is that of the auxiliary ego, the representation of absentee people or of delusions, hallucinations, symbols, ideals, animals, and objects. They make the protagonist's world real, concrete, and tangible.

Bodily Contact. In the course of making the protagonist's world real and dynamic, numerous problems emerge, as in the use of bodily contact, for instance. Bodily contact has been, to some extent, a taboo in all psychotherapies. Yet, when a nurse sees a patient suffering, she cannot help but touch him and say, "Now, Jack, don't worry, it will be all right." Her touch may mean more to the boy than the words she speaks, not in an overtly sexual way but as a sort of maternal, protective approach to him.

A psychoanalyst who would become in any way physically personal with his patient would be ostracized. But in the psychodramatic approach to human relations, the therapist is interested in following the model of life itself and, within limits, in making therapeutic use of the bodily-contact technique. This technique is obviously contraindicated if it is used to gratify the need of the therapist, but it is indicated if it gives the patient, not only in words but in action, the warmth and immediacy of pulsating life in an area in which he is in need.

For instance, if a young woman patient suffers a profound alienation from her husband or her family, the therapist can give her an auxiliary ego, either male or female, and can expect the auxiliary ego to be warm and personal, to put his arm around the patient's shoulders, and, if indicated, to go beyond that. Where to draw the ethical, aesthetic, and therapeutic limit is a great problem. But a person cannot be an auxiliary ego—a mother, father, son, or whatever—unless he lives it. If he does not live it, the role becomes abstract, unfeeling, and untherapeutic.

Of course, the therapist can get into real trouble this way, as a case in a large hospital illustrates.

The case involved a young woman patient who was engaged to be married; she was profoundly depressed and very much in need of affection. The therapist gave her an auxiliary ego to portray the man to whom she was engaged. According to the rules, the auxiliary fiance became very warm, put his arms around her, and kissed her. He did not go too far but far enough to arouse the ire of the patient's father, who happened to be a Senator. When he heard about the session, he immediately called up the superintendent of the hospital and asked him:

What's the big idea, to allow a perfect stranger to make love to my daughter on a stage?

The superintendent answered:

Senator, this is therapy. It isn't anything but therapy. We are trying to treat your daughter. Don't you send her or your wife to gynecologists, obstetricians, and other specialists when they need professional attention, and don't these doctors use all kinds of methods that may be a little embarrassing? What do you have against psychotherapy when it becomes a little bit real?

And so the whole thing was smoothed over, the daughter improved, and a good method was found to calm down even a Senator.

Role-Playing. This is another important surplus-reality technique. Here a person may be trained to function more effectively in his reality role, whether he be employer, employee, student, instructor, parent, child, mate, lover, or friend. In the therapeutic setting of psychodrama, the protagonist is free to try and even to fail in this role, for he knows he will be given the opportunity to try again, to try another interpretation and another, until he finally learns new approaches to the situations he fears, approaches that he can then apply in life itself.

Other Techniques. There are still many other effective surplus-reality techniques, such as the empty chair (empty crib, empty pew, empty bed, etc.), the high chair, the magic shop, dream enactment, God technique, rehearsal for the future, existential validation, and the therapeutic community.

The Cosmos

Early in the twentieth century, two philosophies of human relations were particularly popular. One was the philosophy that everything in the universe is packed into the single individual, into the individual psyche. This was particularly emphasized by Sigmund Freud, who thought that the group was an epiphenomenon. For Freud, only the individual counted. The other philosophy was that of Karl Marx. For Marx, everything ended with the social man or more specifically, the socioeconomic man. Very early in his career, the author came to the position that there is another area, a larger world beyond the psychodynamics and sociodynamics of human society—cosmodynamics. Man is a cosmic man, not only a social man or an individual man.

Since time immemorial, man has tried to understand his position in the universe at large and to control the phenomena that determine this position—evolution, birth, death, sex, and the function of the Creator of the world. To do this, man has invented religions, myths, fables. He has submitted himself to stark regimentation in order to comply with the laws of the universe as he conceived them. Buddha's rules, the Ten Commandments, the numerous rituals of the various illiterate cultures—all are testimony to the profound anxiety of man to comply with an invisible value system.

In the age of the atomic bomb and the computer, the conceptions of man have changed radically. The pronouncement that God is dead may be meaningless; He may never have existed. But it is important that men may be able to create Him in their image. The evolution of the future is wide open for speculation. Birth and death may not be terminal but may attain new meaning through scientific discoveries. Even the differences between the sexes may not be fixed but may be transitory. One's sex may be changed. The possibility that millions of other beings exist on other planets raises questions that man has never confronted as clearly as now.

Just like the functions of time, space, and reality, the function of the cosmos must be so integrated into the therapeutic setting that it has experiential and existential value for the protagonist. Within the framework of psychodrama, by means of its numerous methods, cosmic phenomena can be integrated into the therapeutic process. In the psychodramatic world, the differentiation between the sexes is overlooked and surpassed. The differences in age are also overlooked. The facts of birth and death are overlooked. The unborn and the dead are brought to life on the psychodrama stage.

These externalizations are closely related to the subjectivity and imaginings of the protagonist. A woman who wishes she were born a man may play a man on the psychodrama stage and so correct the injustices of the universe as she perceives them. In reverse, a man may play a woman. An old man may play a child and so correct the loss of childhood or else experience the childhood he feels he never had. Anatomy and physiology and biology do not matter. What matters is the expansion of man in relation to the needs and fantasies he has about himself. He becomes the master of anatomy and physiology instead of the servant. A man can, in the psychodramatic cosmos, also embody animals—dogs, tigers, bears, fish, birds, insects, any actual or imaginary beings—not as a form of regression but as creative involvement. He is free from the fetters of facts and actualities, although not without the highest respect for them. And he has a good foundation to believe, as science has repeatedly taught us, that things are changing and can be further changed, even conditions that seemed for millennia absolutely fixed.

Warming Up

It would be difficult to find an adult who has not witnessed at some time or other an act of warming up. An automobile engine warms up when it is started; track athletes warm up prior to a race; some people make circular motions before signing an important document; singers vocalize before singing a solo. Every act of man begins with warming up.

In the morning a man emerges from a state of sleep in a gradual way, warming up to the process of leaving his bed and assuming the state of wakefulness. Even after he gets out of bed, he may need a prolonged period of warming up to the activities and demands of the day. He yawns, he stretches, he scratches himself, and he ponders the immediate problems that have to be met and solved, such as the choice of clothing and the consumption of breakfast. All this activity can be called a warming up for the business of conducting life through one day. At the end of each day, he begins to unwind. In order to prepare for the cessation of mental and physical activity, he reverses the process he went through that morning and begins to warm up for sleep. Prior to getting into bed, he may snack or smoke or read or watch television or deliberately turn his mind to the habitual, orderly habits of putting the house to bed by locking doors, adjusting the thermostat, etc. Between the warming-up processes of waking from sleep and of putting himself to sleep,

he has a day full of activities, almost all of which must be preceded by warming-up procedures.

There is a circular quality in the relationship of warming up and spontaneity. Warming up initiates spontaneity. Spontaneity, in turn, shortens the period of warming up. At times, warming up and spontaneity are so entwined that they seem to be both cause and effect. In a sense the shorter and more controlled the process of warming up becomes, the greater the degree of spontaneity. Also, the shorter the period of warming up, the more efficient the personality becomes in meeting life situations. The more quickly one can make adjustments prior to beginning a task, the less trial and error is involved in shifting gears, especially in proceeding from one task to another.

One of the goals in creating a good personality is to be aware of and to appreciate the effect of warming up. Efficient warming up may also reduce emotional anxiety. Take, for example, the ubiquitous intrusion of the telephone call. Answering a telephone permits very little opportunity for warming up to the voice on the other end of the line. The usual reinforcement clues, such as the speaker's appearance and the location of the conversation (one expects to talk of bowling in a bowling alley), are absent. The abrupt ring of the telephone, the voice not always clear, the face unseen, and the disruption of one's activity are not designed to aid the answering party in warming up to the conversation. Emotional anxiety may result, therefore, if the individual does not possess adequate spontaneity and an efficient warming-up technique suited to telephone conversation.

Warming up does not mean the same thing as conditioning. Conditioning implies a set relationship between a stimulus and a response. A person may become conditioned to respond to the telephone's ring by arising and answering the call with little or no apparent thought. However automatic that response becomes, he is still confronted with a warming-up task the moment he picks up the telephone. In his conversation he makes preliminary adjustments, and the manner in which he makes them produces reciprocal adjustments in the person calling him. Both prior to the call and during the call, the warming-up process is operating. A conditioned response produces only a singular behavior pattern. Warming up both prepares the subject for the act and is highly involved in structuring the act as it proceeds from singular act to singular act. As the individual warms up to the telephone conversation, he becomes more spontaneous. As he becomes more spontaneous, he continues to warm up to the situation.

In summary, therefore, warming up exists before and in the course of any act whether or not the act is creative, and it is not synonymous with conditioning.

Purely as a sidelight, it is interesting to note that high-speed electronic computers do not possess these warming-up and spontaneous principles. The gigantic electronic brains possess phenomenal conditioned responses but lack the ingenuity of man's reciprocal responses to situations.

Creativity-Spontaneity-Cultural Conserve Triad

Creativity. Creativity manifests itself in any series of creative states or creative acts. One example is the creation of new organisms capable of surviving on land at the time that animal life was confined to the sea. A new animal organism arose when it underwent, through the evolutional process, certain physical changes. This process may be called biological creativity. A second example is the Sermon on the Mount as it emerged, however unformed, for the first time from the mind of Jesus. This is a form of religious creativity. A third illustration is musical creativity, such as the music of Beethoven's Ninth Symphony at the moment it was being created by him in contrast to the same music as a finished product, separated from the composer himself.

Spontaneity. Creativity is a sleeping beauty that, to become effective, needs a catalyzer. The arch catalyzer of creativity is spontaneity, a form of energy that is unconservable. It emerges and is spent in a moment; it must emerge to be spent and must be spent to make place for new emergence, like some animals that are born and die in the love act. It is a truism to say that the

universe cannot exist without physical and mental energy that can be conserved. But it is important to realize that without the other kind of energy, the unconservable one, the creativity of the universe could not start and could not run. Creativity would come to a standstill.

Spontaneity operates in the present. It propels a person toward an adequate response to a new situation or a new response to an old situation. Thus, while creativity is related to the act itself, spontaneity is related to the warming up, to the readiness for the act.

Here follow three types of spontaneity: The first type is a novel response to a situation that is not adequate for that situation. Psychotics, for example, may state that two times two equals five, certainly a novel response but hardly adequate. Children, too, burst with spontaneity and have a wide range of novel experiences, but the creative value of their responses is often doubtful, at least from the point of view of the adult world, just as the creative value of the novel responses of psychotics is doubtful from the point of view of normal people.

The second type of spontaneity is a stereotype variety. It consists of a response that is adequate to the situation but that lacks sufficient novelty or significant creativity to be fruitful for the situation. The comedian's repetitive reaction to a situation soon loses its novelty, and, although it may continue to provoke some laughter, it loses spontaneity with each repetition.

The third type of spontaneity is the high-grade creativity variety of genius. In this type an adequate response is accompanied by characteristics that are both novel and creative. The resulting phenomenon may be in the form of an act or a substantive article, such as a poem, story, art object, or piece of machinery. To be truly spontaneous, the results must be in some way new and useful for some purpose.

Cultural Conserve. The finished product of the creative process is the cultural conserve, the latter word coming from *conservare*, to guard. The cultural conserve is anything that preserves the values of a particular culture. It may take the form of a material object—such as a book, film, building, or musical composition—or it may appear as a highly set pattern of behavior—such as a religious ceremony, theatrical performance of a written play, fraternity initiation, or inaugural ceremony for the President of the United States. As a repository of the past, cultural conserves preserve and continue man's creative ego. Without them man would be reduced to creating spontaneously the same forms to meet the same situations day after day. For example, a cultural conserve such as the dictionary makes it unnecessary for men to redefine words every time they wish to communicate. In addition to providing continuity for the heritage of human existence, the cultural conserve plays an even more significant role as the springboard for enticing new spontaneity toward creativity.

There is a danger in the overreliance of mankind on the cultural conserve. This danger is inherent both in the conserve's state of finality and in its abuse by mankind. Once conserved, spontaneous creativity—however supreme it may be in itself—is, by definition, no longer spontaneous.

Here-and-Now

The concept of the here-and-now has assumed great importance in psychiatry in the last 50 years. In 1919 the author wrote:

The meaning of the decision is in this moment, the here-and-now, even if you have lived through all the instants of the past and will live through all the instants of the future.

In 1922 the author wrote:

How does a moment emerge? A feeling must be related to the object of the feelings, a thought must be related to the object of the thoughts, a perception must be related to the object of the perceptions, a touch must be related to the object of touching. You are the object of my feelings, the object of my thoughts, the object of my perceptions, the object of my touch. Such is an encounter in the here-and-now.

In 1931 the author wrote:

Both Freud and Jung have studied man as an historical development; the one from the biological, the other from the cultural aspect. On the other hand, our approach has been that of *direct* experiment, man in action, man thrown into action, the moment not a part of history but history a part of the moment—*sub species momenti.*

In 1940 the author wrote:

The moment of being, living and creating has been the stepchild of all universally known philosophical and therapeutic systems. The reasons for this are that the moment is difficult to define, that it has appeared to most philosophers as but a fleeting transition between past and future, without real substance; that it is intangible and unstable and therefore an unsatisfactory basis for a system of theoretical and practical philosophy. Some phenomenon on a different plane than that presented by the moment itself had to be found which was tangible and capable of clear definition, but to which the moment was *integrally* related. I believe that I accomplished this in analyzing "cultural conserves." The cultural conserve is a concept in the light of which the dynamic meaning of the moment can be reflected and evaluated and this becomes a frame of reference.

And in 1941 the author wrote:

The first step toward a philosophy of the moment is to define and establish the moment as a concept in its own right. A study of the moment in experimental situations, parallel to and as a follow-up of a philosophical analysis of the subject, provides one method of arriving at a definition of the moment. In the establishment of a point of reference, three factors must be emphasized: the *status nascendi,* the *locus* and the *matrix.* These represent different phases of the same process. There is nothing without its locus, no locus without its status nascendi, and no status nascendi without its matrix.

Encounter

In the center of the group process is the concept of the encounter. The term encounter covers numerous areas of living: It means to be together, to meet one another, the contact of two bodies, seeing, observing, touching, feeling the other person, withdrawing and uniting, understanding one another, intuitive insight through silence or movement, language or gestures, kiss or embrace, becoming one.

The word encounter contains as a root the word counter, derived from the Latin *contra,* against, and thus encounter denotes the meeting of opposing forces. It includes not only loving relations but also hostile and threatening ones, confronting one another, acting in spite, and quarreling.

Encounter is a unique experience that occurs only once and is irreplaceable. A touch and contact between two bodies, as in a psychodrama session, is a personal outburst of interaction that is unrehearsed. It is a challenge not only to the acting protagonist but also to all the participants. They witness an experience in the making. Encountering is, therefore, at the core of psychodramatic experience. The encounter comes first. Perception or interpretive analysis comes second. It cannot be exchanged through other forms of expression, other individuals, a book, or a letter.

Encounter means that two persons not only meet but also experience and comprehend one another, each with his whole being. It is not a circumscribed contact like a professional meeting of a therapist with a patient, nor is it an intellectual contact (teacher and pupil) or a scientific contact (a transaction between an observer and an object). The participants in an encounter are not pushed into the situation by an external force. They are there because they want to be there. The encounter is unprepared; it is not conducted or rehearsed in advance. There is in every encounter an element of surprise.

Encounter is essentially different from what the psychoanalysts call transference, and it is also different from what the psychologists call empathy. It does not negate transference, and it does not negate empathy. Rather it includes transference and empathy and gives them their natural function in the entire process. It moves from I to Thou and from Thou to I. It is two-feeling. It is tele.

Tele

When the group speaks for itself, sets its own pace, and develops its own concepts, what holds the group together? What establishes a group as an enduring, stable, and ongoing process? There must be factors operating among the individual members of the group that stimulate reciprocal relations among them. Shared values and common goals must lead to the cohesiveness of group action.

When the author began work with groups, no term in literature described such affects as group stability, group cohesion, and group integration. The author introduced the term *tele*, the Greek word meaning far. Previously it had been used not as an isolated term, but always in various combinations: telencephalon, telepathy, telephone, television, and the like. Taking over such concepts as transference from the individual situation would not have satisfied the requirements of the group situation. By definition, transference tends to produce dissociation of interpersonal relations. In contrast, tele strengthens association and promotes continuity, security, stability, reciprocity, and cohesiveness of groups. In the construction of a conceptual framework, it is advantageous to introduce concepts that are indigenous to the field rather than to force alien concepts on a new situation.

Tele is the constant frame of reference for all forms and methods of psychotherapy, including not only professional methods of psychotherapy, like psychoanalysis, psychodrama, and group psychotherapy but also nonprofessional methods like faith healing and methods that have apparently no relation to psychotherapy, such as Chinese thought reform.

Allport says that the author

defines tele as "insight into," "appreciation of," and "feeling for" the "actual make-up" of the other person. Thus defined, it is indeed the foundation of all sound therapy, as it is of all wholesome human relationships. Occasionally it may grow out of a previous transference situation, but I suspect that normally tele is present from the outset and increases as sessions continue. Only at certain periods it is obscured by an onrush of transference (or, rarely, counter-transference), and it may occasionally break down altogether, with the result that the therapeutic relationship depends on the presence of tele, and thereby differs in this respect only because the patient's distress thrusts his inner needs forward, with the result that projections and transference and hostility sometimes obscure for the time being the basic telic relationship.

Neither transference nor empathy could

explain in a satisfactory way the emergent cohesion of a social configuration. Social configurations consist of two or multiple ways of interaction. They are social wholes, not the point of view of one particular person. Empathy and transference are parts of a more elementary and more inclusive process, tele. It is an objective social process functioning with transference as a psychopathological outgrowth and empathy as an aesthetic outgrowth. The process of reciprocation does not enter into the meaning of empathy, and transference is considered the factor responsible for dissociation and disintegration in social groups. Tele is the factor responsible for the increased mutuality of choices surpassing chance possibility and responsible for the increased rate of interaction among members of a group.

Tele operates on the wish level, the social desire level, the choice level, and the behavioral level of a relationship. It has, besides, a conative, a cognitive aspect.

It can be hypothesized that the greater the sociometric distance between a person and others in their common social space, the more inaccurate will be his social evaluation of their relationship to him and to each other. He may guess accurately how A, B, and C feel toward him, but he may have only a vague perception of how A feels about B, A feels about C, B feels about C, B feels about A, etc.

Tele is the interpersonal experience growing out of person-to-person and person-to-object contacts from the birth level on and gradually developing the sense for interpersonal relations; some real process in one person's life situation is sensitive and corresponds to some real process in another person's life situation, and there are numerous degrees, positive and negative, of these interpersonal sensitivities. The tele process is an objective system of interpersonal relations.

A feeling complex which goes out from a person does not run wildly into space but goes to a certain other person, and that other person, in turn, does not accept this passively, like a robot, but responds actively with another feeling complex. One tele may become interlocked with another tele, a pair-relation being formed. In the original application the subject is faced with persons and situations which have meaning for him. Some of the most effective methods of training in sensitivity are the various psychodrama techniques, especially role reversal.

Co-Conscious and Co-Unconscious States

Free associations of A may be a path to the unconscious of A—that is, to the unconscious content of A. The free associations of B may be a path to the unconscious of B—that is, to the unconsciously repressed content of B. But can the unconscious material of A ever link naturally and directly with the unconscious material of B. Freud ignores the matter. His hypothesis of the unconscious and the interpretation of resistance is significant only in the dimension of a single psyche.

When one moves from one person to another, the concept of the individual unconscious becomes unsatisfactory for explaining both movements, from the present situation of A to his unconscious, U_1, and from the present situation of B to his unconscious, U_2. One must either modify the meaning of unconscious by looking for a counterpoint, a sort of musical key that is able to relate every event in the unconscious of A to every event in the unconscious of B, or one must look for concepts so constructed that the objective indication for their existence comes not from the resistances of a single psyche but from a still deeper reality in which the unconscious tracks of several individuals are interlocked, a co-unconscious.

Jung postulates that every person has, besides a personal unconscious, a collective unconscious. Jung does not apply the collective unconscious to concrete collectivities in which people live. Nothing is gained in turning from a personal to a collective unconscious if, on the way, the anchorage to the concrete, whether individual or group, is diminished. Had Jung turned to the group by developing techniques like group psychotherapy or sociodrama, he might have gained a concrete position for his theory of a collective unconscious; as it is, he removed the individual anchorage but did not establish a safe collective anchorage as a counter position. The problem here is not the collective images of a given culture or of mankind but the specific relatedness and cohesiveness of a group of individuals on the unconscious level.

Role

Role can be defined as the actual and tangible form that the individual self takes. The role is the functioning form a person assumes in the specific moment he reacts to a specific situation in which other persons or objects are involved. The symbolic representation of this functioning form is perceived by the person and by others. The form is created by past experiences and the cultural patterns of the society in which the person lives and may be satisfied by the specific type of his productivity. Every role is a fusion of private and collective elements. Every role has two sides, a private and a collective side.

Role vs. Ego and Self. It has been hypothesized that understanding of human behavior is more easily facilitated by means of the role concept than by any other concept. It is a more operational concept than the concept of ego and more descriptive than the concept of self.

The tangible points of crystallization of the ego are the roles in which it manifests itself. The roles and the relations between them are the most important phenomena within a given culture. It is simpler to speak of the roles of a person than of his ego. Ego has mysterious, metapsychological side orientations. But the expression of behavior in terms of roles is not new. The universal cultivation of drama has made this a part of our common-sense knowledge. Dramatists have repeatedly described in literary terms what today is defined in technical terms. However, such roles as King Lear, Macbeth, and Romeo are not created before the eyes of the audience. The step from the texts of the playwrights to scientific texts requires a return to the original formation of a role *in statu nascendi.*

The approach to the problem of verifying the role process is most promising in experiments with roles in laboratory settings. In such settings, persons are placed in an experimental climate with the task of improvising and creating roles on the spur of the moment. The people who are used for these experiments are required to use their spontaneity rather than their memory. A psychodramatic theatre can be easily transformed into a laboratory setting by the adequate selection of subjects, controls, recordings, and trained observers.

Role-playing comes before the emergence of the self. Roles do not emerge from the self; the self emerges from roles. This is, of course, a hypothesis that appeals only to the sociometrist and the behavioral scientist, but that may be rejected by the Aristotelian, the theologian, and the metapsychologist. The sociometrist will point out that the playing of roles is not an exclusively human trait, that roles are also played by animals. They can be observed taking sexual roles, roles of nest-builders, and leader roles, for instance.

If the self came before the roles and roles emerged from the self, one would have to assume that the roles were already embedded in the self and that they emerged by necessity. Pre-established as they would then be, they would have to assume predetermined forms. Such a· theory would be difficult to accept in a dynamic, changing, self-creative world. One would be in the same position as the theologians of the past, who assumed that man is born with a soul and that from that original given soul everything man does or sees or feels emerges or comes forth. For the modern theologian it should be of advantage to think of the soul as an entity that evolves and creates itself from millions of small beginnings. The soul is then not in the beginning but in the end.

Role Reversal. Role reversal is important both as a learning technique for children and adults and as a method of therapy for individuals and social groups. Role reversal is the heart of role-playing theory as demonstrated in psychodrama and sociodrama.

Here are some hypotheses about the nature of reversal:

Role reversal increases the strength and stability of the child's ego. Ego is here defined as identity with himself.

Role reversal tends to diminish the dependency of the child on the parent, but it tends also to increase his ability to dominate the parent because the child has gained a profound knowledge of him through inside information.

Frequent role reversal of the child with persons superior in age and experience increases his sensitivity for an inner life more complex than his own. In order to keep up with them on their internal role level, which is far above the overt level of the role, he has to be resourceful. He becomes prematurely skilled in the management of interpersonal relations.

The excess desire to reverse roles with the mother is due to an early appreciation and perception of her roles. Frequency of role reversal with the father increases as the perception of the father's roles becomes clearer to the child.

The technique of role reversal is the more effective the nearer in psychological, social, and ethnic proximity the two individuals are: mother-child, father-son, husband-wife.

Role reversal is an effective technique for socializing one ethnic group to the other. The greater the ethnic distance between two social groups is, the more difficult is the application of role reversal.

The empathy of individuals or representatives of groups for the internal experiences of other individuals or representatives of groups —what they feel, think, perceive, and do— increases with the reciprocal perception of the roles in which they operate. Therefore, the training of auxiliary egos and doubles, as well as of psychotherapists in general, is in the direction of increasing their sensitivity.

The empathy of therapists increases with their training in role perception and role reversal.

Role reversal is a risk and is at times contraindicated when the ego of one person is minimally structured and the ego of the other is maximally structured. Psychotic patients like to play the part of authorities— nurses, doctors, policemen—or of ideal persons—for instance, they like to play God. But when faced with an actual person who embodies authority, they resent interaction and role reversal.

Role reversal is without risk when the two persons who reverse roles with one another are solidly structured.

RULES AND TECHNIQUES

Psychodrama may be applied as a method of individual treatment—one patient with one director or with one director and an auxiliary ego, or one patient and the director. It may also be applied as a method of group treatment with other patients in the group serving as auxiliary egos for one another. In this fashion even individual-centered sessions involve other members of the group. They, in turn, derive therapeutic benefit from this auxiliary ego function, thus intensifying the learning of all those present.

Rules

Action. The patient acts out his conflicts, instead of just talking about them. To this end, a special vehicle or psychodrama stage is ideal, since the special vehicle makes for more intense involvement. But the process sometimes has to take place in an informal room or space when no such specially designed vehicle is available. The process also requires a director or chief therapist and at least one trained auxiliary ego, although the director may be forced to act as an auxiliary ego when no one else is available. Maximal learning is achieved whenever such trained assistant-therapist-actors are used.

Here-and-Now. The patient acts in the here-and-now, regardless of when the actual incident took place or may take place—past, present, or future—or when the imagined incident—which may never take place—was fantasied or when the crucial situation, out of which this present enactment arose, occurred. The patient speaks and acts in the present and not in the past, because the past is related to memory. Speaking in the past tense removes the subject from the immediacy of experience and turns him into a spectator or a storyteller rather than an actor.

One of the notable experiences in psychodrama is the ineffectual, weak, incomplete, and distorted fashion in which recall and reenactment are produced. This phenomenon has been experimentally verified by the immediate re-enactment of scenes that took place only five minutes earlier, using the identical persons involved in the original scene. Both verbal and action recall as well as interpersonal perception were impossible to reproduce, even though all actual partners tried systematically and honestly to recapture what actually happened.

The inability to recall perfectly indicates that such recall is a practical impossibility. Absolute recall does not exist, and correct reproduction is a hardly attainable ideal. Furthermore, spontaneity and presentness are subjugated to correct reproduction and thus disappear. To release spontaneity and increase presentness in the here-and-now, the therapist specifically instructs the patient to make time his servant, not his master, to act as if the incident were happening to him now, so that he can feel, perceive, and act as if it were happening to him for the first time.

Subjectivity. The patient must act out his truth as he feels and perceives it in a completely subjective manner, no matter how distorted it appears to the spectator. The warming-up process cannot proceed properly unless the patient is accepted with all his subjectivity. Enactment comes first, retraining comes later. The therapist must give him the satisfaction of act completion first, before considering retraining for behavior changes.

Maximal Expression. The patient is encouraged to maximize all expression, action, and verbal communication rather than to reduce them. To this end, delusions, hallucinations, soliloquies, thoughts, fantasies, projections—all are allowed to be part of the production. Restraint has to come after expression, although restraint should never be overlooked. Without, however, getting expression *in toto*, restraint can be at best only partial.

Inward Movement. The warming-up process proceeds from the periphery to the center. The director, therefore, does not begin with the most traumatic events in the patient's life. The beginning is on a more superficial level, allowing the self-involvement of the patient to carry him more deeply toward the core. The director's skills are expressed in the construction of the scenes and in the choice of persons or objects needed to assist the patient in his warming up.

Patient Choice. Whenever possible, the patient picks the time, place, scene, and auxiliary ego he requires in the production of his psychodrama. The director serves as dramaturgist in assisting the patient or protagonist. The director and protagonist are partners; at any one moment the director may be more active, but the protagonist always reserves the right to decline the enactment of a scene or to change it.

When the interaction between patient and director becomes negative, with the patient resisting the director as well as the process, the director may do any one of the following: (1) Ask the patient to designate another director if more than one are present. (2) Ask the patient to sit down and watch a mirror production of himself by an auxiliary ego or egos. (3) Turn the direction over to the patient himself, who may then involve others in the group as auxiliary egos. (4) Ask the patient to choose another scene. (5) Explain to the patient why he chose the scene, even though it may not be carried out now. (6) Return to an enactment of the scene at a later time if the patient needs it. (7) Insist on its enactment if the benefits to be derived for the patient are greater than his resistance.

Restraint. Psychodrama is just as much a method of restraint as it is a method of expression. The repressiveness of our culture has attached to expression a value that is often beyond its actual reward. A greatly underestimated and disregarded application of psychodrama lies in such methods as role reversal and the enactment of roles that require restraint, retraining, or reconditioning of excitability. One thinks especially of the chronic bad actor in life, the delinquent or psychopath, whose ability for self-restraint has not been strengthened by his warming up to stresses in life.

Acceptance of Inexpressiveness. The patient is permitted to be as unspontaneous or inexpressive as he is at the time. This rule may seem to be a contradiction of the maximal expression rule, but only apparently so. Maximizing the patient's expression may also refer to his inability to express, his withdrawal, his submerged anger, etc. The therapist must first accept this inability and help the patient to accept himself. Then, gradually, the therapist tries to release the patient from his bonds by such methods as asides, soliloquies, and doubles.

The fact that a patient lacks spontaneity is not a block to psychodramatic production. It is, indeed, the reason for the existence of auxiliary egos—who are trained to support, assist, and strengthen the patient—and techniques such as the soliloquy, the double, the mirror, and role reversal. The person who is unable to be spontaneous as himself, in his own roles, may become extremely spontaneous in role reversal—in the role of his wife, father, baby, or pet dog. His expressiveness grows as his spontaneity increases.

Expressiveness at any price is not necessarily spontaneous. Producing a steady flow of words and actions may be a cover-up for genuine feelings. A patient may be entirely spontaneous, on the other hand, while sitting quietly in a chair or observing others around him.

Interpretation. Interpretation and insight-giving in psychodrama are of a different nature from those processes in the verbal types of psychotherapy. In psychodrama one speaks of action insight, action learning, or action catharsis. It is an integrative process brought about by the synthesis of numerous techniques at the height of the protagonist's warm-up. Psychodrama is actually the most interpretative method there is, but the director acts upon his interpretations in the construction of the scenes. Verbal interpretation may be either essential or entirely omitted at the discretion of the director, because his interpretation is in the act. Verbal interpretation is frequently redundant.

Even when interpretation is given, action is primary. There can be no interpretation without previous action. Interpretation may be questioned, rejected, or totally ineffective, but the action speaks for itself. Furthermore, interpretation is colored by the orientation of the therapist. Thus, a Freudian will interpret from a different framework from an Adlerian, Jungian, or Horneyan. But varied interpretations do not in any way change the value of the production itself.

They merely put interpretation on a less important rung. At times, indeed, interpretation may be destructive rather than constructive; it may be that what the patient requires is not analysis but emotional identification.

Cultural Adaptations. Warming up to psychodrama may proceed differently from culture to culture, and appropriate changes in the application of the method have to be made. It may be impossible to start a psychodrama in the Congo by verbal exchange; it may be necessary to start with singing and dancing. What may be a suitable warm-up in Manhattan may fall flat in Tokyo. Cultural adaptations must be made. The important thing is not how to begin but what one begins.

Three-Part Procedure. Psychodrama sessions consist of three portions: the warm-up, the action, and the postaction sharing by the group. Disturbances in any one of these areas reflect on the total process. However, sharing may at times be of a nonverbal nature. The most suitable way of sharing with a protagonist is often a silence pregnant with emotion or going out to coffee together or making plans to meet again.

Identification with Protagonist. The protagonist should never be left with the impression that he is all alone with his type of problem in the group. The director must draw from the group, in the postaction discussion phase, identifications with the subject. This will increase cohesion, broaden interpersonal perceptions, and establish anchorages in the group for mutually satisfying relations among group members.

When no one in the audience openly identifies with the subject, the protagonist feels denuded, robbed of that most sacred part of himself—his private psyche. Then it is the task of the director to reveal himself as not merely in sympathy with the protagonist but as being or having been similarly burdened. It is not analysis that is indicated here but love and sharing of the self. The only way to repay a person for giving of himself is in kind. Doing so frequently warms up other persons in the audience to come forward in a similar manner, thus involving the audience in a genuine warming up, which once more includes the protagonist and helps to establish closure.

Role-Playing. The protagonist must learn to take the role of all those with whom he is meaningfully related, to experience those persons in his social atom, to experience their relationship to him and to one another. Taking this a step further still, the patient must learn to become in psychodrama that which he sees, feels, hears, smells, dreams, loves, hates, fears, rejects, is rejected by, is attracted to, is wanted by, wants to avoid, wants to become, fears to become, or fears not to become.

The patient has taken unto himself, with greater or lesser success, those persons, situations, experiences, and perceptions from which he is now suffering. In order to overcome the distortions and manifestations of imbalance, he has to re-integrate them on a new level. In role reversal, an excellent method, he can re-integrate, redigest, and grow beyond those experiences that are of negative impact, free himself, and become more spontaneous along positive lines.

Flexibility. The director must trust the psychodrama method as the final arbiter and guide in the therapeutic process. This imperative is so universal that it finds confirmation among psychodramatic director-therapists. When the warm-up of the director is objective, the patient and the group feel the spontaneity of his presence and his availability for their needs. Stated another way, when there is no anxiety in the director's performance, the psychodramatic method becomes a flexible, all-embracing medium leading systematically to the heart of the patient's suffering, enabling the director, the protagonist, the auxiliary egos, and the group members to become a cohesive force, welded together to maximize emotional learning.

Techniques

Therapeutic Soliloquy. A soliloquy is a monologue of the protagonist *in situ*.

A young woman is preparing to go to bed and is combing her hair.

Protagonist (speaking to herself): Why don't I cut my hair short again? It's such a nuisance, this long hair. On the other hand, it really suits me better this way, and I don't look like everybody else.

A therapeutic soliloquy, however, is the portrayal by side dialogues and side actions of hidden thoughts and feelings, parallel with overt thoughts and actions.

The patient, a young woman, is confronting her superior, who has called her on the carpet for participating in civil rights demonstrations. The auxiliary ego, acting as the superior, asks her to account for her whereabouts the previous evening. The patient tells her she went to visit a sick friend. The auxiliary ego says she had evidence that this is not the truth. The director stops the overt action and asks the patient to express how she feels, explaining that her superior won't hear her and will not react, since she could not have known what was going on inside of her in the real situation.

Patient: I really *did* go to that demonstration. She can't do anything to me because I have tenure, but she can make it unpleasant for me.

Director: What do you want to do?

Patient: Give her a raspberry, but, of course, I can't.

Director: Here you can.

(Patient gives a lusty raspberry. Director asks her now to continue the scene as it was and to end it on the reality level.)

Self-Presentation. The protagonist presents himself, his mother, his father, his brother, his favorite professor, etc. He acts all these roles himself in complete subjectiveness, as he experiences and perceives them.

Self-Realization. The protagonist enacts, with the aid of a few auxiliary egos, the plan of his life, no matter how remote this plan may be from his present situation. For instance, a patient is actually an accountant, but for a long time he has been taking singing lessons, hoping to try out for a musical comedy part in summer stock, planning eventually to make the theatre his life's work. In psychotherapy he can explore the effects of success in this venture, possible failure and return to his old livelihood or preparing for still another career, etc.

Hallucinatory Psychodrama. The patient enacts the hallucinations and delusions he is at present experiencing although they may not be so designated by the director. The patient portrays the voices he hears, the sounds emanating from the chair he sits on, the visions he has when the trees outside his window turn into monsters that pursue him. Auxiliary egos enact the various phenomena expressed by the patient and involve him in interaction with them, so as to put the phenomena to a reality test.

Double. The patient portrays himself, and an auxiliary ego also represents the patient, establishing identity with him by moving, acting, and behaving like him.

The patient is in bed, preparing to get up in the morning. The auxiliary ego lies down on the stage alongside him, taking the same bodily posture.

Auxiliary ego: What's the use of waking up? I have nothing to live for.

Patient: Yes, that's true, I have no reason for living.

Auxiliary ego: But I am a very talented artist. There have been times when life has been very satisfying.

Patient: Yes, but it seems a long time ago.

Auxiliary ego: Maybe I can get up and start to paint again.

Patient: Well let's try to get up first, anyway, and see what will happen.

(Both patient and auxiliary ego get up, go through the motions of washing, shaving, brushing teeth—all the while moving together as if they were one. The auxiliary ego becomes the link through which the patient may try to reach out into the real world.)

Multiple Double. The protagonist is on the stage with several doubles of himself, each portraying another part of the patient —one as he is now, another as he was five years ago, a third as he was when at three years of age he first heard that his mother had died, another how he may be 20 years hence. The multiple representations of the patient are simultaneously present and act in sequence, one continuing where the other left off.

Mirror. When the patient is unable to represent himself, in word or in action, an auxiliary ego is placed on the action portion of the psychodramatic space. The patient remains seated in the group portion. The auxiliary ego re-enacts the patient, copying his behavior, trying to express his feelings in word and movement, showing the patient, as if in a mirror, how other people experience him.

The mirror may be exaggerated, employing techniques of deliberate distortion in order to arouse the patient to come forth and change from a passive spectator into an active participant—an actor—to correct what he feels is not the right enactment and interpretation of himself.

Role Reversal. The patient, in an interpersonal situation—for instance, in a scene with his mother—steps into his mother's shoes while the mother steps into those of her son. The mother may be the real mother, as is done in psychodrama *in situ,* or she may be represented by an auxiliary ego. In role reversal, the son is now enacting his mother, the mother enacting the son. Distortions of interpersonal perception can be brought to the surface, explored, and corrected in action. The son must warm up to how his mother may be feeling and perceiving him. The mother goes through the same process.

A mother and her eight-year-old daughter, Kay, show how they argue for ten minutes every morning during the winter as to what clothing the child should wear to school. After their own roles have become clear, the mother is asked to take the role of Kay, and the daughter is asked to take the role of her mother. They are instructed to change place in space, to assume the role of the other, the posture and position each had. Kay stretches a foot in the role of her mother, shows authority and certainty, whereas in her own role her anxiety was very evident. Mother now has to subdue her ebullience and restrain herself to be her somewhat withdrawn daughter. Both open their eyes wide at the image each holds before the other. The mother remarks when this scene is ended: "Am I really as aggressive as Kay portrayed me? My poor Kay!"

Future Projection. The patient portrays in action how he thinks his future will shape itself. He picks the point in time—or is assisted by the director to do so—the place and the people, if any, with whom he expects to be involved at that time.

The patient is studying to be an English teacher and has his bachelor's degree. He has been working on his M.A. for almost eight years but is unable to complete it. The future-projection technique shows him three years hence, teaching his first course in English at the university. The entire audience is his class. He is asked to face them and inspire them with the beauty of the English language.

Patient: My name is Mr. Johnson: It is a very ordinary and yet a beautiful name. I should like to welcome you here today by asking you all to introduce yourselves to one another. But remember, that name stands for you. Try to present it in such a way that it sings, that it reaches out to the other person as if to say, "Here I am. Who are you?"

Dream Presentation. The patient enacts a dream instead of telling it. He takes the position he usually has in bed when sleeping. Before lying down and taking this position, he warms up to the setting separately. The director asks him when and where he had this dream, what the room looks like, the location and size of the bed, the color of his pajamas, whether he wears top and bottom or sleeps in the nude, whether he sleeps alone, with the light on or off, with the window open or closed, and how long it normally takes him to fall asleep. In the lying position the patient is asked to breathe deeply and evenly, as he does in sleep, to move in bed as he does ordinarily while asleep, and to relax and let himself drift off as though into sleep.

Director: Try, without telling me about it, to visualize in your mind the beginning, the middle, and the end. Do you see it? Just answer yes or no.

(Patient fixes the various images somewhat in his mind's eye.)

Director: Where are you in the dream? Do you see yourself? Yes? Then step out of the dream. What are you doing—walking, swimming, sitting, running, what?

Patient: I do not see myself. I am in the dream.

Director: You are acting, doing something.

Patient: Yes, I am flying over the rooftops of houses.

Director: Do you see the rooftops? Get up and start to take a position resembling flying. Here, stand on top of this table.

(Patient climbs on table, leans forward somewhat.)

Patient: Yes, I see the rooftops. In fact, I'm hardly able to fly over them. Sometimes it seems I'm going to crash into them.

Director: Where are these buildings, and what are they?

Patient: This is a residential section. In fact, as I realize now, this is the suburb where I live.

Director: Do you see your house?

Patient: No, but I seem to sense this is my section.

Director: Are you the only one who is flying? Are you alone?

Patient: No, I'm carrying a bundle in my arms.

Director: In both arms, or only in one? Look at your arms.

(Patient looks down at his arms, which appear to be carrying something, then drops his left arm.)

Patient: My right arm.

Director: What is in the bundle? Do you know its contents?

Patient (amazed, looking intently at his right arm, crooked around an object): It's a baby.

Director: Whose?

Patient: My parents'; it's my baby sister. We are 18 years apart in age.

(Director motions to an auxiliary ego to come up on the stage to represent the baby. The director asks the auxiliary ego to kneel in such a way that the top of her head is approximately at the height of the patient's right elbow. The director asks the protagonist to hold her as best he can.)

Director: What are you doing there, flying with her?

Patient: I'm carrying her with me through life, protecting her from harm, but I'm not very sure that I'm able to do this. I seem to have trouble keeping her aloft with me.

Director: Are you afraid?

Patient: Afraid—but also very angry.

Director: Angry at whom? The baby?

Patient: No, at fate. Why should I be saddled with this responsibility? She is my parents' child, not mine.

Director: In the actual dream, do you speak to your baby sister?

Patient: No.

Director: Well, here you can. (This is a psychodramatic extension of the dream.)

Director (to auxiliary ego): Talk to your older brother.

Auxiliary ego: I'm a bit scared flying this high. Do you hold me carefully?

Patient: I'm doing my best, but you are very heavy.

Auxiliary ego: You won't drop me, will' you?

Patient: I can't, though, frankly, I'd like to.

Auxiliary ego: Why? Are you angry at me for being here with you?

Patient: Not at you, but, after all, I'm not ready for such responsibility yet. I'm just starting college, and you're a tiny infant.

Auxiliary ego: I like you. You are my big, strong brother.

Director: What happens next in the dream?

Patient: I clutch her, and the dream just fades off.

Director: You do not see any conclusive ending? Concentrate for a moment.

Patient: No, I just wake up in a cold sweat.

(Director dismisses auxiliary ego, returns patient to the position of the sleeper, back in bed.)

Director: You wake up in a cold sweat.

Patient: Yes, I'm thoroughly soaked.

Director: Sounds like a very frightening dream. Obviously, you wish it had not ended this way.

Patient: I even wish it had never started.

Director: Yes, of course. You see, in psychodrama, we can change the dream. When you are there, at night, things happen to you that appear to be out of your control. But, after all, it is you who produced the dream because of your fears and anxieties. We believe that, if we can help you to change your dream pattern, to train your unconscious, so to speak, the next time you are dreaming, your dreams will change in character, you will be in better control. Now, let's see how you wish to change your dream.

Patient: I don't want to have this dream at all.

Director: Yes, I can see that, but what would you like to do instead?

Patient: I would want to have a good talk with my parents.

Director: Fine, let's have a good talk with your parents. Get up and pick a mother and father from the group, two auxiliary egos to represent them.

(Patient does so and sets up the living room of their house.)

Patient: Gee Mom, Dad, I know you have both been very ill in the past year, and, being the the oldest son, I feel terribly burdened by the responsibility of the two younger kids, especially Alice. Timmy is already older and not quite such a problem, but Alice is just a little infant.

Director: Tell them as brutally as possible what is on your mind. After all, these are not your real parents, merely stand-ins. They will not be hurt by anything you say or feel or do.

Patient (blurts out): Why the devil did you have to go and have a menopause baby? Don't you think you have enough complications? Mother works. The housekeeper is terrible; she doesn't even speak English. Is my kid sister going to learn broken English? And don't you care what she eats? That dope can't even cook. All the kid gets is cereals and mashed banana.

(Mother and father respond, try to soothe the patient. He reverses roles with them and, finally, feels more reassured that his parents still have the major responsibility for the child.)

Dream presentation is the unique contribution of psychodrama to dream therapy. One can go into enactment over and beyond the actual dream, include actual and latent material, and, even more important, retrain the dreamer rather than interpret the dream for him. Interpretation is in the act itself.

Therapeutic Community. This is a community in which disputes and conflicts between individuals and groups are settled under the rule of therapy instead of the rule of law. The entire population, patients and staff alike, are responsible for the welfare of every other person, participate in the therapeutic process, and have equal status.

Hypnodrama. Hypnosis is sometimes induced on the psychodrama stage. The hypnotized patient is free to act and move about. He is given auxiliary egos to help him portray his drama. Hypnodrama is a merging of hypnotherapy with psychodrama.

Psychodramatic Shock. The patient is asked to throw himself back into a hallucinatory experience while it is still vivid. He does not describe it; he must act. He puts his body in the position in which it was then, in the space he was in, at the time of day or night when this incident actually occurred. He may select a staff member to recreate the hallucinatory involvement.

The patient may resist being placed again into the horrifying experience from which he has just emerged. His natural bent is to forget, not to talk about it, to leave it behind. He is full of fears that his newfound freedom may be shattered. The mere recall frightens him, and the idea of enactment frightens him still more. The psychodramatic director explains that the purpose is to learn control, not merely to relive the experience, that re-enactment will help him build resources against recurrence.

Once the patient has warmed himself up again into the psychotic state and has thoroughly enacted it, the director stops him and helps the patient realize that he can construct his own inner controls.

Improvisation. The patient is brought into the psychodrama theatre or the life situation without any prior preparation. The director has structured the situation in advance with the aid of auxiliary egos. The subject is then asked to warm up to the situation as he would if it were actually happening to him.

The patient is told he is in his car, driving on the highway. He is alone. Suddenly he hears a siren and a police car comes alongside, then ahead of him. The policemen stops him, walks over to him, demands to see his license, and gives him a tongue-lashing because he was driving 20 miles over the speed limit. He gives him a ticket for speeding.

Or:

The subject enters a cafeteria. An auxiliary ego, obviously the worse for indulgence in alcohol, approaches him and asks for money.

Numerous sets of standard situations have been devised, and they enable the director and group members to get a profile of the action potential of the individual that paper-and-pencil tests are unable to uncover.

Didactic Psychodrama. In this teaching method, auxiliary egos, nurses, social workers, psychologists, and psychiatrists take the role of a patient, in a situation of everyday occurrence, such as a patient who refuses to obey rules as they are applied in a hospital or clinic. The psychodrama students also take their own professional roles. The training situations are structured according to typical conflicts with which they are familiar or which they are likely to face in their professional roles. Several versions of how to deal with the obstreperous patient can be represented by various students. Real patients need not be involved.

Another teaching application is to have staff members sit in on actual patient session, becoming involved as seems necessary. In this technique, the patient represents himself, and the staff members represent themselves. Role reversal between a staff member and the patient intensifies learning, with each getting a new perception of their relationship, the responsibility in being a staff member, and the agony of being a patient.

It seems obvious that some sort of bias must operate in every type of social investigator, whether he be a case interviewer, a participant observer, an intelligence tester, a psychoanalyst, or a sociometrist. It follows, therefore, that no experiment in the social sciences can be entirely controlled unless and until the social investigator himself is explored and his bias brought under control. An attempt to accomplish this under laboratory conditions would be extremely difficult because of the lack of adequate motivation for both the investigator and his subjects to undertake such a program. A life situation cannot easily be manufactured under laboratory conditions.

In psychodramatic work, however, the very atmosphere and purpose require the presentation of life situations, on the one hand, and analysis of the total situation on the other. Psychodramatic work partakes automatically of investigating the social investigator because its major tools for treatment, the director and the auxiliary egos, cannot effectively be used unless they are continuously examined and maintained at their keenest temper. Therefore, the psychodramatic procedure presents itself as doubly fitted to investigate every type of social investigator in his natural setting and to protect the results of his work from any admixture of bias.

Psychodrama and Narcosynthesis. Under the influence of drugs, the patient relives certain experiences or, after having undergone drug therapy, needs to integrate his experience as it unfolded inside of him while he was unable to communicate those experiences. There are two variables: the drug—for instance, thiopental sodium (Pentothal sodium®, Abbott)—and the enactment of the inner worlds. The question here is which variable contributes what to the treatment.

Family Psychodrama. Husband and wife or mother and child are treated as a combine, often facing each other, rather than separately, because separate from each other they may not have any tangible mental ailment. In the course of this approach the family members may reverse roles, double for each other, and, in general, serve as each other's auxiliary ego.

Videotape and Television in Psychodrama. Television is a medium in which interpersonal action of the moment is the final desideratum. It is a medium which is continuously changing, and in which the attention of the participants is shifting from one task to another without warning. Under these conditions, split-second judgment and responsive spontaneity will be most rigorously challenged. One of the earliest studies of the use of videotape and television for group psychotherapy and psychodrama was made by the author in 1942.

Psychodrama's main features—the group or audience, the director, a staff of egos, the emergence of one or more protagonists, and the dramatic action between them—can be maintained in television productions. It is of great therapeutic values that the total process of interaction between group members is televised.

CLINICAL EXAMPLES

Psychodrama of Adolf Hitler

Christs and Napoleons are frequently embodied by mental patients, but a pseudo-Hitler is apparently unique in the literature. The author treated such a patient in 1941, at the beginning of World War II, and first reported the case in 1956. Here are a few highlights of the case of Karl Miller, a German immigrant, who was caught by the Hitler contagion.

The therapist is in his office. The door opens, and the nurse comes in.
Nurse: Doctor, there is a man outside. He wants to see you.
Therapist: You know I can't see anyone. I'm about to give a session in the theatre, and the students are waiting.
Nurse: He claims he has an appointment. He does not want to give his name.
Therapist: Try to find out who he is and what he wants.
(Nurse leaves and returns.)
Nurse: He insists that he has an appointment with you. He won't go away.
Therapist: Well, let him come in.
(The door opens, and a man enters. He is in his early forties. Therapist and man look at each other; their eyes meet. The man looks familiar.)
Karl (challengingly): Don't you know who I am?
Therapist: I'm sorry, I don't.
Karl (sharply): Well, my name is Adolf Hitler.
(The therapist is taken aback. Indeed, the man looks the part—the same hypnotic eyes, the way of brushing his hair, the moustache.
The therapist rises from his seat and thinks, "He carries his body the same way, makes the same gestures, speaks in the same shrieking, penetrating voice.")
Therapist: Of course, now I recognize you. (The therapist is flustered and uneasy; he sits down again and tries to be as formal as possible.) Won't you sit down, Mr. Hitler?
(Karl takes a seat. The therapist opens his record book.)
Therapist: Your first name, please?
Karl: But don't you know? Adolf!
Therapist: Oh, yes, Adolf Hitler. Where do you live?
Karl (surprised and annoyed): In Berchtesgaden, of course!
Therapist: In Berchtesgaden, oh yes. But why have you come to me?
Karl: Don't you know? Didn't she tell you?
Therapist: Who?
Karl: My wife.
Therapist: Oh, yes, now I remember.
(The therapist recalls that about three months ago a woman came to see him. She spoke of her husband, who owned a meat market on Third Avenue in the heart of Yorkville. She was depressed, and she cried. She said, "My husband has changed; he is sick. His real name is Karl, and now he calls himself Adolf. He believes he is Hitler. I don't know what to do with him." The therapist said, "Why don't you let him come to see me?" Now here he is.)
Karl: Is there anything you can do for me?
Therapist: I may, but first tell me what happened.
Karl (becoming excited again): But didn't she tell you? I organized the party for him, and he took my name. I wrote *Mein Kampf*

but he took it away from me! I was in jail for him for two years. He took everything I have—my inspiration, my brainpower, my energy. Right now, as I'm sitting here, he takes it all from me, every minute. That scoundrel! I can't stop him; maybe you can. (He puts his head on the therapist's shoulder and weeps.) Oh, help me, help me! I will make you the chief of all the doctors in the Third Reich.

(The therapist begins to feel more at home in the situation. He reaches for the telephone and speaks to the nurse. A moment later, two men come in—one fat, one skinny. The therapist performs the introductions.)

Therapist: Mr. Goering, Mr. Hitler; Mr. Goebbels, Mr. Hitler. (The two men are male nurses, trained auxiliary egos. Karl accepts them without question, is happy to see them, and shakes hands with them. He seems to know them well.)

Therapist: Gentlemen, let us all go into the theatre. Mr. Hitler wishes to make an announcement.

(All four proceed to the psychodrama theatre.)

The opening session is crucial for the course of psychodramatic treatment. The therapist has a clue, which Karl's wife gave him. She had come home after a short vacation and had seen the walls of their apartment covered with Hitler's pictures. All day long her husband had stood before the mirror trying to imitate Hitler's speech and the way he ate and walked. Karl neglected his business and took a job as doorman of a motion picture house so he could wear a uniform and make converts for the cause. He and his wife no longer slept in the same bedroom; he had his own room. He did not seem to care for her anymore. She asked him what all this meant, but he became violently angry. Theoretically, this incident would have been an excellent clue for the first episode; however, it might throw off the production because at this moment the wife has no reality for him; in psychodramatic jargon, he has not warmed up to this episode. But he is intrigued with the fellows who portray Goering and Goebbels.

In the psychodrama theatre, the therapist suggests that Karl present his case to the German people. The theatre is filled with nurses, patients, doctors, and students. Karl steps forward and makes an announcement to the German People, speaking over a public address system. He states that he is the real Hitler; the other is an imposter. The German people should eject the imposter! He will return triumphantly to Germany to take over the helm. The group receives his proclamation with spontaneous applause. A few scenes follow swiftly: Karl returns to Germany on a boat. He calls a meeting of the war cabinet, planning with his ministers the future of the Third Reich. He ends the first session with a moving scene at the grave of his mother, whom he had lost at the age of 18.

For many weeks the psychodrama group has sessions with Karl at regular intervals. He is provided with all the characters he needs to put his plans of conquering the world into operation (technique of self-realization). He seems to know everything in advance; many things he presents on the stage come very close to what actually took place years later. He appears to have a special sense for fitting himself into moods and decisions that were made thousands of miles apart from him. In fact, at times the group members speculate whether Karl is not the real Hitler and the other in Germany his double. They have the strange experience of feeling the real Hitler among them, working desperately to find a solution for himself. They see him often alone with his mother or sweetheart, bursting out in tears, fighting with astrologists for an answer when he is in doubt, praying in his solitude to God for help, knocking his head on the wall, fearing that he may become insane before he can attain the great victory. At other times, he portrays moods of great desperation, feelings that he has failed and that the Reich will be conquered by its enemies. In one of these moods, he steps upon the stage and declares that the time has come for him to end his life. He asks all the Gestapo leaders who fill the audience—from Goering, Goebbels, von Ribbentrop, and Hess down to the last man— to die with him. He orders that the music of Gotterdammerung be played to accompany the death orgy. He shoots himself in front of the audience. Many years later, when the real Hitler killed himself and his wife in his Berlin bunker, the therapist recalled the strange coincidence that the poor butcher from Yorkville should have anticipated the future of world history so closely.

Many times, Karl and the therapist stand alone on the stage, eye to eye, involved in conversation. "What's the matter with me?" he says, "Will this torture never end? Is it real, or is it a dream?" Such intimate dialogues prove to be of unique value for the progress of therapy. It is at the height of psychodramatic production that rare levels of intensive reflection are reached.

One day, due to the intimate rapport Karl has established with "Goering" and "Goebbels" in the production of his inner life, he begins to become more intimate with them. During an intermission of one session he says to Goering:

"Hello, Goering, what do you think of the joke I made on the stage today?" And they laugh together. But suddenly Karl swats Goering. Goering responds in kind, and a regular fist-fight takes place on the spot, during which Karl takes a bad beating. Later they enjoy a glass of beer together. From then on, the ice gradually melts.

The result of the physical contact between Karl and Goering is that Karl permits the auxiliary ego to call him Adolf, and he calls him Herman. They act like pals; their relationship is full of homosexual undertones. From then on Herman begins to get an inside hold on Karl's thoughts and feelings. The psychodrama group begins to use this relationship as a therapeutic guide, for now Karl is able to accept correction from Herman. The productions on the stage are greatly facilitated by getting clues from the auxiliary ego as to how to direct the production.

The point is that a therapist who is unable to establish a working rapport with a noncooperative patient in a physician-patient situation may be able to produce one by means of the psychodramatic method. In the case of the pseudo-Hitler, who was noncooperative to an extreme, it was possible to warm him up to a level of communication when an auxiliary ego portrayed the role of Goering in an episode relevant to his psychotic world. Once Karl had established rapport with the auxiliary ego on the psychodramatic stage, he was able to develop a relationship with the private person, a therapeutic nurse, who was playing Goering. Karl began to communicate spontaneously with him on a realistic level. This was the turning point in the therapeutic process.

About three months after treatment begins, a strange event occurs. The group is gathered in the theatre, waiting for Karl's next session. Goering comes to the therapist.

Auxiliary ego: Adolf wants a haircut.

Therapist: Well, call a barber.

(This is the first time since Karl fell ill that he has allowed anyone to touch his hair. A barber comes and cuts his hair according to Karl's instructions—on stage. When the ceremony is over, the barber starts to pack his instruments, getting ready to leave. Suddenly, Karl looks sharply at the group, at the therapist, then at the barber.)

Karl (pointing at his moustache): Take this off! The barber immediately soaps Karl's face and applies the razor. The moustache is gone. A tense silence has descended on the audience.)

Karl (rising from his chair, pointing at his face): It's gone, it's gone, it's gone, it's over!

(Starting to weep) I lost it, I lost it! Why did I do it? I shouldn't have done it!

Gradually, changes take place in Karl from session to session—changes in his body and behavior, the look in his eyes, his smile, the words he speaks. Still later he asks to be called Karl and not Adolf. He asks his wife to come to the sessions. For the first time in many months, he kisses her in a scene on the stage.

These episodes, from a large psychodramatic protocol, illustrate the rapid diagnostic picture a protagonist may give, often within a single psychodramatic session. The patient made a good social recovery and returned to Germany a few years later, after the war. His case proves the hypothesis that acting-out techniques are the choice for acting-out syndromes.

The highlight of the sessions with Karl was the intense participation of the group. The longer the sessions went on, the more it became apparent that the true hero of this psychodrama was the audience. After the second session, Karl began to sit in the audience as one of the members of the group, and he became the center of attractions and repulsions. At times the group became involved in the production to such a degree that everyone, without exception, sided with Karl; at other times, everyone became involved in a negative way and reacted as if Karl were the real Hitler. Many episodes resulting from the interactions were acted out on the stage, mixing the events in Karl's delusion with the actualities of the group.

Sociograms and role diagrams, which were compared from session to session, showed that there were a few little Hitlers in the group. A magnificent panorama of the contemporary world emerged in bold relief, caught in the miniature mirror of this group. Careful analysis of the responses, as well as of the production, suggested that the real Adolf Hitler might have profited greatly if he had participated in psychodramatic sessions during his adolescence and that World War II might have been averted or, at least, have taken a different form.

Karl learned to see his own private paranoiac world in the perspective of the larger world that he had unconsciously provoked. He gave us a number of clues, suggesting the dynamic forces operating in the development of his mental syndrome. Why did he want to become Hitler? He said once: "I had a dream since I was a little boy to conquer the world or destroy it, and I imitated Hitler because he tried the same." What helped him to recover from his obsession? He said: "I was surprised to see in the group so many others besides me who had the dream of becoming Hitler. That helped me."

Psychodrama of an Obsessional Neurosis

William is a likable, fair-haired youngster of 18. He seems quiet and rather well-mannered, and his intelligence is well above average. In a number of preliminary interviews with the therapist, William has displayed remarkable honesty, and this trait carries over onto the psychodramatic stage.

William's problem is a severe form of obsessional neurosis. He thinks of people dying. He has vague images, not of the people themselves but of things related to their deaths—funeral parlors, cemeteries, and the like—which cause him to feel anxious. To combat this feeling he employs several devices. For instance, he coughs loudly and frequently, hoping to disrupt the unpleasant train of thought. In the meantime, he disturbs the entire household, and the coughing is not at an end. Out of this primary cough arises a secondary cough, which is almost a nervous reflex, and after this stage William begins to cough because he is hoarse—a tertiary stage. This cycle may go on for several days at a time.

William also seeks relief in loud talking, usually swearing at the images that disturb him, trying to drive them away by a name-calling process. In doing so, he upsets all the people with whom he lives. Sometimes he starts to shout vile imprecations while walking through the streets. More often he is at home, and the noise disturbs everyone in the house. Patterns of profanity tend to creep into his ordinary conversation. His parents are continually having to take him to task, and he gets the name of bad boy.

One way to get relief at times from his feelings of anxiety is to take a bath. Again, he annoys the other members of his social atom, for he frequently feels it necessary to take baths in the middle of the night. Sometimes he is content to let the water run, and the noise of the running water is sufficient to take his thoughts away from unpleasant things. Inevitably, he disturbs others.

These manifestations and the resulting criticism of his behavior have brought William to a point where he fears the return of his unpleasant thoughts rather than the thoughts themselves. His feeling of anxiety has become a fear of fear itself. He becomes subject to this fear whenever he passes a funeral parlor or a cemetery, whenever he reads a word that has unpleasant associations. His thoughts become a continual battleground on which part of his psyche fights back at the fears engendered by the other part.

After a short interview with William, the psychodramatic director selects a staff member to act as an auxiliary ego to represent Williams' outward self and tells William to portray his own inner thoughts.

William is not sure about the role he is to portray. The staff member, his auxiliary ego, has never met him before and tries to get him to describe the processes of thought he undergoes at times of stress and anxiety. William, who seems most anxious for the portrayal to be an honest one, keeps repeating that he cannot see the point of the scene. The staff member persuades him to go ahead and act whatever role and situation comes into his mind.

A scene is finally chosen in which William is walking past a funeral parlor on his way to his club. He describes the scene to the audience:

William: This scene is at the intersection of two streets in New York. I am walking down the street to the club to have a swim, and I am just rounding the corner.

(The staff member, as William's auxiliary ego, follows William like a shadow as he walks around the circular stage. He tries to copy William in everything but speech, and here he is forced to push the dialogue in order to stimulate William.)

Auxiliary ego: I wonder who I'm going to meet today.

William: I see Jim down there ahead.

Auxiliary ego: I've got to get in some work at that racing start today.

William: I always was afraid of the water. I'll never learn to dive and swim.

Auxiliary ego: There's nothing wrong with the water. It's perfectly safe. The only thing is, I can't seem to let go of the edge of the pool.

William: Two more blocks and I'll be there. I guess I'll walk a little faster.

Auxiliary ego: I wonder what those fellows up ahead are doing? Four or five, aren't there?

William (opposite the funeral parlor): I won't look over there. I've got to do something. I guess I'll concentrate on going swimming. I don't want to spoil the whole day. It will if it keeps on like this.

Auxiliary ego: I'd better not look over there.

William (looking upward): It's getting cold—I hope it doesn't rain. Ha! (Obvious relief) I'm past there already. There's the club ahead, there. When I get there, I'll be safe. There will be nothing to disturb my imagination there!

Auxiliary ego: What happened with those cars back there? I heard the brakes, but I'd better not look.

William: If I hurry in and get into the pool, I'll be all right.

(The scene ends here. William seems relieved.)

The psychodramatic director asks William

whether, during the scene, he did not feel the urge to cough, as certainly would have happened in real life. William claims that he felt no real anxiety during the scene. Another scene is tried, without any preparation, in which William is reading a newspaper. The results are similar to those in the preceding scene. William avoids all but the most obscure references to the things he fears. When the psychodramatic director interrupts to ask him why he does not swear or cough, he explains that he does not have any feeling of panic. He says that he is not warmed up to the part. On the stage, William does exactly what he would do in real life—he avoids all references to or thoughts of those things that create deep panic in him.

During these two scenes, the auxiliary ego has had an opportunity to see which ideas elicit responses from William and which seeds of thought fall on barren ground. Therefore, he can guide his actions in future scenes accordingly.

This situation on the psychodramatic stage may be compared to that which takes place inside a gasoline engine at the moment the starting pedal is pressed. The auxiliary ego tries to supply the spark: he tries to bridge the gap that exists between his own mental processes and those of the patient. If he succeeds, he ignites the fuel of ideas, and as long as fresh ideas continue to be supplied, the spontaneity remains on a high level. Then, just like the driver whose engine has begun a comfortable hum, one may expect progress.

In the analysis immediately following the two scenes, the psychodramatic director makes this comment: "William *wants* to work himself up! He must be encouraged so that he comes to a complete presentation."

William has attempted, for the first time, to portray his obsessions on the psychodramatic stage. He has failed, it is true, but in the very moment of failure he recognizes that the fault lies largely within himself. He admits this when he says that he is not warmed up, that he cannot seem to act the part. He does not realize it at the time, but this is actually a part of the process by which he will become warmed up in the future. He is beginning to get an idea of what is expected of him on the psychodramatic stage. He has had some experience, however slight, in one of its most difficult techniques. Gradually, he will be able to act out, on a psychodramatic level, those fears from which he flees in actual life. The scenes in which William has appeared, if taken as part of this process, cannot be deemed failures.

Now the psychodramatic director tries another tack. He gives his reasons in a discussion that follows the scene: "When a person has a clear delu-sion—if it is really clear and systematic—the person may be able to give a picture of what he experiences which is clear in every detail. But when we are dealing with people who have nothing but a rudimentary idea of their delusions, the auxiliary egos are at sea as to what to do. Then the technique is to increase the proportions of their ideas—not to present mere copies—insofar as we have been able to discover them."

The psychodramatic director gets William to describe the undertaking establishment he passes so often, the sight of which disturbs him so greatly. Then he selects two staff members to portray the undertaker and his wife. He tells William to direct the scene by telling the actors how he would imagine it. The directorial method here employed is known as the projection technique. William, however, claims that he has never allowed his fears to go that far and, therefore, has no mental picture of what goes on inside the funeral parlor. Consequently, the psychodramatic director instructs the staff members to go ahead on their own and to depict not a copy of a real undertaking parlor but a wholly imaginary one, with every detail magnified and exaggerated. The purpose is to depict an undertaking establishment that confirms William's fears of what a real one must be like.

The result is a macabre performance tinged at all times with the grotesque. The staff workers are highly imaginative, and, gradually, four or five corpses take ghostly shape on the stage as the actors make physical comments and comparisons and, now and then, a grimly humorous remark. Several spectators become extremely uneasy during this scene, and William is among them. Still, when the psychodramatic director questions him at the conclusion of the scene, he says that he had never allowed himself to think about the life within a funeral parlor. Two other scenes are improvised by staff members, portraying happenings in a funeral parlor, and William, as a spectator, is given a picture he might have imagined had his fears permitted him to go so far. This technique gives him something he has never been able to produce by himself, either consciously or unconsciously. It furnishes a basis for future conjecture on his part.

In the discussion after these scenes, the technique employed shows its first effect. A hitherto hidden piece of information is forthcoming from William: He has actually met the undertaker who runs this funeral parlor, the exterior of which is so familiar to him. Up to this time William has persistently denied knowing him, but now it appears that he has met him and that the incident occurred at a gas station two blocks away from the funeral parlor. William is at once requested to portray this scene with the aid of the auxiliary ego with whom he worked previously.

It is in this scene that the auxiliary ego is first able to perform his function for William properly. Indeed, he also acts as a starter for William in the preparation.

The real scene, as described by William, contained two or three lines of dialogue and lasted no more than 30 seconds. William protests that he cannot see what the psychodramatic director will be able to get out of it. The auxiliary ego, however, persuades William to allow the scene to continue beyond what actually happened, pointing out that the director would like to know what William's reactions might have been if he had had a longer conversation with the undertaker. William finally agrees, and the following scene takes place:

The scene is a gas station. William plays himself. The undertaker is played by the auxiliary ego. William is in the gas station when the undertaker appears and puts money into the cigarette machine.

Auxiliary ego: Have you seen the attendant around anywhere?

William (staring at the ground): I guess he's out back, working on a car.

Auxiliary ego: He's never here when I want him—always out back or out to lunch.

William: I don't know. I guess so. I'm around here a lot of time.

Auxiliary ego: Do you do any work here?

William: No, just hang around.

Auxiliary ego: Well, say, I need a part-time assistant over at my place. How would you like to work for me? (William begins to shake his head slowly but doesn't say anything.) It would only take a couple of hours in the afternoon or evening, running errands and answering the phone. I could afford to pay pretty well for your time.

William: Well I don't think I'd have the time. I have homework.

Auxiliary ego (interrupting): Oh, you'd have plenty of time for that at my place. I just need someone to be there while I'm out and to do occasional errands and odd jobs. You'd have plenty of time for your homework.

William: Well, I have a sort of job already, running errands for people on the block.

Auxiliary ego: You don't make much at that, do you? I could afford to pay you ten dollars a week to start.

William: Well, I do pretty well on this other job.

Auxiliary ego: How much do you make a week?

William: Oh, three, four—sometimes five dollars a week.

Auxiliary ego: But I could pay you ten, and you'd be sure of it. Ten dollars a week—steady money—is not something to be sneezed at. That's for just being around to answer the phone and run a few errands. You'd have plenty of time for yourself and your homework.

William: Well, I don't know. You see, these people on our block sort of depend on me to do their errands. I wouldn't want to disappoint them.

Auxiliary ego: I realize that, but, after all, when you can make more than twice as much, and be sure of it! Why, I should think you could tell them, and they'd understand. (During this speech, the auxiliary ego tries to put his hand on William's shoulder. William pulls away, avoiding his touch.)

William: Well, they kind of count on me, and I wouldn't want to disappoint them.

Auxiliary ego: Sure you won't change your mind?

William: No, I wouldn't want to disappoint those people.

Auxiliary ego: Well, in case you do change your mind, let me know. You know where my place is, don't you?

William: Yeah, but I don't think. . . .

Auxiliary ego: Fine! Let's see, you're William—William Morrow.

William (barely audible): Yes.

Auxiliary ego: Yes, I thought I knew you. I had heard you were a good worker. That's why I wanted to hire you. You live right down the block, don't you?

William (pauses): Yes.

Auxiliary ego: In case something comes up, I'll drop you a card or come down to see you. I really need an assistant badly, and I may be able to pay a little more than ten dollars a week. I'll have to see. What number do you live at?

William: Right down the street. In the next block.

Auxiliary ego: You're sure you won't change your mind? (William simply shakes his head and looks away.) Now, let me see. What number was that you said you lived at?

William (after a pause): Sixty-five.

Auxiliary ego: Fine, fine! I'll see you soon. In case you change your mind in the meantime, drop into my place. I'll be glad to see you.

Throughout the scene, William presents an astonishing contrast to his usual self. He looks at the auxiliary ego only once or twice during the dialogue. Most of the time he looks at the ground, and occasionally he turns his head away. He is very nervous and plays with a chair on the stage. He keeps this chair, like a bulwark, between him and the auxiliary ego, and when the latter moves past it and attempts to put his hand on William's shoulder, the patient involuntarily pulls away.

Here, at last, William finally accepts the auxiliary ego—in the role of the undertaker. William is afraid of this person and everything for which he stands, and his fear shows in his voice, in his gestures, and even in the ideas he expresses on the psychodramatic stage. He clings desperately to a flimsy excuse to keep from taking an excellent job. He does not want this job because he is afraid, but he does not want to admit this fear, either to himself or to his auxiliary ego.

In this scene, William has achieved a certain catharsis. The original meeting with the undertaker consumed only a few seconds.

In view of his actions on the psychodramatic stage, it does not seem possible that he could have subjected this man to any long drawn-out scrutiny. The picture he carried away from that meeting must have been a shadowy one, even as his fears have become shadowy things through his refusal to confront them. Here, on the psychodramatic stage, William is given an opportunity to study this terrifying creature at greater length. The undertaker is presented to him as a normal man, and many of the blank spaces in the original picture are now filled in. The fear of the unknown has been replaced by knowledge. This is the first step and, indeed, the *sine qua non* for the removal of that fear.

The psychodramatic director now suggests a scene to take place in William's home. William is to be thinking about this encounter with the undertaker, and his ego conflict is to be portrayed by himself and his auxiliary ego. The latter must now make a complete about-face and become the part of William's mental processes that mirrors the fears, while William himself is to represent the part that fights them.

During the preparation, William shows a great advance over his previous effort. Before, he had been unsure of himself because he did not know what he was expected to do. Now he knows almost exactly what is required of him, and the assistance of the auxiliary ego is invaluable to him.

Although he still cannot translate his fears into actions, he knows that certain things upset him and that others do not. He cites the scene between the undertaker and his wife as one that might have taken place in his mind. He says that his fears do not lie in that direction, that their basis is not in the gory details of death but rather in the idea that lies behind death. He says to the auxiliary ego: "You can talk all you want to about bloody corpses without upsetting me. It's just words like 'funeral parlor,' 'undertaker,' and things like that which start me off." He tends to visualize scenes and people, like the funeral parlor and the undertaker, "as if someone had suddenly turned on a hidden motion picture machine." These visualized scenes also start attacks of anxiety.

The auxiliary ego suggests to William that he try to visualize the meeting with the undertaker at the start of the scene. And thus begins a new scene in which the staff member functions again as William's double ego.

At the start of the scene there is a long pause. William obviously has a hard time breaking through his fears. Therefore, the auxiliary ego begins to talk for him, starting the warming up for William.

Auxiliary ego: Funny, I can't seem to keep from thinking about his face. I keep seeing him again the way he was in the gas station.

William: I'd better not think about him.

Auxiliary ego: Yes, but I can't seem to stop. He was a funny-looking guy.

William (in a very surly tone): Wanted to know where the attendant was.

Auxiliary ego: Why wasn't the attendant there, anyway? He should have been.

William: Why couldn't he have had the change in his pocket instead of having to ask for the attendant?

Auxiliary ego: Why did he have to come there, anyway? It's almost two blocks away from his place.

William: He could have gotten his cigarettes in a cigarette place. Why did he have to come to a gas station to get his cigarettes?

Auxiliary ego: Maybe the attendant is a friend of his. Or maybe he gets something else there . . . . (William coughs.)

William (coughing): Why did this have to happen to me? Why me, of all people? (Coughs.)

Auxiliary ego: He should have known the attendant was out back. He shouldn't have had to ask me. He has a funny voice, anyway.

William: Why does this sort of thing always have to happen to me? (Coughs)

Auxiliary ego: And then he offered me a job. As if I'd ever take a job in his place!

William (coughs): Better not think about that! (Coughs.)

Auxiliary ego: But I can't help it. Just because it's an undertaking parlor is no reason why I should keep on thinking about it.

William: I don't want to think about it.

Auxiliary ego: But I do. Those brass plates. "Funeral Parlor."

William: In gold letters.

Auxiliary ego: I wonder why they shine them so? You'd think they would paint them black instead of making them so bright.

William (coughs): It's nothing to brag about. (Coughs.) Well, better not think about it. Guess I'll try to read this newspaper.

Auxiliary ego: Oh-oh! Don't want to read that page!

William: No, sir! I'll turn it over and see what's on the next page.

Auxiliary ego: Who wants to read funeral notices, anyway?

William (coughs): There's nothing to them, anyway. (Coughs.)

Auxiliary ego: (coughs, which brings an immediate responding cough from William.) The first one was Charles B. Rogers. I wonder what he was like?

William (coughs): Better not think about him. (Coughs.)

Auxiliary ego: They had a picture of him.

William: Oh, why did I have to see that?

Auxiliary ego: He's a funny-looking duck. Kind of like that undertaker I met in the gas station.

William: There I go again! Why must I think about him? Or gas stations? Now every time I think about gas stations, I'll start thinking about him again. (William is quite excited during this speech. His voice is much louder than it has heretofore been.)

Auxiliary ego: And that place of his! (Coughs.) I wonder what it's like inside?

William: No, I don't. I don't even want to think about the outside! (Coughs.)

Auxiliary ego: I suppose his friend knows what it's like inside. I wonder if he lives in there?

William (coughs): I wouldn't want to live in there! (Coughs.)

Auxiliary ego: I wonder if he has any friends? I suppose he must have. I wonder what they're like?

William: I suppose even an undertaker has to have friends. I don't want to be one of them! (Coughs.)

Auxiliary ego: No, sir! I don't even want to go near him!

William (coughs): I don't even want to think about him!

Auxiliary ego: Or his place.

William: Guess I'll get up and go for a walk. Anything to get my mind off him! (They get up and turn to go left.)

Auxiliary ego: Oh-oh! I don't want to go that way!

William (turning right): No, sir! I'll go this way!

Throughout this scene, neither William nor his auxiliary ego used many gestures. Except for a desultory bit of pantomime when he was supposed to be reading the paper, William spent the entire time rubbing the palm of his left hand with the thumb and fingers of his right. The auxiliary ego attempted at all times to duplicate these actions. William used this continual rubbing to alleviate the tension caused by his anxiety. The auxiliary ego, who had started to use this gesture for no reason other than imitation, found it an excellent antidote for the tension he, too, felt as the scene progressed. William's tension was caused by anxiety, which stemmed from his fear of the ideas being presented to him. The auxiliary ego was also laboring under a strain, but his anxiety arose from a different source. He was trying to fire each speech the instant William ceased uttering his lines. To do this, he, like a chess player, had to keep thinking several moves ahead. But he was denied the advantage of taking whatever time he needed. He always had to be prepared, and several times he was forced to discard whole trains of thought while he shifted to meet William's changing ideas. Despite this basic difference in attitude, the same physical release—hand-rubbing—served as an outlet for both.

The auxiliary ego coughed twice during the scene. He did this deliberately, to see how it would affect William. The first time his auxiliary coughed, William immediately echoed him. Later, the auxiliary ego's cough seemed to have no effect. And what of William's own coughing? In the interview immediately after the scene, the director asked William if he was aware that he had coughed. William said that he had coughed deliberately, to make the scene seem real. But when the director asked him how often he had done so, he replied, "Three or four times." As a matter of actual fact, William coughed 18 times. On the psychodramatic stage, William reproduced the physical symptoms of his obsession. The scene would seem to have forced him into a relapse. But what is actually taking place is a channeling of his fears.

To continue channeling William's fears, the psychodramatic director selects a final scene for the session. William had accepted the production on the stage of what goes on inside an imaginary funeral parlor, something he had not dared imagine for himself. In this final scene, William is asked to take the logical next step—to go inside this imaginary funeral parlor and accept the job he was offered in the gas station scene, to inhabit this imaginary setting.

While preparing the scene with his auxiliary ego, William at first displays extreme reluctance. He points out that he would not take the job for a salary two or three times as large as the one offered. When pressed, he admits that he would not take it for $100 a week; later he amplifies this figure to $1,000,000. The auxiliary ego persuades him to accept the job by saying that it is intended as a test. This shows the cumulative effect of all the scenes in which William has thus far participated on the psychodramatic stage. In the first part of the session he would not have consented to this test. Now he can be persuaded to try it, although he does so with obvious reluctance and a certain amount of trepidation.

Auxiliary ego: Why, hello, William. Glad to see you!

William (staring at the floor): Hello.

Auxiliary ego: Well, well! So you decided to change your mind about taking that job after all! That's fine!

William: I guess so. What do I have to do?

Auxiliary ego: Nothing right now. Just sit down and make yourself comfortable. Would you like to look around first? Come on! I'll show you the place.

(The auxiliary ego, as the undertaker, shows William where various things are located in the office, then takes him to a basement room, where the bodies are kept until the funerals. William stops at the point that represents the door of this room and contents himself with peering vaguely inside. Then the auxiliary ego points to the wall telephone.)

Auxiliary ego: This is an extension of the upstairs phone. In case the phone rings and you're down here, you can answer it without having to go upstairs.

William: But I wouldn't be down here, would I?

Auxiliary ego: Well, no. Probably not. But you might be down here doing some odd job or other, and it would save you the trip upstairs.

William: I thought I was just supposed to run errands and answer the phone. I thought I would have time to do my homework.

Auxiliary ego: So you will, so you will. It's just that once in a while there are a few things to be done down here. You won't mind that, will you?

William: I guess not.

Auxiliary ego: (as they are returning to the office): Once in a while I may need a hand bringing in the bodies, but that's not very heavy work. (Here William starts to say something, but the auxiliary ego interrupts.) They come in light pine boxes, and they don't weigh very much. (William walks almost to the edge of the stage and stares at the back of the audience. The auxiliary ego continues.) Right now, there's nothing to do. (William sighs and returns, sitting down at the desk.) I guess you can sit here and start in on your homework. (The auxiliary ego now goes back to the basement room and opens one of the coffins.) Say, William, could you bring me

some of that formaldehyde? There's a bottle on the shelf over there. (William goes to the shelf and takes down a bottle. He hesitates, but then the auxiliary ego speaks again.) Just bring it down here to me. (William does this and starts back upstairs again.) Just a minute. Don't go yet. I can use a hand here. (He pantomimes filling a syringe with formaldehyde.) Now, I want you to take the wrist here and press so that the vein sticks out— like this. (He pantomimes this action.)

William: I'd rather not.

Auxiliary ego: Why not? (Pause.) Oh, come on! It won't bite you!

William (barely audible): Show me how you did that again.

Auxiliary ego: You take it like this and put one finger here and one here. Then you press down, like this. (William bends down very slowly and copies the pantomime. His neck is very stiff and he tries to hold his head as far away from the corpse as possible.) That's fine! Kind of cold, isn't it? (William lets go of the hand.) Hey! Wait till I'm through! There we are. Nothing to it after all, was there?

Here, at last, William is brought to the very threshold of his fears. Here, on the psychodramatic stage, he has been shown the handiwork of death, and he has held the cold hand of a corpse in his. In talking with him afterward, the therapist learned that he had been able to visualize the hand at the time. His actions on the stage were convincing evidence of this fact, and the end of the scene brought him obvious relief.

Here, in this crucial situation, the interested spectator stands, as it were, on a peak. Now he can see clearly the road by which William has been brought to this point, and the direction in which he will be led. The carefully organized and integrated plan that has been followed by the psychodramatic director becomes apparent.

William, in trying to escape his fears, had come to a mental cul-de-sac. A speech in one of his scenes shows us how fraught with discomfort that blind alley must have been. In thinking of his meeting with the undertaker, William cries out: "There I go again! Why must I think about him? Or gas stations? Now every time I think about gas stations, I'll start thinking about him again."

One readily sees how impossible it was for William to maintain this position with regard to his fears. In attempting to close the door on them, he had left himself open to another set of fears. By these chains of associations, fears would one day have filled his entire mental world.

Therefore, the director began the treatment by coaxing William out of his hiding place and bringing him face to face with the fears from which he was trying to run. In this difficult operation, the auxiliary ego was an invaluable tool. The psychodramatic director, assisted by the auxiliary ego, continued to represent, on a symbolic level, the reality underlying William's fears. William would not have been willing to receive and deal with that reality otherwise. The director accomplished it by a well-planned and skillfully executed use of his therapeutic instruments.

The road that lies ahead in William's case is an interesting one. The reader can readily envisage him portraying the role of the undertaker, perhaps directing his auxiliary ego in the conduct of his calling. He may be called on to act the part of a relative of a person about to die or someone dying and thinking about his funeral or even someone who is already dead and for whom arrangements must be made. He may eventually find himself cast as Death in a psychodrama that would strike at the very root of his fears.

Whatever procedure is followed will tend to diminish the importance of the auxiliary ego's functions. The auxiliary ego will then begin to be dominated by the patient, as the latter begins to master the fears that have held him in thrall. There will be less and less need, perhaps none at all, for the auxiliary ego to act as a starter.

William himself will be able to take the corpse's hand in his and say with confidence: "There we are. Nothing to it after all, was there?" The psychodramatic director, with the aid of the auxiliary ego, has shown him the way.

The pattern of conduct or the method of approach the director exhibited in William's case shows an important deviation from the regular psychodramatic procedure, which makes the subject the chief source of initiative in the dramatization of symptoms. William had never been inside a funeral parlor. He had no knowledge of what went on in such a place. Interviews and analysis in the preparatory phase did not elicit any satisfactory information from him in regard to dreams or fantasies of any sort relating to this topic. He even violently objected to hearing anything about it. In this deadlock, the director turned to a method that may have projected some of his own bias into the treatment situation: he and a number of his assistants, instead of the patient, became the source of initiative. They constructed on the stage the atmosphere of a funeral parlor in several variations, and they let these variations pass before the patient's eyes, watching him carefully for reactions. By a combination of empathy into the patient's psychological life and a constructive ingenuity of their own, they produced, without any design on the part of the patient, something he needed, although it was not of his

creation. His own imaginative expectancy fell into step with one of these atmospheres. Thus, by means of an experience that was just as much extraconscious as it was extraunconscious, the patient attained a very effective catharsis.

The social investigators in the case, the psychodramatic director and the auxiliary egos, created for the patient something that had not previously existed for him, and they were faced with the necessity of exploring the product of their own imagination in order to compensate for a lack of the patient, thus consciously manufacturing a psychodramatic error.

Psychodrama of a Dream

This session was presented strictly in the here-and-now. Up to the last minute, the therapist did not know for certain that the Radio and Television Center of France would film the psychodramatic session he was to conduct on the afternoon of September 1, 1964, at the Faculté de Médecine at the Sorbonne.

The therapist asked for volunteers, and a couple, Pierre and Michele, stepped forward. The first scene was a confrontation of the two protagonists and a brief explanation of their dilemma after seven years of marriage. They had come to the point of total disillusionment and were ready to bring their marriage to an end. In the second scene Michele proposed that they bring her mother-in-law into the session because she appeared to be the main reason for Pierre's desire to return to America and discontinue the marriage. The scene with the mother-in-law, represented by an auxiliary ego, brought the feelings of resentment on all sides to a climax. In the third scene the therapist met Michele's children, her father Jacques, and her mother Lise. The fragmentary character of the family displayed difficulties in communication, a bilingual marriage, and a sexless life. In the fourth scene it became evident that Michele had a dream at the beginning of the courtship, which was apparently a prophetic anticipation that the marriage would end in failure. In the next scene the dream was acted out by Michele. She claimed it was the strongest dream she ever had and was as clear today as when she dreamed it. In the sixth scene, efforts for reconciliation and readaptation failed. Both partners were reluctant to go on with the marriage.

The session concluded with the participation of the audience, consisting of several hundred doctors and students, married couples, and single people. Many stepped forward to share the two protagonists' roles with them. Many had similar problems, and the sharing of the group became the climax of the psychodrama.

In psychodramatic dream presentation the therapist instructs the protagonist, "Don't tell the dream, but act it out." The patient goes to bed. He must enact every detail, recapitulating the natural process of living. The patient first assumes the role of a sleeper before he can be a dreamer. Concretization of the situation is brought about in the here-and-now instead of in an unrelated presentation and instead of just analyzing in an unrelated way.

Therapist: Michele, you will act out your dream.

Michele: I remember the place.

Therapist: The place. Where was the place? Don't tell me too much, just answer my questions.

Michele: It was in the small apartment of my mother.

Therapist: In the small apartment of your mother?

Michele: Yes.

Therapist: Your mother lived with you in the house.

Michele: Yes.

Therapist: What is her name?

Michele: Lise.

Therapist: Lise. Where is she now?

Michele: Well, she's an art teacher.

Therapist: She's an art teacher just like your father, Jacques?

Michele: Yes.

Therapist: And so you live with your mother, alone?

Michele: Yes.

Therapist: Do you see the room before you?

Michele: Very well, yes.

Therapist: Now, describe the room to me. What kind of a bed do you have?

Michele: It's a very small bed.

Therapist: A couch, a double bed, a single bed?

Michele: No, a single bed.

Therapist: A single bed. Try to describe the room. How many windows do you have in it?

Michele: Only one window.

Therapist: One window. Where does it go to, the window?

Michele: In front.

Therapist: In front of what street do you have there?

Michele: Well, on uh . . . .

Therapist: On a boulevard? What's the name of the street?

Michele: The roof of a small market.

Therapist: The roof of a small market. A meat market or what kind of market?

Michele: No, it is empty. It is not used anymore.

Therapist: It is not used anymore. Where is the bed?

Michele: The bed is here with a red blanket.

Therapist: A red blanket! That's right! I remember it now myself. It was a red blanket, and now, where is the bathroom?

Michele: It's outside.

Therapist: Outside, where?

Michele: In a little corridor.

Therapist: In a little corridor.

Michele: Yes.

Therapist: Let me see where it is. Let's walk for a minute. Here?

Michele: It's there.

Therapist: It's there. And you go through a door into the corridor, right?

Michele: Yes. I think it was in spring.

Therapist: In spring. Do you remember the day?

Michele: Not at all, no.

Therapist: Was it day or night?

Michele: It was night.

Therapist: It was at night. And you have the room alone?

Michele: Yes, I was alone, and I was sleeping.

Therapist: You were sleeping. Now the bed is here, right here. And you go to bed.

Michele: Yes.

Therapist: Well, then, go to bed. (Michele makes a sleeping motion by putting her hands along her cheek.) No. In psychodrama you have to reproduce the dream; you have to do it here. (Takes Michele over to the couch.) Now, that's wonderful. It's very nicely arranged. You have a bed here. Now, but you see in psychodrama you have to act it out. Before you go to bed, what do you do? Do you sleep in your clothes?

Michele: I sleep in my nightgown. (Goes to lie down on the couch.)

Therapist: No, no. You undress yourself first, don't you? All right, go through the motions. (Michele pretends to take off clothes.) You can't do it that way. Fiction is not permitted. You have to go through the motions so that we get the feeling that you are undressing yourself.

Michele: Yes.

Therapist: All right. A little bit.

(Michele takes off her cardigan sweater. She goes through the motions of undressing herself, step by step.)

Michele: I am putting the things on the chair.

Therapist: That's it. That's the spirit. You put it on the chair. Then you see the psychodrama dream comes back to you by doing that. You warm yourself up to it, and you warm me up to it, and everybody here is warmed up to it, Michele. And now what do you put on?

Michele: My nightgown.

Therapist: You are a beautiful girl, really. Look at her, very charming. Let me see, what do you put on?

Michele: I put on my nightgown.

Therapist: What kind of nightgown is it? Where is the nightgown? Let me see the closet.

Michele: Where is it? Here.

Therapist: In the middle of the room?

Michele: No, by the wall here. I take the things from the drawer.

Therapist: Take it out. What do you take out?

Michele: A white nightgown.

Therapist: A white nightgown. That is nice. White, are you sure?

Michele: Oh, yes.

Therapist: You remember.

Michele: Yes.

Therapist: Are you still wearing white nightgowns now?

Michele: Yes.

Therapist: That is your preference.

Michele (laughs): Yes.

Therapist: That's very nice. Well, and so it's a white nightgown. You put it on then, go ahead. Oh, let me look at you. Now, do you go to the bathroom?

Michele: Yes.

Therapist: All right then, go ahead. Do what you always do.

Michele: I fix my hair; I brush my teeth.

Therapist: You fix your hair; you wash your teeth. All right, let me look at your teeth. Some girls don't wash their teeth properly. Oh, your teeth are all right. Very good. And now?

Michele: And then I am going to bed.

Therapist: You're going to bed. And when you go to bed, do you turn the light out?

Michele: No, I'm reading usually. Should I start to read?

Therapist: Start to read; start to warm up to the act of reading.

Michele: Yes. And I'm reading a story.

Therapist: And so you are reading.

Michele: And I relax.

Therapist: You relax. Now you are coming closer and closer to sleep, right? Do you have your head on a pillow?

Michele: Yes.

Therapist: How many pillows?

Michele: Only one.

Therapist: Only one pillow. (Michele turns on her left side.) Do you sleep on your left side? That's how you always start?

Michele: Yes, I sleep easier that way.

Therapist: And what do you do with your arms, with your hands?

Michele: I sleep like that. (Folds her arms over her body.)

Therapist: You sleep like that. What do you do with your legs?

Michele: Usually they are like that. (Bends her legs under her.)

Therapist: They are just like that. You always sleep with your legs bent.

Michele: Yes, especially when I start to sleep.

Therapist: When you start to sleep, you bend them, and you just crawl together, right? You crawl together.

Michele: Yes.

Therapist: And now, you try to close your eyes. Now close your eyes and try to fall asleep, deep asleep. Try to fall asleep, deep asleep. Breathe deep. I'm breathing with you. Breathe deep. Deeper and deeper, that's it, deeper and deeper and deeper. (Very hypnotic speech.) That's right. And you fall—asleep. Now, recall your dream. Recall the dream, Michele. And now, I get you out of that trance. And now try to concentrate on the first part of the dream. Do you see it? What is first in the dream, do you see that?

Michele: Well.

Therapist: Don't tell me now. Do you see it?

Michele: Yes.

Therapist: You see it.

Michele: Yes.

Therapist: You see it. Do you see yourself in the dream?

Michele: Yes.

Therapist: What do you do in the dream? Get up and let us see how you are in the dream. Come on, get out of bed. (Michele stands up, moves sleepily.) Are you standing? Sitting? What are you doing in the dream?

Michele: I am in the Metro. (Stands up.)

Therapist: In the Metro. Oh, then let's go to the Metro, come on. You are in the Metro. What is the Metro, the subway?

Michele: The subway. (Makes long parallel movements at side of her body to indicate a train.)

Therapist: What are you doing in the Metro?

Michele: I am standing.

Therapist: You are standing. And what have you on, anything?

Michele: Yes, I'm dressed up normally.

Therapist: All dressed up normally. Is it dark, is it night, is it day?

Michele: It's very dark. I don't see much.

Therapist: You don't see much. Are you alone?

Michele: No.

Therapist: Who is there?

Michele: It's filled up with people.

Therapist: Filled with people.

Michele: Very, very crowded.

Therapist: Very, very crowded.

Michele: We are close together.

Therapist: You are close together.

Michele: Yes.

Therapist: Maybe let's have a few people here. Come close together. Let's see how it is. (Motions to some members of the audience, who get up and crowd around Michele.) Now they are all close together.

Michele: Yes.

Therapist: Yah, in the Metro. And you are in the middle. (To people surrounding Michele) Let her be in the middle, don't crowd her out. Why don't you all go there, and here's Michele. (To Michele) Is this how it is? Are there too many people here?

Michele: No, much more, much more.

Therapist: Much more, much more. And are they talking to you?

Michele: No, not at all. Everybody was dumb.

Therapist: Everybody was dumb.

Michele: Yes, and I didn't. . . .

Therapist: "I don't." Be in the present.

Michele: I don't see their faces; I don't feel them there.

Therapist: You don't feel them; they are just there.

Michele: Well, there are people, but they are very. . . .

Therapist: Are they men or women?

Michele: I don't know.

Therapist: You don't know.

Michele: I don't care.

Therapist: You don't care.

Michele: I'm lonely.

Therapist: You are alone there.

Michele: With a lot of people.

Therapist: Are you thinking of something?

Michele: Well, no.

Therapist: Are you feeling good, are you feeling good?

Michele: No, I feel empty, not explainable.

Therapist: Are you feeling comfortable; are you feeling depressed, sad?

Michele: No, no special feeling.

Therapist: No special feeling. Not explainable. You are just there. And what happens next?

Michele: Well the Metro goes very, very fast.

Therapist: The Metro, let's see, goes very, very fast. Let's see the motion. It goes very, very fast. Try to go very, very fast.

(Crowd surrounding Michele pretends to be hanging on to straps overhead and begins to sway back and forth.)

Michele: And then sometimes it stops.

Therapist: Sometimes it stops.

(People around Michele bump into each other suddenly and stop swaying.)

Michele: And I get mixed up. I don't know where to go.

Therapist: You don't know where to go.

Michele: No, I don't know if I have to stop in that station or in another one.

Therapist: You don't know where to stop.

Michele: Yes.

Therapist: You are very confused about it.

Michele: Yes. I feel empty and. . . .

Therapist: You feel empty, and you don't know where to stop.

Michele: No. That's it. And I feel completely mixed up.

Therapist: Are you in motion, or are you always standing still?

Michele. I am standing still.

Therapist: Standing still. With all these people. You don't know where to stop, and you are empty inside.

Michele: And finally. . . .

Therapist: Finally what?

Michele: Well, I want to go down the Metro and stop somewhere.

Therapist: Do you eventually go?

Michele: Well, it was not possible.

Therapist: Not possible. Why?

Michele: The Metro doesn't stop anymore.

Therapist: The Metro does not stop anymore.

Michele: No.

Therapist: Well, that is terrible. What are you doing now?

Michele: Well, I feel very. . . .

Therapist: Very what?

Michele: Full of anguish.

Therapist: Full of anguish.

Michele: Yes.

Therapist: Are you trembling? Are you crying?

Michele: No, not at all, no manifestations. Nobody can see.

Therapist: Nobody can see it, only you?

Michele: And I don't even know if there are other people in the Metro. I suppose there are some people, but very few people.

Therapist: The Metro doesn't stop anymore, and here you are all alone, and there is nobody to help you.

Michele: No, and the Metro goes very, very fast.

Therapist: The Metro goes faster and faster, and it doesn't stop.

(Crowd around Michele sways back and forth rapidly.)

Michele: I don't know where I go. And after hours like that. . . .

Therapist: Hours? Hours go by. Long time?

Michele: Long time.

Therapist: Long time. Hours and hours go by, and it doesn't stop. And what happens next?

Michele: The Metro finally stops.

Therapist: The Metro finally stops. Where?

Michele: Well, in the country, very, very far away.

Therapist: In the country very, very far away. Is it in America?

Michele: No.

Therapist: No. You don't know?

Michele: I didn't have that problem then.

Therapist: Oh, I see. (Laughs.)

Michele: No, very far away. It was completely unknown to me.

Therapist: Completely unknown to you.

Michele: In the country.

Therapist: In the country. What kind of a country is it? Do you know the streets? Does it look like French country?

Michele: Well, it was French country; trees and. . . .

Therapist: Trees. Do you see the trees?

Michele: Yes.

Therapist: What type of trees do you see?

Michele: It was not a far country at all, but just country.

Therapist: Beautiful country. Sun shining?

Michele: Yes, it was morning.

Therapist: Morning? It was morning. You remember that? You see it?

Michele: Yes.

Therapist: It's a blue sky?

Michele: Light blue, yes.

Therapist: Do you walk? Do you walk out of the Metro now?

Michele: Yes, I. . . .

Therapist: Then walk, walk, come on, walk.

Michele: I walked here, and then I was seeking for a road.

Therapist: You are seeking for a road. You seek for a road. Well, do you find a road?

Michele: No, no.

Therapist: You don't find a road.

Michele: I didn't find any road; I was lost.

Therapist: You were lost!

Michele: And I didn't have any money.

Therapist: You have no money. Maybe I can help you out, Michele. You have no money.

Michele: No.

Therapist: No. And what are you doing now?

Michele: Well, I don't know. I was there and full of anguish.

Therapist: No money. . . . What?

Michele: Full of anguish.

Therapist: Full of anxiety.

Michele: Yes. And then the dream stopped. It was the end. I woke up but. . . .

Therapist: Just a moment. What is the last thing you remember? What is the last picture you see—country, trees?

Michele: Well, the landscape and me wandering about like that.

Therapist: Do you wander in the countryside, into the streets?

Michele: There were no streets; it was only grass. . . .

Therapist: Only grass and trees.

Michele: Yes, and the sky, that's all.

Therapist: That's all. You are all alone, no money.

Michele: No money. . . .

Therapist: How do you know that you had no money? For what do you need money?

Michele: I felt it, you know. I felt that. . . .

Therapist: That you have no money.

Michele: No money, no name, nothing.

Therapist: Nothing. That is the last thing you remember. Now, let's go back to bed. You are in bed now. The dream has been re-enacted, and now you go back to bed and sleep. Go back to bed to sleep in the same position. Now you close your eyes, and you are sleeping again, yes?

Michele: Yes.

Therapist: Now tell me, does the dream wake you up?

Michele: I think so. The anguish wakes me up.

Therapist: The anguish wakes you up. And you suddenly get up. Get up.

Michele: I get up.

Psychodramatic Shock

This protocol is taken from a televised session at Camarillo State Hospital, California, in May 1964. The session was entirely unrehearsed. The protagonist was selected on the spot and taken by surprise; taken equally unaware were the 2,600 patients in the wards who followed the session on closed-circuit television. The group present consisted of doctors, nurses, social workers, attendants, and students. This television tape is shown weekly at the hospital and is viewed by the patients for therapeutic purposes.

Tim, the protagonist, is 20 years old and has had several previous admissions involving alcoholism. The session consists of several scenes. In the first scene Tim improvises going home. He is confronted by his mother and father. The encounter ends in a hostile discussion in which

Tim threatens to return to the hospital rather than live with his parents. In the second scene he looks for employment but fails to get his old job back or to get a new one.

In the third scene he is confronted with his girlfriend, Monica, who simultaneously with him had a breakdown and was placed in a different mental hospital. When he hears the voice of his girlfriend, portrayed by an auxiliary ego, he has a complete breakdown, a psychodramatic shock, in which he is unable to find himself. He is resuscitated by the action of the director. In the protocol presented here, it becomes clear that he is unable and unwilling to hold the affection of Monica. In a later scene he hallucinates a dream. The last scene is dedicated to sharing with his companions.

Therapist: Tim, do you have a girlfriend?

Tim: No, not any more.

Therapist: What? What happened to her?

Tim: We broke up.

Therapist: When?

Tim: We were engaged.

Therapist: Why did you break up with her. What happened?

Tim: Uh. . . .

Therapist: What?

Tim: She talked about other guys all the time, and it got on my nerves.

Therapist: Other guys?

Tim: Yeah, she was bugging me. She took off the ring at times and went out with another guy. She was mad at me because I didn't have a car.

Therapist: She was engaged to you, and you gave her an engagement ring? What's her name?

Tim: Her name is Monica.

Therapist: Monica. Is she still around, Tim?

Tim: She's supposed to be in a state hospital in Indiana.

Therapist: Did you telephone her?

Tim: Oh no, I got into this hospital before she landed there. She went and got engaged to another guy, and when I landed in here, she cracked up.

Therapist: She cracked up. Would you like to call her up at the other hospital and see what she says?

Tim: Yeah, yeah, that's what I've been wanting to do for a long time.

Therapist: All right, telephone her. Go ahead. What is her name?

Tim: Monica Rodriquez.

Therapist: All right, call up the hospital. See what she thinks.

Tim: All right. (Telephones.) Uh, could I somehow speak to Monica Rodriquez? I don't know what ward she's on or anything. You say she's here? Could I talk to her, please?

(Long pause. Suddenly Tim breaks down and sobs heart-rendingly. He puts his arms on the table and his head on top of his forearms. He cannot seem to stop crying. The therapist goes over to him and gently strokes his head.)

Therapist (soothingly): What's the matter, Tim? What is it, Tim? Come on, tell me, what is it?

Tim: I don't want to. . . .

Therapist: She doesn't want to talk to you?

Tim: Yes, that's it. She wouldn't want to talk to me. She said those things—she said those things! (Gradually stops sobbing.)

Therapist: Yes, well, I'll tell you something. She is there on the telephone. She wants to talk to you. Give her a chance, Tim. Here she is. (Points to auxiliary ego, who picks up a phone.)

Auxiliary ego: Who's that?

Tim (listens intently, starts to smile, wipes his tears off his face): This is Tim. You remember me!

Auxiliary ego: Sure, I remember you. How have you been?

Tim: Oh, pretty good.

Auxiliary ego: How are you getting along?

Tim: Well, I'm here at the state hospital, and I got a job in a TV studio, and I may go on a visit home pretty soon. . . .

Therapist (interrupting): Don't forget you are right now out of the hospital.

Tim: Oh.

Auxiliary ego: It's nice of you to call me. I guess I haven't acted very nice to you. Why did we get mixed up? What happened between us?

Tim: I don't know. I didn't have a car, and you were pretty angry about that.

Auxiliary ego: That was stupid of me.

Tim: Well, I could understand your feelings. That's why I let you go out with Jim.

Auxiliary ego: It didn't work out with Jim either.

Tim: Yes, I heard about that.

Auxiliary ego: You know, I've been quite sick.

Tim: So have I. You think we should get back together again?

Auxiliary ego: Do you want to?

Tim: I'm not sure, but I'll come over to your place. Do you still live at the same place?

Auxiliary ego: I don't want us to get sick again over this.

Tim: No, I know how you feel.

Auxiliary ego: I did miss you, though.

Tim: I missed you quite a lot, quite a lot. I really did miss you. I'm not sure I should come over again. I might start drinking again. I don't know if drinking's my problem or not. Maybe it's you.

Auxiliary ego: It could be me and your drinking both.

Tim: I didn't really drink that much. It used to mess me up in my job and everything else.

Auxiliary ego: I don't want to mess you up again.

Tim: No, I wouldn't want to hurt you anymore than I did either.

Auxiliary ego: You messed me up pretty good too, you know.

Tim: I know. (Seems quite relaxed, at ease, and frank with her.)

Auxiliary ego: We were really going at it hot and strong there for a while.

Tim: Yeah, we were. (Laughs.) It's funny.

Auxiliary ego: It's not funny!

Tim: No. I was real sadistic about the whole affair. Man, waking you up in the middle of the night and giving you a bad time when you had to go to work in the morning. Maybe I just haven't grown up yet. Maybe I shouldn't see you for a while.

Auxiliary ego: Are you still drinking?

Tim (aside): Man, I'm ready for a drink right now! (To Monica) No, no, on my 20th birthday I cut a recipe out of a magazine, and I'm going to have this special on my 21st birthday. It's called a guster ball, you make it with Schlitz, and maybe I can invite you to that party.

Auxiliary ego: I don't think I'm ready for any party just now. (Tim does not answer.) Are you working?

Tim: Uh, yeah, I've been looking for a job all day, and I'm pretty sure I'll get one. I've just got to keep trying. I still need a little support from my folks.

Auxiliary ego: I wish you'd come and see me when you're feeling better. But don't come when upset, because you upset me, too. I get upset, too.

Tim: I guess I shouldn't call for a while. Well, after I get a job and a car, maybe I'll drop by, and we can go to a drive-in or something.

Auxiliary ego: Call me again then.

Tim: All right. (Hangs up the phone.)

Therapist: Well, Tim, I understand some of your difficulties now. You love that girl Monica, right? And you didn't have a car, and maybe you were cruel to her. What do you mean? You didn't warm up to her properly and make love to her?

Tim: Oh, I did, I did. That's where we got mixed up.

Therapist: Oh, I see. Did you get intimate with her?

Tim: Very.

Therapist: Very. Did she like it?

Tim: At times she called me filthy.

Therapist: She called you filthy. Love is not filthy, is it?

Tim: No. (Is very serious now.)

Therapist: And then what happened? You had no car. What did you mean by that?

Tim: Well, she always wanted to go places, which I understood, but I didn't have a car. And we were engaged at the time, and she said she'd like to go out with Jim.

Therapist: Who is Jim?

Tim: Oh, he had a car and an airplane.

Therapist: Do you know Jim?

Tim: I only met him twice.

Therapist: What kind of a guy is he? Is he older than you are?

Tim: Yeah, he was a pretty nice guy. She was older than me, in fact. She's 22.

Therapist: Oh, Monica is older than you are. And Jim is older than both of you?

Tim: Yeah.

Therapist: Hm. And she liked Jim, too?

Tim: She liked Jim very much. She got engaged to him after she broke up with me. I went with her first.

Therapist: She was a virgin when you met her?

Tim: Pardon?

Therapist: Was she a virgin?

Tim: No.

Therapist: No. But she became a virgin after you met her? Was she?

(Laughter.)

Tim: Now wait. She told me all about it.

Therapist: Oh, I understand. And so you were heartbroken after she left you.

Tim: Yes, in fact, that's when I really started drinking.

Therapist: That's when you started drinking. Where do you go drinking, in your neighborhood?

Tim: At first it was just in the neighborhood, and then a guy had this big Buick, so we cruised all around town and everywhere. There was a burlesque show, and we had a good time there.

Therapist: You got drunk, hm?

Tim: Oh, yeah, I got drunk. He had to drive. I didn't want to in my condition.

Therapist: That was wise. And now, Tim, you are now back in the community. Would you go drinking now? You have talked with Monica. Do you feel like going to a speakeasy and drinking again? How do you feel, really? Be honest!

Tim: No, I wouldn't. After I cried. . . .

Therapist: Crying helped you. Do you often cry?

Tim: Yes.

Therapist: When she upsets you, huh?

Tim: When I get upset.

Therapist: Would you like to have her back?

Tim: Yes.

Therapist: Do you think there is a chance?

Tim: No, no.

Therapist: She broke off with Jim. You don't think there is a chance?

Tim: Uh, 'cause it would just drive me to the same old rotten crap all over again. (Here he gets tense again.)

Therapist: Is she the only girl you had?

Tim: No, no, no.

Therapist: You have others?

Tim: Yeah.

Therapist: But this is the one you love most.

Tim: Yeah, the one I love most. (Seems to be balancing on the balls of his feet, swaying, unhappy.)

Therapist: Italian?

Tim: No, she's Mexican, a lot of Indian in her 'cause she has high cheekbones.

Therapist: Wonderful! Beautiful girl!

Tim: Beautiful.

Therapist: Too bad, isn't it?

Tim: Yeah, it's rough.

Therapist: Imagine, you felt ready to get married to her, hm? Have you ever imagined that with her? What would you have had, a church wedding? What kind of a wedding?

Tim: Oh, we weren't going to have that. Because she's Catholic, and I was going to change my religion for her. That's how much I loved her.

Therapist: You were going to become a Catholic and go to the priest, hm?

Tim: No, we weren't going to do that. We said it would be a simple wedding.

Therapist: A simple wedding. How did your mother feel about her?

Tim: Well, I brought her to our house with her sister one night. We felt gay, and, after they were gone, my Dad said, "God, those two dames act awful giddy." And that hurt me, 'cause he didn't have a good impression of them.

Therapist: She didn't make a good impression on your Dad?

Tim: No.

Therapist: What about your Mom?

Tim: Same difference.

Therapist: Same difference. Then you didn't have support from your family, hm?

Tim: No, I didn't. I didn't have any backing.

Therapist: Would you go back to Monica if she would have you?

Tim (more determined now): No, I want to find another girl.

Therapist: You want to find another girl, and so that is your decision. You'd like to find another girl, and you want to stop drinking.

Tim: Yes, 'cause I'll land back in here if I do. It happens every time.

Therapist: It happens every time. How many times have you been in the hospital?

Tim: This is my third time.

Therapist: Your third.

Tim: I was in General Hospital before.

Therapist: In General Hospital, and then you came here. Always drinking.

Tim: Yeah, every time I started drinking.

Therapist: What do you drink when you drink?

Tim: I usually start with beer, and then pretty soon we start buying a half pint. You know, I'm not an alcoholic, but it just gets me down and makes me guilty about it.

Therapist: Tell me something, when you drink, do you get violent?

Tim: Uh, no, no. I'm usually just a little depressed. I thought at one time there I might have gotten violent, but I didn't. I walked out of a bar. I felt the people were against me.

SUMMARY

People live within the framework of time, space, and reality, but time-learning, space-learning, and reality-learning cannot take place and be improved unless they are tested in an experimental setting, where they are experienced, expressed, practiced, and re-integrated within the framework of a psychotherapy modeled after life itself. Otherwise, the split between the experiences of time, space, and reality in life itself and their representations within the therapeutic process may remain unrelated. The situation is paradoxical if pathologies are entirely neglected or insufficiently considered in a test situation. Thus, it is imperative that the therapist transfer these phenomena from life itself into the therapeutic setting and back from the therapeutic setting into life.

The processes of concretization of living, fantasied experiences, and spontaneous time, as tested out in psychodrama sessions, differ in intensity, duration, and perspective. Some of the greatest difficulties encountered in behavioral contexts are deficiencies in time, in complementary warm-ups, and in the estimation of future consequences of present behavior.

Research into the psychopathology of spatial configurations should be carried out in laboratory settings, where the practical assessment of proximity and distance, of movements to and fro, horizontal and vertical can be tested.

The psychopathology of reality and fantasies of reality can be studied in psychodramatic laboratory settings especially the concretization of symbols, dream symbols, delusions, and hallucinations. The process of symbolization is taken out of the domain of language and interpretation and put into the more inclusive domain of concrete action.

Psychodrama is a form of psychotherapy which is modeled after life. It offers great flexibility for growth and emotional learning. Man, in the psychodramatic situation, is free from the fetters of facts and actualities, although not without the highest respect for them. He has a good foundation to believe that things are changing, as science has repeatedly taught us. In psychodrama, he can take his own dreams, hopes, and aspirations and create his own new world. This is not a plea for escape from reality but just the opposite—a plea for creativity in a psychodramatic world which may one day become true.

If an individual is enabled to experience himself acting in a spontaneous and creative manner in relation to others and experiences others accepting and loving him, he will tend to develop a new perception of himself. This will have a beneficial effect upon his life and his life space.

REFERENCES

Allport, G. W. Comments on: J. L. Moreno, transference, countertransference, and tele—their relation to group research and group psychotherapy. Group Psychother., *7:* 307, 1954.

Bischof, L. J. *Interpreting Personality Theories.* Harper and Row, New York, 1970.

Dreikurs, R., and Corsini, R. J. Twenty years of group psychotherapy. Amer. J. Psychiat., *110:* 567, 1954.

Ezriel, H. A. psycho-analytic approach to group treatment. Brit. J. Med. Psychol. *23:* 59, 1950.

Fromm-Reichmann, F., and Moreno, J. L., editors. *Progress in Psychotherapy.* Grune & Stratton, New York, 1956.

Moreno, J. L. Homo juvenis. *In Einladung zu einer Begegnung.* G. Kiepenheuer, Berlin, 1914.

Moreno, J. L. Die Gottheit als Redner. In *Der Neue Daimon,* p. 17, J. L. Moreno, editor. Anzengruber Verlag, Vienna, 1919.

Moreno, J. L. Interpersonal therapy and the psychopathology of interpersonality relations. Sociometry, *1:* 9, 1937.

Moreno, J. L. Mental catharsis and the psychodrama. Sociometry, *3:* 209, 1940.

Moreno, J. L. The philosophy of the moment and the spontaneity theater. Sociometry, *4:* 206, 1941.

Moreno, J. L. *Psychodrama.* Beacon House, New York, 1946.

Moreno, J. L. *The Theater of Spontaneity. Beacon House,* New York, 1947.

Moreno, J. L. *The First Book on Group Psychotherapy.* Beacon House, New York, 1957.

Moreno, J. L., editor. *International Handbook of Group Psychotherapy.* Philosophical Library, New York, 1966.

Moreno, J. L., and Dunkin, W. S. The function of the social investigator in experimental psychodrama. Sociometry, *4:* 392, 1941.

Moreno, J. L., and Fischel, J. K. Spontaneity procedures in television broadcasting with special emphasis on interpersonal relation systems. Sociometry, *5:* 7, 1942.

Moreno, J. L., and Moreno, Z. T. *Psychodrama.* Beacon House, New York, 1959.

Sacks, J. Group psychotherapy and psychoanalysis, historical note. Group Psychother., *13:* 199, 1960.

5

Accelerated Interaction:
A Time-Limited Approach Based on
the Brief Intensive Approach

Frederick H. Stoller, Ph.D.

INTRODUCTION AND DEFINITION

Accelerated interaction is a recent development in the use of groups for the purpose of personal change which utilizes continuous group interaction over several days as its major source of impetus. Other important ingredients of this new approach are time-limited contact, negation of the illness model, and the promotion of plans for the future.

Succinctly, accelerated interaction proposes that people can sit down together for several days and engage in an intense, meaningful, and memorable experience leading to important and enduring changes. Of prime importance is the experience of being deeply involved with others, honestly focusing on the here and now. The total gestalt of what impinges upon a participant may be of more importance than the specific techniques that are introduced.

In a certain sense, the development of the group therapy movement has been an extension of individual psychotherapy. The length of sessions and duration of treatment have paralleled the older movement, and group practice has not developed its own rhythms. Most of the important concepts have been borrowed from the

Reprinted with permission from the *International Journal of Group Psychotherapy*.

dyadic situation. The group experience offers unique opportunities and is potentially a process which has a power in its own right. Accelerated interaction places great emphasis upon enhancing the resources which are inherent in the group.

Several concepts are central to accelerated interaction: an ahistorical focus, avoidance of the mental illness model, emphasis upon the responsibility of the individual for his own fate, and concentration upon the future and upon the potential of people rather than upon their difficulties. These are trends which are found in the views of the following influential figures: Maslow, Rogers, Jourard, Berne, and Bach. (It is clear that developments such as accelerated interaction represent a climate of thought current within the helping professions.) It also partially reflects the sensitivity training movement (Bradford et al.). The particular combination of developments is unique, however, as is the attempt to put them to immediate use.

Accelerated interaction has been adapted to a number of different settings. For clarity the most general model will be described: a group of individuals who come together on a weekend for an intensive group experience. The motives and purposes of these individuals, usually strangers to one another, resemble those of most private-practice clients.

THE TERMS OF THE CONTRACT

Service relationships always involve agreements over fees, type of service to be rendered, and the scope of the responsibility carried by both parties. The contractual terms in the typical therapeutic relationship are usually quite explicit about the fee as well as the time and length of the individual appointments. The duration of the service is kept indefinite with the understanding that the relationship will terminate when both parties feel sufficient benefit has been obtained. Expectations of patients and therapists as to length of time involved in therapy often differ markedly (Garfield and Wolpin).

It is highly questionable whether most therapeutic alliances end in a rational manner; a large proportion terminate for many reasons other than therapeutic considerations. Indeterminate therapeutic relationships raise problems which are not often considered. The effect of not having a limited time in which to work undermines the sense of urgency of both parties. Apparently, a patient can even become accustomed to paying high fees without necessarily developing a high motivation for termination. Put in its most exaggerated form, it is as if both parties are saying, "If we don't get to it this year, we'll get to it next year." Evidence is accumulating that effective change is not necessarily a function of long-term therapy (Wolberg; Schlien).

The Time Limitation

Within the framework of accelerated interaction, the contract is always time-limited. In the weekend program the group meets at 8 P.M. on Friday and runs until midnight or later. Members reconvene at 10 A.M. Saturday morning and again meet until at least midnight or beyond. On Sunday the group meets between 10 A.M. and 6 P.M. Meals are eaten together. Except for an evening follow-up meeting about six weeks later, this constitutes the limit of the time commitment of all the participants.

At the beginning of each group, the leader states, as explicitly as he can, what is going to occur. He outlines the hours of the meeting, the goals of the group as he anticipates them, the general content of the interaction as he sees it, and the role he intends to play in the group. It is felt that this sets the tone of the experience from the very beginning: honest, direct, and open communication.

When there is only a limited time available, a built-in urgency is likely. In a sense, everyone, including the group leader, realizes that unless an individual comes to terms with himself and his world during the weekend, a unique opportunity will have passed. The motivation of everyone concerned heightens, and the participants exert a degree of effort they are unlikely to make in other situations. It can be said that a crisis situation has been provided. Given an urgent situation, marked involvement, and a sense of special opportunity, the possibility of breakthrough is maximized.

One of the difficulties of a prolonged psychotherapeutic relationship is its inherent dependency. Therapeutic contracts of unlimited duration enhance the dependency which is already a prominent quality of many seeking help. This type of difficulty is almost totally circumvented in accelerated interaction. Not only does the multiple group identification dilute dependency upon a single individual, as is common to groups, but the time-limited contract creates expectancies leading to independence from the group leader. It has been my experience that long-term dependency situations do not occur. When given the expectation that they will be able to take care of themselves, people do a remarkable job of doing just that.

THE STRUGGLE WITHIN THE ARENA

In any therapeutic situation the therapist sets most of the rules of the encounter:

what will be talked about, the nature of interventions, and the emotional tone to be sought. The nature of these rules are largely determined by the therapist's personal qualities, his image of man, and his concept of how change is brought about. Above all, the therapist's expectancies, as communicated to participants, color the proceedings and the results.

At the opening of an accelerated interaction session, the group leader states the goals that are being sought and, to some extent, the manner in which they will be pursued. He may make a statement such as this: "We are going to be together continuously for a good period of time and we will get to know each other pretty well. I am going to ask you to do something here that is very difficult. We are going to try to talk to each other as directly and as honestly as possible. As we get to know one another, we are going to try to spell out the kinds of reactions aroused in us: how the others make us feel and how they make us behave toward them. In a very real sense the world is going to shrink down to this group. Your behavior in the group will represent a fair sample of your way of being in the world, and you will have ample opportunity to change aspects of yourself which you find are both unrewarding and unnecessary. We will be much more interested in what goes on between us than in going into history. If I, or anyone, feels you are going too far afield from what we think is important or relevant, we will let you know. It is our hope that you will come away from this weekend having dropped a number of your masks and that you will find that, without them, you are freer and more sure of what you want and of what you are capable."

Dropping Masks

Once the stage is set, participants seem willing to give up the search for historical explanation. They recognize everyone's tendency to say, in effect, "Let me explain to you why I have to be the way I am," and when alternate routes are provided, they have a way of ridiculing any attempt to invest heavily in explanation or speculation. This is not to say that personal history has no place in the arena; it can contribute to how much a person lets himself be known. Some individuals remain a mere outline, and after a weekend together, others may not know whether this person has any brothers or sisters, whether he is rich or poor, whether he has had an easy life or a hard one. Rather than the content it is the quality with which facts about one's self are shared that is important. Thus, a relatively minor incident or seemingly unimportant relationship shared with the group in such a way that they are moved and touched is more valuable than a momentous event told in a detailed but mechanical fashion.

The way people talk and the manner in which they permit themselves to experience one another constitutes the principal struggle within the group arena. Most people are rarely able to sustain direct, honest, adult-to-adult communication over any appreciable portion of time. Ordinarily the goal is to have an interesting or amusing but, above all, comfortable time together. When serious goals are involved, maneuver becomes the prime ingredient of social intercourse.

Where the manifest purpose is to solve personal difficulties, such as in group psychotherapy, interaction style undergoes still another change. Basically, it can be categorized as: "Don't touch me!" In a purposeful search with others, people tend to explain themselves away, justify their particular stance, bemoan their burdens, or paint monochromatic self-portraits. The very style of talking is often distinctive: the shrillness of self-justification, the studied reasonableness of explanation, and the quickened rush to accumulate grievances.

Talking about "problems" is a subtle way of building barriers rather than bridges. Ostensibly the purpose is to present difficulties the person encounters in his life. Most characteristically, it involves framing the words in such a way that the individual discusses the problem as if it were something outside himself. Because there is an apparent attempt to deal with what is relevant to the therapeutic goal, the avoidant nature of the maneuver can be very elusive. Nevertheless, the object is actually to talk about "something" rather than focus on one's way of moving through the world. In the continuous group, people can see that a person's impact upon the world is of more urgency than problem-solving.

To show oneself to others in a face-to-face encounter is to be vulnerable and exposed. To be open reveals our weaknesses, inadequacies, inconsistencies, guilts, and inner wishes. It is the enormous energy that goes into remaining hidden which constitutes much of the difficulties and limitations with which we struggle. Without our disguises, we have a potential for greater use of our resources of intellect and organization, a greater depth of feeling as well as a greater strength and resilience for recovering from disappointment and injury. An important key to personal change lies in permitting oneself to drop some masks, staying with the consequences of this exposure, and learning that the masks are not so necessary. The accelerated group gives time and opportunity for this to happen.

Because the nature of the interaction constitutes the major struggle, the rules of the arena are of prime importance. An individual's current stance and his accumulated impact as reflected by his group participation become the main interest. Anything that tends to move too far afield from this is minimized. Anything that would tend to dilute genuine contact is discouraged. The group experience becomes the prime mechanism of change.

THE GROUP LEADER AS PARTICIPANT AND MODEL

If the group experience is the major vehicle of change, the group leader's major responsibility is in setting up experiences which provide such opportunities. The demands placed on him are less in the direction of applying techniques and categorization and more in setting the tone and atmosphere of the group, actively rather than passively. He acts as a model for the group style from his opening statement.

If it is the aim of an accelerated interaction group to attain a sustained experience in direct, adult-to-adult interaction, the leader must set the pace. He is the member of the group who is less fearful of direct encounter, who has the most feeling for the group direction. He is more skillful at providing feedback and is particularly adept at presenting it in a helpful way, that is, in providing the individual with alternatives to his customary behavior.

Not only should the group leader be open and honest but he should refrain from establishing himself in a superior or inferior relationship to anyone else in the group. The conventional role of psychotherapist militates against this because the therapist sees people within the context of a theoretical framework, is bound to a set of techniques, and is provided with a special kind of knowledge about the individual. Ultimately the group leader must learn to read his own inner responses to people and it is to these that he must direct his attention. Constant contact with a person provides an accumulation of responses which has a special relevance; a sense of what living with the person is like is a particular advantage of the intensive group. It is an inevitable phenomenon that an individual's behavior in the group, over a period of time, is a direct reflection of his way of moving through the world.

By leaning heavily upon his own personal reactions, a group leader runs the risk of perceiving a person through his own set of distortions rather than as that person actually rubs up against the world. Group settings become especially valuable under these circumstances; the group leader is only one voice in a consensus and it is the consensus with which the individual must ultimately deal. If a leader's response is not echoed by the rest of the group, the leader should accept this as a special distortion of his own rather than an accurate reflection of the person's impact. In this fashion, the group gives the leader the freedom to be a truly reactive person.

Being confronted by a group consensus, rather than an individual reaction, has powerful consequences. It is particularly compelling when the involvement with the other group participants is intense. The individual's regard for the others and his concern for their feelings about him is often a highly potent force for change. However, it should not be assumed that group reaction is a sufficient condition for inducing change in behavior and attitudes. A member must often be helped to relate to the group differently.

If the group leader wishes the experience to be characterized by openness and sharing, he can do no less than lead the way. Rather than remaining a distant figure who lives and breathes only as a therapist, he must be a very real person. Only to the degree that he presents himself as a variegated human being filled with the juices of human frailities and assets does he get the same behavior from others. To this end the group leader may share specific details about himself; in particular, aspects of his own difficulties and struggles which seem to parallel those of other participants. Often this results in the group leader's entering into a mutual exploration with others. At times the group leader is able to make a personal breakthrough for himself, unburdening some unnecessary and troublesome manner of functioning. Not every group presents such an opportunity but the leader should conduct himself so as to be open to such a self-therapeutic possibility.

Holding oneself to a very restricted role, attempting to keep others at a distance, guarding one's responses and ordering them so as to create a particular effect in someone else are exhausting ways of conducting oneself. It takes an inordinate amount of energy to maintain roles and stances; the more intensive the situation, the more burdensome they can be. Free of the necessity to constrict himself, a group leader can enter a very grueling and demanding endeavor without excess strain. In fact, following 24 to 30 hours of almost continuous psychotherapy, a group leader may emerge feeling exhilarated and renewed. Fatigue is temporary, while the positive features have a way of lingering. A well-conducted and well-functioning accelerated interaction group will renew and fulfill the group leader almost as much as it does the other participants.

In order for this to be so, the leader must not be chained to theory, and particularly, not to systems which tend to categorize people. There is a tremendous temptation to lean on diagnostic frameworks and on various ways of ordering behavior. Clinical caution often engenders fear and inhibition on the part of the therapist. However, such structure gets between the one who relies on it and the direct experience of the other person. In the same fashion, leaning upon case history material gives a biased and generally derogatory picture of the person. The only way to meet someone in the intensive group is as they appear in direct interaction.

The mental illness-mental health model is particularly inappropriate in the arena of intensive encounter. Such a framework forces one person to function as the authority who passes judgment on another's health. It is quite apparent that the very act of judging highlights certain features, and an appreciation of the individual's potential is invariably missed. When judgment as to the mental health (or illness) of the person is inconsequential to the purpose at hand, new aspects of the individual emerge. It can be argued that viewing people within the mental-illness framework does not, of necessity, force a downgrading approach, that it is possible to develop the freedom to appreciate the person for what he could be within the more conventional clinical approach. But, as currently practiced, conventional therapy does not foster this appreciation. A group leader in an accelerated group experience functions much more effectively the more he relegates his clinical training to the background.

THE NATURE OF THE INTENSIVE GROUP

A number of phenomena emerge when the group experience is concentrated in time which are rarely found in other group therapy situations. These new phenomena represent important ingredients for the growth experience which have not been appreciated until now and which require considerable investigation before they are fully understood or their dimensions clearly seen.

At the present stage of development, it is appropriate to point only to some observable characteristics of such groups. More objective examination is possible and will be the object of further study. As a preliminary, the following observations should be noted:

1. The higher the level of involvement with others, the higher the level of tension and concentration. In the conventional group, meeting periodically, tension rises within each session and breaks at the end. In each new session the group tension must begin building once more, though it may start at a slightly higher level. Over many sessions there is a gradually rising curve of tension and involvement consisting of a series of peaks and valleys.

In the weekend session, the curve of tension and involvement is not broken but shows a continuous, sharp rise. As a consequence, levels of tension and involvement are reached which are rarely encountered in the conventional therapeutic setting. This is evidenced by tremendous interest in and concern for fellow group members. Under these circumstances, groups are generally able to get beyond the usual poses and stances inherent in most social contacts, even that very special social situation called group psychotherapy. Participants become less concerned with "looking good" and more concerned with closely experiencing the others. Above all, people grow together and are genuinely moved by one another's struggles. The way in which people talk to one another alters in a marked manner, and communication is designed to foster closeness and openness rather than distance and camouflage.

2. The participants' sense of time and place undergoes profound alterations. In view of the crowded series of events and interactions as well as the physical restriction, such changes are understandable. There seems to be some value in experiencing social interaction under other than customary hit-and-run circumstances. New views of conventional social practices are provided for the participants against the background of this new experience.

Within the experience itself, the sense of prolonged time has two specific advantages. A feeling of having lived with other individuals yields a new dimension for appreciating the consequences of intimate involvement with him. This is very different from experiencing another in short bursts, particularly when he is only talking about his life situation rather than living through it. It is equally true for married couples: their prolonged intimacy is inevitably excluded from observation and comment by others and involves such a history of maneuvering that helpful intervention is rare.

The unusual social arrangement of time and place sets the occasion aside as something special and out of the ordinary. Expectations for such special events are different, as is the investment of effort. Placing a change-inducing experience in a setting that stands out from routine life has consequences that are not entirely appreciated and that need investigation.

3. Within the confines of the brief intensive group, mask-wearing and role-playing become extremely fatiguing; their usual cost in terms of energy is rarely appreciated because such behavior is so ubiquitous in everyday life. Within the intensive group, the effort that it takes to maintain a particular mask becomes evident. With the mounting strain of holding a usual distancing and alienating pose, the likelihood of change is increased. There is likely to emerge genuine concern and regard for others, an uncharacteristic strength and humanity, a lessening in self-justification, a reaching into the self for sharing with others, and a determination

and dedication to seek out goals congruent with actual desires.

Avoiding and distancing postures can be maintained relatively easily over the conventional time span of most therapy sessions. Being together for many months, as happens in long-term therapy, does not necessarily facilitate mask-dropping: people may simply accommodate to each other's disguises and collude so that no one is ever put in a position of really being touched by anyone else. Being together continuously, however, in the context of honest and direct encounter, highlights the considerable effort that goes into maintaining the pose. When people talk together without the necessity for sustaining their usual front, the difference in the tone and quality of their self-presentation is startlingly different. Conventional psychotherapeutic modalities rarely attain this.

4. Behavioral breakthroughs occur within the accelerated group. It invariably happens that various participants will begin to show different facets of themselves. With change, different feedback is received. When people begin to talk to one another with an unmistakable quality of honesty and directness, the regard and appreciation they receive is highly reinforcing; such regard is earned in the crucible of the group struggle.

Considerable doubt may be entertained as to whether a sudden breakthrough is effective, whether it can feasibly replace the long-term growth learning and insight, which are the goals of conventional therapy. For the most part, in conventional therapy, people work on only one aspect of themselves at a time, and behavioral change rarely takes place in highly charged, emotional circumstances. The electric quality of the intensive group experience appears to provide a different type of learning situation. There is good reason to believe that significant portions of new behavior remain as parts of the individual's behavioral repertory. The actual incidence of such outcomes, as well as their extensiveness, will have to be studied in the years to come. However, it is premature to assume that substantial and last-ing changes in life styles and attitudes cannot occur in a brief, intensive experience.

5. Intense elation and excitement is a consistent and unique element in this type of group. Exactly why it occurs (and why it occasionally does not occur) is not entirely clear and should be studied carefully. It would be of some use to speculate as to what might be involved.

The excitement and elation occur in the later phases of the group experience and often extend for a week or two beyond. However, they are transitory effects and fade away. Group excitement seems to occur only after successful struggle. It seems to be a feeling which says in effect: "I have placed myself on the line before others, and they have seen something of me without my usual protection. Not only have I come through this relatively unscathed, but people feel better about me than I dared hope."

Part of the feeling of courage, triumph, and enhanced self-regard is the sense of there being alternatives. The participant can now see many new possibilities for himself. Even the fact that he is only growing toward a new stance rather than having attained it has exciting possibilities.

The feeling of self-regard which increases in the closing phases of the group is accompanied by an emerging appreciation for the other group members. Continuously growing involvement is accompanied by a rich mixture of feelings: concern, identification, directness, honesty, helpfulness, the joy of participating in someone else's growth, as well as the friendship that is synonymous with mutuality. All these contribute, in immeasurable fashion, to the inner and outer excitement which is so unique to the brief, intensive group experience.

It is likely that elation is not central to the important changes that can occur in accelerated interaction. Experience has shown that extremely important breakthroughs can occur without the excitement and should not be confused with more important, but less spectacular, processes which are operating. Nevertheless, it does represent a phenomenon as yet little understood and whose potential for impelling movement and providing reinforcement is only beginning to be appreciated. Most exciting of all, it may provide participants with a feeling of what is possible when one conducts one's life with openness and honesty. Should this be the case, the final phase of the intensive group may be an instance in which true adult growth is possible, in contrast to the reparative or "band-aid" aspect of most psychotherapy.

It should be apparent from the impressionistic observations that have been presented that the intensive group involves characteristics and processes that differ appreciably from those of the more conventional group. These qualities have an interest and importance which are compelling to anyone who has experienced them. It is highly likely that they represent extremely potent forces for movement which have been only dimly suspected in the past. In any event, they deserve more study, and some of the preliminary work for these studies is now being initiated.

THE AFTERMATH OF THE STRUGGLE

Accelerated interaction has a very specific goal: appreciable change on the part of the participants. Success implies significantly different conduct. It may involve embarking on a new course, dealing differently with people, or making a series of decisions which have heretofore been impossible. Less explicitly but perhaps of more importance, it may enable an individual to approach new crises in a more creative and growth-inducing manner than has been thought possible.

Self-understanding, in the sense that it enables a person to talk more about himself, to explain himself away, is irrelevant. Words, insofar as they are brought in as ammunition for self-justification, are considered to be the antithesis of meaningful change. When people really change, when they drop an aspect of themselves, there is a tendency to move on to new things. What has been left behind is something they no longer care about; there is little need to explain it, understand it, or rationalize it. With real change there is a tendency to react more quickly and spontaneously, to feel right about a particular response without having to question oneself or to speculate about what others will think or how they will react.

Accelerated interaction is a rich experience in which a great variety of reactions, stimuli, ideations, identifications, and responses impinge upon an individual within a relatively brief period of time. Such a wealth of stimulation creates a state which can only be characterized as "stirred up." It is as if a person comes to a group experience with an internal organization. The experience stirs him up and causes the internal organization to undergo a state of excitation and movement. When he begins to settle down, his internal structure settles back into a state of greater stability. But it now represents a new organization which is not quite the same.

The degree of change differs among individuals. There are those who undergo a marked and startling change that is noticeable to anyone who has any enduring contact with them. There are others who seem to behave as before but meet crises in a different fashion and can recognize that they now arrive at solutions which are more purposeful and less self-defeating. Some feel differently about themselves and others; their emotional framework becomes much more pleasing to themselves. Still others find a renewed faith in themselves; it is as if they had undergone a self-validating experience. For many there is a realization of strengths and resources within themselves of which they had been only dimly aware. But, of course, there are those who show little or no change and for whom the experience can be said to have been a failure.

The gains and breakthroughs which follow a group experience take some time to jell. Follow-up sessions are held approximately six weeks following the original group experience. It would appear to take approximately that long for the original elation to fade and for the new aspects of the individual to have emerged and stabilized. At this interval, some estimate of the permanence of the gains can be made. If the gains are temporary, they will have faded within six weeks; judged too early, the person may be in a state of flux which will give a misleading picture of the final result. It is still premature to evaluate how long gains made in this very brief situation will last, but informal inquiries have revealed breakthroughs that have been maintained for at least a year.

Another type of growth has been found in persons who have gone through a number of marathon group experiences. Their entire initial experience may have revolved around whether or not they could permit themselves to be touched by others. Upon entering a second group experience, the person may involve himself in a very different manner than he did in the first group; his struggle will be of a different order and, as a consequence, will permit him to deal with different aspects of himself. There is reason to believe that people can engage in step-by-step growth with successive group experiences providing they are not permitted to grow "group-wise," to learn how to get by in a group of this sort by playing the game.

On the basis of purely subjective observation, approximately 20 per cent of the participants do not get the kind of gain from accelerated interaction that is sought. About 1 or 2 per cent undergo actual harm in that they seem worse after the experience than before. How to determine who will not benefit and, in particular, who will be harmed is not easy. While it is clear that motivation is as important here as it is in any approach, many who are ambivalent become mobilized by the momentum of the group. Diagnostic or psychopathological considerations are not as central for determining who might be harmed as might be assumed. Many whose involvement with mental illness would seem to rule them out have made enormous gains. In contrast, some who have had the most difficulty in

the group have had no history of disturbance. The need to maintain a rigid role may be the most important feature for anticipating difficulties. But this is strictly speculative and cannot now be used as a basis for screening.

On the assumption that the risks are actually quite small in contrast to the probable gains, participants are now taken into groups as they apply. Sometimes the feelings of the group leader toward a prospective participant, whether he finds he wants to spend a long period of time with him, are the best indicator.

VARIATIONS AND APPLICATIONS

The primary technical consideration for accelerated interaction is that a group meet continuously over several days and that it be time-limited. Two or three days would seem to be optimal as judged by experience. More time does not necessarily mean more will be accomplished by the participants. Parkinson's law is applicable to psychotherapy: people will take the time allotted to them to achieve the goals they seek.

Settings for marathon groups vary with the demands of the situation. However, the author's preference is for home settings; many of the groups are held in my own home with my wife participating. It should be noted, however, that the attitude of the participants, particularly the group leader, is far more important than the setting. One of my most effective groups was held in an abandoned dormitory of a prison, as sterile a setting as can be imagined.

Many clinicians assume that the intensive group experience is too powerful for people who have undergone hospitalization or profound disorganization, but it is my experience that such people are not bruised by the experience and often achieve considerable gains. The primary limitation would seem to be for persons whose resources are too limited or who are too bogged down in immediate reality difficul ties. If there is no room in which to apply new behavior or patterns, such people quickly become overwhelmed by the demands of their lives.

This can be clearly seen in an institutional setting. Accelerated interaction has been applied in mental hospitals and prisons for drug addicts, and the structure of institutional life is such that it is very difficult to sustain the gains that are frequently achieved. Because of this, it has become advantageous to think of this approach as facilitating the individual's utilization of the institutional program. In this sense, accelerated interaction may be utilized to promote a greater degree of meaningful participation on the part of immates rather than as a primary tool to change life styles.

It should be re-emphasized that precise time goals are important. Attempts to prolong the therapeutic relationship for purposes of support undermine the growth potential of this experience. If necessary, it is preferable to have the individual undergo another accelerated experience; the growth under this situation is often much more meaningful than if the initial experience is prolonged.

SUMMARY

Accelerated interaction is a new approach mainly characterized by continuous group interaction over several days with a very definite time limit to the therapeutic contact. It utilizes the urgency and independence fostering qualities of the time-limited contact while taking advantage of the impact of intimate group life. Elements of the group process emerge under continuous interaction which are scarcely realized under most conventional circumstances and which have profound implications for promoting social change in people. By stressing involvement, honesty, directness, and mutuality, the accelerated group promotes an intense experience in living with people which opens many possibilities for personal growth. The role of the group leader shifts from that of commentator and technician to that of participant who reacts in an immediate fashion. Holding such groups in homes rather than the usual office or clinic setting places the emphasis on personal growth and new possibilities for living instead of on correcting defective functioning. In addition, accelerated interaction has advantageous applications for institutional programs.

REFERENCES

Bach, G. R. *Intensive Group Psychotherapy.* Ronald Press, New York, 1954.

Berne, E. *Transactional Analysis in Psychotherapy.* Grove Press, New York, 1961.

Bradford, L. P., Gibb, J. R., and Benne, K. D., editors. *T-Group Theory and Laboratory Method.* Wiley, New York, 1964.

Garfield, S. L. and Wolpin, M. Expectations regarding psychotherapy. J. Nerv. Ment. Dis., *137:* 353, 1963.

Jourard, S. M. *The Transparent Self.* Van Nostrand, Princeton, 1964.

Maslow, A. H. *Toward a Psychology of Being.* Van Nostrand, Princeton, 1962.

Rogers, C. R. *On Becoming a Person.* Houghton-Mifflin, Boston, 1961.

Schlien, J. M. Time-limited psychotherapy: an experimental investigation of practical values and theoretical implications. J. Counsel. Psychol., *4:* 318, 1957.

Stroller, F. H. Accelerated Interaction: A Collective Presentation by Members of ''Swing,'' a Professional Cooperative of Group Psychotherapists. Mimeographed paper, 1964.

Wolberg, L. R. Introduction. In *Short-Term Psychotherapy,* L. R. Wolberg, editor. Grune & Stratton, New York, 1965.

6

The Marathon Group:
Intensive Practice of
Intimate Interaction

George R. Bach, Ph.D.

INTRODUCTION

Like all effective group psychotherapeutic programs, the marathon is a group practicum in intimate, authentic human interaction. One of the unique aspects of the marathon technique is an intensification and acceleration of transparency and genuine encounter by a deliberate instigation of group pressure focused on behavioral change.

In the course of conducting more than 12,000 therapeutic group hours with a great variety of patients, it is clinically observable that for many patients the 50-minute individual hour or the one- to two-hour group sessions are not long enough for either patient or therapist to take off their social masks, that is, to stop playing games and start interacting truthfully,

From *Psychological Reports,* vol. 18, 1966, pp. 995–1002. The information contained in this paper was presented May 5, 1964, at the 120th annual meeting of the American Psychiatric Association in Los Angeles, California, and then prepared in manuscript form on October 6, 1964. Although much clinical work and a great deal of research have been done since that time, the need for a description of the basic procedure seems still needed; hence, the manuscript in its original form is made available.

authentically, and transparently. It takes a longer session for people in our culture to switch from the marketing stance of role-playing and image-making, which they must practice in the workaday world, to feel free to come out straight and strong, not hidden behind oblique "sick" roles or other so-called resistance.

Clinical experience has shown that the group pressure, rather than the therapist's individual interventions and interpretations given privately, is a major vehicle which can move people effectively and quickly from impression-making and manipulative behavior toward honest, responsible, spontaneous leveling with one another. But it takes time for the therapeutic group to generate influence-pressure in intensity and work-oriented kind, sufficient to produce behavioral change. It takes time, also, for group members to display their individual ways of acting within the group which simulates their ways of being and acting in the world. It takes time for therapists and peers to discern the potential and to suggest change. Finally, it also takes time to experience the change, experiment with it, and practice it here and now while participating in shaping the learning culture of the therapeutic group. All of this—becoming transparent, leveling, exposing to influence-pressure, attempting changes, and practicing new behavior—we believe, is a natural gestalt, a unit of learning experience which should not be broken up into bits and pieces but should occur as a whole, mediating a significant turning point, a big step toward becoming what one can be!

Customary schedules of group therapy tend to break up this experiential learning unit. One-, two-, or even three-hour office meetings are not enough therapeutically, although staff time and fee economics make them universally accepted schedules. The author has tried long hour groups and also weekend retreats and closely spaced groups (every other evening). With each of these schedules he noticed that there are always a few patients who "slip by" the experience, always waiting and ready to level truthfully with their peers, but never quite coming out openly transparent in time for the group to get hold of them fully for feedback, confrontation, and pressure to change. These brief interrupted groups rarely generate the right amount and kind of influence-pressure to make a crucial impact on the resistant learner. The brief group is an ideal playground for time-wasting, psychiatric games such as diagnosing (labeling), safaris into phantasies, psychological archaeology, playing psychoanalysis with transference interpretation, collusive acceptance of people's irrational self-propaganda as to who is the best therapist, best patient, etc.

SETTING AND STRUCTURE

Searching for a practical solution, the author was delighted to discover in 1963 that a group of younger colleagues (Roger Wickland and Frederick Stoller) had independently developed in a psychiatric hospital setting all-day-long types of group therapeutic sessions which were effective in producing therapeutic changes in "difficult" patients. Adopting this approach to private practice patients, the author reactivated the old weekend-retreat program, but with a new twist: no interruptions, continuous meetings for two days, no subgrouping, no socializing, minimal breaks,

clear-cut ground rules, and admission of people seriously interested in changing themselves rather than the universe. The revision is a success thanks to the author's consultant, Dr. Stoller, who, working as cotherapist in the very first marathon ever done with private patients, has helped the author significantly to improve the old weekend live-in program.

Currently, marathon group therapy retreats take place in a secluded private setting where a selected group of 10 to 14 participants can stay together for two, three, or four days. The enrollment fee, which includes room and board, ranges from $90.00 to $300.00 per participant, depending on duration, setting, and staff. The minimum fee per actual group therapy hour is $3.00.

Scheduling

The actual schedule of a particular marathon varies, depending on setting and the members' goals and values. In the standard procedures members meet nonstop throughout the first night, without sleeping for 24 hours or longer. The marathon terminates in nonverbal, silent communication exercises, conducted in pairs. This is followed by a "closure-party" in which subgrouping is resumed. Thus, a gradual reentry into the conventional social atmosphere is reluctantly made. The entire session may be recorded and a feedback follow-up is scheduled four to eight weeks later, which is designed to reinforce those decisions for change which have been emerging during the marathon itself. In the author's institute practice, the marathon retreats for private patients are systematically integrated with the regular group therapy program. Most patients are first seen individually (briefly) and then assigned to a regular two- to four-hour weekly therapy group. Marathon retreat experiences are interspersed at intervals of three to six months. Some marathons are specialized for marital couples, executives of business organizations, or an advanced training session for group psychotherapists or social science researchers.

Awareness

The author conceptualizes the marathon therapeutic process as a practicum in authentic communication, based on freedom from social fears conventionally associated with transparency.

The unique opportunity of participating in honest encounter on a day-and-night basis produces psychological intimacy among the participants. This gives them a taste for what can be achieved with significant others everywhere.

As subjective truths are shared, irrational and ineffectual behavior appears incongruent, to be dropped in favor of new, more intimate, and competent behavioral patterns. The latter emerge and are practiced in the course of the marathon. Orientation is ahistorical, emphasizing "what" and "how now" rather than "why" and "where from."

Full Participation

The genuine productivity of every group member is the therapist's mission, which he procures by whatever means at his disposal. One of the other missions of the therapist is to maximize group feedback and enhance the opportunity for genuine encountering of and exposure to group pressure. For these reasons the marathon is not unlike a pressure cooker in which phony steam boils away and genuine emotions (including negative ones) emerge. The group atmosphere is kept focused every moment on the objectives at hand: to produce change in orientation and new ways of dealing with old crucial problems (creativity).

Every member is a co-therapist and co-responsible for the relative success or failure of any given marathon meeting. Thus, the two or more professional co-therapists will, if and when they genuinely feel it, take their turns to participate "patient-wise," that is, as whole persons rather than just in a technical role-wise form. Decisions for change and serious commitment to follow through in life action are frankly elicited. Follow-up sessions will inquire into their validity.

Selection

Concerning selection, prospective marathon participants are not sorted out in the traditional psychiatric-diagnostic sense but rather on the basis of attitudes toward self-change and group constellation. Before admittance "marathonians" must convince one and preferably both professional co-therapists that they are anxious to make significant changes in their customary ways of acting and being in this world. This presumes some degree of basic self-understanding of what one now is and what one can potentially become. The purpose of the marathon is to awaken and strengthen further feelings for new directions and movement toward self-actualization in mutual intimate concert with others who are also growing. Marathons create a social climate for inter-peer growth stimulation, a sort of psychological fertility.

The marathon group therapeutic experience is most fully effective with those who wish to exchange their own ways of acting and being in this world and who are ready to quit blaming others and environment for their present unsatisfactory lot. New patients who initially tend to play the psychiatric game: "*I* am sick—*You* cure me" may be admitted to initiation types of marathons whose specific mission is to knock out blamesmanship and other false, irrational, socially destructive operations (Bach, 1954) by which people preserve, cuddle, and justify their sick roles. A patient who has given up his game of "I am sick—You, Doctor, and you-all (group) do something and take care of me" is a person ready to behave like a problem-solving adult. Such an individual can quickly learn to accept rational group pressure as a useful means of strengthening his still weak and new character. Therapeutic group pressure need not be misused irrationally (Bach, 1956) and immaturely as a substitute for individuality or as some social womb into which one may regressively crawl and hide in fearful alienation from the big, bad competitive world of adult "fighters." The regressive tendency to depend on the group is counteracted by the demand for everyone to act as therapist to everyone.

The work burden of trying to be an effective co-therapist and agent of change to others fatigues all marathonians over the long work hours. It takes devotion mixed with constructive aggression to get people to take off image masks and put on honest faces. It takes patience and energy to break down resistances against change which all well-entrenched behavioral patterns—however irrational—will put up as part of a person's phony self-esteem. The exhaustion and fatigue produced by the marathon procedure lead to refusal to spend any energy on acting-up or acting-out. Tired people tend to be truthful. They do not have the energy to play games.

THERAPEUTIC EFFECTS

It also takes disciplined, concerted group cooperation to create properly focused, selective group pressure. Behavioral change is not created by unilateral influence, or chaotic, disorganized free-for-all, cathartic group-emotions per se. Marathons are not tension-relieving, cathartic acting-out groups. They generate rather high levels of emotional tensions which stimulate cognitive re-orientation for their relief. Generally two new modes of acting, feeling, and being emerge during a marathon: *transparency of the real self*, which (being accepted and reinforced by the peer group) leads to *psychological intimacy* within the peer group. This sequence from transparency to intimacy is a natural development, because what alienates people from one another are the masks they put on, the roles they take, the images they try to create, and many of the games they play. Parenthetically, there are a few intimacy-producing games played by explicit mutual awareness and consent. These interpersonal stances alienate because they make it harder to know a person and to know where one stands with him. Interpersonal uncertainty is experienced as psychologically dangerous and anxiety-evoking until authenticity and transparency are reciprocally practiced. One or both parties may have hidden ulterior motives which usually turn out to be exploitive or destructive. Unless a person displays himself transparently, one never knows when to come on with him and when to get off or when to give, when to get or when to give up. One must remain alienated, on guard against the possibility of psychological ambush, that is, to be seduced into spilling one's guts, to expose one's vulnerability, to get one's expectations up, only to be let down, even "destroyed." The con artist's use of the double bind—you are damned if you do and damned if you don't—is psychologically lethal, for friends have no effective defenses against the double bind.

In the course of the long work hours of marathon therapy, a transition from this self-defensive alienation and exploitative game-playing to psychological intimacy is revealed for everyone present to see.

Entering a marathon group implies submitting to a set of ground rules. The importance of these rules is such that they have been termed Ten Marathon Commandments. How explicit these rules are made depends upon the sophistication of the particular group; many participants grasp them without their having to be concretely outlined. However, there are groups which require that the rules be clearly laid out, and individual participants may behave in such a manner as to force the rules to be spelled out. In any case, these rules must be crystal clear in the minds of the group leaders and will act as a guide for their direction of the sessions. The following, then, are the basic group rules of the marathon. (The following section of the chapter was drafted by Dr. Bach and edited by Dr. Stoller after they had worked both together and independently with marathon groups for two years. The Ten Marathon Commandments, their purpose and evolution, will be discussed in detail in *The 300-Year Weekend*, by G. R. Bach, J. Gibb, G. Hoover, and F. Stoller.)

THE TEN MARATHON COMMANDMENTS

(1) To stay together in the same place and not leave until the group breaks or ends at its prearranged time. Everyone communicates with the whole group. Everyone attends to and reacts to how each individual acts in the group situation. This means that there must be no subgrouping, such as is common at ordinary social gatherings and parties. Only during official group breaks and at the end of the session do people break up into subgroups.

(2) Creature comforts are to be taken care of on a self-regulatory basis. Eating will be done within the rules of the group, usually on a buffet basis without disrupting the continuity of the group proceedings. Participants can move about to different chairs, lie down on the floor, indulge in exercises within the sights and sounds of the group arena. Brief breaks for exercising, sleeping, or changing clothes will be decided on by each group as a whole. At the conclusion, most groups treat themselves to a closure-party, and some groups schedule a follow-up meeting.

(3) The group leader is bound by the same rules as everyone else, except that in order to keep his services alert he has the privilege, during every 24 hours of work, to rest up to four hours away from the group. During his absence, the group continues the meeting on a self-regulatory basis with every group member responsible for the uninterrupted continuation of the group proceedings and the enforcement of the ground rules. (A group leader in top physical condition may become so involved in the proceedings that he may choose not to exercise his resting privilege.)

(4) All forms of physical assault or threats of physical violence are outlawed.

Attacks must be confined to verbal critiques. However, there are no limits as to the straightforward use of Anglo-Saxon words or slang.

(5) Legitimate, professionally correct group procedures such as psychodrama, awareness-expansion exercises, sensitivity training, transactional games analyses, etc., may be used temporarily during a marathon, but only under very special circumstances. We have found that the use of a technique may retard rather than facilitate the slow, natural emergence of trust, transparency, and intimacy. Any routine use of any group-process technique, however valuable it may be in other settings, is definitely contraindicated in the marathon group situation.

(6) The encountering experience is a four-phase process. Individual expressions are reacted to; these reactions are shared in a feedback; the feedback in turn generates counterreactions; these come from the original expressers as well as from the rest of the group. Members are expected to facilitate each of these phases by active participation in the following manner.

(a) Members share true feelings as clearly and transparently as possible. The expresser is himself responsible for drawing and keeping the full attention of the group onto himself. No one should wait to be brought out. Every participant is expected to put himself voluntarily into the focus of the group's attention, to seek out the group and to turn attention to himself, preferably a number of times. This applies to everybody, including the official group leaders. There are no observers, only active participants.

By being an attentive audience, the group rewards the expresser. The expresser will remain in focal position (or "hot seat") until his feeling-productivity wanes and/or until the expresser himself has had enough of the hot seat, or until group interest and group pressure are dissipated.

(b) In the feedback reactions to the expresser, no holds are barred. Candid leveling is expected from everyone, which means participants explicitly share and do not hide or mask their here-and-now, on-the-spot reactions to one another. Tact is out and brutal frankness is in. Any phony, defensive, or evasive behavior (such as playing psychiatric games or reciting old lines) is fair game for the group's critique and verbal attack. Ought's-manship (advising others how to solve their problems) can deteriorate into a time-consuming, dulling routine which suppresses spontaneous encounter. Excessive advice-giving is, therefore, undesirable.

(c) Trying to make people feel better is not the purpose of the marathon. Self-appointed, tactful diplomats, amateur protectors, and "Red Cross nurses" distract and dilute the leveling experience. Any kind of protective cushioning or cuddling spoils (for the central hot seat person) the experience of standing up alone to the group, as he must to the world. Cushioning interventions should be held in abeyance until a participant has had the opportunity to express the full range of his being in the group and to feel the group's reaction to him.

7. "Show me now—Do not tell me when" is the marathon leitmotif. Owning up to feelings here-and-now and sharing them is the mode of participation. Telling the group about how one behaves outside the group and how he then and there reacted in bygone times and other places—back home or back at the office—is only warm-up material. The thing to do is for each member to let himself feel his presence in the group and let the currently active impact of the others get to him.

The modes of participation recommended in the four preceding paragraphs provide each group member with the opportunity to become better aware of how he is in the group and in what directions he may want to change and to try out new ways of being in the group.

8. "As you are in the group, so you are in the world." As the members learn to exchange feelings in the group, a pattern of participation automatically emerges which the group will mirror back to the individual member. In the long hours of a marathon one cannot help being seen for what

he really is and to see what he may become. The marathon group simulates the world of emotionally significant others; and the ways in which the member relates to this world reflect the core pattern of his being. The group members' reactions give cues as to the effect his behavior patterns have on the world. He has the option to try out new, improved ways of being.

9. Group members' changes and improvements in participation will be attended by the group. Giving affectionate recognition to growth and new learning is as much in order as cuddling, defensive behavior is out of order as cited in paragraph 6(c). Reinforcement of new learning is the loving side of critical leveling as mentioned in part of paragraph 7.

10. While nothing is sacred within the group, the information gained during a marathon weekend is confidential in the nature of professionally privileged communication. Nothing is revealed to anyone outside. Objective research reporting in anonymous format is the only exception to this rule of discretion.

SUMMARY

The Ten Commandments, the ground rules for marathon participants given above, are not arbitrary rules or conventions. Rather, they emerged gradually and painfully in years of clinical experience with interaction groups generally and with marathon groups in particular. Respecting these basic ground rules does not necessarily guarantee success for a given marathon. But we do know that respecting the work spirit of the situation facilitates the exciting metamorphosis of an assembly of role-playing strangers into a creatively intimate, authentically sharing communion. Since the marathon leader likes to facilitate and partake of this metamorphosis, he has a vested, professional, and personal interest in keeping anybody from distracting him and the group from this beautiful and valuable experience.

REFERENCES

Bach, George R. *Intensive Group Psychotherapy.* Ronald Press, New York, 1954.

Bach, George R. Pathological aspects of therapeutic groups. Group Psychother., *9:* 133, 1956.

Bach, George R. and Wyden, P. *Intimate Enemy: How To Fight Fair in Love and Marriage.* Morrow, New York, 1969.

7

Group Therapy and
the Small-Group Field: An Encounter

Morris B. Parloff, Ph.D.

INTRODUCTION

The small-group field appears to be confronted with a phenomenon that aspires to the rarely used accolade of "breakthrough." An ill-defined set of techniques has been broadly applied to groups of "normals," professionals, and paraprofessionals. The claims made concerning the consequences of such procedures are extravagantly immodest on the part of both proponents and adversaries.

The advocates describe these groups as a much needed antidote to current social ills and as a prophylactic agent against the further inroads of our sick culture on man's sacred humanness. Opponents see these groups as representing a force which subverts the basic tenets of our culture, undermines Christian morality, and debases the field of group psychotherapy.

While there is little agreement regarding the definition or characteristics of groups variously labeled as personal growth, human relations, sensory awareness, sensitivity training, self-awareness, leadership training, love-ins, psychological karate, etc., it is generally agreed that they represent a potent force for great benefit or great mischief.

Reprinted with permission from the *International Journal of Group Psychotherapy, 20*: 267, 1970.

DEFINITION

Rogers has characterized the intensive encounter group as "perhaps the most significant social invention of this century" (1968, p. 268), and Burton has said, "all of us who do encountering work believe that something unique, transporting, and unifying has been found which is unmatched thus far by classical psychotherapy."

It has not, however, escaped notice that, as with any powerful force, these groups have the potential for harm as well as good. One of the more grandiose characterizations was aired on the floor of the U. S. House of Representatives. A Congressman, on the basis of information made available to him, concluded that the impact of such group experiences resulted in "confusion, frustration, and wholesale disorientation among our unsuspecting people." He also believes that such groups are being employed as "a tool to indoctrinate the masses for a 'planned change' in the United States" (Rarick, 1969, p. 4666).

Clearly these groups have powerful credentials for a claim on our attention. Not only are they described as potent but they appear to produce their powerful impact in a relatively short period of time, and they emphasize procedures not classically employed by the professional psychotherapist. The psychotherapist, usually apathetic in response to novel theoretical formulations, is excited by the development of new and apparently powerful procedures and techniques. It is not always necessary that their claims be substantiated before he is willing to adopt them. The author's purpose is to review the available evidence in order to assess whether these dramatic innovations represent a valid breakthrough in psychotherapy's body of theory and practice, or simply another hernia.

Specifically, it is to consider (1) the nature of the current small-group phenomenon, (2) the cultural context in which these groups have developed and flourished, (3) the evidence concerning effects and effectiveness, (4) the contribution, actual and potential, of the encounter groups to group psychotherapy practice, (5) the role and responsibility of professional group psychotherapists, and (6) some conclusions.

NATURE OF THE SMALL-GROUP PHENOMENON

Small-group theory is no more uniform and monolithic than conventional group psychotherapy theory. One approach to the problem of differentiating among the new varieties of small groups is to identify them in terms of the relative emphasis they place on the study of dynamics of *groups* as contrasted to the study of the dynamics of *individuals* in the group.

The Process-Centered Group

Initially the T-groups of the National Training Laboratories (NTL) and the Group Relations Conference of the Tavistock Institute both placed primary emphasis on the study of small-group processes and only incidentally on the dynamics of individual members. The residential conferences of each follow a similar format of major "exercises": small group (T-group or study group), large group, intergroup, and theory. The small-group aspect of the program was developed as an educational device and emphasized the experiential basis of learning. These types of groups became increasingly popular and provided the basis for the present plethora of personal growth and development groups. While the focus of NTL has shifted somewhat toward the individual dynamics, the Tavistock program and its American counterpart, the Group Relations Center of the Washington School of Psychiatry (WSP), have maintained their focus on the group per se. Both of these centers have in fact gravitated toward the study of even larger interactional processes: between groups, between group and institution, among groups within an institution, and among institutions. The attention of the members of the "study group" is directed to such group-based issues as leadership, authority, and the role of group members *vis-à-vis* the group's primary task. Efforts by members to introduce personal material in such groups is interpreted by the consultant only in terms of the role which such behavior plays for the group.

The group-centered emphasis is also found in varying degrees in groups which have as their specific aim the improved functioning of institutions. Organizations such at NTL, Western Training Laboratories, Boston University's Human Relations Center, and UCLA's Institute of Industrial Relations all conduct groups as a management training procedure. These institutional growth groups usually include lectures and group problem-solving exercises as well as sensitivity training. These groups may be used in training community leaders, securing labor-management harmony, promoting better understanding between police and community, etc. Such groups usually stress group process in order to assist institutions and organizations to fulfill their primary missions. The group experts assist the participants to identify problems in formal structure and in the relationships among staff members.

The process-centered groups tend to be conducted by highly professional organizations which undertake to exercise close control over the training and selection of their group leaders.

The Individual-Centered Group

The classification "individual-centered group" is intended to include all groups which are primarily concerned with the behavior, feelings, fantasies, and motivations of the individual. Most such groups that are not specifically psychotherapy groups limit themselves to the goal of education and do not wittingly undertake the treatment of patients. These individual-centered groups encompass personal growth, human potential, self-awareness, encounter, confrontation, gestalt, sensory awareness, and human relations, and have also borne such labels as truth labs, marathons, and T-groups. Perhaps the best known of these groups is the T-group, a term that is widely used to refer to all members of this proliferating class. The term "encounter group," however, recently introduced by Rogers, is more descriptive, and will, therefore, be used here interchangeably with the term "individual-centered group" to denote all members of the class.

The proponents of encounter groups do not appear to be interested in the amelioration of suffering and the overcoming of disability—the classical concerns of the psychotherapist—but aim, instead, at assisting the individual to attain new, increased, and sustained experiences of joy and self-fulfillment. Clearly the group leaders are less concerned with "head shrinking" than with "mind expanding" (Parloff, 1970). The attractive goals of such groups as described in their brochures include assisting the individual to achieve self-realization, fulfillment, peak experiences, body integration, peace, unity, joy, authenticity, love, openness, and honesty.

The general format is that of a small, unstructured, face-to-face group averaging about ten to fifteen members. Such groups meet for a relatively brief span of days during which the group meetings are massed rather than spaced. The techniques employed are aimed at stimulating intense, candid, highly personal interactions and confrontations. The leader may act as a model for the participants in that he expresses his own feelings "openly and honestly," and except in such groups as Synanon and the psychological karate types of groups, he is warm, accepting, and strongly supportive. He thus illustrates the role of ideal group member and encourages the direct expression of feelings. While many of these groups place heavy emphasis on the experience of warmth, love, and total acceptance in the group, others emphasize direct expressions of hostility and physical displays of aggression. It appears, then, that while some group leaders prefer to train their group members to turn to each other for help, others find it equally useful to train the members to turn on each other for help.

The techniques employed include the familiar verbal interactions but also stress nonverbal exercises and games that have been devised to assist participants to overcome their usual resistances and social inhibitions. Such techniques include meditating, introspecting, exercising, fantasizing, touching, tapping, holding, hugging, dancing, wading, stripping, and the like.

A time-extended version of the encounter group has been given a special designation, "the marathon group," in recognition of its prolonged and sustained duration and stress. The time span of a marathon group may range from an afternoon to 36 or even 48 continuous hours (Casriel and Deitch, 1968; Stoller, 1968; Bach, 1966, 1967a, 1967b, 1967c; Mintz, 1967, 1969). The special value of this practice lies in the claim that by developing a high level of intensity and fatigue, group members will achieve a corresponding weakening or dissolution of their usual defensive patterns.

In contrast to the group-centered, the individual-centered groups may or may not have institutional sponsorship. With a few notable exceptions, persons who decide to lead individual-centered groups are self-selected rather than appointed by an organization on the basis of formal training, supervision, and demonstrated competence. As a consequence the quality of leadership of encounter groups is highly variable. Leaders range from the highly trained mental health professional to the "compleat" novice.

As these groups proliferate, it becomes clear that they attract participants who would ordinarily seek psychotherapy. The clients of the groups appear to be drawn primarily from young and middle-aged members of the middle class. The groups are especially attractive to students and professionals—particularly mental health practitioners themselves. These groups have been very aptly described as group therapy for normals (Weschler et al., 1962); however, the definition of normal is becoming increasingly ambiguous.

The issue of whether these groups are primarily educational or therapeutic in intent seems to many encounter group practitioners a meaningless and unnecessary distinction. While the initial goals of the T-group were clearly limited to the study of group processes, the current trend toward use of the group for personal growth, self-knowledge, and peak experiences has confounded the issue.

The NTL has attempted to reestablish this important distinction in its recent policy statement: "Insofar as it is possible to distinguish between education and psychotherapy, NTL Institute programs are applied for educational, not psychotherapeutic, purposes. The Institute does not design or conduct programs to cure or alleviate pathological, mental or emotional conditions" (NTL, 1959, p. 7). However, review of the brochures of many encounter group leaders suggests that, as with zealots of any new truth, their major aim is to spread enlightenment. They offer their truths promiscuously to all comers. There is little evidence that unaffiliated encounter group leaders attempt to screen out patients from nonpatients. This is a difficult enough task for the professional and a frankly impossible one for the layman. Neither the popularity of the concept of the "cultural neurosis" nor the encounter

movement's failure to recognize the qualifications for patienthood make the problem any easier.

THE CULTURAL CONTEXT

Although the group movement did not spring Minervalike from the Jovian brow of the NTL, the author shall not undertake here to trace the vagaries of its growth. Excellent summaries of this history have already been written (Yalom, 1970; Gottschalk and Pattison, 1969). Rather one should consider the cultural epoch which generated the movement and continues to sustain it. It is important to recognize that the popularity of these groups has been nurtured by the same powerful social forces that have produced other significant changes within our culture and in current psychotherapy practice.

The social changes that are reflected in these groups may be characterized as belonging to a "counterculture" in terms of implicit and explicit values. The encounter groups emphasize direct action, freedom, growth, and direct expression of feelings.

Every age attempts to define man as he should be and presumably could be if he were given the opportunity. Today the humanist-existentialist view of man has taken root in the credibility crevices which seam our political and social structure. The culture is blamed for thwarting man's desire for self-actualization, love, and intimacy. Middle-class man, having satisfied his primary physical needs for shelter and food, *pace* Maslow, has looked about for residual deprivation and has become keenly aware of his alienation. He experiences a sense of meaninglessness in the mere attainment of what had earlier been touted as the good life. (This is wittily illustrated by a pampered dog who is the heroine of a children's book by Maurice Sendak. She had pillows, round and square, her own comb and brush, two different bottles of pills, eyedrops, eardrops, a thermometer, a red wool sweater, two windows to look out of, two bowls to eat from, and a master who loved her. Yet, she decided to leave home, explaining, "I am discontented. I want something I do not have. There must be more to life than having everything!") Man's attention has shifted from his belly to his belly button and, now, to that of his neighbor.

The exacerbation of the "adolescent" conflict between dependence and independence, passivity and dominance, alienation and intimacy, reserve and openness is seen as an important contribution and problem of our culture. The term "cultural neurosis" has been devised to describe a pervasive malaise.

The wish to change an unfortunate external state is frequently seen as occasion for changing one's internal state. Groups have classically played an important role in the achievement of this goal. It has now been rediscovered that small groups may provide reassuring, enlightening, and edifying sets of experiences of varying durability—from permanent conversion to transistory titillation. The encounter groups are now being advertised as the treatment of choice for the cultural neurosis.

Rogers, in the role of spokesman for the new social movement, states that he is offering participants a set of clearly counter-posed values: ". . . becoming more spontaneous, flexible, closely related to their feelings, open to their experience, and closer and more expressively intimate in their interpersonal relationships" (1967a, p. 275).

Since encounter groups appear to be counterculture manifestations, they have been vigorously attacked by conservative individuals and groups who are not pleased to learn that their values have suddenly gone out of style. Troubled people, they believe, should be encouraged to bear their burdens privately, not to bare them publicly.

One aspect of the counterculture rebellion is its distrust of the overly rational. Thoughts, fumblingly expressed in words, fall notoriously short of the ideal of clarity and absolute honesty. Verbal communications require interpretation and may there-fore obscure meanings as often as they clarify them. Only feelings and personal experience can be trusted. These have a compelling sense of immediacy and conviction that far exceed that of rational thought. The more intense the feeling, the more intense the associated conviction. This trend is also reflected in the extraordinary increase in the use of psychedelic drugs as well as the current popularity of audience participation in the theater.

According to the existentialist, the most pervasive problems experienced by members of this society are boredom, fear of intimacy, fear of self-disclosure, and lack of commitment. While it may be argued that these problems do not fall uniquely in the area of competence of the psychotherapist, he is appropriately concerned when encounter group leaders undertake to treat individuals who either could be more usefully treated by psychotherapy or are so precariously balanced that the intensity of the group experience may precipitate serious decompensation.

The untrained encounter group leader can evade this sobering responsibility by pointing to the growing debate within the psychiatric community regarding the meaning of the term mental illness. The fact that this concept is largely a metaphor encourages the erroneous interpretation that the problem of differentiating between the psychiatric patient and nonpatient is purely one of semantics without identifiable referents or significant consequences.

The controversy over the encounter group as an inadvertent therapeutic arena is aggravated by a growing antiprofessional bias, clearly reflected in increased skepticism regarding the value of graduate training for the psychotherapist. "Often, he [the student] becomes so burdened with theoretical and diagnostic baggage that he becomes *less* able to understand the inner world of another person as it seems to that person. Also, as his professional training continues, it all too often occurs that his initial warm liking for other persons is submerged in a sea of psychiatric and psychological evaluation, and hidden under an all-enveloping professional role" (Rogers,

1965, p. 106). The concern regarding the negative effect of training is echoed by Carkhuff.

Such questions, coupled with the real scarcity of trained individuals equipped to deal with the pressures of the community psychiatry programs, may contribute to the entrance of nonprofessionals into the group field. To the professional, however, this is an explanation, not an excuse. He views with jaundice the burgeoning number of paraprofessionals who treat parapatients in encounter groups. One of the reasons may be that these parapatients tend to be young, well-to-do, intelligent, highly motivated, verbal, successful, and only moderately disturbed. In short, they would make ideal psychotherapy patients.

THE EFFECTS OF THE NEW GROUPS

The kinship between group therapists and "new group" practitioners is perhaps most clearly illustrated in their unanimous avoidance of systematic and rigorous assessment of the effects of their efforts. The new group leaders, while eloquent and rhapsodic in describing the functions and goals of their groups, are quite inarticulate in presenting evidence of consequences. Outcome research here, as in group therapy, is sporadic, ill-designed, and inconclusive.

In part, the reluctance of the encounter group practitioner to subject his work to objective scrutiny stems from the bias which scorns the "uptight" investigator who demands objective evidence. The practitioner appears to share the view expressed in *Man of La Mancha*: "Facts are the enemy of truth."

The undeniable fact, however, is that the small-group movement is still growing and large numbers of people are attending these groups. This would appear to be a powerful testimonial to their effectiveness, but the question remains: Effectiveness for what? What kinds of changes occur, with what kinds of individuals, and under what kinds of conditions? As in the field of psychiatry this sort of research has yet to be done. It is with these reservations in mind that I shall undertake to scan the reports in the literature. Two basic questions are addressed here: (1) Are the stated goals achieved? (2) What are the dangers and negative effects?

Achievement of Goals

The major aims of small groups can be grouped into three categories: (1) enhancing organizational efficiency, (2) enhancing interpersonal skills, and (3) enhancing the sense of well-being.

1. **Enhanced Organizational Efficiency.** Process-centered groups have as one of their aims training participants to experience and to recognize group forces and their own contribution to them. The test of such training is its practical application in expediting the work of task-oriented groups in the "back-home" situation.

One of the most sophisticated reviews of this sizable literature has recently been completed by Campbell and Dunnette. I shall therefore cite their conclusions, with which I am in agreement. They bring in a Scotch verdict: ". . . the assumption that T-group training has positive utility for organizations must necessarily rest on shaky ground. It has been neither confirmed nor disconfirmed."

2. **Enhanced Interpersonal Skills.** There are a number of reports which purport to show that experience in T-groups and encounter groups produces increased skills in communication, independence, flexibility, increased self-awareness, and sensitivity to others' feelings. These changes are not only observed in the group but are apparently maintained in the "back-home" setting. Comparisons of individuals who have completed a group experience and those who have not suggest that the experimental subjects show two to three times as many "changes" as do the control subjects. According to Bunker, for example, approximately one-third of group subjects ($N =$

229) tended to show increases in openness, receptivity, tolerance of differences, and operational skills in interpersonal relationships, and improved understanding of self and others; only 15 to 20 per cent of the control group (N = 125) showed such changes. An even higher percentage of favorable change in group participants (64%) was reported by Boyd and Elliss.

While there is evidence in support of positive effects of T-group training, a number of problems exist in these studies. One of the difficulties is that the amount of change reported appears to vary with the source of the judgments. The trainee's opinion of the effectiveness of his behavioral change tends to be far more optimistic than that of observers. For example, Miles reported that of 34 high school principals who had participated in NTL programs, 82 per cent indicated improved functioning subsequent to their training. Ratings by their ''back-home'' colleagues, however, indicated that only 30 per cent had undergone changes. The fact that the participant's own responses are more enthusiastic than those of his associates was also found by Taylor.

Campbell and Dunnette summarize the evidence for change: ''In absolute terms about 30 per cent to 40 per cent of the trained individuals were reported as exhibiting some sort of perceptible change.'' These findings must be interpreted with caution, since there are two obvious methodological problems.

The interpretation of data submitted by judges is difficult in that peers tend to assign less change to colleagues who completed a group training experience than do either their superiors or subordinates (Valiquet, 1964). Compounding the serious problem of judge bias is the fact that these studies are based solely on opinions obtained at the conclusion of the training period. In the absence of a pretraining baseline the results are of questionable value.

3. **Enhanced Sense of Well-Being.** A number of encounter group leaders view the major function of the group as simply providing an intense emotional experience.

This shifts the criterion for assessing success to the internal subjective state of the participant. If it is assumed that reaction to the encounter groups are to be treated as private events, such as aesthetic appreciation or recreational enjoyment, then such reports may be assumed to have face validity. The individual may take that which he chooses, or is capable of choosing, from the opportunity provided.

That most participants retrospectively report global satisfaction with their group experience is indicated by the survey findings of three investigators. Perhaps the most careful study was that conducted by Rogers (1967a), who was able to obtain responses to his questionnaire from 82 per cent (481) of clients who had participated in groups which he had led. Three-fourths reported that it had been a helpful, positive experience: 30 per cent stated that the experience had been ''constructive,'' and 45 per cent described it as a ''deeply meaningful, positive experience.'' An additional 19 per cent checked that it had been ''more helpful than unhelpful'' (1967a, p. 273).

Approximately the same degree of participant satisfaction, 78 per cent, is implied by Bach (1968), who states that his analysis of the self-reports of 612 participants is supportive of the clinical impressions reported by his colleague Stoller. Stoller is quoted as stating that only 20 per cent of participants do not get the kind of gain they seek and about 1 or 2 per cent undergo actual harm (cited in Bach, 1968, p. 246). An earlier report by Bach is even more sanguine, for he reports of 400 group members: ''Ninety per cent of these Marathon Group participants . . . have evaluated their 24- to 40-hour group encounters as 'one of the most significant and meaningful experiences' of their lives'' (1967b, p. 1147).

Mintz (1969) also undertook to obtain follow-up reports from group participants and found that of 93 subjects who evaluated their experiences immediately after the termination of the marathon group, 66 per cent reported that they had profited greatly and 30 per cent reported that they had profited moderately. In a sample of 80 who evaluated their marathon group experience after a minimum period of three months or longer, 46 per cent had profited greatly and 41 per cent had profited moderately. A further analysis of the data reported by Mintz reveals that the rate of decline in enthusiasm appears to be differentially related to whether the participant is himself a psychotherapist or not. While 70 per cent of the nontherapists report immediately upon group termination that they are greatly profited, only 34 per cent still report after three months or more that they were greatly profited. On the other hand, psychotherapists tend to maintain their enthusiasm—or possibly increase it: 62 per cent in the immediate response period report having profited greatly, while 67 per cent in the follow-up period report similarly.

These studies permit investigators to conclude that most of the clients who choose to respond to the inquiries of their former group leaders report that they "gained something" from the experience. Neither Bach nor Mintz provided information regarding the number of eligible respondents who failed to reply to these questionnaires, and they do not attempt to compare the characteristics of the responder and nonresponder samples. Besides the issue of response bias, there are three other methodological problems which further limit the value of these studies. (1) There are no control groups to aid in assessing the impact of techniques, leader personality, style, level of training, length of meeting time, and other such obvious variables. (2) Measures were not taken prior to the group experience but only after the group had disbanded. This acts to increase the opportunity for rater bias. (3) The measures used are global rather than specific. It is not possible to determine the specific nature of the changes experienced—e.g., interpersonal sensitivity, empathy, warmth, objectivity, and other such presumed goals of the encounter groups.

When investigators have attempted to identify specific rather than general changes induced by encounter-type groups, e.g., changes in self-concept, changes in inner- or outer-directedness, and changes in attitude and personality, the findings are less positive. Stock found that the individuals who reported the greatest degree of change in their self-percepts were also those who had become much less sure of what kinds of people they were. Kassarjian attempted to determine whether sensitivity training influenced participants to become more "other-directed," as is claimed by some, or more "inner-directed," as claimed by others. He failed to find any reliable directional shifts in ten groups of subjects compared on measures taken before and after training. Kassarjian concluded that social character may not be one of the variables affected by such training. Students who were exposed to a program of sensitivity training were reported by Massarik and Carlson as showing no significant change in such standard personality measures as the CPI (cited in Dunnette, 1962), the MMPI, F-scale (Kernan, 1964), and the Cattell 16 Personality Factor Questionnaire (Cadden et al., 1969).

The paucity of standardized scales employed makes it difficult to assess the nature of attitude and personality changes that may be fostered in encounter groups. Of the attitude scales employed, only the FIRO-B appeared to give positive results (Smith, 1964; Schutz and Allen, 1966).

In summary, participants in encounter groups report favorable reactions and are frequently described by others as showing improved interpersonal skills. The evidence is meager that such participants undergo significant attitude change or personality change, and evidence that group training improves organizational efficiency is not compelling. What is clearest is that these groups provide an intensive affective experience for many participants. In this sense, the groups may be described as potent. As is the case with all potent agents, they may be helpful when properly administered, inert in "subclinical" dosages, and noxious when excessive or inappropriate.

Dangers

It is apparent from the public press and from an increasing number of articles appearing in professional journals that the enthusiasm for encounter groups is not universal. The public fear is that the very popularity of these groups may ultimately endanger society by encouraging the spread of values inimical to the standards and morality of our culture. The professional fear is that encounter group participation may produce psychonoxious effects in the individual during and/or after his group participation.

The evidence of the impact of encounter groups on our cultural values is unclear and even more inferential than are the inadequate data on its effect on the individual participant. Those who insist on ascribing a major role to such groups in either undermining or saving our society may be doing the encounter group much too much honor. The author proposes, therefore, to finesse the first issue and to limit this discussion to the area of primary professional concern to the group psychotherapist, namely, the assessment of the evidence of psychological and emotional damage to group participants.

Clinicians are becoming increasingly concerned about the sheer number of "new" patients who report that their earlier participation in one or another of the encounter groups precipitated serious emotional disturbances. While it is entirely appropriate to recognize that the clinician may be exposed to a highly selected sample—that is, those individuals who have had "bad trips" rather than those who have had favorable experiences—these observations cannot be lightly dismissed. Lazarus who is no stranger to experimentation with new techniques, has recently written that the number of patients who are "victims of encounter groups is becoming so large as to constitute a new 'clinical entity.'"

Three major areas of negative effects shall be reviewed: (1) psychosis and other serious emotional reactions; (2) mild to moderate emotional disturbances; and (3) "re-entry" problems.

1. **Psychosis and Other Serious Emotional Reactions.** A number of case reports have cited compelling instances of psychotic and near psychotic reactions to encounter group exposure (for example, Odiorne, 1963; Marmor, quoted in Hoover, 1967; Jaffe and Scherl, 1969). A cursory review of these findings may give the impression that the association between encounter group attendance and serious pathological reactions is quite high. This may reflect only an increased incidence of negative reports rather than an increase of untoward reactions. However, both trends may be true.

The clinician who becomes aware that someone has suffered a serious breakdown subsequent to a group experience is understandably concerned; he is eager to inform his colleagues of the negative effects of the seemingly promiscuous and amateurish application of encounter groups to a wide spectrum of clients. He may not be much comforted by evidence that the occurrence of such gross reactions may be relatively rare with respect to the total number of persons who participate in groups. He is concerned only that pathological reactions occur at all. If a group experience is capable of precipitating severe psychological reactions, then the clinician will wish to take action to minimize this risk.

Granting the seriousness of even a single instance in which an individual is so stressed by a group experience as to become grossly disturbed, one should consider the evidence regarding the incidence of such events.

Rogers (1967a), who has achieved a considerable reputation as both a therapist and researcher, particularly in the field of assessing the effects of psychotherapy, reported that of a total sample of 587 (sample size was computed on the basis of Rogers' report that the follow-up data from 481 Ss represented an 82 per cent return) subjects whom he treated in some forty groups, only two participants showed a psychotic reaction during or immediately following the intensive group experience. A further statement by Rogers suggests that he is including in this analysis only those cases in which psychoses were not transitory, for he states, "On the other side of the picture is the fact that individuals have also lived through what were clearly psychotic episodes, and lived through them very constructively, in the context of a basic encounter group" (1967a, p. 273). These data suggest that in Rogers' groups enduring psychotic reactions occurred in only 0.3 per cent of the reporting participants. It is not clear, however, what proportion suffered transitory psychotic episodes during the life of the group.

It is noted that in Bach's discussion of a study of 400 marathon group participants, he does not report a single instance of a seriously pathological reaction. He states ". . . but no one, so far, has ever complained of any real emotional or social damage to himself" (1967b, p. 1147). A subsequent report by Bach based on the cumulative sample of 612 "research subjects," although less optimistic, supports his earlier findings: ". . . we do not know of any instance of permanent deterioration due to marathon-group shock" (1968, p. 246). Similarly, Mintz's (1969) follow-up study, based on a sample of 173 respondents and the observation of a minimum of 279 participants, fails to mention the occurrence of any psychotic reactions.

The reports of these three encounter group practitioners, based on a sample of approximately 1500 group participants, suggests that the incidence of psychoticlike reactions is quite small. There are, however, conflicting reports from other participants, observers, and researchers.

An unusually high incidence of psychopathological reactions was reported by Gottschalk (1966), and subsequently by Gottschalk and Pattison (1969). Gottschalk participated in one group and observed two others in the course of a two-week Human Relations Laboratory. Here only his observations of psychotic and severe reactions shall be considered. In a group of 11 in which he was a member, Gottschalk diagnosed "one borderline acute

psychotic withdrawal reaction" and "two severe emotional breakdowns with acute anxiety." In another group of ten participants, he found "one frank psychotic reaction" and "two severe depressive reactions with anxiety." In a third group of 11 he found no severe emotional reactions (1966, p. 475; Gottschalk and Pattison, 1969, p. 833) Thus, of 32 participants, two (6.5%) showed psychotic reactions and 4 (12.5%) showed severe disruptions in performance. In total, the reports suggest that 19 per cent of the participants were seriously disturbed by their group experience.

A preliminary report of a research study conducted at Stanford University (Lieberman et al., in preparation) on the effects of encounter group experiences is based on a sample of 209 university students. As of the time of this writing, one student had suffered a manic state and another student had become "severely anxiously depressed." This suggests that approximately 1 per cent of the participants were seriously disturbed by the group experience. A third student committed suicide, but the role of the encounter group seems minimally implicated.

Another case report, this one originating at the Menninger School of Psychiatry (Lima and Lievano, 1968, personal communication), claims that two of 11 psychiatric residents who participated in the same T-group suffered "psychotic breakdowns" (18%), and one more became psychotic some seven months after (sic) the group had ended.

The difference between the low casualty rate reported by the encounter group practitioners (less than 1%) and the higher rates reported by other sources (1% to 19%) may be attributable to a number of factors other than the obvious interest of the practitioner in presenting his work in a favorable light.

Competence and Skills of Leaders. The encounter group leaders whose work is cited here are expert, and, therefore, members of their groups may suffer less risk than do participants in groups led by less expert group leaders. The hypothesis that untoward reactions are attributable to the inadequacies of the group leaders is an appealing and popular one. Bach (1968) notes that many instances of "flip-outs" have come to his attention but that these occurred in groups that were conducted by leaders who were incompetent in both the clinical and group-dynamics areas. Greatest leadership skill is required in both the control of the anxiety levels which are stimulated within the group—i.e., in the monitoring of "regressive levels" (Scheidlinger, 1968)—and in the therapeutic use of such experiences.

Differential Significance Assigned to Transitory Emotional Disturbances. Encounter group practitioners and nonpractitioners place different weight on evidences of transitory psychotic manifestations. Practitioners, unlike observers, participants, and researchers, may tend not to report such episodes, for on the basis of their experience, they have become inured to the occurrence of brief, intensive reactions, even those of psychoticlike proportions. Observers and others who have less experience with such groups may not share the leaders' reassuring breadth of familiarity with such phenomena and will tend to report each instance as evidence of important untoward consequences. The occurrence of intense emotional stress in group members may be highly valued by leaders as evidence of the power of the "medicine." Powerful medicine promises powerful change. It is very reassuring to know that "something is happening."

For some encounter group leaders the mere fact that an individual may have a psychotic reaction is not taken as unequivocal evidence of an undesirable response. Concern is tempered by a rather optimistic view of the potential gains for the disturbed individual. It is argued that he will ultimately be benefited as his personality is reintegrated in a new and more constructive manner. The expectation that psychotic disruptions may permit more effective integrations of personality is not new in the field of psychiatry, but compelling demonstrations of the beneficial effects of psychotic reactions, particularly those which endure beyond the life of the group,

have yet to be made. The group leader who encourages psychotic regressions must be prepared to provide a high level of professional service to his group members during and after the period of the group's existence. It cannot be assumed that a psychotic episode, without appropriate therapeutic interventions, will automatically lead to more effective personality integrations. Our back wards are filled with patients who even after many years have failed to attain maximum benefit from their psychoses.

Limitation of Follow-Up Information. Since the leaders of brief intensive groups have contact with group members only for the duration of the groups, they usually remain unaware of the occurrence of negative consequences in members following termination of the groups. The clinician, on the other hand, sees only the casualties and not the successes.

2. **Mild to Moderate Emotional Disturbances.** Each individual responds to the stress of group participation with homeostatic mechanisms. When he is unable to invoke his usual defenses or when the level of stress exceeds his capacity to compensate, symptoms of varying degrees of pathology may be evidenced. While the reports suggest that mild to moderate disturbances are not uncommon, it is usually difficult to determine whether and to what degree the reactions are transitory or enduring.

A psychiatrist who was acting as the psychiatrist-in-residence at a two-week group reported that the total incidence of emotional disturbances requiring his care was approximately 0.5 per cent (Sata, personal communication). Another psychiatrist who attended a lab sponsored by the same parent organization found that approximately 10 to 15 per cent of the participants consulted the lab psychiatrist for such complaints as anxiety, depression, agitation, and insomnia (Yalom et al., 1970). An even higher rate of pathological reactions among participants in similar groups was reported by Gottschalk. Of 32 members in three groups not only did six subjects (19%), as previously noted, have serious pathological reactions, but an additional nine subjects (28%) showed milder but substantial psychological disturbances. Thus, the incidence of emotional disturbances in these three groups appears to be a phenomenal 47 per cent.

While Rogers (1967a) does not present direct evidence of the frequency with which negative experiences occurred among his group participants, he stated that a number (unspecified) found it necessary to seek psychotherapy to deal with the feelings that were stimulated but left unresolved in the "workshop groups." He added that in the absence of more specific information about each individual case, it is not possible to determine whether this observation is to be interpreted as a negative or positive outcome. While the assessment of negative or pathological responses usually requires a professional judgment, one may properly infer negative reactions from the self-reports of the participants. I am not here concerned with whether the participant was merely disappointed with his experience but whether he experienced it as damaging.

The follow-up study by Rogers (1967a) indicates that of the 481 subjects who assessed their group experiences after a period of two to 12 months, only two individuals described it as "mostly damaging"; another six cases described it as "more unhelpful than helpful" and 21 classified it as "mostly frustrating, annoying, or confusing." Thus, of those reporting, only 6 per cent reported negative reactions. It is not known, of course, how the 106 nonresponders would have described their reactions to the group experience.

Based on a survey of 612 marathon group participants, Bach reported that only four (0.6%) could be classed as having been damaged by the experience, that is, clients ". . . who get 'hurt' and stay hurt . . ." (1968, p. 246). Mintz's study revealed that only two respondents (2.5%) of a sample of 80 subjects, reporting after a minimum of three months following their group experience, indicated an increase in symptoms: ". . . increase in anxiety and depression lasting for several weeks" (1969, p. 94).

In brief, the reports of mild to moderate emotional disturbances that occur *during* the group experience range from 0.5 per cent to 28 per cent; negative reactions that endure *subsequent* to the group experience range from 0.6 per cent to about 6 per cent.

Critics of encounter groups have suggested that participants may sustain significant injury in ways not ordinarily reported in the usual survey studies. They refer not simply to increasing instances of physical injury—contusions, strains, sprains, and broken limbs—as a consequence of relatively uninhibited expressions of feelings, but to the intensive group and individual assaults on a member's sensibilities. Too often, when a group member finds some group practices, particularly those involving physical intimacy or invasion of privacy, personally offensive, his reaction is explained simply as an instance of hypersensitivity or an indulgence in overly "precious" thinking. Some humanists, however, have begun to voice objection to group activities which, in the name of reverence for everyone's essential humanness, subject the individual to dehumanizing and humiliating experiences (Koch, 1969).

The clinician, researcher, and potential client will be more benefited by the identification of factors that contribute importantly to psychological accidents than by the derivation of reliable "morbidity" tables estimating the probabilities of serious emotional breakdowns among encounter group participants. The reports currently available provide little evidence concerning the influences of such variables as client, leader, group composition, techniques, duration, and setting. There is little to guide the clinician other than the commonsense advice to select participants with good ego-strength and ability to cope with stress (Jaffe and Scherl, 1969). The prospective group member, in turn, is urged to select a group leader who has been "well trained" and is "skillful." The meaning of these terms is obscure, not only to the prospective client but apparently to many aspiring group leaders as well.

3. **"Re-entry" Problems.** There is evidence that some participants experience problems on returning to their homes and to the workaday world. Rogers (1967a), for example, has noted that an individual who attends an encounter group may be moved to recognize and confront marital tensions that he had previously sought to ignore. This experience, coupled with his greater openness and honesty, may lead to encounters at home of such candidness that the marriage may ultimately be endangered. The danger is enhanced if the spouse has not also been exposed to group participation. Rogers further observes that the sexual component of the warm and loving feelings which may develop between group members can constitute "a profound threat to their spouses if these feelings are not worked through satisfactorily in the workshops" (1967a, p. 274).

A nondiscriminating, single-minded adherence to the rediscovered ideal of directness and openness in one's interpersonal relationships may be greeted by one's employer and co-workers with more restrained joy than was evinced by the encounter group leader and one's fellow participants. Some encounter group graduates appear to have overlooked the point that skills in communication are not limited to directness but include the accurate assessment of the recipient's receptivity to the communication.

What appears to be seized upon by some participants is the attractiveness of an absolute and infallible standard: all behavior should be uniformly truthful, honest, direct, open, and unhesitatingly spontaneous. Compromise with these high standards is unerringly recognized as a falling-away from grace and as evidence of hypocrisy. This approach dismisses as misguided the socialization process which attempts to convey the complexities of Murray's (1938, pp. 136-137) tpmo formulas—the relation of the nature and intensity of one's behavior to the time, place, mode, and object.

There are reports that individuals are deeply moved by their experiences and appear to undergo rapid and radical changes akin to a conversion experience. One of the most common expressions of this type of dramatic change is the conversion of laymen, after a single workshop, lab, or T-group into encounter group leaders. So widespread is this extraordinary parthenogenetic transmutation that the authors of the NTL *Standards for the Use of Laboratory Method* twice allude to the phenomenon. They emphasize, "No capabilities as a T-Group trainer or consultant should be assumed as a result of participation in one or more basic laboratories or other short-term experiences" (1969, p. 11).

The change in self-concept may affect other areas of participants' lives. Some individuals are so impressed by their new self that they attempt to undo earlier life decisions regarding marriage, jobs, etc., that were made by the old self. This can be tragic when the new self melts.

For some group participants the reality of the encounter group is more attractive than the seemingly bland, cold, hypocritical, and compromising world. As a consequence, a new breed of escapists is developing—the group addicts. Once hooked, these people move from group to group in their attempt to regain the elusive "peak experience" and "meaningful" interchange with others.

In brief, there is evidence that emotional disturbances—serious and mild, transitory and enduring—may be precipitated by encounter group experiences. This finding is not challenged even by the encounter group's warmest and most enthusiastic supporters. The reports do little, however, to advance knowledge regarding the relevant variables responsible for negative effects. It is difficult to interpret meaningfully materials based on a wide variety of groups of varying purposes, techniques, leadership skills, composition, and duration.

The reported incidence of pathological reactions, however, does appear to be somewhat more ominous in the writings of participants, observers, and psychotherapists than in the publications of encounter group leaders. The issue of assessing the extent of iatrogenic reactions to encounter groups is analogous to the problem of interpreting military reports of casualties. Much depends on the size of the sample that is selected as the reference population from which a rate is computed. To the leader of a ten-man squad, three casualties represent "heavy" losses; to the commander of a company of 200 men of which the squad is a part, these three casualties are "light." Similarly, those associated with a single encounter group in which one or two serious emotional reactions are observed will be impressed by the high casualty rate. The group leader who has conducted 40 or 50 groups and uses some 400 to 600 participants as his baseline experience will be less disquieted by the occurrence of a relatively few pathological reactions. While all agree that every effort must be made to reduce or eliminate such reactions, encounter group leaders also appear to be sustained by one or more assumptions which act to minimize the potential threat posed by clients who suffer psychotic or other serious reactions to encounter group experiences. Encounter group leaders seem to believe that: (1) such responses are merely transitory; (2) they are potentially beneficial as they may make the individual accessible to personality reorganization; and (3) the potential benefits outweigh the risks.

The last assumption should be considered, as it is basic to the problem of making recommendations to prospective participants. Clearly, there is a degree of risk involved in encounter group participation, but the studies fail to shed much light on the critical problems of risk of what, risk for whom, and risk under what conditions. Clinicians are left, then, to make their day-to-day decisions on the basis of clinical experience and professional biases regarding the selection of appropriate subjects and the prerequisite training for group leaders. That the individual may experience stress as a result of "treatment" may not in itself be a sufficient basis for rejecting the treatment form. In some instances the possibility of increasing a patient's discomfort may be viewed as an acceptable risk in the light of the potential gain. Surgery presents the classical example of this phenomenon, for it always produces some new symptoms. Frequently, useful medicines

have side effects. Whether the risk of iatrogenic effects of interventions are tolerable depends on the seriousness of the condition being treated, the probability that the treatment will achieve a more desirable state, and the intensity and duration of the discomfort concomitant to such treatment.

The individuals who present themselves for encounter groups are presumably not seriously disturbed. If they are, then all responsible practitioners are agreed that they do not belong in encounter groups. Participation in encounter groups may be classed as an elective cosmetic operation rather than as an urgent life-saving procedure. If the analogy is apt, how much risk should one be willing to take? This is a highly individual choice, and ideally it should be made by each candidate on the basis of unambiguous information and expert opinion regarding his suitability. Unfortunately, neither of these conditions can be adequately fulfilled. The degree of risk an individual might be willing to endure in order to "grow," "self-actualize," and experience himself more deeply is a highly personal matter. The acceptable risk level might be somewhat less for the same individual if the goal is to learn more about group processes and to improve organizational efficiency.

Having only the evidence currently available in the public press and professional journals, the circumspect clinician who wishes to advise prospective group participants regarding possible dangers can, with confidence, offer only the following kind of advice: participation in most encounter groups is likely to be more dangerous than attending an office Christmas party and somewhat less dangerous than skiing.

THE CONTRIBUTION OF THE ENCOUNTER GROUP TO GROUP PSYCHOTHERAPY

Encounter group practices are of interest to psychotherapists, and particularly to group psychotherapists, because of their claimed advantages in (a) accelerating the development of conditions prerequisite for the treatment process, (b) attaining goals overlapping with those of psychotherapy despite use of techniques different from those emphasized by therapists, and (c) expediting the training of mental health practitioners.

Development of Prerequisite Treatment Conditions

Most psychotherapists believe that the process of therapy involves three conditions: (1) stimulating or re-creating in the treatment setting the patient's emotional conflicts, (2) increasing his accessibility to new experience (via support, permissiveness, confidence in the potency of the treatment, etc.), and (3) introducing those procedures which the therapist assumes will bring about therapeutic change. The first two steps are common to all forms of therapy while the third is determined by the theoretical assumptions favored by the therapist. The encounter group approaches may have a special contribution to make in establishing the first two conditions.

In addition to the usual group therapy procedures, the encounter group adds an expanding repertoire of verbal and nonverbal exercises. Direct interchange, including varying degrees of physical contact and intimacy, is encouraged. The techniques include a wide spectrum: sensory awareness, role-playing, meditating, fatiguing, wrestling, rocking, restraining, dancing, fantasizing, "spread-eagling," "crotch-eyeballing," etc. The nature and range of the techniques suggested seem to be limited only by the ingenuity and *chutzpah* of the leader. There appears to be an escalation in the race among technique-innovators to invent procedures which are stimulating, exciting, and, above all, different. As a consequence the unique advantages of varying degrees of nudity in groups are undergoing a thorough scrutiny at such research centers as Esalen. It has been reported that some groups have discovered the distinctive benefits of nonsexual

manipulation of nude participants (Lawrence, 1969). Hopefully by the time this volume is published, the advantages of frankly sexual manipulation will also have been discovered.

The capacity of some of these groups quickly to establish an atmosphere of warmth, mutual acceptance, and love is by now well-documented. Their techniques are effective both with groups of complete strangers and with groups of individuals who have pregroup relationships, some of which are expected to continue after the group terminates.

Overlapping Goals—Different Techniques

Both encounter groups and therapy groups appear to share such aims as aiding group members to become increasingly sensitive to their impact on others and to their own misperceptions and distortions, and helping them to learn more effective ways of relating. In the encounter group, such goals are the end points of the training program, while in the therapy group, increased awareness and the acquisition of new social skills are only intermediate goals. The ultimate goals in psychotherapy are relieving the patient's discomfort and assisting him to function more effectively, not only in the group but in his life situations. Further, the group therapist is concerned not only with "teaching" new patterns of behavior but with helping the patient to unlearn old ones, and with increasing the patient's capacity to discriminate between present life situations and earlier ones.

The group therapist, particularly the analytic rather than "existential" or "supportive" therapist, deals with the member's group behavior principally as it provides clues to the patient's underlying motives. The central concern is with covert processes, and only secondarily with overt behavior. In the encounter group, the interest in group behavior is in highlighting group-shared motivations and conflicts.

The group therapist is interested in the techniques employed by encounter group leaders not only because both groups share some of the same goals but also because the encounter group leader claims to be able to achieve the shared goals relatively quickly. More importantly, the encounter group leader claims to reach these goals by the use of techniques and approaches not usually employed by psychotherapists.

One of the major contributions of encounter group practice for the analytic group therapist may be the development of procedures which facilitate rapid group formation and group cohesion. The heightened psychological stimulation achieved appears to increase suggestibility and emotional contagion, thus producing a climate characterized as group formative regression. The analytic therapist, unlike the encounter group leader, does not regard this level of group functioning as an end point but attempts to utilize it in the development of "therapeutic regression"—temporal and topographical. It may be possible for the psychoanalytically oriented therapist to adopt some of the group formative procedures of the encounter group in order to accelerate the process of analyzing resistances, defenses, transferences, distortions, free association, dream, and fantasies.

An objection frequently raised by classical therapists is that the encounter groups emphasize the "affective" and "here and now" at the expense of insight into the underlying, unresolved emotional conflicts of the past. These psychotherapists believe that an interpretation may produce useful insight if it is well-timed and/or correct. Such an interpretation is accompanied by an affective response. It may be debated whether the useful insight and affective response occur because the interpretation is "correct" and, therefore, convincing, or whether the compelling nature of the insight is due less to its accuracy than to the degree of associated emotional experience.

In the author's view, the encounter group procedures which enhance the affective experience of the participants may be useful to the insight-oriented psychotherapist even if they do not arise as a result of conventional interpretation. If the patient can be assisted to experience an intense affective state, then he will be accessible to a plausible and congenial interpretation which appears to explain that emotional state. It seems to be in the nature of man to seek to understand the meaning of any powerful experience.

> Tiger got to hunt,
> Bird got to fly;
> Man got to sit and wonder,
> "Why, why, why?"
>
> Tiger got to sleep,
> Bird got to land;
> Man got to tell himself
> he understand.
>
> (Vonnegut, 1968, p. 124)

The view that "interpretations" offered after affective arousal have useful impact is supported by a study conducted by Hoehn-Saric et al.

Analytically oriented group psychotherapists, such as Mintz (1967), have found it very useful to employ arm wrestling, rocking, restraining, holding, etc., in order to assist individual members to "get in touch with their feelings" and to stimulate recall of repressed and suppressed material. These and other encounter group procedures may assist the analytically oriented group therapist to accomplish the mediating goal of re-creating emotional conflicts of the past in the present group situation.

The encounter group has been used by psychotherapists to supplement treatment programs for their patients. Group therapists are now undertaking marathon groups with their patients in order to deal with group resistances, to stimulate strong affective experiences for patients, and to provide them with a further opportunity to intensively explore their interpersonal relationships.

Therapists recognize that a strong emotional experience is not necessarily therapeutic per se; however, patients who are gifted intellectualizers and well practiced in the art of obsessing may find the affect-arousing stimulation of the encounter group particularly useful. It may provide an important step in the total treatment process.

The therapist and patient can then collaborate to utilize this new experience in the subsequent "working through" process.

Training of Mental Health Practitioners

Many training programs for professional therapists are being expanded to include trainee participation in one or more sensitivity training groups. The Annual Institutes sponsored by the American Group Psychotherapy Association (AGPA) have increasingly veered from didactic workshop training to an almost exclusive concentration on training via the experiential "process group" and encounter group. These personal growth groups play an important training role in a variety of psychotherapist training programs, including the Group Psychotherapy Training Program of the Washington School of Psychiatry and that of the New York State Psychiatric Institute (Berger, 1969). Many universities have made attendance at T-groups part of the required training for psychologists, psychiatrists, public health workers, etc.

While the encounter group may be a particularly useful procedure for dramatically demonstrating certain group phenomena to the trainee, in my view, it is not a substitute for participation as a patient in a psychotherapy group.

THE ROLE AND RESPONSIBILITY OF THE PROFESSIONAL GROUP THERAPIST

If the preceding discussion is a fair representation of the nature, bases, effects, and usefulness of encounter groups, what stance should the professional group psychotherapist adopt *vis-à-vis* such groups?

Typically the public pronouncements and recommendations emanating from professional organizations and their spokesmen are represented as being motivated exclusively by a wholesome and selfless interest

in furthering the welfare of the society. That what is seen as furthering the welfare of the public happens to be highly correlated with what enhances the welfare of the profession is dismissed as a coincidence. In this case the author believes he does not need to invoke a disclaimer regarding conflict of interests.

The welfare of the group psychotherapist does not seem particularly threatened by the new group movement. The inherent dangers of the current trends are far more ominous for the established T-groups and group process organizations than for the professional group therapy societies. Group dynamics organizations are being threatened with extinction by the influx of self-appointed—and self-annointed—encounter group leaders from two sides: the professional group therapist and the overzealous and undertrained layman. Gresham's law—bad money drives out the good —may have an analogous application for these groups. Its corollary certainly holds: Good money brings in bad leaders. This possibility has not been overlooked by those most concerned. Recently the NTL has published the first of what promises to be a series of statements specifying standards of ethical practice, training of leaders, and a guide to the selection of suitable clients. Such efforts are to be applauded and vigorously supported. One must, however, resist the temptation to identify as the sole problem the fact that the leadership of the small-group field has been infiltrated by psychodynamic illiterates. While it may be an exhilarating exercise to hurl polemic missiles at this group, at this point no one has the authority to enforce acceptance of recommended standards or the power to impose sanctions on those who violate them.

It is highly probable that ultimately some formal organizations will be identified as authorized to offer appropriate training, and perhaps still other practitioner-organized societies will arise to monitor the ethical practices of the encounter group leaders. In any event, the author does not see the AGPA as a likely candidate to take on these responsibilities.

The fact that no professional society of

encounter group practitioners has yet been constituted leaves the field without minimal standards for assessing qualifications of potential leaders and without a formal set of ethical standards. While such practitioners are not usually liable to malpractice suits, since they do not "hold themselves out" as offering treatment, they still are legally responsible under tort law for any injury—physical or emotional—which their clients sustain. Clients who believe that they have been injured may sue for damages "in order to be made whole again." That the pursuit of such legal recourse has not become a more common practice suggests that it may not provide adequate protection, is not widely recognized, or is not justified.

The professional group therapist frequently becomes preoccupied with the question of whether or not the nonclinically trained encounter group leader is perpetrating psychotherapy on his witting or unwitting clients. A related question, but not identical, is whether psychiatric patients are being "treated" in encounter groups. Both questions are an embarrassment and are better tabled. Psychotherapy cannot be defined either by evidence of its unique effects or by its professionally specialized and restricted techniques. Psychotherapy is defined simply by intent. The nonclinically trained encounter group leader does not publicly undertake to offer psychotherapy. He is, therefore, not performing psychotherapy. It would be difficult to prove that someone is performing psychotherapy accidentally or against his will.

The second question revolves about the definition of the state of being a patient. While the professional psychotherapist appears to be able to discriminate individuals into two classes—psychiatric patients and nonpatients—this is admittedly a difficult task. Many challenges have been made of the concept of the "psychiatric" patient and of the entire concept of mental illness. The problem has not been clarified by the psychotherapist's reluctance clearly to define the limits of patienthood. The waters are further muddied by the fact that the term has recently been extended by therapists to include the nonpatient class of

"cultural neuroses." If the trained professional extends the limits of the class designation, "patient," he must expect that at any given time one or more patients will be found frolicking on the encounter group floor. The therapist, presumably, is not objecting because such patients are being effectively treated but because they are not being helped or are, indeed, being injured in some way. This concern invites the clinician to choose among a number of alternative courses of action. He could, for example, attempt to prevent the nonclinically trained from leading such groups, or he could encourage such leaders to seek further training, supervision, consultation, etc., or he might, himself, offer to provide such services to leaders, or he might choose to deliver service directly to the group members.

These alternatives are painfully familiar to the medical psychotherapist, who over the years has somewhat reluctantly been forced into the position of training the nonmedical practitioner. The psychiatrists' efforts to enforce the exclusion of the "layman" from the field of psychotherapy have proved to be impracticable. The author predicts no greater success with regard to encounter group leaders.

While he is sensitive to the fact that untrained encounter group leaders—particularly those not exposed to clinical practice or to professional societies which can enforce ethical practice—constitute a serious problem, he is also aware that exhortation and finger-wagging are tiresome and unprofitable exercises. It is his intention, therefore, primarily to address professional group therapists—among them those who may have already undertaken to lead encounter groups and those who aspire to roles of leader, supervisor, consultant, and adviser.

The group therapist who elects to offer his services to the encounter group leader must be modest about the areas of his competence. By virtue of the clinician's training and experience, he can be of greatest help to the nonclinician group leader in aiding him to recognize the limitations of the participant's capacities to withstand stress and to recognize those clients who require psychiatric referral. Given the opportunity, the group therapist might also be useful in the selection of members and the composition of groups.

The group therapist must recognize, however, that his clinical training does not automatically equip him to conduct such groups. The effective leadership of encounter groups requires an intimate knowledge of group processes, a facility with a wide range of techniques, and a knowledge of when to employ them consistent with the level of group development. The clinician who wishes to lead encounter groups for his patients or for nonpatients must supplement his training. A plausible description of minimal training requirements is given in a recent NTL brochure: *Standards for the Use of Laboratory Methods in NTL Programs* (1969).

While the author has chosen to emphasize the potential value of encounter group techniques for the clinician, he does not imply that the group therapist is to be encouraged to use these techniques for the treatment of acute and chronically disturbed patients.

It is appropriate that the therapist be familiar with the approach and procedures of the encounter groups in order to determine whether they have anything to offer him in increasing his usefulness in the treatment of his patients. The group therapist is primarily concerned with providing his patients with the opportunity to recognize their needs and conflicts in order that they be better prepared to find gratification outside of the group. The encounter group, however, emphasizes the direct gratification, albeit in attenuated form, of needs and wishes for closeness, affection, love, sex, and even pain. It is not appropriate that the group psychotherapist impulsively adopt procedures simply because they exist or that he shift his practice from leading therapy groups for the emotionally disturbed to conducting "sheltered workshops" for the alienated, disenchanted, and unloved.

The group therapist may be called upon to assess the suitability of patients and other clients for membership in an encounter group. If the recommendation is to be made independent of knowledge of the qualifications of the prospective group leader or of the particular nature of the group procedures to be employed, then the decision must be made solely on the strengths and weaknesses of the individual in question. A permissive group atmosphere may not be particularly useful to those who require more, rather than less, ego controls, such as the characteristically hostile, the chronically asocial, the psychotic, and the flagrantly hysteric.

Ethical Standards

Professional group therapists are guided by the ethical standards developed and enforced by their own professions and professional societies. These standards will, of course, be applied by the professional in the conduct of encounter groups. While it may be unnecessary, therefore, to spell out in detail all relevant ethical considerations, the author believes it is appropriate to emphasize three principles which are basic to sound clinical practice: (1) informed consent, (2) freedom of choice, and (3) establishment of safeguards.

1. **Informed Consent.** Prior to entrance into the encounter group the patient/client should be provided with as full information as possible to permit him to make a decision as to whether the purposes, leadership, techniques, duration, costs, etc., are acceptable to him. The ideal of providing adequate information is, like all ideals, a goal to be striven for but not likely to be attained in any absolute sense. The prospective participant has, in fact, little opportunity to assess in advance the skills and intentions of the leaders, the nature of the specific exercises in which he will be expected to take part, and the likely consequences of his group participation.

If it were possible to present the candidate with complete information sufficient for him to make an intelligent choice, then it would be possible to invoke the principle of "consenting adults." The idea that mutually consenting adults may engage in private acts which are not injurious to others is gaining acceptance. As human beings we may have reservations about the morality of some acts, and we may as profession-' als offer some opinions about possible negative psychological consequences; however, once the prospective participant has been apprised of these possibilities the right of decision remains with him. Unfortunately, the responsible group leader cannot invoke the principle of consenting adults, for it will usually be impossible to provide a group candidate with all information prerequisite for meaningful "informed consent." The leader must, therefore, retain responsibility for selection and for the consequences of an individual's group experiences.

The problem of meeting the conditions for informed consent is complicated, because leaders may wish the subjects to remain in ignorance about the nature and purposes of certain procedures. This decision is presumably justified by the rationale that the effects of certain procedures will be enhanced if they are presented "spontaneously" and in a context conducive to their usefulness. These considerations may be valid, but they require that the leader undertake to further protect the individual by guaranteeing the right of free choice and by providing the necessary safeguards.

One of the dangers of withholding information is that the leader may not be able to anticipate which of the practices may be offensive to the participant. Many leaders will assume this risk in the hope that in the course of the group a climate will be established in which the participant will find certain activities inoffensive which he might otherwise have found objectionable.

The implementation of the principle of informed consent is particularly difficult because the validity of the information provided may be highly debatable. The client organization—church, school, industry— employs the services of group trainers and consultants in the hope that a specified goal or set of goals may be achieved. Responsible group relations organizations will undertake to tailor the group experience to the particular client needs specified (Schein and Bennis, 1965); however, some group leaders assume that no modification of procedure is required. They appear to believe that the indiscriminate and stereotyped attempts at breaking down defenses, the induction of regressions, and the "Zen Master" scrutiny of group process are invariably useful in the service of any and all goals. At best, such an approach may be irrelevant, and, at worst, a damaging breach of contract.

2. **Freedom of Choice.** Since the prerequisite conditions of informed consent are difficult to achieve, it is necessary that scrupulous attention be paid to preserving the client's right of free choice. This includes the client's right to withdraw from any given activity or from the group itself without being exposed to pressures from the group members or leadership. The principle of free choice is not to be violated even when the practitioner is confident that his own motivation is simply that of doing good unto the client. Ethical standards require that proper respect be shown for the convictions, sensibilities, and values of the clients. It is unethical to attempt to impose any morality on the subject that is contrary to his own.

The group leader must be prepared to protect the individual member from the subtle and overt pressures exerted by the group to force the "deviant" member to conform to the group norms. The mere announcement that participants are free to decline participation is no assurance that the rights of the nonconformist will be protected. The group leader must actively protect the participants' freedom of decision. Free choice can only be exercised when the individual is not threatened by humiliation, reprisal, rejection, or ridicule.

A special problem is presented by the practice of some industries and universities of requiring employees and students to participate in encounter-type groups. Ethical considerations require that such potential group members be excused from the group if they prefer not to participate. It is necessary that the sponsoring agency be familiarized with and respect the principle of free choice. No adverse action should be taken against those who decline to enter such groups.

3. **Establishment of Safeguards.** It is the leader's responsibility to provide adequate facilities and resources to protect the subject against the possibility of psychological or physical injury. The most relevant safeguards are, of course, the leader's sensitivity to the psychological states of the participants and his skillful regulation of stress levels in order not to exceed the coping abilities of the individuals involved.

The skilled therapist is careful to permit an optimal level of regression, namely, a level which does not overwhelm the patients' capacity to utilize primary-process materials constructively. The skills required in the stimulation of regression and, more importantly, in the promotion of the effective use of such material by the observing, synthesizing, and controlling ego cannot be assumed to be present in the casually trained or untrained encounter group leader. The leader must also assume responsibility for dealing with crisis situations should they arise and for making use of appropriate referrals as indicated. The leader must be willing to remove from the group any individual who may harm others or himself by his continued participation in the group.

CONCLUSIONS

The burgeoning growth of the encounter groups, which may now be nearing its asymptote, cannot be dismissed as a fad. Such groups will survive after the more bizarre aspects fade, just as the basic tenets of psychoanalysis survived the period of "wild analyis."

There is evidence that the majority of participants report satisfaction with their encounter group experience and indicate that it helped them to feel more related to themselves and to others. There is but little evidence that such subjective changes are enduring or that these changes are followed by behavioral, personality, or performance improvements. As with any intensive and emotionally stimulating experiences, they result in transitory emotional disturbances in some participants and enduring pathological changes in a few.

While leadership training and the adherence to sound ethical practices cannot guarantee elimination of negative effects, they can do much to minimize their occurrence. The dangers of indiscriminate application of these procedures by undisciplined leaders to the psychologically unstable are apparent.

Some of the principles and techniques of the encounter group may be usefully explored by the analytic group psychotherapist in order to expedite the treatment of patients. However, a number of group therapists appear to be moving in the direction of leading encounter groups of nonpatients. The therapist's primary responsibility remains with patients—psychotic, schizoid, depressed, obsessive, compulsive, phobic, anxious, and sociopathic. He has no special responsibility or unique competence in dealing with others who have as their primary goals the seeking of a new purpose and new meaning in life.

Man's ultimate motivation appears to be that of finding and maintaining a state of happiness. It is not surprising, therefore, that over the centuries various proposals have been put forth for the achievement of this goal. What is surprising is how few proposals have emerged and how recurrent these few are. The encounter group movement appears to proffer only one of the classical views. Necessarily, it conflicts with other classical prescriptions. The author will not presume to enter into the philosophical debate over which is the true *summum bonum*. He suggests only that concepts such as the reification of openness and honesty, the celebration of the body, and regard for one's inner experiences deserve no less respect than the set which urges the benefits of self-denial, self-discipline, and self-mastery as prerequisites to the joy of competence, intellectual achievement, and productivity. Both views are due the reverence accorded to age and survival. Neither has led to a Golden Age. However, the individual who has access to alternative views and alternative routes to happiness may be less despairing when he finds himself at a road block.

Admittedly the fields of "small groups" and of group psychotherapy, like society itself, are in flux. The basic challenge is the familiar one summarized by Whitehead: "The art of progress is to preserve order amid change and to assure change amid order."

REFERENCES

Bach, G. R. The marathon group: intensive practice of intimate interaction. Psychol. *18:* 995, 1966.

Bach, G. R. Marathon group dynamics: I. Some functions of the professional group facilitator. Psychol. Rep. *20:* 995, 1967.

Bach, G. R. Marathon group dynamics: II. Dimensions of helpfulness: therapeutic aggression. Psychol. Rep. *20:* 1147, 1967.

Bach, G. R. Marathon group dynamics: III. Disjunctive contacts. Psychol. Rep. *20:* 1163, 1967.

Bach, G. R. Discussion. Int. J. Group Psychother. *18:* 244, 1968.

Berger, M. M. Experimental and didactic aspects of training and therapeutic group approaches. Amer. J. Psychiat., *126:* 845, 1969.

Boyd, J. B. and Elliss, J. D. *Findings of Research into Senior Management Seminars.* Hydro-Electric Power Commission of Ontario, Toronto, 1962.

Bunker, D. R. Individual application of laboratory training. J. Applied Behav. Sci., *1:* 131, 1965.

Burton, A. *Encounter.* Jossey-Bass, San Francisco, 1969.

Cadden, J. J., Flach, F. F., Blakeslee, S., and Charlton, R., Jr. Growth in medical students through group process. Amer. J. Psychiat., *126:* 862, 1969.

Campbell, J. P., and Dunnette, M. D. Effectiveness of T-group experiences on managerial training and development. Psychol. Bull., *70:* 73, 1968.

Carkhuff, R. R. Requiem or reveille. In: *Sources of Gain in Counseling and Psychotherapy.* B. G. Berenson and R. R. Carkhuff, editors. pp. 8–20. Jossey-Bass, San Francisco, 1967.

Casriel, D. H., and Deitch, D. The Marathon: Time-extended group therapy. In: *Current Psychiatric Therapies,* J. H. Masserman, editor. Grune & Stratton, New York, 1968.

Dunnette, M. D. Personnel management. Annual Rev. Psychol., *13:* 285, 1962.

Gottschalk, L. A. Psychoanalytic notes on T-groups at the human relations laboratory, Bethel, Maine. Comprehensive Psychiat., *7:* 472, 1966.

Gottschalk, L. A., and Pattison, E. M. Psychiatric perspectives on T-groups and the laboratory movement: an overview. Amer. J. Psychiat., *126:* 823, 1969.

Hoehn-Saric, R., Frank, J. D., and Gurland, B. J. Focused attitude change in neurotic patients. J. Nerv. Ment. Dis., *147:* 124, 1968.

Hoover, E. The great group binge. West Magazine, Los Angeles Times, Jan. 8, pp. 8–13, 1967.

Jaffe, S. L., and Scherl, D. J. Acute psychosis precipitated by the T-group experiences. Arch. Gen. Psychiat., *21:* 443, 1969.

Kassarjian, H. H. Social character and sensitivity training. J. Applied Behav. Sci., *1:* 433, 1965.

Kernan, J. P. Laboratory human relations training: its effects on the "personality" of supervisory engineers. Dissert. Abs., *25:* 665, 1964.

Koch, S. Psychology cannot be a coherent science. Psychology Today, *3:* 14, 1969.

Kuehn, J. L., and Crinelia, F. M. Sensitivity training: interpersonal overkill and other problems, Amer. J. Psychiat., *126:* 841, 1969.

Lawrence, S. B. Psychology in action. Video tape and other therapeutic procedures with nude marathon groups. Amer. Psychologist, *24:* 476, 1969.

Lazarus, A. A. *Behavior Therapy and Beyond.* McGraw-Hill, New York, 1970.

Lieberman, M. A., Miles, M., Yalom, I. D., and Golde, P. *Encounter Groups: Process and Outcome—A Controlled Study* (in preparation).

Lima, F. P., and Lievano, J. E. Personal communication, 1968.

Miles, M. B. Changes during and following laboratory training: a clinical-experimental study. J. Applied Behav. Sci., *1:* 215, 1965.

Mintz, E. E. Time-extended marathon groups. Psychotherapy: Theory, Research and Practice, *4:* 65, 1967.

Mintz, E. E. Marathon groups: a preliminary evaluation. J. Contemp. Psychother., *1:* 91, 1969.

Murray, H., et al. *Explorations in Personality.* Oxford, New York, 1938.

National Training Laboratory, *Standards for the Use of Laboratory Method in NTL Institute Programs.* NTL Institute, Washington, D.C., 1969.

Odiorne, G. S. The trouble with sensitivity training. Training Directors Journal, *10:* 9, 1963.

Parloff, M. B. Assessing the effects of headshrinking and mind-expanding. Int. J. Group Psychother. *20:* 14, 1970.

Rarick, J. R. Sensitivity training. Congressional Record-House of Representatives, June 10, 1969, H4666, 1969.

Rogers, C. R. The therapeutic relationship: recent theory and research. Austral. J. Psychol., *17:* 95, 1965.

Rogers, C. R. A conversation with the father of Rogerian therapy. Psychology Today, *1:* 20, 1967.

Rogers, C. R. The process of the basic encounter group. In: *Challenges of Humanistic Psychology*, J. F. G. Bugental, editor. McGraw-Hill, New York, 1967.

Rogers, C. R. Interpersonal relationships: year 2000. J. Applied Behav. Sci., *4:* 265, 1968.

Sata, L. Personal communication, 1967.

Scheidlinger, S. The concept of regression in group psychotherapy. Int. J. Group Psychother., *18:* 3, 1968.

Schein, E. H., and Bennis, W. G., editors. *Personal and Organizational Change Through Group Methods: The Laboratory Approach.* Wiley, New York, 1955.

Schutz, W. C., and Allen, V. L. The effects of a T-group laboratory on interpersonal behavior. J. Applied Behav. Sci., *2:* 265, 1966.

Glossary*

Aberration, mental. Pathological deviation from normal thinking. Mental aberration is not related to a person's intelligence. *See also* Mental illness.

Abreaction. A process by which repressed material, particularly a painful experience or a conflict, is brought back to consciousness. In the process of abreacting, the person not only recalls but relives the repressed material, which is accompanied by the appropriate affective response. *See also* Catharsis.

Accelerated interaction. An alternate term for marathon group session that was introduced by one of its co-developers, Frederick Stoller. *See also* Group marathon.

Accountability. The responsibility a member has for his actions within a group and the need to explain to other members the motivations for his behavior.

Acid. Slang for lysergic acid diethylamide (LSD).

Acrophobia. Fear of high places.

Acting out. An action rather than a verbal response to an unconscious instinctual drive or impulse that brings about temporary partial relief of inner tension. Relief is attained by reacting to a present situation as if it were the situation that originally gave rise to the drive or impulse. *See also* Therapeutic crisis.

Actional-deep approach. Group procedure in which communication is effected through various forms of nonverbal behavior as well as or in place of language to produce character change. It is a technique used in psychodrama. *See also* Actional-superficial approach, Activity group therapy, Verbal-deep approach, Verbal-superficial approach.

Actional-superficial approach. Group procedure in which specific activities and verbal communication are used for limited goals. Verbal interchange and patient-to-patient interaction are of relatively minor therapeutic significance, and the groups are usually large. *See also* Actional-deep approach, Verbal-deep approach, Verbal-superficial approach.

Action group (A-group). Group whose purpose is to discuss a problem—community, industrial, or organizational—and to formulate a program of action. Emphasis is put on problem-solving rather than on developing awareness of self and group process. *See also* T-group.

Active therapist. Type of therapist who makes no effort to remain anonymous but is forceful and expresses his personality definitively in the therapy setting. *See also* Passive therapist.

Activity group therapy. A type of group therapy introduced and developed by S. R. Slavson and designed for children and young adolescents, with emphasis on emotional and active interaction in a permissive, nonthreatening atmosphere. The therapist stresses reality-testing, ego-strengthening, and action interpretation. *See also* Actional-deep approach; Activity-interview method; Bender, Lauretta; Play therapy.

Activity-interview method. Screening and diagnostic technique used with children. *See also* Activity group therapy.

Actualization. Process of mobilizing one's potentialities or making them concrete. *See also* Individuation.

---

* Edited by Ernesto A. Amaranto, M.D.

I

Adaptational approach. An approach used in analytic group therapy. Consonant with Sandor Rado's formulations on adaptational psychodynamics, the group focuses on the maladaptive patterns used by patients in the treatment sessions, on how these patterns developed, and on what the patients must do to overcome them and stabilize their functioning at self-reliant, adult levels. New methods of adaptation are practiced by the group members in the therapeutic sessions and later in their regular interpersonal relationships. *See also* Social adaptation.

Adapted Child. In transactional analysis, the primitive ego state that is under the parental influence. The adapted Child is dependent, unexpressive, and constrained. *See also* Natural Child.

Adler, Alfred (1870–1937). Viennese psychiatrist and one of Freud's original followers. Adler broke off from Freud and introduced and developed the concepts of individual psychology, inferiority complex, and overcompensation. A pioneer in group psychotherapy, he believed that the sharing of problems takes precedence over confidentiality. He also made contributions in the understanding of group process. *See also* Individual psychology, Masculine protest.

Adolescence. Period of growth from puberty to maturity. The beginning of adolescence is marked by the appearance of secondary sexual characteristics, usually at about age 12, and the termination is marked by the achievement of sexual maturity at about age 20. *See also* Psychosexual development.

Adult. In transactional analysis, an ego state oriented toward objective, autonomous data-processing and estimating. It is essentially a computer, devoid of feeling. It is also known as neopsychic function.

Affect. Emotional feeling tone attached to an object, idea, or thought. The term includes inner feelings and their external manifestations. *See also* Inappropriate affect, Mood.

Affect, blunted. A disturbance of affect manifested by dullness of externalized feeling tone. Observed in schizophrenia, it is one of that disorder's fundamental symptoms, according to Eugen Bleuler.

Affection phase. Last stage of group treatment. In this phase the members experience reasonable equality with the therapist and dwell on affectionate contact with each other in a give-and-take atmosphere rather than dwelling on dependency or aggression. *See also* Inclusion phase, Power phase.

Affective interaction. Interpersonal experience and exchange that are emotionally charged.

Affectualizing. In transactional analysis, the expression of emotions or feelings in group or individual treatment as part of a pasttime or game. It is distinguished from the expression of authentic feelings, which are characteristic of intimacy.

Afro-American. American Negro of African ancestry. This term has significance for blacks who seek a deeper and more positive sense of identity with their African heritage. *See also* Black separatism.

After-session. Group meeting of patients without the therapist. It is held immediately after a regular therapist-led session. *See also* Alternate session, Premeeting.

Agency. The striving and need to achieve in a person. Agency manifests itself in self-protection, the urge to master, self-expansion, and repression of thought, feeling, and impulse. *See also* Communion.

Aggression. Forceful, goal-directed behavior that may be verbal or physical. It is the motor counterpart of the affects of rage, anger, and hostility.

Aggressive drive. Destructive impulse directed at oneself or another. It is also known as the death instinct. According to contemporary psychoanalytic psychology, it is one of the two basic drives; sexual drive is the other one. Sexual drive operates on the pleasure-pain principle, whereas aggressive drive operates on the repetition-compulsion principle. *See also* Aggression, Libido theory.

Agitation. State of anxiety associated with severe motor restlessness.

Agnosia. Disturbance of perception characterized by inability to recognize a stimulus and interpret the significance of its memory impressions. It is observed in patients with organic brain disease and in certain schizophrenics, hysterics, and depressed patients.

Agoraphobia. Fear of open places. *See also* Claustrophobia.

Agranulocytosis. A rare, serious side effect, occurring with some of the psychotropic drugs. The condition is characterized by sore throat, fever, a sudden sharp decrease in white blood cell count, and a marked reduction in number of granulocytes.

A-group. *See* Action group.

Alcoholics Anonymous (A.A.) An organization of alcoholics formed in 1935. It uses certain group methods, such as inspirational-supportive techniques, to help rehabilitate chronic alcoholics.

Algophobia. Fear of pain.

Allergic jaundice. *See* Jaundice, allergic.

Alliance. *See* Therapeutic alliance, Working alliance.

Allport's group relations theory. Gordon W. Allport's theory that a person's behavior is influenced by his personality and his need to conform to social forces. It illustrates the interrelationship between group therapy and social psychology. For example, dealing with bigotry in a therapy group enhances the opportunity for therapeutic experiences because it challenges the individual patient's need to conform to earlier social determinants or to hold on to familiar but restrictive aspects of his personality.

Alternate session. Scheduled group meeting held without the therapist. Such meetings are held on a regular basis in between therapist-led sessions. Use of this technique was originated by Alexander Wolf. *See also* After-session, Premeeting.

Alternating role. Pattern characterized by periodic switching from one type of behavior to another. For example, in a group, alternating role is observed among members who switch from the role of the recipient of help to the giver of help.

Alternating scrutiny. *See* Shifting attention.

Altruism. Regard for and dedication to the welfare of others. The term was originated by Auguste Comte (1798–1857), a French philosopher. In psychiatry the term is closely linked with ethics and morals. Freud recognized altruism as the only basis for the development of community interest; Bleuler equated it with morality.

Ambivalence. Presence of strong and often overwhelming simultaneous contrasting attitudes, ideas, feelings, and drives toward an object, person, or goal. The term was coined by Eugen Bleuler, who differentiated three types: affective, intellectual, and ambivalence of the will.

Amnesia. Disturbance in memory manifested by partial or total inability to recall past experiences.

Amphetamine. A central nervous system stimulant. Its chemical structure and action are closely related to ephedrine and other sympathomimetic amines. *See also* Sympathomimetic drug.

Anal erotism. *See* Anal phase.

Anal phase. The second stage in psychosexual development. It occurs when the child is between the ages of one and three. During this period the infant's activities, interests, and concerns are centered around his anal zone, and the pleasurable experience felt around this area is called anal erotism. *See also* Genital phase, Infantile sexuality, Latency phase, Oral phase, Phallic phase.

Analysis. *See* Psychoanalysis.

Analysis in depth. *See* Psychoanalysis.

Analysis of transference. *See* Psychoanalysis.

Analytic psychodrama. Psychotherapy method in which a hypothesis is tested on a stage to verify its validity. The analyst sits in the audience and observes. Analysis of the material is made immediately after the scene is presented.

Anchor. Point at which the patient settles down to the analytic work involved in the therapeutic experience.

Antianxiety drug. Drug used to reduce pathological anxiety and its related symptoms without influencing cognitive or perceptual disturbance. It is also known as a minor tranquilizer and a psycholeptic drug. Meprobamate derivatives and diazepoxides are typical antianxiety drugs.

Anticholinergic effect. Effect due to a blockade of the cholinergic (parasympathetic and somatic) nerves. It is often seen as a side effect of phenothiazine therapy. Anticholinergic effects include dry mouth and blurred vision. *See also* Paralytic ileus.

Antidepressant drug. Drug used in the treatment of pathological depression. It is also known as a thymoleptic drug and a psychic energizer. The two main classes of antidepressant drugs are the tricyclic drugs and the monoamine oxidase inhibitors. *See also* Hypertensive crisis, Monoamine oxidase inhibitor, Tinnitus, Tricyclic drug.

Antimanic drug. Drug, such as lithium, used to alleviate the symptoms of mania. Lithium is particularly effective in preventing relapses in manic-depressive illness. Other drugs with antimanic effects are haloperidol and chlorpromazine.

Antiparkinsonism drug. Drug used to relieve the symptoms of parkinsonism and the extrapyramidal side effects often induced by antipsychotic drugs. The antiparkinsonism drug acts by diminishing muscle tone and involuntary movements. Antiparkinsonism agents include benztropine, procyclidine, biperiden, and trihexphenidyl. *See also* Cycloplegia, Mydriasis.

Antipsychotic drug. Drug used to treat psychosis, particularly schizophrenia. It is also known as a major tranquilizer and a neuroleptic drug. Phenothiazine derivatives, thioxanthene derivatives, and butyrophenone derivatives are typical antipsychotic drugs. *See also* Autonomic side effect, Dyskinesia, Extrapyramidal effect, Major tranquilizer, Parkinsonismlike effect, Reserpine, Tardive oral dyskinesia.

Antirepression device. Technique used in encounter groups and therapeutic groups to break through the defense of repression. In encounter groups, such techniques are frequently nonverbal and involve physical contact between group members. In therapeutic groups, dream analysis, free association, and role-playing are some antirepression techniques.

Anxiety. Unpleasurable affect consisting of psychophysiological changes in response to an intrapsychic conflict. In contrast to fear, the danger or threat in anxiety is unreal. Physiological changes consist of increased heart rate, disturbed breathing, trembling, sweating, and vasomotor changes. Psychological changes consist of an uncomfortable feeling of impending danger accompanied by overwhelming awareness of being powerless, inability to perceive the unreality of the threat, prolonged feeling of tension, and exhaustive readiness for the expected danger. *See also* Basic anxiety, Fear.

Apathetic withdrawal. *See* Withdrawal.

Apathy. Want of feeling or affect; lack of interest and emotional involvement in one's surroundings. It is observed in certain types of schizophrenia and depression.

Apgar scores. Measurements taken one minute and five minutes after birth to determine physical normality in the neonate. The scores are based on color, respiratory rate, heart beat, reflex action, and muscle tone. Used routinely, they are particularly useful in detecting the effects on the infant of drugs taken by the pregnant mother.

Aphasia. Disturbance in speech due to organic brain disorder. It is characterized by inability to express thoughts verbally. There are several types of aphasia: (1) motor aphasia—inability to speak, although understanding remains; (2) sensory aphasia—inability to comprehend the meaning of words or use of objects; (3) nominal aphasia—difficulty in finding the right name for an object; (4) syntactical aphasia—inability to arrange words in proper sequence.

Apperception. Awareness of the meaning and significance of a particular sensory stimulus as modified by one's own experiences, knowledge, thoughts, and emotions. *See also* Perception.

Archeopsychic function. *See* Child.

Arteriosclerotic cardiovascular disease. A metabolic disturbance characterized by degenerative changes involving the blood vessels of the heart and other arteries, mainly the arterioles. Fatty plaques, deposited within the blood vessels, gradually obstruct the flow of blood. Organic brain syndrome may develop when cerebral arteries are involved in the degenerative process.

Ataractic drug. *See* Major tranquilizer.

Ataxia. Lack of coordination, either physical or mental. In neurology it refers to loss of muscular coordination. In psychiatry the term intrapsychic ataxia refers to lack of coordination between feelings and thoughts; the disturbance is found in schizophrenia.

Atmosphere. *See* Therapeutic atmosphere.

Attention. Concentration; the aspect of consciousness that relates to the amount of effort exerted in focusing on certain aspects of an experience.

Attitude. Preparatory mental posture with which one receives stimuli and reacts to them. Group therapy often involves itself in defining for the group members their attitudes that have unconsciously dominated their reactions.

Auditory hallucination. False auditory sensory perception.

Authenticity. Quality of being authentic, real, and valid. In psychological functioning and personality, it applies to the conscious feelings, perceptions, and thoughts that a person expresses and communicates. It does not apply to the deeper, unconscious layers of the personality. *See also* Honesty.

Authority figure. A real or projected person in a position of power; transferentially, a projected parent.

Authority principle. The idea that each member of an organizational hierarchy tries to comply with the presumed or fantasied wishes of those above him while those below him try to comply with his wishes. *See also* Hierarchical vector, Political therapist, Procedural therapist.

Autism. *See* Autistic thinking.

Autistic thinking. A form of thinking in which the thoughts are largely narcissistic and egocentric, with emphasis on subjectivity rather than objectivity and without regard for reality. The term is used interchangeably with autism and dereism. *See also* Narcissism.

Autoerotism. Sexual arousal of self without the participation of another person. The term, introduced by Havelock Ellis, is at present used interchangeably with masturbation. In psychoanalysis, autoerotism is considered a primitive phase in object-relationship development, preceding the narcissistic stage. In narcissism there is a love object, but there is no love object in autoerotism.

Autonomic side effect. Disturbance of the autonomic nervous system, both central and peripheral. It may be a result of the use of anti-psychotic drugs, particularly the phenothiazine derivatives. The autonomic side effects include hypotension, hypertension, blurred vision, nasal congestion, and dryness of the mouth. *See also* Mydriasis.

Auxiliary ego. In psychodrama, a person, usually a member of the staff, trained to act out different roles during a psychodramatic session to intensify the therapeutic situation. The trained auxiliary ego may represent an important figure in the patient's life. He may express the patient's unconscious wishes and attitudes or portray his unacceptable self. He may represent a delusion, hallucination, symbol, ideal, animal, or object that makes the patient's psychodramatic world real, concrete, and tangible. *See also* Ego model Hallucinatory psychodrama, Mirror, Multiple double.

Auxiliary therapist. Co-therapist. *See also* Co-therapy.

Back-home group. Collection of persons that a patient usually lives with, works with, and socializes with. It does not include the members of his therapy group. *See also* Expanded group.

Bag. Slang for area of classification, interest, or skill. Bringing together members of a group with different bags makes it initially difficult to achieve a feeling of group cohesiveness but later provides the potential for more productive interchange and deeper cohesiveness.

Basic anxiety. As conceptualized by Karen Horney, the mainspring from which neurotic trends get their intensity and pervasiveness. Basic anxiety is characterized by vague feelings of loneliness, helplessness, and fear of a potentially hostile world. *See also* Anxiety, Fear.

Basic skills training. The teaching of leadership functions, communication skills, the use of group processes, and other interpersonal skills. National Training Laboratories' groups include this training as part of the T-group process. *See also* East-Coast-style T-group.

Behavioral group psychotherapy. A type of group therapy that focuses on overt and objectively observable behavior rather than on thoughts and feelings. It aims at symptomatic improvement and the elimination of suffering and maladaptive habits. Various conditioning and anxiety-eliminating techniques derived from learning theory are combined with didactic discussions and techniques adapted from other systems of treatment.

Behind-the-back technique. An encounter group procedure in which a patient talks about himself and then turns his back and listens while the other participants discuss him as if he were physically absent. Later he "returns" to the group to participate in further discussions of his problems.

Bender, Lauretta (1897–). American psychiatrist who has done extensive work in the fields of child psychiatry, neurology, and psychology. She employed group therapy, particularly activity group therapy, with inpatient children in the early 1940's.

Berne, Eric (1910–1970). American psychiatrist. He was the founder of transactional analysis, which is used in both individual and group therapy. *See also* Transactional group psychotherapy.

Bestiality. Sexual deviation in which a person engages in sexual relations with an animal.

Bieber, Irving (1908–). American psychiatrist and psychoanalyst who has done extensive work in the field of homosexuality. He originated the first major scientific study of male homosexuality published as *Homosexuality; A Psychoanalytic Study*.

Bio-energetic group psychotherapy. A type of group therapy developed by Alexander Lowen that directly involves the body and mobilizes energy processes to facilitate the expression of feeling. Verbal interchange and a variety of exercises are designed to improve and coordinate physical functioning with mental functioning.

Bion, Walter R. British psychoanalyst of the Kleinian school. He introduced concepts dealing largely with the group as a whole. He was one of the European workers who demonstrated the use of open wards in mental hospitals and who developed the concept of therapeutic milieu. *See also* Leaderless therapeutic group, Pairing, Therapeutic community.

Bisexuality. Existence of the qualities of both sexes in the same person. Freud postulated that both biologically and psychologically the sexes differentiated from a common core, that differentiation between the two sexes was relative rather than absolute, and that regression to the common core occurs to varying degrees in both normal and abnormal conditions. An adult person who engages in bisexual behavior is one who is sexually attracted to and has contact with members of both sexes. He is also known in lay terms as an AC-DC person. *See also* Heterosexuality, Homosexuality, Latent homosexuality, Overt homosexuality.

Black separatism. Philosophy that blacks, in order to develop a positive identity, must establish cultural, socioeconomic, and political systems that are distinctively black and separate from white systems. *See also* Afro-American.

Blank screen. Neutral backdrop on which the patient projects a gamut of transferential irrationalities. The passivity of the analyst allows him to act as a blank screen.

Blind self. The behavior, feelings, and motivations of a person known to others but not to himself. The blind self is one quadrant of the Johari Window, a diagrammatic concept of human behavior. *See also* Hidden self, Public self, Undeveloped potential.

Blind spot. Area of someone's personality that he is totally unaware of. These unperceived areas are often hidden by repression so that he can avoid painful emotions. In both group and individual therapy, such blind spots often appear obliquely as projected ideas, intentions, and emotions.

Blind walk. A technique used in encounter groups to help a member experience and develop trust. As a group exercise, each member picks a partner; one partner closes his eyes, and the other leads him around, keeping him out of dangerous places. The partners then reverse roles. Later, the group members discuss their reactions to the blind walk.

Blocking. Involuntary cessation of thought processes or speech because of unconscious emotional factors. It is also known as thought deprivation.

Blunted affect. *See* Affect, blunted.

Body-contact-exploration maneuver. Any physical touching of another person for the purpose of becoming more aware of the sensations and emotions aroused by the experience. The technique is used mainly in encounter groups.

Boundary. Physical or psychological factor that separates relevant regions in the group structure. An external boundary separates the group from the external environment. A major internal boundary distinguishes the group leader from the members. A minor internal boundary separates individual members or subgroups from one another.

Brainwashing. Any technique designed to manipulate human thought or action against the desire, will, or knowledge of the person involved. It usually refers to systematic efforts to indoctrinate nonbelievers. *See also* Dog-eat-dog period, Give-up-itis.

Breuer, Josef (1842–1925). Viennese physician with wide scientific and cultural interests. His collaboration with Freud in studies of cathartic therapy were reported in *Studies on Hysteria* (1895). He withdrew as Freud proceeded to introduce psychoanalysis, but he left important imprints on that discipline, such as the concepts of the primary and secondary process.

Brill, A. A. (1874–1948). First American analyst (1908). Freud gave him permission to translate several of his most important works. He was active in the formation of the New York Psychoanalytic Society (1911) and remained in the forefront of propagators of psychoanalysis as a lecturer and writer throughout his life.

Brooding compulsion. *See* Intellectualization.

Bull session. Informal group meeting at which members discuss their opinions, philosophies, and personal feelings about situations and people. Such groups are leaderless, and no attempt is made to perceive group process, but the cathartic value is often great. It is also known as a rap session.

Burned-out anergic schizophrenic. A chronic schizophrenic who is apathetic and withdrawn, with minimal florid psychotic symptoms but with persistent and often severe schizophrenic thought processes.

Burrow, Trigant L. (1875–1951). American student of Freud and Jung who coined the term group analysis and later developed a method called phyloanalysis. Much of Burrow's work was based on his social views and his opinion that individual psychotherapy places the therapist in too authoritarian a role to be therapeutic. He formed groups of patients, students, and colleagues who, living together in a camp, analyzed their interactions.

Catalepsy. *See* Cerea flexibilitas.

Cataphasia. *See* Verbigeration.

Cataplexy. Temporary loss of muscle tone, causing weakness and immobilization. It can be precipitated by a variety of emotional states.

Catecholamine. Monoamine containing a catechol group that has a sympathomimetic property. Norepinephrine, epinephrine, and dopamine are common catecholamines.

Category method. Technique used in structured interactional group psychotherapy. Members are asked to verbally rate one another along a variety of parameters—such as appearance, intelligence, and relatedness.

Catharsis. Release of ideas, thoughts, and repressed materials from the unconscious, accompanied by an affective emotional response and release of tension. Commonly observed in the course of treatment, both individual and group, it can also occur outside therapy. *See also* Abreaction, Bull session, Conversational catharsis.

Cathexis. In psychoanalysis, a conscious or unconscious investment of the psychic energy of a drive in an idea, a concept, or an object.

Cerea flexibilitas. Condition in which a person maintains the body position he is placed into. It is a pathological symptom observed in severe cases of catatonic schizophrenia. It is also known as waxy flexibility or catalepsy.

Chain-reaction phenomenon. Group therapy situation in which information is passed from one group to another, resulting in a loss of confidentiality. This phenomenon is common when members of different groups socialize together.

Chemotherapy. *See* Drug therapy.

Child. In transactional analysis, an ego state that is an archaic relic from an early period of the person's life. It is also known as archeopsychic function. *See also* Adapted Child, Natural Child.

Chlorpromazine. A phenothiazine derivative used primarily as an antipsychotic agent and in the treatment of nausea and vomiting. The drug was synthesized in 1950 and was used in psychiatry for the first time in 1952. At present, chlorpromazine is one of the most widely used drugs in medical practice.

Circumstantiality. Disturbance in the associative thought processes in which the patient digresses into unnecessary details and inappropriate thoughts before communicating the central idea. It is observed in schizophrenia, obsessional disturbances, and certain cases of epileptic dementia. *See also* Tangentiality, Thought process disorder.

Clarification. In transactional analysis, the attainment of Adult control by a patient who understands what he is doing, knows what parts of his personality are involved in what he is doing, and is able to control and decide whether or not to continue his games. Clarification contributes to stability by assuring the patient that his hidden Parent and Child ego states can be monitored by his Adult ego state. *See also* Decontamination, Interpretation.

Class method. Group therapy method that is lecture-centered and designed to enlighten patients as to their condition and provide them with motivations. Joseph Pratt, a Boston physician, first used this method at the turn of the century to help groups of tuberculous patients understand their illness. *See also* Didactic technique, Group bibliotherapy, Mechanical group therapy.

Claustrophobia. Fear of closed places. *See also* Agoraphobia.

Client-centered psychotherapy. A form of psychotherapy, formulated by Carl Rogers, in which the patient or client is believed to possess the ability to improve. The therapist merely helps him clarify his own thinking and feeling. The client-centered approach in both group and individual therapy is democratic, unlike the psychotherapist-centered treatment methods. *See also* Group-centered psychotherapy, Nondirective approach.

Closed group. Treatment group into which no new members are permitted once it has begun the treatment process. *See also* Open group.

Clouding of consciousness. Disturbance of consciousness characterized by unclear sensory perceptions.

Coexistent culture. Alternative system of values, perceptions, and patterns for behavior. The group experience leads to an awareness of other systems as legitimate alternatives to one's own system.

Cognition. Mental process of knowing and becoming aware. One of the ego functions, it is closely associated with judgment. Groups that study their own processes and dynamics use more cognition than do encounter groups, which emphasize emotions. It is also known as thinking.

Cohesion. *See* Group cohesion.

Cold turkey. Abrupt withdrawal from opiates without the benefit of methadone or other drugs. The term was originated by drug addicts to describe their chills and consequent goose flesh. This type of detoxification is generally used by abstinence-oriented therapeutic communities.

Collaborative therapy. A type of marital therapy in which treatment is conducted by two therapists, each of whom sees one spouse. They may confer occasionally or at regular intervals. This form of treatment affords each analyst a double view of his patient—the way in which one patient reports to his analyst and the way in which the patient's mate sees the situation as reported to the analyst's colleague. *See also* Combined therapy, Concurrent therapy, Conjoint therapy, Family therapy, Group marital therapy, Marriage therapy, Quadrangular therapy, Square interview.

Collective experience. The common emotional experiences of a group of people. Identification, mutual support, reduction of ego defenses, sibling transferences, and empathy help integrate the individual member into the group and accelerate the therapeutic process. S. R. Slavson, who coined the phrase, warned against letting the collective experience submerge the individuality of the members or give them an opportunity to escape from their own autonomy and responsibility.

Collective family transference neurosis. A phenomenon observed in a group when a member projects irrational feelings and thoughts onto other members as a result of transferring the family psychopathology from early childhood into the therapeutic group situation. The interpretation and analysis of this phenomenon is one of the cornerstones of psychoanalytic group therapy. *See also* Lateral transference, Multiple transference.

Collective unconscious. Psychic contents outside the realm of awareness that are common to mankind in general, not to one person in particular. Jung, who introduced the term, believed that the collective unconscious is inherited and derived from the collective experience of the species. It transcends cultural differences and explains the analogy between ancient mythological ideas and the primitive archaic projections observed in some patients who have never been exposed to these ideas.

Coma. A profound degree of unconsciousness with minimal or no detectable responsiveness to stimuli. It is seen in conditions involving the brain—such as head injury, cerebral hemorrhage, thrombosis and embolism, and cerebral infection—in such systemic conditions as diabetes, and in drug and alcohol intoxication. In psychiatry, comas may be seen in severe catatonic states.

Coma vigil. A profound degree of unconsciousness in which the patient's eyes remain open but there is minimal or no detectable evidence of responsiveness to stimuli. It is seen in acute brain syndromes secondary to cerebral infection.

Combined therapy. A type of psychotherapy in which the patient is in both individual and group treatment with the same or two different therapists. In marriage therapy, it is the combination of married couples group therapy with either individual sessions with one spouse or conjoint sessions with the marital pair. *See also* Collaborative therapy, Concurrent therapy, Conjoint therapy, Co-therapy, Family therapy, Group marital therapy, Marriage therapy, Quadrangular therapy, Square interview.

Coming on. A colloquial term used in transactional analysis groups to label an emerging ego state. For example, when a patient points his finger and says "should," he is coming on Parent.

Command automation. Condition closely associated with catalepsy in which suggestions are followed automatically.

Command negativism. *See* Negativism.

Common group tension. Common denominator of tension arising out of the dominant unconscious fantasies of all the members in a group.

Each member projects his unconscious fantasy onto the other members and tries to manipulate them accordingly. Interpretation by the group therapist plays a prominent role in bringing about change.

Communion. The union of one living thing with another or the participation of a person in an organization. It is a necessary ingredient in individual and group psychotherapy and in sensitivity training. Both the leader-therapist and the patient-trainee must experience communion for a successful learning experience to occur. *See also* Agency.

Communion-oriented group psychotherapy. A type of group therapy that focuses on developing a spirit of unity and cohesiveness rather than on performing a task.

Community. *See* Therapeutic community.

Community psychiatry. Psychiatry focusing on the detection, prevention, and early treatment of emotional disorders and social deviance as they develop in the community rather than at large, centralized psychiatric facilities. Particular emphasis is placed on the environmental factors that contribute to mental illness.

Compensation. Conscious or, usually, unconscious defense mechanism by which a person tries to make up for an imagined or real deficiency, physical or psychological or both.

Competition. Struggle for the possession or use of limited goods, concrete or abstract. Gratification for one person largely precludes gratification for another.

Complementarity of interaction. A concept of bipersonal and multipersonal psychology in which behavior is viewed as a response to stimulation and interaction replaces the concept of reaction. Each person in an interactive situation plays both a provocative role and a responsive role.

Complex. A group of inter-related ideas, mainly unconscious, that have a common affective tone. A complex strongly influences the person's attitudes and behavior. *See also* God complex, Inferiority complex, Mother Superior complex, Oedipus complex.

Composition. Make-up of a group according to

sex, age, race, cultural and ethnic background, and psychopathology.

Compulsion. Uncontrollable impulse to perform an act repetitively. It is used as a way to avoid unacceptable ideas and desires. Failure to perform the act leads to anxiety. *See also* Obsession.

Conation. That part of a person's mental life concerned with his strivings, instincts, drives, and wishes as expressed through his behavior.

Concretization of living. As used in psychodrama, the actualization of life in a therapeutic setting, integrating time, space, reality, and cosmos.

Concurrent therapy. A type of family therapy in which one therapist handles two or more members of the same family but sees each member separately. *See also* Collaborative therapy, Combined therapy, Conjoint therapy, Family therapy, Group marital therapy, Marriage therapy, Quadrangular therapy, Square interview.

Conditioning. Procedure designed to alter behavioral potential. There are two main types of conditioning—classical and operant. Classical or Pavlovian conditioning pairs two stimuli—one adequate, such as offering food to a dog to produce salivation, and the other inadequate, such as ringing of a bell, which by itself does not have an effect on salivation. After the two stimuli have been paired several times, the dog responds to the inadequate stimulus (ringing of bell) by itself. In operant conditioning, a desired activity is reinforced by giving the subject a reward every time he performs the act. As a result, the activity becomes automatic without the need for further reinforcement.

Confabulation. Unconscious filling of gaps in memory by imagining experiences that have no basis in fact. It is common in organic brain syndromes. *See also* Paramnesia.

Confidentiality. Aspect of medical ethics in which the physician is bound to hold secret all information given him by the patient. Legally, certain states do not recognize confidentiality and can require the physician to divulge such information if needed in a legal proceeding. In group psychotherapy this ethic is adhered to by the members as well as by the therapist.

Confirmation. In transactional analysis, a re-

confrontation that may be undertaken by the patient himself. *See also* Confrontation.

Conflict. Clash of two opposing emotional forces. In a group, the term refers to a clash between group members or between the group members and the leader, a clash that frequently reflects the inner psychic problems of individual members. *See also* Extrapsychic conflict, Intrapsychic conflict.

Conflict-free area. Part of one's personality or ego that is well-integrated and does not cause any conflicts, symptoms, or displeasure. Conflict-free areas are usually not analyzed in individual analysis, but they become obvious in the interaction of an analytic group, where they can then be analyzed.

Confrontation. Act of letting a person know where one stands in relationship to him, what one is experiencing, and how one perceives him. Used in a spirit of deep involvement, this technique is a powerful tool for changing relationships; used as an attempt to destroy another person, it can be harmful. In group and individual therapy, the value of confrontation is likely to be determined by the therapist. *See also* Encounter group, Existential group psychotherapy.

Confusion. Disturbance of consciousness manifested by a disordered orientation in relation to time, place, or person.

Conjoint therapy. A type of marriage therapy in which a therapist sees the partners together in joint sessions. This situation is also called triadic or triangular, since two patients and one therapist work together. *See also* Collaborative therapy, Combined therapy, Concurrent therapy, Family therapy, Group marital therapy, Marriage therapy, Quadrangular therapy, Square interview.

Conscious. One division of Freud's topographical theory of the mind. The content of the conscious is within the realm of awareness at all times. The term is also used to describe a function of organic consciousness. *See also* Preconscious, Unconscious.

Consciousness. *See* Sensorium.

Consensual validation. The continuous comparison of the thoughts and feelings of group members toward one another that tend to modify and correct interpersonal distortions. The term was introduced by Harry Stack Sullivan. Previously, Trigant Burrow referred to consensual observation to describe this process, which results in effective reality-testing.

Contact situation. Encounter between individual persons or groups in which the interaction patterns that develop represent the dynamic interplay of psychological, cultural, and socioeconomic factors.

Contagion. Force that operates in large groups or masses. When the level of psychological functioning has been lowered, some sudden upsurge of anxiety can spread through the group, speeded by a high degree of suggestibility. The anxiety gradually mounts to panic, and the whole group may be simultaneously affected by a primitive emotional upheaval.

Contamination. In transactional analysis, a state in which attitudes, prejudices, and standards that originate in a Parent or Child ego state become part of the Adult ego state's information and are treated as accepted facts. *See also* Clarification, Decontamination.

Contemporaneity. Here-and-now.

Contract. Explicit, bilateral commitment to a well-defined course of action. In group or individual therapy, the therapist-patient contract is to attain the treatment goal.

Conversational catharsis. Release of repressed or suppressed thoughts and feelings in group and individual psychotherapy as a result of verbal interchange.

Conversion. An unconscious defense mechanism by which the anxiety that stems from an intrapsychic conflict is converted and expressed in a symbolic somatic symptom. Seen in a variety of mental disorders, it is particularly common in hysterical neurosis.

Cooperative therapy. *See* Co-therapy.

Co-patients. Members of a treatment group exclusive of the therapist and the recorder or observer. Co-patients are also known as patient peers.

Coprolalia. The use of vulgar, obscene, or dirty words. It is observed in some cases of schizophrenia. The word is derived from the Greek words *kopros* (excrement) and *lalia* (talking). *See also* Gilles de la Tourette's disease.

Corrective emotional experience. Re-exposure, under favorable circumstances, to an emotional situation that the patient could not handle in the past. As advocated by Franz Alexander, the therapist temporarily assumes a particular role to generate the experience and facilitate reality-testing.

Co-therapy. A form of psychotherapy in which more than one therapist treat the individual patient or the group. It is also known as combined therapy, cooperative therapy, dual leadership, multiple therapy, and three-cornered therapy. *See also* Role-divided therapy, Splitting situation.

Counterdependent person. *See* Nontruster.

Countertransference. Conscious or unconscious emotional response of the therapist to the patient. It is determined by the therapist's inner needs rather than by the patient's needs, and it may reinforce the patient's earlier traumatic history if not checked by the therapist.

Co-worker. Professional or paraprofessional who works in the same clinical or institutional setting.

Creativity. Ability to produce something new. Silvano Arieti describes creativity as the tertiary process, a balanced combination of primary and secondary processes, whereby materials from the id are used in the service of the ego.

Crisis-intervention group psychotherapy. Group therapy aimed at decreasing or eliminating an emotional or situational crisis.

Crisis, therapeutic. *See* Therapeutic crisis.

Crystallization. In transactional analysis, a statement of the patient's position from the Adult of the therapist to the Adult of the patient. *See also* Ego state.

Cultural conserve. The finished product of the creative process; anything that preserves the values of a particular culture. Without this repository of the past, man would be forced to create the same forms to meet the same situations day after day. The cultural conserve also entices new creativity.

Cultural deprivation. Restricted participation in the culture of the larger society.

Current material. Data from present interpersonal experiences. *See also* Genetic material.

Cyclazocine. A narcotic antagonist that blocks the effects of heroin but does not relieve heroin craving. It has been used experimentally with a limited number of drug addicts in research programs.

Cycloplegia. Paralysis of the muscles of accommodation in the eye. It is observed at times as an autonomic side effect of phenothiazine and antiparkinsonism drugs.

Dance therapy. Nonverbal communication through rhythmic body movements, used to rehabilitate people with emotional or physical disorders. Pioneered by Marian Chase in 1940, this method is used in both individual and group therapy.

Data. *See* Current material, Genetic material.

Death instinct. *See* Aggressive drive.

Decision. In transactional analysis, a childhood commitment to a certain existential position and life style. *See also* Script analysis.

Decompensation. In medical science, the failure of normal functioning of an organ, as in cardiac decompensation; in psychiatry, the breakdown of the psychological defense mechanisms that maintain the person's optimal psychic functioning. *See also* Depersonalization.

Decontamination. In transactional analysis, a process whereby a person is freed of Parent or Child contaminations. *See also* Clarification.

Defense mechanism. Unconscious intrapsychic process. Protective in nature, it is used to relieve the anxiety and conflict arising from one's impulses and drives. *See also* Compensation, Conversion, Denial, Displacement, Dissociation, Idealization, Identification, Incorporation, Intellectualization, Introjection, Projection, Rationalization, Reaction formation, Regression, Repression, Sublimation, Substitution, Symbolization, Undoing.

Defensive emotion. Strong feeling that serves as a screen for a less acceptable feeling, one that would cause a person to experience anxiety if it appeared. For example, expressing the emotion of anger is often more acceptable to a group member than expressing the fear that his anger covers up. In this instance, anger is defensive.

Déjà entendu. Illusion of auditory recognition. *See also* Paramnesia.

Déjà vu. Illusion of visual recognition in which a new situation is incorrectly regarded as a repetition of a previous experience. *See also* Paramnesia.

Delirium. A disturbance in the state of consciousness that stems from an acute organic reaction characterized by restlessness, confusion, disorientation, bewilderment, agitation, and affective lability. It is associated with fear, hallucinations, and illusions.

Delusion. A false fixed belief not in accord with one's intelligence and cultural background. Types of delusion include:
Delusion of control. False belief that one is being manipulated by others.
Delusion of grandeur. Exaggerated concept of one's importance.
Delusion of infidelity. False belief that one's lover is unfaithful; it is derived from pathological jealousy.
Delusion of persecution. False belief that one is being harrassed.
Delusion of reference. False belief that the behavior of others refers to oneself; a derivation from ideas of reference in which the patient falsely feels that he is being talked about by others.
Delusion of self-accusation. False feeling of remorse.
Paranoid delusion. Oversuspiciousness leading to false persecutory ideas or beliefs.

Dementia. Organic loss of mental functioning.

Denial. An unconscious defense mechanism in which an aspect of external reality is rejected. At times it is replaced by a more satisfying fantasy or piece of behavior. The term can also refer to the blocking of awareness of internal reality. It is one of the primitive or infantile defenses.

Dependence on therapy. Patient's pathological need for therapy, created out of the belief that he cannot survive without it.

Dependency. A state of reliance on another

for psychological support. It reflects needs for security, love, protection, and mothering.

Dependency phase. *See* Inclusion phase.

Depersonalization. Sensation of unreality concerning oneself, parts of oneself, or one's environment. It is seen in schizophrenics, particularly during the early stages of decompensation. *See also* Decompensation.

Depression. In psychiatry, a morbid state characterized by mood alterations, such as sadness and loneliness; by low self-esteem associated with self-reproach; by psychomotor retardation and, at times, agitation; by withdrawal from interpersonal contact and, at times, a desire to die; and by such vegetative symptoms as insomnia and anorexia. *See also* Grief.

Derailment. *See* Tangentiality.

Derealization. Sensation of distorted spatial relationships. It is seen in certain types of schizophrenia.

Dereism. Mental activity not concordant with logic or experience. This type of thinking is commonly observed in schizophrenic states.

Detoxification. Removal of the toxic effects of a drug. It is also known as detoxication. *See also* Cold turkey, Methadone.

Diagnostic and Statistical Manual of Mental Disorders. A handbook for the classification of mental illnesses. Formulated by the American Psychiatric Association, it was first issued in 1952 (DSM-I). The second edition (DSM-II), issued in 1968, correlates closely with the World Health Organization's *International Classification of Diseases.*

Dialogue. Verbal communication between two or more persons.

Didactic psychodrama. Psychodrama used as a teaching method. It is used with persons involved in the care of psychiatric patients to teach them how to handle typical conflicts.

Didactic technique. Group therapeutic method given prominence by J. M. Klapman that emphasizes the tutorial approach. The group therapist makes use of outlines, texts, and visual aids to teach the group about themselves and

their functioning. *See also* Class method, Group bibliotherapy, Mechanical group therapy.

Differentiation. *See* Individuation.

Dilution of transference. Partial projection of irrational feelings and reactions onto various group members and away from the leader. Some therapists do not believe that dilution of transference occurs. *See also* Multiple transference, Transference.

Dipsomania. Morbid, irrepressible compulsion to drink alcoholic beverages.

Directive-didactic approach. Group therapy approach characterized by guided discussions and active direction by the therapist. Various teaching methods and printed materials are used, and autobiographical material may be presented. Such an approach is common with regressed patients in mental institutions.

Discussion model of group psychotherapy. A type of group therapy in which issues, problems, and facts are deliberated, with the major emphasis on rational understanding.

Disinhibition. Withdrawal of inhibition. Chemical substances such as alcohol can remove inhibitions by interfering with functions of the cerebral cortex. In psychiatry, disinhibition leads to the freedom to act on one's own needs rather than to submit to the demands of others.

Displacement. An unconscious defense mechanism by which the affective component of an unacceptable idea or object is transferred to an acceptable one.

Disposition. Sum total of a person's inclinations as determined by his mood.

Dissociation. An unconscious defense mechanism by which an idea is separated from its accompanying affect, as seen in hysterical dissociative states; an unconscious process by which a group of mental processes are split off from the rest of a person's thinking, resulting in an independent functioning of this group of processes and thus a loss of the usual inter-relationships.

Distortion. Misrepresentation of reality. It is based on historically determined motives.

Distractability. Inability to focus one's attention.

Diversified reality. A condition in a treatment situation that provides various real stimuli with which the patient may interact. In a group, the term refers to the variety of personalities of the co-members, in contrast with the one personality of the analyst in the dyadic relationship.

Doctor-patient relationship. Human interchange that exists between the person who is sick and the person who is selected because of training and experience to heal.

Dog-eat-dog period. Early stage of Communist brainwashing of American prisoners during the Korean War. During this period, as described by former Army psychiatrist William Mayer, the Communists encouraged each prisoner to be selfish and to do only what was best for himself. *See also* Give-up-itis.

Dominant member. The patient in a group who tends to monopolize certain group sessions or situations.

Double. *See* Mirror.

Double-bind. Two conflicting communications from another person. One message is usually nonverbal and the other verbal. For example, parents may tell a child that arguments are to be settled peacefully and yet battle with each other constantly. The concept was formulated by Gregory Bateson.

Double-blind study. A study in which one or more drugs and a placebo are compared in such a way that neither the patient nor the persons directly or indirectly involved in the study know which is being given to the patient. The drugs being investigated and the placebo are coded for identification.

Dream. Mental activity during sleep that is experienced as though it were real. A dream has both a psychological and a biological purpose. It provides an outlet for the release of instinctual impulses and wish fulfillment of archaic needs and fantasies unacceptable in the real world. It permits the partial resolution of conflicts and the healing of traumata too overwhelming to be dealt with in the waking state. And it is the guardian of sleep, which is indispensable for the proper functioning of mind and body during the waking state. *See also* Hypnagogic hallucination, Hypnopompic hallucination, Paramnesia.

Dreamy state. Altered state of consciousness

likened to a dream situation. It is accompanied by hallucinations—visual, auditory, and olfactory—and is believed to be associated with temporal lobe lesions. *See also* Marijuana.

Drive. A mental constituent, believed to be genetically determined, that produces a state of tension when it is in operation. This tension or state of psychic excitation motivates the person into action to alleviate the tension. Contemporary psychoanalysts prefer to use the term drive rather than Freud's term, instinct. *See also* Aggressive drive, Instinct, Sexual drive.

Drop-out. Patient who leaves group therapy against the therapist's advice.

Drug therapy. The use of chemical substances in the treatment of illness. It is also known as chemotherapy. *See also* Maintenance drug therapy.

DSM. *See Diagnostic and Statistical Manual of Mental Disorders.*

Dual leadership. *See* Co-therapy.

Dual therapy. *See* Co-therapy.

Dyad. A pair of persons in an interactional situation—such as husband and wife, mother and father, co-therapists, or patient and therapist.

Dyadic session. Psychotherapeutic session involving only two persons, the therapist and the patient.

Dynamic reasoning. Forming all the clinical evidence gained from free-associative anamnesis into a psychological reconstruction of the patient's development. It is a term used by Franz Alexander.

Dyskinesia. Involuntary, stereotyped, rhythmic muscular activity, such as a tic or a spasm. It is sometimes observed as an extrapyramidal side effect of antipsychotic drugs, particularly the phenothiazine derivatives. *See also* Tardive oral dyskinesia.

Dystonia. Extrapyramidal motor disturbance consisting of uncoordinated and spasmodic movements of the body and limbs, such as arching of the back and twisting of the body and neck. It is observed as a side effect of phenothiazine drugs and other major tranquilizers. *See also* Tardive oral dyskinesia.

East-Coast-style T-group. Group that follows the traditional National Training Laboratories orientation by developing awareness of group process. The first T-groups were held in Bethel, Maine. *See also* Basic skills training, West-Coast-style T-group.

Echolalia. Repetition of another person's words or phrases. It is a psychopathological symptom observed in certain cases of schizophrenia, particularly the catatonic types. Some authors consider this behavior to be an attempt by the patient to maintain a continuity of thought processes. *See also* Gilles de la Tourette's disease.

Echopraxia. Imitation of another person's movements. It is a psychopathological symptom observed in some cases of catatonic schizophrenia.

Ecstasy. Affect of intense rapture.

Ego. One of the three components of the psychic apparatus in the Freudian structural framework. The other two components are the id and the superego. Although the ego has some conscious components, many of its operations are automatic. It occupies a position between the primal instincts and the demands of the outer world, and it therefore serves to mediate between the person and external reality. In so doing, it performs the important functions of perceiving the needs of the self, both physical and psychological, and the qualities and attitudes of the environment. It evaluates, coordinates, and integrates these perceptions so that internal demands can be adjusted to external requirements. It is also responsible for certain defensive functions to protect the person against the demands of the id and the superego. It has a host of functions, but adaptation to reality is perhaps the most important one. *See also* Reality-testing.

Ego-coping skill. Adaptive method or capacity developed by a person to deal with or overcome a psychological or social problem.

Ego defense. *See* Defense mechanism.

Ego ideal. Part of the ego during its development that eventually fuses with the superego. It is a social as well as a psychological concept, reflecting the mutual esteem as well as the dis-illusionment in child-parent and subsequent relationships.

Egomania. Pathological self-preoccupation or self-centeredness. *See also* Narcissism.

Ego model. A person on whom another person patterns his ego. In a group, the therapist or a healthier member acts as an ego model for members with less healthy egos. In psychodrama, the auxiliary ego may act as the ego model.

Ego state. In Eric Berne's structural analysis, a state of mind and its related set of coherent behavior patterns. It includes a system of feelings directly related to a given subject. There are three ego states—Parent, Adult, and Child.

Eitingon, Max (1881–1943). Austrian psychoanalyst. An emissary of the Zurich school, he gained fame as the first person to be analyzed by Freud—in a few sessions in 1907. Later he became the first chief of the Berlin Psychoanalytic Clinic, a founder of the Berlin Psychoanalytic Institute, and a founder of the Palestine Psychoanalytic Society.

Elation. Affect characterized by euphoria, confidence, and enjoyment. It is associated with increased motor activity.

Electrocardiographic effect. Change seen in recordings of the electrical activity of the heart. It is observed as a side effect of phenothiazine derivatives, particularly thioridazine.

Electroconvulsive treatment. *See* Shock treatment.

Emotion. *See* Affect.

Emotional deprivation. Lack of adequate and appropriate interpersonal or environmental experiences or both, usually in the early developmental years. Emotional deprivation is caused by poor mothering or by separation from the mother.

Emotional insight. *See* Insight.

Emotional support. Encouragement, hope, and inspiration given to one person by another. Members of a treatment group often empathize with a patient who needs such support in order to try a new mode of behavior or to face the truth.

Empathy. Ability to put oneself in another person's place, get into his frame of reference, and understand his feelings and behavior objectively. It is one of the major qualities in a successful therapist, facilitator, or helpful group member. *See also* Sympathy.

Encounter group. A form of sensitivity training that emphasizes the experiencing of individual relationships within the group and minimizes intellectual and didactic input. It is a group that focuses on the present rather than concerning itself with the past or outside problems of its members. J. L. Moreno introduced and developed the idea of the encounter group in 1914. *See also* Here-and-now approach, Intervention laboratory, Nonverbal interaction, Task-oriented group.

Encountertapes. Tape recordings designed to provide a group with guidelines for progressive interaction in the absence of a leader. They are copyrighted by the Bell & Howell Company and are available commercially from their Human Development Institute in Atlanta, Georgia.

Epileptic dementia. A form of epilepsy that is accompanied by progressive mental and intellectual impairment. Some believe that the circulatory disturbances during epileptic attacks cause nerve cell degeneration and lead to dementia.

Epinephrine. A sympathomimetic agent. It is the chief hormone secreted by the adrenal medulla. In a state of fear or anxiety, the physiological changes stem from the release of epinephrine. Also known as adrenaline, it is related to norepinephrine, a substance presently linked with mood disturbances in depression.

Eros. *See* Sexual drive.

Erotomania. Pathological preoccupation with sexual activities or fantasies.

Esalen massage. A particular type of massage taught and practiced at the Esalen Institute, a growth center at Big Sur, California. The massage lasts between one and a half and three hours and is intended to be an intimate, loving communion between the participants. A variation is the massage of one person by a group. The massage is given without words.

Ethnocentrism. Conviction that one's own group is superior to other groups. It impairs one's ability to evaluate members of another group realistically or to communicate with them on an open, equal, and person-to-person basis.

Euphoria. An altered state of consciousness characterized by an exaggerated feeling of well-being that is inappropriate to apparent events. It is often associated with opiate, amphetamine, or alcohol abuse.

Evasion. Act of not facing up to or of strategically eluding something. It consists of suppressing an idea that is next in a thought series and replacing it with another idea closely related to it. Evasion is also known as paralogia and perverted logic.

Exaltation. Affect consisting of intense elation and feelings of grandeur.

Exhibitionism. A form of sexual deviation characterized by a compulsive need to expose one's body, particularly the genitals.

Existential group psychotherapy. A type of group therapy that puts the emphasis on confrontation, primarily in the here-and-now interaction, and on feeling experiences rather than on rational thinking. Less attention is put on patient resistances. The therapist is involved on the same level and to the same degree as the patients. *See also* Encounter group.

Expanded group. The friends, immediate family, and interested relatives of a group therapy patient. They are the people with whom he has to relate outside the formal therapy group. *See also* Back-home group.

Experiencing. Feeling emotions and sensations as opposed to thinking; being involved in what is happening rather than standing back at a distance and theorizing. Encounter groups attempt to bring about this personal involvement.

Experiential group. *See* Encounter group.

Experiential stimulator. Anything that stimulates an emotional or sensory response. Several techniques, many of them nonverbal, have been developed for encounter groups to accomplish this stimulation. *See also* Behind-the-back technique, Blind walk.

Extended family therapy. A type of family therapy that involves family members, beyond the nuclear family, who are closely associated with it and affect it. *See also* Network, Social network therapy, Visitor.

Exteropsychic function. *See* Parent.

Extrapsychic conflict. Conflict that arises between the person and his environment. *See also* Intrapsychic conflict.

Extrapyramidal effect. Bizarre, involuntary motor movement. It is a central nervous system side effect sometimes produced by antipsychotic drugs. *See also* Dyskinesia.

Extratherapeutic contact. Contact between group members outside of a regularly scheduled group session.

Facilitator. Group leader. He may be the therapist or a patient who emerges during the course of an encounter and who channels group interaction. He is also known as the session leader.

Fag hag. Slang, derogatory expression often used by homosexuals to describe a woman who has become part of a homosexual social circle and has assumed a central role as a mother figure.

Family neurosis. Emotional maladaptation in which a person's psychopathology is unconsciously inter-related with that of the other members of his family.

Family therapy. Treatment of a family in conflict. The whole family meets as a group with the therapist and explores its relationships and process. The focus is on the resolution of current reactions to one another rather than on individual members. *See also* Collaborative therapy, Combined therapy, Concurrent therapy, Conjoint therapy, Extended family therapy, Group marital therapy, Marriage therapy, Quadrangular therapy, Square interview.

Fantasy. Day dream; fabricated mental picture or chain of events. A form of thinking dominated by unconscious material and primary processes, it seeks wish-fulfillment and immediate solutions to conflicts. Fantasy may serve as the matrix for creativity or for neurotic distortions of reality.

Father surrogate. Father substitute. In psychoanalysis, the patient projects his father image onto another person and responds to that person unconsciously in an inappropriate and unrealistic manner with the feelings and attitudes he had toward the original father.

Fausse reconnaissance. False recognition. *See also* Paramnesia.

Fear. Unpleasurable affect consisting of psychophysiological changes in response to a realistic threat or danger to one's existence. *See also* Anxiety.

Federn, Paul (1871–1950). Austrian psychoanalyst, one of Freud's earliest followers, and the last survivor of the original Wednesday Evening Society. He made important original contributions to psychoanalysis—such as the concepts of flying dreams and ego feeling—and was instrumental in saving the minutes of the Vienna Psychoanalytic Society for subsequent publication.

Feedback. Expressed response by one person or a group to another person's behavior. *See also* Sociometric feedback, Transaction.

Feeling-driven group. A group in which little or no attention is paid to rational processes, thinking, or cognition and where the expression of all kinds of emotion is rewarded. *See also* Affectualizing, Encounter group, Existential group psychotherapy.

Ferenczi, Sandor (1873–1933). Hungarian psychoanalyst, one of Freud's early followers, and a brilliant contributor to all aspects of psychoanalysis. His temperament was more romantic than Freud's, and he came to favor more active and personal techniques, to the point that his adherence to psychoanalysis during his last years was questioned.

Field theory. Concept postulated by Kurt Lewin that a person is a complex energy field in which all behavior can be conceived of as a change in some state of the field during a given unit of time. Lewin also postulated the presence within the field of psychological tensions—states of readiness or preparation for action. The field theory is concerned essentially with the present field, the here-and-now. The theory has been applied by various group psychotherapists.

Fliess, Wilhelm (1858–1928). Berlin nose and throat specialist. He shared an early interest with Freud in the physiology of sex and entered into a prolonged correspondence that figures importantly in the records of Freud's self-analysis. Freud was influenced by Fliess's concept of bisexuality and his theory of the periodicity of the sex functions.

Focal-conflict theory. Theory elaborated by Thomas French in 1952 that explains the current behavior of a person as an expression of his method of solving currently experienced personality conflicts that originated very early in his life. He constantly resonates to these early-life conflicts.

Focused exercise. Technique used particularly in encounter groups to help participants break through their defensive behavior and express such specific emotional reactions as anger, affection, and joy. A psychodrama, for instance, may focus on a specific problem that a group member is having with his wife. In playing out both his part and her part, he becomes aware of the emotion he has been blocking.

Folie à deux. Emotional illness shared by two persons. If it involves three persons, it is referred to as *folie à trois*, etc.

Forced interaction. Relationship that occurs in a group when the therapist or other members demand that a particular patient respond, react, and be active. *See also* Structured interactional group psychotherapy.

Ford negative personal contacts with Negroes scale. A scale that measures whites' negative social contacts with blacks. *See also* Kelley desegregation scale, Rosander anti-Negro behavior scale, Steckler anti-Negro scale, Steckler anti-white scale.

Ford negative personal contacts with whites scale. A scale that measures blacks' negative personal contacts with whites. It helps assess the extent to which negative social contacts influence prejudiced attitudes, thus contributing to the theoretical basis for the employment of interracial group experiences to reduce prejudice. *See also* Kelley desegregation scale, Rosander anti-Negro behavior scale, Steckler anti-Negro scale, Steckler anti-white scale.

Formal operations. Jean Piaget's label for the complete development of a person's logical thinking capacities.

Foulkes, S. H. (1923–   ). English psychiatrist and one of the organizers of the group therapy movement in Great Britain. His work combines Moreno's ideas—the here-and-now, the socio-genesis, the social atom, the psychological network—with psypchoanalytic views. He stresses the importance of group-as-a-whole phenomena. *See also* Group analytic psychotherapy, Network.

Free association. Investigative psychoanalytic technique devised by Freud in which the patient seeks to verbalize, without reservation or censor, the passing contents of his mind. The conflicts that emerge while fulfilling this task constitute resistances that are the basis of the analyst's interpretations. *See also* Antirepression device, Conflict.

Free-floating anxiety. Pervasive, unrealistic fear that is not attached to any idea or alleviated by symptom substitution. It is observed particularly in anxiety neurosis, although it may be seen in some cases of latent schizophrenia.

Freud, Sigmund (1856–1939). Austrian psychiatrist and the founder of psychoanalysis. With Josef Breuer, he explored the potentialities of cathartic therapy, then went on to develop the analytic technique and such fundamental concepts of mental phenomena as the unconscious, infantile sexuality, repression, sublimation, superego, ego, and id formation and their applications throughout all spheres of human behavior.

Fulfillment. Satisfaction of needs that may be either real or illusory.

Future projection. Psychodrama technique wherein the patient shows in action how he thinks his future will shape itself. He, sometimes with the assistance of the director, picks the point in time, the place, and the people, if any, he expects to be involved with at that time.

Galactorrhea. Excessive or spontaneous flow of milk from the breast. It may be a result of the endocrine influence of phenothiazine drugs.

Gallows transaction. A transaction in which a person with a self-destructive script smiles while narrating or engaging in a self-destructive act. His smile evokes a smile in the listener, which is in essence an encouragement for self-destruction. *See also* Hamartic script.

Game. Technique that resembles a traditional game in being physical or mental competition conducted according to rules but that is used in the group situation as an experiential learning device. The emphasis is on the process of the game rather than on the objective of the game. A game in Eric Berne's transactional analysis refers to an orderly sequence of social maneuvers with an ulterior motive and resulting in a psychological payoff for the players. *See also* Hit-and-run game, Million-dollar game, Pastime, Survival, Transactional group psychotherapy.

Game analysis. In transactional analysis, the analysis of a person's social interactions that are not honest and straightforward but are contaminated with pretenses for personal gain. *See also* Script analysis, Structural analysis.

Genetic material. Data out of the personal history of the patient that are useful in developing an understanding of the psychodynamics of his present adaptation. *See also* Current material.

Genital phase. The final stage of psychosexual development. It occurs during puberty. In this stage the person's psychosexual development is so organized that he can achieve sexual gratification from genital-to-genital contact and has the capacity for a mature, affectionate relationship with someone of the opposite sex. *See also* Anal phase, Infantile sexuality, Latency phase, Oral phase, Phallic phase.

Gestalt therapy. Type of psychotherapy that emphasizes the treatment of the person as a whole—his biological component parts and their organic functioning, his perceptual configuration, and his inter-relationships with the outside world. Gestalt therapy, developed by Frederic S. Perls, can be used in either an individual or a group therapy setting. It focuses on the sensory awareness of the person's here-and-now experiences rather than on past recollections or future expectations. Gestalt therapy employs role-playing and other techniques to promote the patient's growth process and to develop his full potential. *See also* Nonverbal interaction.

Gilles de la Tourette's disease. A rare illness that has its onset in childhood. The illness, first described by a Paris physician, Gilles de la Tourette, is characterized by involuntary muscular movements and motor incoordination accompanied by echolalia and coprolalia. It is considered by some to be a schizophrenic condition.

Give-up-itis. Syndrome characterized by a giving up of the desire to live. The alienation, isolation, withdrawal, and eventual death associated with this disease syndrome were experienced by many American prisoners during the Korean War, particularly in the early stages of Communist brainwashing. *See also* Dog-eat-dog period.

Go-around. Technique used in group therapy, particularly in structured interactional group psychotherapy, in which the therapist requires that each member of the group respond to another member, a theme, an association, etc. This procedure encourages participation of all members in the group.

God complex. A belief, sometimes seen in therapists, that one can accomplish more than is humanly possible or that one's word should not be doubted. The God complex of the aging psychoanalyst was first discussed by Ernest Jones, Freud's biographer. *See also* Mother Superior complex.

Gould Academy. Private preparatory school in Bethel, Maine, that has been used during summers as the site of the human relations laboratories run by the National Educational Association.

Grief. Alteration in mood and affect consisting of sadness appropriate to a real loss. *See also* Depression.

Group. *See* Therapeutic group.

Group action technique. Technique used in group work to help the participants achieve skills in interpersonal relations and improve their capacity to perform certain tasks better on the job or at home; technique, often involving physical interaction, aimed at enhancing involvement or communion within a new group.

Group analysand. A person in treatment in a psychoanalytically oriented group.

Group analytic psychotherapy. A type of group therapy in which the group is used as the principal therapeutic agent and all communications and relationships are viewed as part of a total field of interaction. Interventions deal primarily with group forces rather than with individual forces. S. H. Foulkes applied the term to his treatment procedure in 1948. It is also known as therapeutic group analysis. *See also* Phyloanalysis, Psychoanalytic group psychotherapy.

Group apparatus. Those people who preserve order and ensure the survival of a group. The internal apparatus deals with members' proclivities in order to maintain the structure of the group and strengthen cohesion. The therapist usually serves as his own apparatus in a small therapy group; in a courtroom, a bailiff ensures internal order. The external apparatus deals with the environment in order to minimize the threat of external pressure. The therapist usually acts as his own external apparatus by setting the time and place for the meetings and making sure that outsiders do not interfere; in a war, combat forces act as the external apparatus.

Group bibliotherapy. A form of group therapy that focuses on the use of selected readings as stimulus material. Outside readings and oral presentations of printed matter by therapist and patients are designed to encourage verbal interchange in the sessions and to hold the attention of severely regressed patients. This approach is used in the treatment of large groups of institutionalized patients. *See also* Class method, Didactic technique, Mechanical group therapy.

Group-centered psychotherapy. A short-term, nonclinical form of group therapy developed by followers of Carl Rogers and based on his client-centered method of individual treatment. The therapist maintains a nonjudgmental attitude, clarifies the feelings expressed in the sessions, and communicates empathic understanding and respect. The participants are not diagnosed, and uncovering techniques are not employed.

Group climate. Atmosphere and emotional tone of a group therapy session.

Group cohesion. Effect of the mutual bonds between members of a group as a result of their concerted effort for a common interest and purpose. Until cohesiveness is achieved, the group cannot concentrate its full energy on a common task. *See also* Group growth.

Group dynamics. Phenomena that occur in groups; the movement of a group from its inception to its termination. Interactions and interrelations among members and between the members and the therapist create tension, which maintains a constantly changing group equilibrium. The interactions and the tension they create are highly influenced by individual members' psychological make-up, unconscious instinctual drives, motives, wishes, and fantasies. The understanding and effective use of group dynamics is essential in group treatment. It is also known as group process. *See also* Group mobility, Psychodynamics.

Group grope. Belittling reference to procedures used in certain encounter groups. The procedures are aimed at providing emotional release through physical contact.

Group growth. Gradual development of trust and cohesiveness in a group. It leads to awareness of self and of other group process and to more effective coping with conflict and intimacy problems. *See also* Group cohesion.

Group history. Chronology of the experiences of a group, including group rituals, group traditions, and group themes.

Group inhibition. *See* Group resistance.

Group marathon. Group meeting that usually lasts from eight to 72 hours, although some sessions last for a week. The session is interrupted only for eating and sleeping. The leader works for the development of intimacy and the open expression of feelings. The time-extended group experience culminates in intense feelings of excitement and elation. Group marathon was developed by George Bach and Frederick Stoller. *See also* Accelerated interaction, Nude marathon, Too-tired-to-be-polite phenomenon.

Group marital therapy. A type of marriage therapy that makes use of a group. There are two basic techniques: (1) Inviting the marital partner of a group member to a group session. The other group members are confronted with the neurotic marriage pattern, which gives them new insights and awareness. (2) Placing a husband and wife together in a traditional group of patients. This method seems indicated if the spouses are unable to achieve meaningful intimacy because they fear the loss of their individual identity at an early phase of the marriage, before a neurotic equilibrium is established. *See also* Collaborative therapy, Combined therapy, Concurrent therapy, Conjoint therapy, Family therapy, Quadrangular therapy, Square interview.

Group mind. Autonomous and unified mental life in an assemblage of people bound together by mutual interests. It is a concept used by group therapists who focus on the group as a unit rather than on the individual members.

Group mobility. Spontaneity and movement in

the group brought about by changes in the functions and roles of individual members, relative to their progress. *See also* Group dynamics.

Group-on-group technique. Device used in T-groups wherein one group watches another group in action and then gives feedback to the observed group. Frequently, one group breaks into two sections, each taking turns in observing the other. The technique is intended to sharpen the participants' observation of individual behavior and group process.

Group phenomenon. *See* Group dynamics.

Group pressure. Demand by group members that individual members submit and conform to group standards, values, and behavior.

Group process. *See* Group dynamics.

Group psychotherapy. A type of psychiatric treatment that involves two or more patients participating together in the presence of one or more psychotherapists, who facilitate both emotional and rational cognitive interaction to effect changes in the maladaptive behavior of the members. *See also* Behavioral group psychotherapy, Bio-energetic group psychotherapy, Client-centered psychotherapy, Communion-oriented group psychotherapy, Crisis-intervention group psychotherapy, Existential group psychotherapy, Group analytic psychotherapy, Group bibliotherapy, Group-centered psychotherapy, Individual therapy, Inspirational-supportive group psychotherapy, Psychoanalytic group psychotherapy, Repressive-inspirational group psychotherapy, Social network therapy, Structured interactional group psychotherapy, Traditional group therapy, Transactional group psychotherapy.

Group resistance. Collective natural aversion of the group members toward dealing with unconscious material, emotions, or old patterns of defense.

Group ritual. Tradition or activity that any group establishes to mechanize some of its activities.

Group stimulus. Effect of several group members' communicating together. Each member has a stimulating effect on every other member, and the total stimulation is studied for therapeutic purposes. *See also* Transactions.

Group therapy. *See* Group psychotherapy.

Group tradition. Activity or value established historically by a group. It determines in part the group's manifest behavior.

Group value. Relative worth or standard developed by and agreed on by the members of a group.

Guilt. Affect associated with self-reproach and need for punishment. In psychoanalysis, guilt refers to a neurotic feeling of culpability that stems from a conflict between the ego and the superego. It begins developmentally with parental disapproval and becomes internalized as conscience in the course of superego formation. Guilt has normal psychological and social functions, but special intensity or absence of guilt characterizes many mental disorders, such as depression and antisocial personality. Some psychiatrists distinguish shame as a less internalized form of guilt.

Gustatory hallucination. False sense of taste.

Hallucination. A false sensory perception without a concrete external stimulus. It can be induced by emotional and by organic factors, such as drugs and alcohol. Common hallucinations involve sights or sounds, although any of the senses may be involved. *See also* Auditory hallucination, Gustatory hallucination, Hypnagogic hallucination, Hypnopompic hallucination, Kinesthetic hallucination, Lilliputian hallucination, Tactile hallucination, Visual hallucination.

Hallucinatory psychodrama. A type of psychodrama wherein the patient portrays the voices he hears and the visions he sees. Auxiliary egos are often called on to enact the various phenomena expressed by the patient and to involve him in interaction with them, so as to put them to a reality test. The intended effect on the patient is called psychodramatic shock.

Hallucinogenic drug. *See* Psychotomimetic drug.

Hamartic script. In transactional analysis, a life script that is self-destructive and tragic in character. *See also* Gallows transaction, Script, Script antithesis, Script matrix.

Healthy identification. Modeling of oneself, consciously or unconsciously, on another person who has sound psychic make-up. The identification has constructive purposes. *See also* Imitation.

Herd instinct. Desire to belong to a group and to participate in social activities. Wilfred Trotter used the term to indicate the presence of a hypothetical social instinct in man. In psychoanalysis, herd instinct is viewed as a social phenomenon rather than as an instinct. *See also* Aggressive drive, Sexual drive.

Here-and-now. Contemporaneity. *See also* There-and-then.

Here-and-now approach. A technique that focuses on understanding the interpersonal and intrapersonal responses and reactions as they occur in the on-going treatment session. Little or no emphasis is put on past history and experiences. *See also* Encounter group, Existential group psychotherapy.

Heterogeneous group. A group that consists of patients from both sexes, a wide age range, differing psychopathologies, and divergent socioeconomic, racial, ethnic, and cultural backgrounds. *See also* Homogeneous group.

Heterosexuality. Sexual attraction or contact between opposite-sex persons. The capacity for heterosexual arousal is probably innate, biologically programmed, and triggered in very early life, perhaps by olfactory modalities, as seen in lower animals. *See also* Bisexuality, Homosexuality.

Hidden self. The behavior, feelings, and motivations of a person known to himself but not to others. It is a quadrant of the Johari Window, a diagrammatic concept of human behavior. *See also* Blind self, Public self, Undeveloped potential.

Hierarchical vector. Thrust of relating to the other members of a group or to the therapist in a supraordinate or subordinate way. It is the opposite of relating as peers. It is also known as vertical vector. *See also* Authority principle, Horizontal vector, Political therapist.

Hit-and-run game. Hostile or nonconstructive aggressive activity indiscriminately and irresponsibly carried out against others. *See also* Game, Million dollar game, Survival.

Homogeneous group. A group that consists of patients of the same sex, with similarities in

their psychopathology, and from the same age range and socioeconomic, racial, ethnic, and cultural background. *See also* Heterogeneous group.

Homosexuality. Sexual attraction or contact between same-sex persons. Some authors distinguish two types: overt homosexuality and latent homosexuality. *See also* Bisexuality, Heterosexuality, Inversion, Lesbianism.

Homosexual panic. Sudden, acute onset of severe anxiety, precipitated by the unconscious fear or conflict that one may be a homosexual or act out homosexual impulses. *See also* Homosexuality.

Honesty. Forthrightness of conduct and uprightness of character; truthfulness. In therapy, honesty is a value manifested by the ability to communicate one's immediate experience, including inconsistent, conflicting, or ambivalent feelings and perceptions. *See also* Authenticity.

Hook. In transactional analysis, to switch one's transactions to a new ego state. For example, a patient's Adult ego state is hooked when he goes to the blackboard and draws a diagram.

Horizontal vector. Thrust of relating to the therapist or other members of the group as equals. It is also known as peer vector. *See also* Authority principle, Hierarchical vector, Political therapist.

House encounter. Group meeting of all the persons in a treatment facility. Such a meeting is designed to deal with specific problems within the therapeutic community that affect its functioning, such as poor morale and poor job performances.

Hydrotherapy. External or internal use of water in the treatment of disease. In psychiatry the use of wet packs to calm an agitated psychotic patient was formerly a popular treatment modality.

Hyperactivity. Increased muscular activity. The term is commonly used to describe a disturbance found in children that is manifested by constant restlessness and movements executed at a rapid rate. The disturbance is believed to be due to brain damage, mental retardation, emotional disturbance, or physiological disturbance. It is also known as hyperkinesis.

Hyperkinesis. *See* Hyperactivity.

Hypermnesia. Exaggerated degree of retention and recall. It is observed in schizophrenia, the manic phase of manic-depressive illness, organic brain syndrome, drug intoxication induced by amphetamines and hallucinogens, hypnosis, and febrile conditions. *See also* Memory.

Hypertensive crisis. Severe rise in blood pressure that can lead to intracranial hemorrhage. It is occasionally seen as a side effect of certain antidepressant drugs.

Hypnagogic hallucination. False sensory perception that occurs just before falling asleep. *See also* Hypnopompic hallucination.

Hypnodrama. Psychodrama under hypnotic trance. The patient is first put into a hypnotic trance. During the trance he is encouraged to act out the various experiences that torment him.

Hypnopompic hallucination. False sensory perception that occurs just before full wakefulness. *See also* Hypnagogic hallucination.

Hypnosis. Artificially induced alteration of consciousness of one person by another. The subject responds with a high degree of suggestibility, both mental and physical, during the trancelike state.

Hypochondriasis. Exaggerated concern with one's physical health. The concern is not based on real organic pathology.

Hypotension, orthostatic. *See* Orthostatic hypotension.

Hysterical anesthesia. Disturbance in sensory perception characterized by absence of sense of feeling in certain areas of the body. It is observed in certain cases of hysterical neurosis, particularly the conversion type, and it is believed to be a defense mechanism.

Id. Part of Freud's concept of the psychic apparatus. According to his structural theory of mental functioning, the id harbors the energy that stems from the instinctual drives and desires of a person. The id is completely in the unconscious realm, unorganized and under the influence of the primary processes. *See also* Conscious, Ego, Preconscious, Primary process, Superego, Unconscious.

Idealization. A defense mechanism in which a

person consciously or, usually, unconsciously overestimates an attribute or an aspect of another person.

Ideas of reference. Misinterpretation of incidents and events in the outside world as having a direct personal reference to oneself. Occasionally observed in normal persons, ideas of reference are frequently seen in paranoid patients. *See also* Projection.

Ideational shield. An intellectual, rational defense against the anxiety a person would feel if he became vulnerable to the criticisms and rejection of others. As a result of his fear of being rejected, he may feel threatened if he criticizes another person—an act that is unacceptable to him. In both group and individual therapy, conditions are set up that allow the participants to lower this ideational shield.

Identification. An unconscious defense mechanism in which a person incorporates into himself the mental picture of an object and then patterns himself after this object; seeing oneself as like the person used as a pattern. It is distinguished from imitation, a conscious process. *See also* Healthy identification, Imitation, Role.

Identification with the aggressor. An unconscious process by which a person incorporates within himself the mental image of a person who represents a source of frustration from the outside world. A primitive defense, it operates in the interest and service of the developing ego. The classical example of this defense occurs toward the end of the oedipal stage, when the male child, whose main source of love and gratification is the mother, identifies with his father. The father represents the source of frustration, being the powerful rival for the mother; the child cannot master or run away from his father, so he is obliged to identify with him. *See also* Psychosexual development.

Idiot. *See* Mental retardation.

I-It. Philosopher Martin Buber's description of damaging interpersonal relationships. If a person treats himself or another person exclusively as an object, he prevents mutuality, trust, and growth. When pervasive in a group, I-It relationships prevent human warmth, destroy cohesiveness, and retard group process. *See also* I-Thou.

Ileus, paralytic. *See* Paralytic ileus.

Illusion. False perception and misinterpretation of an actual sensory stimulus.

Illustration. In transactional analysis, an anecdote, simile, or comparison that reinforces a confrontation or softens its potentially undesirable effects. The illustration may be immediate or remote in time and may refer to the external environment or to the internal situation in the group.

Imbecile. *See* Mental retardation.

Imitation. In psychiatry, a conscious act of mimicking another person's behavior pattern. *See also* Healthy identification, Identification.

Impasse. *See* Therapeutic impasse.

Improvement scale. In transactional analysis, a quantitative specification of a patient's position in terms of improvement in the course of therapy.

Improvisation. In psychodrama, the acting out of problems without prior preparation.

Impulse. Unexpected, instinctive urge motivated by conscious and unconscious feelings over which the person has little or no control. *See also* Drive, Instinct.

Inappropriate affect. Emotional tone that is out of harmony with the idea, object, or thought accompanying it.

Inclusion phase. Early stage of group treatment. In this phase, each group member's concern focuses primarily on belonging and being accepted and recognized, particularly by the therapist. It is also known as the dependency stage. *See also* Affection phase, Power phase.

Incorporation. An unconscious defense mechanism in which an object representation is assimilated into oneself through symbolic oral ingestion. One of the primitive defenses, incorporation is a special form of introjection and is the primary mechanism in identification.

Individual psychology. Holistic theory of personality developed by Alfred Adler. Personality development is explained in terms of adaptation to the social milieu (life style), strivings toward perfection motivated by feelings of inferiority, and the interpersonal nature of the person's problems. Individual psychology is applied in group psychotherapy and counseling by Adlerian practitioners.

Individual therapy. A type of psychotherapy in which a professionally trained psychotherapist treats one patient who either wants relief from disturbing symptoms or improvement in his ability to cope with his problems. This one therapist-one patient relationship, the traditional dyadic therapeutic technique, is opposed to other techniques that deal with more than one patient. *See also* Group psychotherapy, Psychotherapy.

Individuation. Differentiation; the process of molding and developing the individual personality so that it is different from the rest of the group. *See also* Actualization.

Infantile dynamics. Psychodynamic integrations, such as the Oedipus complex, that are organized during childhood and continue to exert unconsciously experienced influences on adult personality.

Infantile sexuality. Freudian concept regarding the erotic life of infants and children. Freud observed that, from birth, infants are capable of erotic activities. Infantile sexuality encompasses the overlapping phases of psychosexual development during the first five years of life and includes the oral phase (birth to 18 months), when erotic activity centers around the mouth; the anal phase (ages one to three), when erotic activity centers around the rectum; and the phallic phase (ages two to six), when erotic activity centers around the genital region. *See also* Psychosexual development.

Inferiority complex. Concept, originated by Alfred Adler, that everyone is born with inferiority or a feeling of inferiority secondary to real or fantasied organic or psychological inadequacies. How this inferiority or feeling of inferiority is handled determines a person's behavior in life. *See also* Masculine protest.

Infra reality. Reduced actuality that is observed in certain therapeutic settings. For example, according to J. L. Moreno, who coined the term, the contact between doctor and patient is not a genuine dialogue but is an interview, research situation, or projective test.

Injunction. In transactional analysis, the instructions given by one ego state to another usually the Parent ego state to the Child ego state, that become the basis of the person's lif script decisions. *See also* Permission, Program, Role, Script analysis.

Inner-directed person. A person who is self-motivated and autonomous and is not easily guided or influenced by the opinions and values of other people. *See also* Other-directed person.

Insight. Conscious awareness and understanding of one's own psychodynamics and symptoms of maladaptive behavior. It is highly important in effecting changes in the personality and behavior of a person. Most therapists distinguish two types: (1) intellectual insight—knowledge and awareness without any change of maladaptive behavior; (2) emotional or visceral insight—awareness, knowledge, and understanding of one's own maladaptive behavior, leading to positive changes in personality and behavior.

Inspirational-supportive group psychotherapy. A type of group therapy that focuses on the positive potential of members and stresses reinforcement for accomplishments or achievements. *See also* Alcoholics Anonymous.

Instinct. A biological, species-specific, genetically determined drive to respond in an automatic, complex, but organized way to a particular stimulus. *See also* Drive, Impulse.

Institute of Industrial Relations. A department of the Graduate School of Business Administration at the University of California at Los Angeles. It has conducted sensitivity training laboratories for business and professional people for nearly 20 years.

Insulin coma therapy. A form of psychiatric treatment originated by Manfred Sakel in which insulin is administered to the patient to produce coma. It is used in certain types of schizophrenia. *See also* Shock treatment.

Intellectual insight. *See* Insight.

Intellectualization. An unconscious defense mechanism in which reasoning or logic is used in an attempt to avoid confrontation with an objectionable impulse or affect. It is also known as brooding or thinking compulsion.

Intelligence. Capacity for understanding, recalling, mobilizing, and integrating constructively what one has learned and for using it to meet new situations.

Intensive group process. Group process designed to evoke a high degree of personal interaction and involvement, often accompanied by the expression of strong or deep feelings.

Interaction. *See* Transaction.

Interpersonal conflict. *See* Extrapsychic conflict.

Interpersonal psychiatry. Dynamic-cultural system of psychoanalytic therapy based on Harry Stack Sullivan's interpersonal theory. Sullivan's formulations were couched in terms of a person's interactions with other people. In group psychotherapy conducted by practitioners of this school, the focus is on the patients' transactions with one another.

Interpersonal skill. Ability of a person in relationship with others to express his feelings appropriately, to be socially responsible, to change and influence, and to work and create. *See also* Socialization.

Interpretation. A psychotherapeutic technique used in psychoanalysis, both individual and group. The therapist conveys to the patient the significance and meaning of his behavior, constructing into a more meaningful form the patient's resistances, defenses, transferences, and symbols (dreams). *See also* Clarification.

Interpretation of Dreams, The. Title of a book by Freud. Published in 1899, this work was a major presentation not only of Freud's discoveries about the meaning of dreams—hitherto regarded as outside scientific interest—but also of his concept of a mental apparatus that is topographically divided into unconscious, preconscious, and conscious areas.

Interracial group. *See* Heterogeneous group.

Intervention laboratory. Human relations laboratory, such as an encounter group or training group, especially designed to intervene and resolve some group conflict or crisis.

Intrapersonal conflict. *See* Intrapsychic conflict.

Intrapsychic ataxia. *See* Ataxia.

Intrapsychic conflict. Conflict that arises from the clash of two opposing forces within oneself.

It is also known as intrapersonal conflict. *See also* Extrapsychic conflict.

Introjection. An unconscious defense mechanism in which a psychic representation of a loved or hated object is taken into one's ego system. In depression, for example, the emotional feelings related to the loss of a loved one are directed toward the introjected mental representation of the loved one. *See also* Identification, Incorporation.

Inversion. Synonym for homosexuality. Inversion was the term used by Freud and his predecessors. There are three types: absolute, amphigenous, and occasional. *See also* Homosexuality, Latent homosexuality, Overt homosexuality.

I-Thou. Philosopher Martin Buber's conception that man's identity develops from true sharing by persons. Basic trust can occur in a living partnership in which each member identifies the particular real personality of the other in his wholeness, unity, and uniqueness. In groups, I-Thou relationships promote warmth, cohesiveness, and constructive group process. *See also* I-It.

Jamais vu. False feeling of unfamiliarity with a real situation one has experienced. *See also* Paramnesia.

Jaundice, allergic. Yellowish staining of the skin and deeper tissues accompanied by bile in the urine secondary to a hypersensitivity reaction. An obstructive type of jaundice, it is occasionally detected during the second to fourth week of phenothiazine therapy.

Johari Window. A schematic diagram used to conceptualize human behavior. It was developed by Joseph (Jo) Luft and Harry (Hari) Ingham at the University of California at Los Angeles in 1955. The diagram is composed of quadrants, each representing some aspect of a person's behavior, feelings, and motivations. *See also* Blind self, Hidden self, Public self, Undeveloped potential.

Jones, Ernest (1879–1958). Welsh psychoanalyst and one of Freud's early followers. He was an organizer of the American Psychoanalytic Association in 1911 and the British Psychoanalytical Society in 1919 and a founder and longtime editor of the journal of the International Psychoanalytical Association. He was the author of many valuable works, the most important of which is his three-volume biography of Freud.

Judgment. Mental act of comparing or evaluating choices within the framework of a given set of values for the purpose of electing a course of action. Judgment is said to be intact if the course of action chosen is consistent with reality; judgment is said to be impaired if the chosen course of action is not consistent with reality.

Jung, Carl Gustav (1875–1961). Swiss psychiatrist and psychoanalyst. He founded the school of analytic psychology. *See also* Collective unconscious.

Karate-chop experience. A technique used in encounter groups to elicit aggression in timid or inhibited participants in a humorous way. The timid one stands facing a more aggressive member. Both make violent pseudokarate motions at each other, without making physical contact but yelling "Hai!" as loudly as possible at each stroke. After this exercise, the group members discuss the experience.

Kelley desegregation scale. A scale designed to measure the attitudes of whites toward blacks in the area of school integration. The scale provides a rough measure of racial prejudice and may be of help in ascertaining the effects on prejudice of participation in an interracial group. *See also* Ford negative personal contacts with Negroes scale, Ford negative personal contacts with whites scale, Rosander anti-Negro behavior scale, Steckler anti-Negro scale, Steckler anti-white scale.

Kinesthetic hallucination. False perception of muscular movement. An amputee may feel movement in his missing limb; this phenomenon is also known as phantom limb.

Kinesthetic sense. Sensation in the muscles as differentiated from the senses that receive stimulation from outside the body.

Kleptomania. Pathological compulsion to steal. In psychoanalytic theory, it originates in the infantile stage of psychosexual development.

Latency phase. Stage of psychosexual development extending from age five to the beginning of adolescence at age 12. Freud's work on ego psychology showed that the apparent cessation of sexual preoccupation during this period stems from a strong, aggressive blockade of libidinal and sexual impulses in an effort to avoid the dangers of the oedipal relationships. During the latency period, boys and girls are inclined to choose friends and join groups of their own sex. *See also* Identification with the aggressor, Psychosexual development.

Latent homosexuality. Unexpressed conscious or unconscious homoerotic wishes that are held in check. Freud's theory of bisexuality postulated the existence of a constitutionally determined, though experientially influenced, instinctual masculine-feminine duality. Normally, the opposite-sex component is dormant, but a breakdown in the defenses of repression and sublimation may activate latent instincts and result in overt homoeroticism. Many writers have questioned the validity of a universal latent homoeroticism. *See also* Bisexuality, Homosexuality, Overt homosexuality.

Lateral transference. Projection of long-range attitudes, values, and emotions onto the other members of the treatment group rather than onto the therapist. The patient sees other members of the group, co-patients, and peers in terms of his experiences in his original family. *See also* Collective family transference neurosis, Multiple transference.

Leaderless therapeutic group. An extreme form of nondirective group, conducted primarily for research purposes, such as the investigations of intragroup tensions by Walter R. Bion. On occasion, the therapist interacts verbally in a nonauthoritarian manner, but he generally functions as a silent observer—withholding explanations, directions, and support.

Leadership function. *See* Leadership role.

Leadership role. Stance adopted by the therapist in conducting a group. There are three main leadership roles: authoritarian, democratic, and laissez-faire. Any group—social, therapeutic, training, or task-oriented—is primarily influenced by the role practiced by the leader.

Leadership style. *See* Leadership role.

Lesbianism. Female homosexuality. About 600 B.C. on the island of Lesbos in the Aegean Sea, the poetess Sappho encouraged young women to engage in mutual sex practices. Lesbianism is also known as Sapphism. *See also* Bisexuality, Homosexuality, Latent homosexuality, Overt homosexuality.

Lewin, Kurt (1890–1946). German psychologist who emigrated to the United States in 1933. His work on the field theory has been useful in the experimental study of human behavior in a social situation. He was one of the early workers who helped develop the National Training Laboratories.

Libido theory. Freudian theory of sexual instinct, its complex process of development, and its accompanying physical and mental manifestations. Before Freud's introduction and completion of the dual-instinct theory (sexual and aggressive) in 1920, all instinctual manifestations were related to the sexual instinct, making for some confusion at that time. Current psychoanalytic practice assumes the existence of two instincts: sexual (libido) and aggressive (death). *See also* Aggressive drive, Sexual drive.

Life instinct. *See* Sexual drive.

Life lie. A contrary-to-fact conviction around which a person structures his life philosophy and attitudes.

Life line. A group technique in which each member is asked to draw a line representing his life, beginning with birth and ending with death. Comparison and discussion usually reveal that the shape and slope of the lines are based on a variety of personally meaningful parameters, such as maturity and academic achievement.

Lifwynn Foundation. Organization established by Trigant Burrow in 1927 as a social community in which the participants examined their interactions in the daily activities in which they were engaged. Lifwynn is currently under the direction of Hans Syz, M.D., in Westport, Conn.

Lilliputian hallucination. False perception that persons are reduced in size. *See also* Micropsia.

Lobotomy. Neurosurgical procedure in which one or more nerve tracts in a lobe of the cerebrum are severed. Prefrontal lobotomy is the ablation of one or more nerve tracts in the prefrontal area of the brain. It is used in the treatment of certain severe mental disorders that do not respond to other treatments.

Locus. Place of origin.

Logorrhea. Copious, pressured, coherent speech. It is observed in manic-depressive illness, manic type. Logorrhea is also known as tachylogia, verbomania, and volubility.

LSD (lysergic acid diethylamide). A potent psychotogenic drug discovered in 1942. LSD produces psychoticlike symptoms and behavior changes—including hallucinations, delusions, and time-space distortions.

Lysergic acid diethylamide. *See* LSD.

Macropsia. False perception that objects are larger than they really are. *See also* Micropsia.

Maintenance drug therapy. A stage in the course of chemotherapy. After the drug has reached its maximal efficacy, the dosage is reduced and sustained at the minimal therapeutic level that will prevent a relapse or exacerbation.

Major tranquilizer. Drug that has antipsychotic properties. The phenothiazines, thioxanthenes, butyrophenones, and reserpine derivatives are typical major tranquilizers, which are also known as ataractics, neuroleptics, and antipsychotics. *See also* Dystonia, Minor tranquilizer.

Maladaptive way. Poorly adjusted or pathological behavior pattern.

Mannerism. Stereotyped involuntary activity that is peculiar to a person.

MAO inhibitor. *See* Monoamine oxidase inhibitor.

Marathon. *See* Group marathon.

Marijuana. Dried leaves and flowers of *Cannabis sativa* (Indian hemp). It induces somatic and psychic changes in man when smoked or ingested in sufficient quantity. The somatic changes include increased heart rate, rise in blood pressure, dryness of the mouth, increased appetite, and occasional nausea, vomiting, and diarrhea. The psychic changes include dreamy-state level of consciousness, disruptive chain of ideas, perceptual disturbances of time and space, and alterations of mood. In strong doses, marijuana can produce hallucinations and, at times, paranoid ideas and suspiciousness. It is also known as pot, grass, weed, tea, and Mary Jane.

Marital counseling. Process whereby a trained counselor helps married couples resolve problems that arise and trouble them in their relationship. The theory and techniques of this approach were first developed in social agencies as part of family casework. Husband and wife are seen by the same worker in separate and joint counseling sessions, which focus on immediate family problems.

Marital therapy. *See* Marriage therapy.

Marriage therapy. A type of family therapy that involves the husband and the wife and focuses on the marital relationship, which affects the individual psychopathology of the partners. The rationale for this method is the assumption that psychopathological processes within the family structure and in the social matrix of the marriage perpetuate individual pathological personality structures, which find expression in the disturbed marriage and are aggravated by the feedback between partners. *See also* Collaborative therapy, Combined therapy, Concurrent therapy, Conjoint therapy, Family therapy, Group marital therapy, Marital counseling, Quadrangular therapy, Square interview.

Masculine identity. Well-developed sense of gender affiliation with males.

Masculine protest. Adlerian doctrine that depicts a universal human tendency to move from a passive and feminine role to a masculine and active role. This doctrine is an extension of his ideas about organic inferiority. It became the prime motivational force in normal and neurotic behavior in the Adlerian system. *See also* Adler, Alfred; Inferiority complex.

Masculinity-femininity scale. Any scale on a psychological test that assesses the relative masculinity or femininity of the testee. Scales vary and may focus, for example, on basic identification with either sex or preference for a particular sex role.

Masochism. A sexual deviation in which sexual gratification is derived from being maltreated by the partner or oneself. It was first described by an Austrian novelist, Leopold von Sacher-Masoch (1836–1895). *See also* Sadism, Sadomasochistic relationship.

Masturbation. *See* Autoerotism.

Mattress-pounding. A technique used in encounter groups to mobilize repressed or suppressed anger. A group member vents his resentments by beating the mattress with his fists and yelling. Frequently, the mattress becomes in fantasy a hated parent, sibling, or spouse. After this exercise, the group members discuss their reactions. *See also* Pillow-beating.

Maximal expression. Utmost communication. In psychodrama, it is the outcome of an involved sharing by the group of the three portions of the session: the warm-up, the action, and the post-action. During the action period the patient is encouraged to express all action and verbal communication to the limit. To this end, delusions, hallucinations, soliloquies, thoughts, and fantasies are allowed to be part of the production.

Mechanical group therapy. A form of group therapy that makes use of mechanical devices. As applied in the early 1950's, it required neither a group nor a therapist. An example of this form of therapy is the playing of brief recorded messages over the loudspeaker system of a mental hospital; the same statement, bearing on some elementary principle of mental health, is frequently repeated to secure general acceptance. *See also* Class method, Didactic technique, Group bibliotherapy.

Megalomania. Morbid preoccupation with expansive delusions of power and wealth.

Melancholia. Old term for depression that is rarely used at the present time. As used in the term involutional melancholia, it refers to a morbid state of depression and not to a symptom.

Memory. Ability to revive past sensory impressions, experiences, and learned ideas. Memory includes three basic mental processes: registration—the ability to perceive, recognize, and establish information in the central nervous system; retention—the ability to retain registered information; and recall—the ability to retrieve stored information at will. *See also* Amnesia, Hypermnesia, Paramnesia.

Mental aberration. *See* Aberration, mental.

Mental illness. Psychiatric disease included in the list of mental disorders in the *Diagnostic and Statistical Manual of Mental Disorders* published by the American Psychiatric Association and in the *Standard Nomenclature of Diseases and Operations* approved by the American Medical Association.

Mental retardation. Subnormal general intellectual functioning, which may be evident at birth or may develop during childhood. Learning, social adjustment, and maturation are impaired, and emotional disturbance is often present. The degree of retardation is commonly measured in terms of I.Q.: borderline (68–85), mild (52–67), moderate (36–51), severe (20–35), and profound (under 20). Obsolescent terms that are still used occasionally are idiot (mental age of less than three years), imbecile (mental age of three to seven years), and moron (mental age of eight years).

Methadone. Methadone hydrochloride, a long-acting synthetic narcotic developed in Germany as a substitute for morphine. It is used as an analgesic and in detoxification and maintenance treatment of opiate addicts.

Methadone maintenance treatment. Long-term use of methadone on a daily basis to relieve narcotic craving and avert the effects of narcotic drugs.

Micropsia. False perception that objects are smaller than they really are. *See also* Lilliputian hallucination, Macropsia.

Milieu therapy. Treatment that emphasizes appropriate socioenvironmental manipulation for the benefit of the patient. The setting for milieu therapy is usually the psychiatric hospital.

Million-dollar game. Group game designed to explore the psychological meaning of money and to encourage free, creative thinking. The group is told that it has a million dollars, which is to be used productively in any way, as long as the endeavor actively involves all members of the group. *See also* Game, Hit-and-run game, Survival.

Minnesota Multiphasic Personality Inventory. Questionnaire type of psychological test for ages 16 and over with 550 true-false statements that are coded in 14 scales, ranging from a social scale to a schizophrenia scale. Group and individual forms are available.

Minor tranquilizer. Drug that diminishes tension, restlessness, and pathological anxiety without any antipsychotic effect. Meprobamate and diazepoxides are typical minor tranquilizers, which are also known as psycholeptics. *See also* Major tranquilizer.

Minutes of the Vienna Psychoanalytic Society. Diary of Freud's Wednesday Evening Society (after 1910, the Vienna Psychoanalytic Society) as recorded by Otto Rank, the paid secretary between 1906 and 1915.

Mirror. In psychodrama, the person who represents the patient, copying his behavior and trying to express his feelings in word and movement, showing the patient as if in a mirror how other people experience him. The mirror may exaggerate, employing techniques of deliberate distortion in order to arouse the patient to come forth and change from a passive spectator into an active participant. The mirror is also known as the double. *See also* Auxiliary ego.

Mirroring. A group process by which a person sees himself in the group by the reflections that come back to him in response to the way he presents himself. The image may be true or distorted, depending on the level of truth at which the group is functioning at the time. Mirroring has been used as an exercise in encounter group therapy and as a laboratory procedure in the warming-up period of the psychodrama approach.

Mixed-gender group. *See* Heterogeneous group.

MMPI. *See* Minnesota Multiphasic Personality Inventory.

Mobility. *See* Group mobility.

Monoamine oxidase inhibitor. Agent that inhibits the enzyme monoamine oxidase (MAO), which oxidizes such monoamines as norepinephrine and serotonin. Some of the MAO inhibitors are highly effective as antidepressants. *See also* Tricyclic drug.

Monomania. Morbid mental state characterized by preoccupation with one subject. It is also known as partial insanity.

Mood. Feeling tone that is experienced by a person internally. Mood does not include the external expression of the internal feeling tone. *See also* Affect.

Mood swing. Oscillation of a person's emotional feeling tone between periods of euphoria and depression.

Moron. *See* Mental retardation.

Moses and Monotheism. Title of a book by Freud published in 1939. In this book, Freud undertook a historical but frankly speculative reconstruction of the personality of Moses and examined the concept of monotheism and the abiding effect of the patriarch on the character of the Jews. One of Freud's last works, it bears the imprint of his latter-day outlook and problems.

Mother Superior complex. Tendency of a therapist to play the role of the mother in his relations with his patients. The complex often leads to interference with the therapeutic process. *See also* God complex.

Mother surrogate. Mother substitute. In psychoanalysis, the patient projects his mother image onto another person and responds to that person unconsciously in an inappropriate and unrealistic manner with the feelings and attitudes he had toward the original mother.

Motivation. Force that pushes a person to act to satisfy a need. It implies an incentive or desire that influences the will and causes the person to act.

Mourning. *See* Grief.

Multibody situation. Group situation. The term was originally used in the description of the evolution of social interaction in human beings from narcissism through the dyadic relationship to the three-body constellation of the Oedipus complex to the multibody situation prevailing in groups.

Multiple double. Several representations of the patient, each portraying a part of him—one as he is now, another as he was (for instance, five years ago), another at a crucial moment in his life (for example, when his mother died), a fourth how he may be 20 years hence. The multiple representations of the patient are presented in sequence, each continuing where the last left off. *See also* Auxiliary ego.

Multiple ego states. Many psychological stages, relating to different periods of one's life or to different depths of experience. These states may be of varying degrees of organization and complexity, and they may or may not be capable of being called to awareness consecutively or simultaneously.

Multiple interaction. Group behavior in which many members participate in the transactions, both verbal and nonverbal, at any one moment in the session.

Multiple intragroup transference. *See* Multiple transference.

Multiple reactivity. A phenomenon in which many group members respond in a variety of ways to the provocative role or stimulation afforded by one patient's behavior.

Multiple therapy. *See* Co-therapy.

Multiple transferences. Feelings and attitudes originally held toward members of one's family that become irrationally attached to the therapist and various group members simultaneously. *See also* Collective family transference neurosis, Lateral transference.

Mutism. *See* Stupor.

Mutual support. Expressions of sympathy, understanding, and affection that group members give to one another. *See also* Pairing.

Mydriasis. Dilatation of the pupil. The condition sometimes occurs as an autonomic side effect of phenothiazine and antiparkinsonism drugs.

Nalline test. The use of Nalline, a narcotic antagonist, to determine abstinence from opiates. An injection of Nalline precipitates withdrawal symptoms if opiates have been used recently. The most important use for Nalline, however, is as an antidote in the treatment of opiate overdose.

Narcissism. Self-love. It is linked to autoerotism but is devoid of genitality. The word is derived from Narcissus, a Greek mythology figure who fell in love with his own reflected image. In psychoanalytic theory, it is divided into primary narcissism and secondary narcissism. Primary narcissism refers to the early infantile phase of object relationship development, when the child has not differentiated himself from the outside world. All sources of pleasure are unrealistically recognized as coming from within himself, giving him a false sense of omnipotence.

Secondary narcissism is the type of narcissism that results when the libido once attached to external love objects is redirected back to the self. *See also* Autistic thinking, Autoerotism.

Narcotic hunger. A physiological craving for a drug. It appears in abstinent narcotic addicts.

National Training Laboratories. Organization started in 1947 at Bethel, Maine, to train professionals who work with groups. Interest in personal development eventually led to sensitivity training and encounter groups. The organization is now called the NTL Institute for Applied Behavioral Science. *See also* Basic skills training, East Coast style T-group.

Natural Child. In transactional analysis, the autonomous, expressive, archaic Child ego state that is free from parental influence. *Se also* Adapted Child.

Natural group. Group that tends to evolve spontaneously in human civilization, such as a kinship, tribal, or religious group. In contrast are various contrived groups or aggregates of people who meet for a relatively brief time to achieve some goal.

Negativism. Verbal or nonverbal opposition to outside suggestions and advice. It is also known as command negativism.

Neologism. New word or condensation of several words formed by patient in an effort to express a highly complex idea. It is often seen in schizophrenia.

Neopsychic function. *See* Adult.

Network. The persons in the patient's environment with whom he is most intimately connected. It frequently includes the nuclear family, the extended family, the orbit of relatives and friends, and work and recreational contacts. S. H. Foulkes believes that this dynamically interacting network has a fundamental significance in the production of illness in the patient. *See also* Extended family therapy, Social network therapy, Visitor.

Neuroleptic. *See* Antipsychotic drug, Major tranquilizer.

Neurosis. Mental disorder characterized by anxiety. The anxiety may be experienced and expressed directly, or, through an unconscious psychic process, it may be converted, displaced, or somatized. Although neuroses do not manifest depersonalization or overt distortion of reality, they can be severe enough to impair a person's functioning. The neuroses, also known as psychoneuroses, include the following types: anxiety neurosis, hysterical neurosis, phobic neurosis, obsessive-compulsive neurosis, depressive neurosis, neurasthenic neurosis, depersonalization neurosis, and hypochondriacal neurosis.

Nondirective approach. Technique in which the therapist follows the lead of the patient in the interview rather than introducing his own theories and directing the course of the interview. This method is applied in both individual and group therapy, such as Carl Rogers' client-centered and group-centered therapy. *See also* Passive therapist.

Nontruster. A person who has a strong unfilled need to be nurtured but whose early experience was one of rejection or overprotection. As a defense against repetition of this experience, he develops an overly strong show of independence. Sometimes this independence is manifested in group therapy by a member's constant rejection of support and of attempts by other members to get close to him. *See also* Outsider.

Nonverbal interaction. Technique used without the aid of words in encounter groups to promote communication and intimacy and to bypass verbal defenses. Many exercises of this sort are carried out in complete silence; in others, the participants emit grunts, groans, yells, cries, or sighs. Gestalt therapy pays particular attention to nonverbal expression.

Norepinephrine. A catecholamine that functions as a neurohumoral mediator liberated by postganglionic adrenergic nerves. It is also present in the adrenal medulla and in many areas in the brain, with the highest concentration in the hypothalamus. A disturbance in the metabolism of norepinephrine is considered to be an important factor in the etiology of depression. *See also* Serotonin.

Nuclear family. Immediate members of a family, including the parents and the children. *See also* Extended family therapy, Network, Social network therapy, Visitor.

Nuclear group member. *See* Therapist surrogate.

Nude marathon. Encounter group in which members assemble for an emotional experience of prolonged duration (from a minimum of eight hours to a couple of days), with the added factor of physical nakedness as members go about their activities. The theory is that clothes are themselves defenses against openness, that they connote limiting roles and result in stereotyped responses from others, and that they allow participants to avoid facing conflicts about their own bodies. *See also* Group marathon, Sensory-experiential group.

Nymphomania. Morbid, insatiable need in women for sexual intercourse. *See also* Satyriasis.

Observer. Person who is included but is generally not an active participant in therapy sessions. His observations are later discussed in posttherapy meetings with the staff or supervisor. *See also* Recorder.

Observer therapist. *See* Passive therapist.

Obsession. Persistent idea, thought, or impulse that cannot be eliminated from consciousness by logical effort. *See also* Compulsion.

Oedipus complex. A distinct group of associated ideas, aims, instinctual drives, and fears that are generally observed in children when they are from three to six years of age. During this period, which coincides with the peak of the phallic phase of psychosexual development, the child's sexual interest is attached chiefly to the parent of the opposite sex and is accompanied by aggressive feelings and wishes for the parent of the same sex. One of Freud's most important concepts, the Oedipus complex was discovered in 1897 as a result of his self-analysis. *See also* Totem and Taboo.

Ogre. In structural analysis, the Child ego state in the father that supersedes the nurturing Parent and becomes a pseudo-Parent.

One-gender group. *See* Homogeneous group.

Open group. Treatment group in which new members are continuously added as other members leave. *See also* Closed group.

Oral dyskinesia, tardive. *See* Tardive oral dyskinesia.

Oral phase. The earliest stage in psychosexual development. It lasts through the first 18 months of life. During this period, the oral zone is the center of the infant's needs, expression, and pleasurable erotic experiences. It has a strong influence on the organization and development of the child's psyche. *See also* Anal phase, Genital phase, Infantile sexuality, Latency phase, Phallic phase.

Orientation. State of awareness of one's relationships and surroundings in terms of time, place, and person.

Orthostatic hypotension. Reduction in blood pressure brought about by a shift from a recumbent to an upright position. It is observed as a side effect of several psychotropic drugs.

Other-directed person. A person who is readily influenced and guided by the attitudes and values of other people. *See also* Inner-directed person.

Outsider. In group therapy, a member who feels alienated and isolated from the group. Such a person has usually experienced repetitive rejection in his early life and is wary of trusting people in the present. Often much effort is required by the group and the therapist before the outsider trusts someone. *See also* Nontruster.

Overt homosexuality. Behaviorally expressed homoeroticism as distinct from unconsciously held homosexual wishes or conscious wishes that are held in check. *See also* Homosexuality, Latent homosexuality.

Pairing. Term coined by Walter R. Bion to denote mutual support between two or more group members who wish to avoid the solution of their problems. The term is often used more loosely to denote an attraction between two group members.

Panic. An acute, intense attack of anxiety associated with personality disorganization. Some writers use the term exclusively for psychotic episodes of overwhelming anxiety. *See also* Homosexual panic.

Pantomime. Gesticulation; psychodrama without the use of words.

Paralogia. *See* Evasion.

Paralytic ileus. Intestinal obstruction of the nonmechanical type, secondary to paralysis of the bowel wall, that may lead to fecal retention.

It is a rare anticholinergic side effect of phenothiazine therapy.

Paramnesia. Disturbance of memory in which reality and fantasy are confused. It is observed in dreams and in certain types of schizophrenia and organic brain syndromes. *See also* Confabulation, Déjà entendu, Déjà vu, Fausse reconnaissance, Jamais vu, Retrospective falsification.

Paranoid delusion. *See* Delusion.

Parent. In transactional analysis, an ego state borrowed from a parental figure. It is also known as exteropsychic function.

Parental rejection. Denial of affection and attention to a child by one or both parents. The child in turn develops great affect hunger and hostility, which is directed either outwardly in the form of tantrums, etc., or inwardly toward himself in the form of allergies, etc.

Parkinsonism. Syndrome characterized by rhythmical muscular tremors known as pill rolling accompanied by spasticity and rigidity of movement, propulsive gait, droopy posture, and masklike facies. It is usually seen in later life as a result of arteriosclerotic changes in the basal ganglia.

Parkinsonismlike effect. Symptom that is a frequent side effect of antipsychotic drugs. Typical symptoms are motor retardation, muscular rigidity, alterations of posture, tremor, and autonomic nervous system disturbances. *See also* Phenothiazine derivative.

Partial insanity. *See* Monomania.

Passive therapist. Type of therapist who remains inactive but whose presence serves as a stimulus for the patient in the group or individual treatment setting. *See also* Active therapist, Leaderless therapeutic group, Nondirective approach.

Pastime. In transactional analysis, semistereotyped set of transactions dealing with a certain topic. Unlike Berne's term game, a pastime has no ulterior motive and no psychological payoff.

Patient peers. *See* Co-patients.

Patty-cake exercise. An encounter group technique that involves the palm-to-palm contact made by children in the game of patty-cake. This type of contact is familiar and does not usually arouse much anxiety in participants, yet it allows people to bypass verbal defenses in getting to know each other. After this exercise, the group members discuss their reactions. Also called Hand-dance.

Pecking order. Sequence of hierarchy or authority in an organization or social group. *See also* Hierarchical vector.

Peer co-therapist. Therapist who is equal in status to the other therapist treating a group and who relates to him on an equal level.

Peer-group phenomenon. Interaction or reaction of a person with a group of equals. These phenomena include activities he does within the group that he would probably not do individually outside the group.

Peer identification. Unconscious process that occurs in a group when one member incorporates within himself the qualities and attributes of another member. It usually occurs in members with low self-esteem who would like to feel at one with members who have improved.

Peer vector. *See* Horizontal vector.

Perception. Mental process by which data—intellectual, sensory, and emotional—are organized meaningfully. Through perception, a person makes sense out of the many stimuli that bombard him. It is one of the many ego functions. Therapy groups and T-groups aim to expand and alter perception in ways conducive to the development of the potential of each participant. *See also* Agnosia, Apperception, Clouding of consciousness, Ego, Hallucination, Hysterical anesthesia, Memory.

Perceptual expansion. Development of one's ability to recognize and interpret the meaning of sensory stimuli through associations with past experiences with similar stimuli. Perceptual expansion through the relaxation of defenses is one of the goals in both individual and group therapy.

Permission. In transactional analysis, a therapeutic transaction designed to permanently neutralize the parental injunctions.

Personal growth laboratory. A sensitivity training laboratory in which the primary emphasis is on each participant's potentialities for creativity, empathy, and leadership. In such a laboratory the facilitator encourages most modalities of experience and expression—such as art, sensory stimulation, and intellectual, emotional, written, oral, verbal, and nonverbal expression. *See also* National Training Laboratories.

Personality. Habitual configuration of behavior of a person, reflecting his physical and mental activities, attitudes, and interests and corresponding to the sum total of his adjustment to life.

Personality disorder. Mental disorder characterized by maladaptive patterns of adjustment to life. There is no subjective anxiety, as seen in neurosis, and no disturbance in the capacity to recognize reality, as seen in psychosis. The types of personality disorders include passive-aggressive, antisocial, schizoid, hysterical, paranoid, cyclothymic, explosive, obsessive-compulsive, asthenic, and inadequate.

Perversion. Deviation from the expected norm. In psychiatry it commonly signifies sexual perversion. *See also* Sexual deviation.

Perverted logic. *See* Evasion.

Peter Principle. Theory that man tends to advance to his level of incompetence. The idea was popularized in a book of the same name by Laurence J. Peter and Raymond Hull.

Phallic overbearance. Domination of another person by aggressive means. It is generally associated with masculinity in its negative aspects.

Phallic phase. The third stage in psychosexual development. It occurs when the child is from two to six years of age. During this period, the child's interest, curiosity, and pleasurable experiences are centered around the penis in boys and the clitoris in girls. *See also* Anal phase, Genital phase, Infantile sexuality, Latency phase, Oral phase.

Phantasy. *See* Fantasy.

Phantom limb. *See* Kinesthetic hallucination.

Phenothiazine derivative. Compound derived from phenothiazine. It is particularly known for its antipsychotic property. As a class, the phenothiazine derivatives are among the most widely used drugs in medical practice, particularly in psychiatry. Chlorpromazine, triflupromazine, fluphenazine, perphenazine, and thioridazine are some examples of phenothiazine derivatives. *See also* Anticholinergic effect, Autonomic side effect, Electrocardiographic effect, Mydriasis, Paralytic ileus, Parkinsonismlike effect.

Phobia. Pathological fear associated with some specific type of stimulus or situation. *See also* Acrophobia, Agoraphobia, Algophobia, Claustrophobia, Xenophobia, Zoophobia.

Phyloanalysis. A means of investigating disorders of human behavior, both individual and collective, resulting from impaired tensional processes that affected the organism's internal reaction as a whole. Trigant Burrow adopted the word to replace his earlier term, group analysis, which he first used in 1927 to describe the social participation of many persons in their common analysis. Because group analysis was confused with group psychotherapy of the analytic type, Burrow changed his nomenclature to phyloanalysis.

Pillow-beating. A technique used in encounter groups to elicit pent-up rage in a group member who needs to release it in a physical way. The member beats the pillow and yells angry words until he gets tired. The acceptance of his anger by the group is considered therapeutic. After this exercise, the group members discuss their reactions. *See also* Mattress-pounding.

Placebo. Inert substance prepared to resemble the active drug being tested in experimental research. It is sometimes used in clinical practice for a psychotherapeutic effect. The response to the placebo may represent the response due to the psychological effect of taking a pill and not to any pharmacological property.

Play therapy. Type of therapy used with children, usually of preschool and early latency ages. The patient reveals his problems on a fantasy level with dolls, clay, and other toys. The therapist intervenes opportunely with helpful explanations about the patient's responses and behavior in language geared to the child's comprehension. *See also* Activity group therapy.

Political therapist. A therapist who gives strong weight to the personalities of those above him as far as they impinge on his professional activities. He pays particular attention to the personal and historical aspects of authority. *See also* Authority principle, Hierarchical vector, Procedural therapist.

Popular mind. The primitive, fickle, suggestible, impulsive, uncritical type of mind that Le Bon felt was characteristic of the mass. He was referring to the unorganized crowds who lack leadership.

Postsession. *See* After-session.

Power phase. Second stage in group treatment. In this phase members start expressing anger and hostility—usually directed at the leader, sometimes directed at other members—in an attempt to achieve individuation and autonomy. *See also* Affection phase, Inclusion phase.

Pratt, Joseph H. Boston physician born in 1842 generally considered to be the first pioneer in group psychotherapy in America. He is known for his work with tuberculous patients (1900–1906). He formed discussion groups to deal with the physical aspects of tuberculosis. Later, these groups began discussing the emotional problems that stemmed from the illness. *See also* Class method.

Preconscious. In psychoanalysis, one of the three divisions of the psyche according to Freud's topographical psychology. The preconscious includes all ideas, thoughts, past experiences, and other memory impressions that can be consciously recalled with effort. *See also* Conscious, Unconscious.

Prefrontal lobotomy. *See* Lobotomy.

Prejudice. Adverse judgment or opinion formed without factual knowledge. Elements of irrational suspicion or hatred are often involved, as in racial prejudice.

Premeeting. Group meeting of patients without the therapist. It is held immediately before the regular therapist-led session and is also referred to as warming-up session and presession. *See also* After-session, Alternate session.

Preoccupation of thought. *See* Trend of thought.

Pressure cooker. Slang phrase to describe the high degree of group involvement and emotional pitch sought by certain intensive groups, such as marathon groups.

Primal father. Hypothetical head of the tribe. He is depicted by Freud in *Totem and Taboo* as slain by his sons, who subsequently devour him in a cannibalistic rite. Later, he is promoted to a god. The son who murders him is the prototype of the tragic hero, and the memory of the crime is perpetuated in the conscience of the individual and of the culture.

Primal scene. In psychoanalysis, the real or fantasied observation by a child of sexual intercourse, particularly between his parents.

Primary process. In psychoanalysis, the mental process directly related to the functions of the id and characteristic of unconscious mental activity. The primary process is marked by unorganized, illogical thinking and by the tendency to seek immediate discharge and gratification of instinctual demands. *See also* Secondary process.

Probe. An encounter technique designed for a specific purpose—for instance, to determine motivation for admission to treatment. The technique is commonly used in such drug rehabilitation centers as Odyssey House.

Procedural therapist. A therapist who places the most weight on the written word, on formal rules and regulations, and on the hierarchical system. *See also* Authority principle, Political therapist.

Process-centered group. Group whose main purpose is to study the dynamics of the group itself—how it operates and through what stages it progresses. Such groups often ask the question, "What's going on here?" rather than the encounter group question, "What are you experiencing or feeling?" *See also* Group analytic psychotherapy, Group-centered psychotherapy.

Program. In transactional analysis, the teaching by one of the parents of how best to comply with the script injunction.

Projection. Unconscious defense mechanism in which a person attributes to another the ideas, thoughts, feelings, and impulses that are part of his inner perceptions but that are unacceptable to him. Projection protects the person from anxiety arising from an inner conflict. By externalizing whatever is unacceptable, the person deals with it as a situation apart from himself. *See also* Blind spot, Future projection.

Projective method. Group treatment procedure that uses the spontaneous creative work of the patients. For example, group members make and analyze drawings, which are often expressions of their underlying emotional problems.

Protagonist. In psychodrama, the patient who is the focal point of a psychodramatic session. He is asked to be himself, to portray his own private world on the stage.

Pseudoauthenticity. False or copied expression of thoughts and feelings.

Pseudocollusion. Sense of closeness, relationship, or cooperation that is not real but is based on transference.

Psychic determinism. Freudian adaptation of the concept of causality. It states that all phenomena or events have antecedent causes that operate on an unconscious level, beyond the control of the person involved.

Psychoactive drug. Drug that alters thoughts, feelings, or perceptions. Such a drug may help a person in either individual or group therapy overcome depression, anxiety, or rigidity of thought and behavior while he learns new methods of perceiving and responding.

Psychoanalysis. Freud's method of psychic investigation and form of psychotherapy. As a technique for exploring the mental processes, psychoanalysis includes the use of free association and the analysis and interpretation of dreams, resistances, and transferences. As a form of psychotherapy, it uses the investigative technique, guided by Freud's libido and instinct theories and by ego psychology, to gain insight into a person's unconscious motivations, conflicts, and symbols and thus to effect a change in his maladaptive behavior. Several schools of thought are loosely referred to as psychoanalytic at present. Psychoanalysis is also known as analysis in depth.

Psychoanalytically oriented group psychotherapy. *See* Psychoanalytic group psychotherapy.

Psychoanalytic group psychotherapy. A major method of group psychotherapy, pioneered by Alexander Wolf and based on the operational principles of individual psychoanalytic therapy. Analysis and interpretation of a patient's transferences, resistances, and defenses are modified to take place in a group setting. Although strictly designating treatment structured to produce significant character change, the term encompasses the same approach in groups conducted at more superficial levels for lesser goals. *See also* Collective family transference neurosis, Discussion model of group psychotherapy, Verbal-deep approach.

Psychoanalytic treatment. *See* Psychoanalysis.

Psychodrama. Psychotherapy method originated by J. L. Moreno in which personality make-up, interpersonal relationships, conflicts, and emotional problems are explored by means of dramatic methods. The therapeutic dramatization of emotional problems includes: (1) protagonist or patient, the person who presents and acts out his emotional problems with the help of (2) auxiliary egos, persons trained to act and dramatize the different aspects of the patient that are called for in a particular scene in order to help him express his feelings, and (3) director, leader, or therapist, the person who guides those involved in the drama for a fruitful and therapeutic session. *See also* Actional-deep approach, Analytic psychodrama, Concretization of living, Didactic psychodrama, Hallucinatory psychodrama, Hypnodrama, Improvisation, Maximal expression, Mirror, Re-enactment, Regressive-reconstructive approach, Role-playing, Role reversal, Self-realization.

Psychodramatic director. Leader of a psychodrama session. The director has three functions: producer, therapist, and analyst. As producer, he turns every clue the patient offers into dramatic action. As therapist, he attacks and shocks the patient at times, laughs and jokes with him at times, and becomes indirect and passive at times. As analyst, he interprets and elicits responses from the audience.

Psychodramatic shock. *See* Hallucinatory psychodrama.

Psychodynamics. Science of the mind, its mental processes, and affective components that influence human behavior and motivations. *See also* Group dynamics, Infantile dynamics.

Psychological defense system. *See* Defense mechanism.

Psychological procedure. Any technique intended to alter a person's attitude toward and perception of himself and others. *See also* Group psychotherapy, Psychoanalysis, Psychotherapy.

Psychomotor stimulant. Drug that arouses the patient through its central excitatory and analeptic properties. Amphetamine and methylphenidate are drugs in this class.

Psychopathology. Branch of science that deals with morbidity of the mind.

Psychophysiological disorder. Mental disorder characterized by physical symptoms of psychic origin. It usually involves a single organ system innervated by the autonomic nervous system. The physiological and organic changes stem from a sustained emotional disturbance.

Psychosexual development. Maturation and development of the psychic phase of sexuality from birth to adult life. Its phases are oral, anal, phallic, latency, and genital. *See also* Identification with the aggressor, Infantile sexuality.

Psychosis. Mental disorder in which a person's mental capacity, affective response, and capacity to recognize reality, communicate, and relate to others are impaired enough to interfere with his capacity to deal with the ordinary demands of life. The psychoses are subdivided into two major classifications according to their origin—psychoses associated with organic brain syndromes and functional psychoses.

Psychosomatic illness. *See* Psychophysiological disorder.

Psychosurgery. *See* Lobotomy.

Psychotherapy. Form of treatment for mental illness and behavioral disturbances in which a trained person establishes a professional contract with the patient and through definite therapeutic communication, both verbal and nonverbal, attempts to alleviate the emotional disturbance, reverse or change maladaptive patterns of behavior, and encourage personality growth and development. Psychotherapy is distinguished from such other forms of psychiatric treatment as the use of drugs, surgery, electric shock treatment, and insulin coma treatment. *See also* Growth psychotherapy, Individual therapy, Psychoanalysis.

Psychotomimetic drug. Drug that produces psychic and behavioral changes that resemble psychosis. Unlike other drugs that can produce organic psychosis as a reaction, a psychotomimetic drug does not produce overt memory impairment. It is also known as a hallucinogenic drug. Lysergic acid diethylamide (LSD), tetrahydrocannabinol, and mescaline are examples of psychotomimetic drugs.

Psychotropic drug. Drug that affects psychic function and behavior. Also known as a phrenotropic drug, it may be classified as an antipsychotic drug, antidepressant drug, antimanic drug, antianxiety drug, or hallucinogenic drug. *See also* Agranulocytosis, Orthostatic hypotension.

Public self. The behavior, feelings, and motivations of a person known both to himself and to others. It is a quadrant of the Johari Window, a diagrammatic concept of human behavior. *See also* Blind self, Hidden self, Undeveloped potential.

Quadràngular therapy. A type of marital therapy that involves four people: the married pair and each spouse's therapist. *See also* Collaborative therapy, Combined therapy, Concurrent therapy, Conjoint therapy, Family therapy, Group marital therapy, Marriage therapy, Square interview.

Rank, Otto (1884–1939). Austrian psychoanalyst. He was one of Freud's earliest followers and the long-time secretary and recorder of the minutes of the Vienna Psychoanalytic Society. He wrote such fundamental works as *The Myth of the Birth of the Hero*. He split with Freud on the significance of the birth trauma, which he used as a basis of brief psychotherapy.

Rapport. Conscious, harmonious accord that usually reflects a good relationship between two persons. In a group, rapport is the presence of mutual responsiveness, as evidenced by spontaneous and sympathetic reaction to each other's needs, sentiments, and attitudes. *See also* Countertransference, Transference.

Rap session. *See* Bull session.

Rationalization. An unconscious defense mechanism in which an irrational behavior, motive, or feeling is made to appear reasonable. Ernest Jones introduced the term.

Reaction formation. An unconscious defense mechanism in which a person develops a socialized attitude or interest that is the direct antithesis of some infantile wish or impulse in the

unconscious. One of the earliest and most unstable defense mechanisms, it is closely related to repression; both are defenses against impulses or urges that are unacceptable to the ego.

Reality. The totality of objective things and factual events. Reality includes everything that is perceived by a person's special senses and is validated by other people.

Reality-testing. Fundamental ego function that consists of the objective evaluation and judgment of the world outside the self. By interacting with his animate and inanimate environment, a person tests its real nature as well as his own relation to it. How the person evaluates reality and his attitudes toward it are determined by early experiences with the significant persons in his life. *See also* Ego.

Recall. Process of remembering thoughts, words, and actions of a past event in an attempt to recapture what actually happened. It is part of a complex mental function known as memory. *See also* Amnesia, Hypermnesia.

Recathexis. In transactional analysis, the experiencing of different ego states.

Recognition. *See* Memory.

Reconstructive psychotherapy. A form of therapy that seeks not only to alleviate symptoms but to produce alterations in maladaptive character structures and to expedite new adaptive potentials. This aim is achieved by bringing into consciousness an awareness of and insight into conflicts, fears, inhibitions, and their derivatives. *See also* Psychoanalysis.

Recorder. Person who takes notes during the group or individual therapy session. Also referred to as the recorder-observer, he generally does not participate in therapy. *See also* Observer.

Re-enactment. In psychodrama, the acting out of a past experience as if it were happening in the present so that a person can feel, perceive, and act as he did the first time.

Registration. *See* Memory.

Regression. Unconscious defense mechanism in which a person undergoes a partial or total return to earlier patterns of adaptation. Regression is observed in many psychiatric conditions, particularly schizophrenia.

Regressive-reconstructive approach. A psychotherapeutic procedure in which regression is made an integral element of the treatment process. The original traumatic situation is reproduced to gain new insight and to effect significant personality change and emotional maturation. *See also* Psychoanalysis, Reconstructive psychotherapy.

Reik, Theodor (1888–1969). Psychoanalyst and early follower of Freud, who considered him one of his most brilliant pupils. Freud's book, *The Question of Lay Analysis* was written to defend Reik's ability to practice psychoanalysis without medical training. Reik made many valuable contributions to psychoanalysis on the subjects of religion, masochism, and technique. *See also* Third ear.

Relatedness. Sense of sympathy and empathy with regard to others; sense of oneness with others. It is the opposite of isolation and alienation.

Reparenting. A technique evolved in transactional analysis for the treatment of schizophrenia. The patient is first regressed to a Child ego state, and then missing Parent transactions are supplied and contaminations corrected.

Repeater. Group member who has had experience in another group.

Repetitive pattern. Continual attitude or mode of behavior characteristic of a person and performed mechanically or unconsciously.

Repression. An unconscious defense mechanism in which a person removes from consciousness those ideas, impulses, and affects that are unacceptable to him. A term introduced by Freud, it is important in both normal psychological development and in neurotic and psychotic symptom formation. Freud recognized two kinds of repression: (1) repression proper—the repressed material was once in the conscious domain; (2) primal repression—the repressed material was never in the conscious realm. *See also* Suppression.

Repressive-inspirational group psychotherapy. A type of group therapy in which discussion is intended to bolster patients' morale and help them avoid undesired feelings. It is used primarily with large groups of seriously regressed patients in institutional settings.

Reserpine. An alkaloid extracted from the root of the *Rauwolfia serpentina* plant. It is used primarily as an antihypertensive agent. It was formerly used as an antipsychotic agent because of its sedative effect.

Residential treatment facility. A center where the patient lives and receives treatment appropriate for his particular needs. A children's residential treatment facility ideally furnishes both educational and therapeutic experiences for the emotionally disturbed child.

Resistance. A conscious or unconscious opposition to the uncovering of the unconscious. Resistance is linked to underlying psychological defense mechanisms against impulses from the id that are threatening to the ego. *See also* Group resistance.

Resonance. Unconscious response determined by early life experiences. In a group, a member may respond by fantasizing at a particular level of psychosexual development when another member functions regressively at that level. The unconscious sounding board is constructed in the first five years of life. *See also* Focal-conflict theory.

Retardation. Slowness of development or progress. In psychiatry there are two types, mental retardation and psychomotor retardation. Mental retardation refers to slowness or arrest of intellectual maturation. Psychomotor retardation refers to slowness or slackened psychic activity or motor activity or both; it is observed in pathological depression.

Retention. *See* Memory.

Retrospective falsification. Recollection of false memory. *See also* Paramnesia.

Review session. Meeting in which each member reviews with the group his goals and progress in treatment. It is a technique used in structured interactional group psychotherapy.

Ritual. Automatic activity of psychogenic or cultural origin. *See also* Group ritual.

Role. Pattern of behavior that a person takes. It has its roots in childhood and is influenced by significant people with whom the person had primary relationships. When the behavior pattern conforms with the expectations and demands of other people, it is said to be a complementary role. If it does not conform with the demands and expectation of others, it is known as noncomplementary role. *See also* Identification, Injunction, Therapeutic role.

Role-divided therapy. Therapeutic arrangement in a co-therapy situation when each therapist takes on a specific function in treatment. For example, one therapist may take the role of a provocateur, while the other takes the role of a passive observer and interpreter. *See also* Splitting situation.

Role limit. Boundary placed on the therapist or the patient by virtue of his conscious position in the therapy group. The patient plays the patient, and the therapist plays the therapist; there is no reversal of roles.

Role model. In a therapeutic community or methadone program, an ex-addict who, because of his successful adjustment and similarity of experience with the patient population, becomes a source of positive identification and a tangible proof of success. *See also* Ego model.

Role-playing. Psychodrama technique in which a person is trained to function more effectively in his reality roles—such as employer, employee, student, and instructor. In the therapeutic setting of psychodrama, the protagonist is free to try and to fail in his role, for he is given the opportunity to try again until he finally learns new approaches to the situation he fears, approaches that he can then apply outside. *See also* Anti-repression device.

Role reversal. Technique used in psychodrama whereby an auxiliary ego plays the role of the patient, and the patient plays the role of the other person. Distortions of interpersonal perception are thereby brought to the surface, explored, and corrected.

Role-training. *See* Role-playing.

Roll and rock. An encounter group technique that is used to develop trust in a participant. A person stands, with eyes closed, in a tight circle of group members and is passed around (rolled) from member to member. Then he is placed on his back on the floor, gently lifted by the group members, and rocked back and forth. He is then put back on the floor. After this exercise, the group members discuss their reactions.

Rosander anti-Negro behavior scale. A scale that measures white attitudes toward blacks by asking respondents what their behavior would be in various hypothetical situations involving black participants. The scale can be of aid in determining the degree of prejudice held by whites toward blacks and the influence of a group experience on such prejudices. *See also* Ford negative personal contacts with Negroes scale, Ford negative personal contacts with whites scale, Kelley desegregation scale, Steckler anti-Negro scale, Steckler anti-white scale.

Rosenberg self-esteem scale. A scale designed to measure a person's opinion of himself. Use of this scale gives the therapist a means of evaluating the effect a group experience has on a member's self-esteem.

Saboteur. One who obstructs progress within a group, either deliberately or unconsciously.

Sadism. A sexual deviation in which sexual gratification is achieved by inflicting pain and humiliation on the partner. Donatien Alphonse François de Sade (1740–1814), a French writer, was the first person to describe this condition. *See also* Masochism, Sadomasochistic relationship.

Sadomasochistic relationship. Relationship in which the enjoyment of suffering by one person and the enjoyment of inflicting pain by the other person are important and complementary attractions in their on-going relationship. *See also* Masochism, Sadism.

Satyriasis. Morbid, insatiable sexual needs or desires in men. It may be caused by organic or psychiatric factors. *See also* Nymphomania.

Schilder, Paul (1886–1940). American neuropsychiatrist. He started the use of group psychotherapy at New York's Bellevue Hospital, combining social and psychoanalytic principles.

Schizophrenia. Mental disorder of psychotic level characterized by disturbances in thinking, mood, and behavior. The thinking disturbance is manifested by a distortion of reality, especially by delusions and hallucinations, accompanied by fragmentation of associations that results in incoherent speech. The mood disturbance is manifested by inappropriate affective responses. The behavior disturbance is manifested by ambivalence, apathetic withdrawal, and bizarre activity. Formerly known as dementia praecox, schizophrenia as a term was introduced by Eugen Bleuler. The causes of schizophrenia remain unknown. The types of schizophrenia include simple type, hebephrenic type, catatonic type, paranoid type, schizo-affective type, childhood type, residual type, latent type, acute schizophrenic episode, and chronic undifferentiated type.

Schreber case. One of Freud's cases. It involved the analysis in 1911 of Daniel Paul Shreber's autobiographical account, *Memoirs of a Neurotic,* published in 1903. Analysis of these memoirs permitted Freud to decipher the fundamental meaning of paranoid processes and ideas, especially the relationship between repressed homosexuality and projective defenses.

Screening. Initial patient evaluation that includes medical and psychiatric history, mental status evaluation, and diagnostic formulation to determine the patient's suitability for a particular treatment modality.

Script. In transactional analysis, a complex set of transactions that are adaptations of infantile responses and experiences. The script is recurrent and operates on an unconscious level. It is the mold on which a person's life adaptation is based. *See also* Hamartic script.

Script analysis. The analysis of a person's life adaption—that is, his injunctions, decisions, and life scripts—and the therapeutic process that helps reverse the maladaptive behavior. It is the last phase in transactional analysis. *See also* Game analysis, Structural analysis.

Script antithesis. In transactional analysis, a therapeutic transaction designed to avert temporarily a tragic event in a script. *See also* Script, Script matrix.

Script matrix. Diagram used in transactional analysis to represent two parents and an offspring. It is useful in representing the genesis of life scripts. *See also* Script, Script antithesis.

Secondary process. In psychoanalysis, the mental process directly related to the functions of the ego and characteristic of conscious and preconscious mental activities. The secondary process is marked by logical thinking and by the tendency to delay gratification by regulation of discharge of instinctual demands. *See also* Primary process.

Sedative. Drug that produces a calming or relaxing effect through central nervous system depression. Some drugs with sedative properties are barbiturates, chloral hydrate, paraldehyde, and bromide.

Selective inattention. An aspect of attentiveness in which a person blocks out those areas that generate anxiety.

Self-analysis. Investigation of one's own psychic components. It plays a part in all analysis, although to a limited extent, since few are capable of sustaining independent and detached attitudes for it to be therapeutic.

Self-awareness. Sense of knowing what one is experiencing. For example, realizing that one has just responded with anger to another group member as a substitute for the anxiety felt when he attacked a vital part of one's self concept. Self-awareness is a major goal of all therapy, individual and group.

Self-discovery. In psychoanalysis, the freeing of the repressed ego in a person who has been brought up to submit to the wishes of the significant others around him.

Self-presentation. Psychodrama technique in which the patient plays the role of himself and of related persons (father, mother, brother, etc.) as he perceives them in a completely subjective manner.

Self-realization. Psychodrama technique in which the protagonist enacts, with the aid of a few auxiliary egos, the plan of his life, no matter how remote it may be from his present situation. For instance, an accountant who has been taking singing lessons, hoping to try out for a musical comedy part in summer stock, and planning to make the theatre his life's work can explore the effects of success in this venture and of possible failure and return to his old livelihood.

Sensation. Feeling or impression when the sensory nerve endings of any of the six senses—taste, touch, smell, sight, kinesthesia, and sound—are stimulated.

Sensitivity training group. Group in which members seek to develop self-awareness and an understanding of group processes rather than gain relief from an emotional disturbance. *See also* Encounter group, Personal growth laboratory, T-group.

Sensorium. Theoretical sensory center located in the brain that is involved with a person's awareness about his surroundings. In psychiatry, it is often referred to as consciousness.

Sensory-experiential group. An encounter group that is primarily concerned with the emotional and physical interaction of the participants. The experience itself, not the examination of the group process, is considered the *raison d'être* for the group.

Serotonin. A monoamine that is believed to be a neurohumoral transmitter. It is found in the serum and, in high concentrations, in the hypothalamus of the brain. Recent pharmacological investigations link depression to disorders in the metabolism of serotonin and other biogenic amines, such as norepinephrine.

Session leader. *See* Facilitator.

Sexual deviation. Mental disorder characterized by sexual interests and behavior other than what is culturally accepted. Sexual deviation includes sexual interest in objects other than a person of the opposite sex, such as homosexuality or bestiality; bizarre sexual practices, such as necrophilia; and other sexual activities that are not accompanied by copulation. *See also* Bestiality, Exhibitionism, Homosexuality, Masochism, Sadism.

Sexual drive. One of the two primal instincts (the other is the aggressive drive) according to Freud's dual-instinct theory of 1920. It is also known as eros and life instinct. Its main goal is to preserve and maintain life. It operates under the influence of the pleasure-unpleasure principle. *See also* Aggressive drive, Libido theory.

Shifting attention. A characteristic of group therapy in which the focus changes from one patient to another so that no one patient remains continuously in the spotlight. It is also known as alternating scrutiny. *See also* Structured interactional group psychotherapy.

Shock treatment. A form of psychiatric treatment with a chemical substance (ingested, inhaled, or injected) or sufficient electric current to produce a convulsive seizure and unconsciousness. It is used in certain types of schizophrenia

and mood disorders. Shock treatment's mechanism of action is still unknown.

Sibling rivalry. Competition among children for the attention, affection, and esteem of their parents. The children's jealousy is accompanied by hatred and death wishes toward each other. The rivalry need not be limited to actual siblings; it is a factor in both normal and abnormal competitiveness throughout life.

Slavson, S. R. (1890–   ). American theoretician who pioneered in group psychotherapy based on psychoanalytic principles. In his work with children, from which he derived most of his concepts, he introduced and developed activity group therapy. *See also* Collective experience.

Sleep. A temporary physiological state of unconsciousness characterized by a reversible cessation of the person's waking sensorimotor activity. A biological need, sleep recurs periodically to rest the whole body and to regenerate neuromuscular tissue. *See also* Dream.

Social adaptation. Adjustment to the whole complex of interpersonal relationships; the ability to live and express oneself in accordance with society's restrictions and cultural demands. *See also* Adaptational approach.

Social configuration. Arrangement of interpersonal interactions. *See also* Hierarchical vector, Horizontal vector.

Social instinct. *See* Herd instinct.

Socialization. Process of learning interpersonal and interactional skills according to and in conformity with one's society. In a group therapy setting, it includes a member's way of participating both mentally and physically in the group. *See also* Interpersonal skill.

Social network therapy. A type of group therapy in which the therapist assembles all the persons—relatives, friends, social relations, work relations—who have emotional or functional significance in the patient's life. Some or all of the social network may be assembled at any given time. *See also* Extended family therapy, Visitor.

Social psychiatry. Branch of psychiatry interested in ecological, sociological, and cultural variables that engender, intensify, or complicate maladaptive patterns of behavior and their treatment.

Social therapy. A rehabilitative form of therapy with psychiatric patients. The aim is to improve social functioning. Occupational therapy, therapeutic community, recreational therapy, milieu therapy, and attitude therapy are forms of social therapy.

Sociogram. Diagrammatic portrayal of choices, rejections, and indifferences of a number of persons involved in a life situation.

Sociometric distance. The measurable degree of perception one person has for another. It can be hypothesized that the greater the sociometric distance between persons, the more inaccurate will be their social evaluation of their relationship.

Sociometric feedback. Information that people give each other about how much closeness or distance they desire between them. It is a measure of how social one would like to be with another. An example of sociometric feedback would be the answer by a group member to the question, "With what three members of this group would you prefer to spend six months on a desert island?"

Sociometrist. Social investigator engaged in measuring the interpersonal relations and social structures in a community.

Soliloquy. *See* Therapeutic soliloquy.

Somnambulism. Sleepwalking; motor activity during sleep. It is commonly seen in children. In adults, it is observed in persons with schizoid personality disorders and certain types of schizophrenia.

Splitting situation. Condition in a co-therapy group. A patient is often unable to express opposite feelings toward one therapist. The splitting situation allows him to express contrasting feelings—positive-love feeling and negative-hostile feeling—by directing one feeling at one co-therapist and the opposite feeling at the other cotherapist. *See also* Role-divided therapy.

Splitting transference. Breaking of an irrational feeling or attitude into its component parts, which are then assigned to different persons. For example, ambivalence toward a mother may be expressed in a group by reacting to one member as to a good mother and reacting to another member as to a bad mother.

Square interview. Occasional session in marriage therapy in which both spouses and each spouse's therapist are present. The therapists and sometimes the patients are able to observe, experience, and respond to the transactional dynamics among the four of them, thus encouraging a common viewpoint by all four people involved in marital therapy. *See also* Collaborative therapy, Combined therapy, Concurrent therapy, Conjoint therapy, Group marital therapy, Marriage therapy, Quadrangular therapy.

Square situation. *See* Quadrangular therapy, Square interview.

Squeaky wheel. Person who is continually calling attention to himself. Because of his style of interacting, he is likely to get more than his share of a group's effort and energy.

Status value. Worth of a person in terms of such criteria as income, social prestige, intelligence, and education. It is considered an important parameter of one's position in the society.

Steckler anti-Negro scale. A scale designed to measure the attitude of Negroes toward Negroes. It can be of use in ascertaining the degree of prejudice blacks have against their own race and in evaluating the corrective efficacy of group experience. *See also* Ford negative personal contacts with Negroes scale, Ford negative personal contacts with whites scale, Kelley desegregation scale, Rosander anti-Negro behavior scale.

Steckler anti-white scale. A scale designed to measure the attitudes of Negroes toward whites. It can be used to ascertain the amount of prejudice blacks have against whites and to evaluate the influence of a group experience. *See also* Ford negative personal contacts with Negroes scale, Ford negative personal contacts with whites scale, Kelley desegregation scale.

Stegreiftheater. *See* Theatre of Spontaneity.

Stekel, Wilhelm (1868–1940). Viennese psychoanalyst. He suggested the formation of the first Freudian group, the Wednesday Evening Society, which later became the Vienna Psychoanalytic Society. A man given to intuition rather than to systematic research, his insight into dreams proved stimulating and added to the knowledge of symbols. Nevertheless, his superficial wild analysis proved incompatible with the Freudian school. He introduced the word thanatos to signify death wish.

Stereotypy. Continuous repetition of speech or physical activities. It is observed in cases of catatonic schizophrenia.

Stimulant. Drug that affects one or more organ systems to produce an exciting or arousing effect, increase physical activity and vivacity, and promote a sense of well-being. There are, for example, central nervous system stimulants, cardiac stimulants, respiratory stimulants, and psychomotor stimulants.

Stress immunity. Failure to react to emotional stress.

Stroke. In transactional analysis, a unit of human recognition. Early in life, strokes must involve physical contact; later in life, strokes can be symbolic—such as, "Glad to see you!"

Structural analysis. Analysis of the personality into its constituent ego states. The goal of structural analysis is to establish and maintain the predominance of reality-testing ego states, free from contamination. It is considered the first phase of transactional analysis. *See also* Contamination, Ego state, Game analysis, Ogre, Script analysis, Transactional analysis.

Structured interactional group psychotherapy. A type of group psychotherapy, developed by Harold Kaplan and Benjamin Sadock, in which the therapist provides a structural matrix for the group's interactions. The important part of the structure is that a different member of the group is the focus of the interaction in each session. *See also* Forced interaction, Go-around, Up.

Studies on Hysteria. Title of a book by Josef Breuer and Sigmund Freud. Published in 1895, it described the cathartic method of treatment and the beginnings of psychoanalysis. It demonstrated the psychological origins of hysterical symptoms and the possibility of effecting a cure through psychotherapy.

Stupor. Disturbance of consciousness in which the patient is nonreactive to and unaware of his surroundings. Organically, it is synonymous with unconsciousness. In psychiatry, it is referred to as mutism and is commonly found in catatonia and psychotic depression.

Subjectivity. Qualitative appraisal and interpretation of an object or experience as influenced by one's own feelings and thinking.

Subject session. Group technique, used particularly in structured interactional group psychotherapy, in which a topic is introduced by the therapist or a group member and is then explored by the whole group.

Sublimation. An unconscious defense mechanism in which unacceptable instinctual drives are diverted into personally and socially acceptable channels. Unlike other defense mechanisms, sublimation offers some minimal gratification of the instinctual drive or impulse.

Substituting. Providing a nonverbal alternate for something a patient missed in his early life. Crossing the room to sit beside a group member who needs support is an example of substituting.

Substitution. An unconscious defense mechanism in which a person replaces an unacceptable wish, drive, emotion, or goal with one that is more acceptable.

Suggestibility. State of compliant responsiveness to an idea or influence. It is commonly observed among persons with hysterical traits.

Sullivan, Harry Stack (1892–1949). American psychiatrist. He is best known for his interpersonal theory of psychiatry. *See also* Consensual validation.

Summer session. In structured interactional group psychotherapy, regularly scheduled group session during the therapist's vacation.

Superego. One of the three component parts of the psychic apparatus. The other two are the ego and the id. Freud created the theoretical concept of the superego to describe the psychic functions that are expressed in moral attitudes, conscience, and a sense of guilt. The superego results from the internalization of the ethical standards of the society in which the person lives, and it develops by identification with the attitudes of his parents. It is mainly unconscious and is believed to develop as a reaction to the Oedipus complex. It has a protective and rewarding function, referred to as the ego ideal, and a critical and punishing function, which evokes the sense of guilt.

Support. *See* Mutual support.

Suppression. Conscious act of controlling and inhibiting an unacceptable impulse, emotion, or idea. Suppression is differentiated from repression in that the latter is an unconscious process.

Surplus reality. The intangible, invisible dimensions of intrapsychic and extrapsychic life. The term was coined by J. L. Moreno.

Survival. Game used in a professionally homogeneous group. It is designed to create awareness of one another's talents. An imaginary situation is created in which the members are no longer permitted to continue in their particular professions and must, as a group, find some other activity in which to work together meaningfully and profitably. *See also* Game, Hit-and-run game, Million-dollar game.

Symbolization. An unconscious defense mechanism whereby one idea or object comes to stand for another because of some common aspect or quality in both. Symbolization is based on similarity and association. The symbols formed protect the person from the anxiety that may be attached to the original idea or object. *See also* Defense mechanism.

Sympathomimetic drug. Drug that mimics the actions of the sympathetic nervous system. Examples of these drugs are amphetamine and epinephrine.

Sympathy. Sharing of another person's feelings, ideas, and experiences. As opposed to empathy, sympathy is not objective. *See also* Identification, Imitation.

Symptom formation. *See* Symptom substitution.

Symptom substitution. Unconscious psychic process in which a repressed impulse is indirectly released and manifested through a symptom. Such symptoms as obsession, compulsion, phobia, dissociation, anxiety, depression, hallucination, and delusion are examples of symptom substitution. It is also known as symptom formation.

Tachylogia. *See* Logorrhea.

Tactile hallucination. False sense of touch.

Tangentiality. Disturbance in the associative thought processes in which the patient is unable to express his idea. In contrast to circumstantiality, the digression in tangentiality is such that the central idea is not communicated. It is observed in schizophrenia and certain types of organic brain disorders. Tangentiality is also known as derailment. *See also* Circumstantiality.

Tardive oral dyskinesia. A syndrome characterized by involuntary movements of the lips and jaw and by other bizarre involuntary dystonic movements. It is an extrapyramidal effect occurring late in the course of antipsychotic drug therapy.

Target patient. Group member who is perceptively analyzed by another member. It is a term used in the process of going around in psychoanalytically oriented groups.

Task-oriented group. Group whose main energy is devoted to reaching a goal, finding a solution to a problem, or building a product. Distinguished from this type of group is the experiential group, which is mainly concerned with sharing whatever happens. *See also* Action group.

Tele. In psychodrama, an objective social process that strengthens association and promotes cohesiveness in groups. It is believed to function on the basis of transference and empathy.

Tension. An unpleasurable alteration of affect characterized by a strenuous increase in mental and physical activity.

Termination. Orderly conclusion of a group member's therapy or of the whole group's treatment as contrasted with a drop-out that is not advised by the therapist.

T-group (training group). A type of group that emphasizes training in self-awareness and group dynamics. *See also* Action group, Intervention laboratory, National Training Laboratories, Sensitivity training.

Thanatos. Death wish. *See also* Stekel, Wilhelm.

Theatre of Spontaneity (Stegreiftheater). Theatre in Vienna which improvised group processes and which was developed by J. L. Moreno, M.D.

Theoretical orientation. Alignment with a hypothetical point of view already espoused by a person or group.

Therapeutic agent. Anything—people and/or drugs—that causes healing in a maladaptive person. In group therapy, it refers mainly to people who help others.

Therapeutic alliance. Conscious relationship between therapist and patient in which each implicitly agrees that they need to work together by means of insight and control to help the patient with his conflicts. It involves a therapeutic splitting of the patient's ego into observing and experiencing parts. A good therapeutic alliance is especially necessary during phases of strong negative transference in order to keep the treatment going. It is as important in group as in dyadic psychotherapy. *See also* Working alliance.

Therapeutic atmosphere. All therapeutic, maturational, and growth-supporting agents—cultural, social, and medical.

Therapeutic community. Ward or hospital treatment setting that provides an effective environment for behavioral changes in patients through resocialization and rehabilitation.

Therapeutic crisis. Turning point in the treatment process. An example is acting out, which, depending on how it is dealt with, may or may not lead to a therapeutic change in the patient's behavior. *See also* Therapeutic impasse.

Therapeutic group. Group of patients joined together under the leadership of a therapist for the purpose of working together for psychotherapeutic ends—specifically, for the treatment of each patient's emotional disorders.

Therapeutic group analysis. *See* Group analytic psychotherapy.

Therapeutic impasse. Deadlock in the treatment process. Therapy is in a state of imminent failure when there is no further insight or awareness and sessions are reduced to routine meetings of patient and therapist. Unresolved resistances and transference and countertransference conflicts are among the common causes of this phenomenon. *See also* Therapeutic crisis.

Therapeutic role. Position in which one aims to treat, bring about an improvement, or provide alleviation of a distressing condition or state.

Therapeutic soliloquy. Psychodrama technique that involves a patient's portrayal—by side dialogues and side actions—of his hidden thoughts and feelings that parallel his overt thoughts and actions.

Therapeutic transaction. Interplay between therapist and patient or among group members that is intended to improve the patient.

Therapist surrogate. Group member who—by virtue of experience, intuition, or training—is able to be an effective group leader in the absence of or in concert with the group therapist. He is also known as a nuclear group member. *See also* Leaderless therapeutic group.

There-and-then. Past experience rather than immediate experience. *See also* Here-and-now.

Thinking. *See* Cognition.

Thinking compulsion. *See* Intellectualization.

Thinking through. The mental process that occurs in an attempt to understand one's own behavior and gain insight from it.

Third ear. Ability to make use of intuition, sensitivity, and awareness of subliminal cues to interpret clinical observations of individual and group patients. First introduced by the German philosopher Frederic Nietzsche, it was later used in analytic psychotherapy by Theodor Reik.

Thought deprivation. *See* Blocking.

Thought process disorder. A symptom of schizophrenia that involves the intellectual functions. It is manifested by irrelevance and incoherence of the patient's verbal productions. It ranges from simple blocking and mild circumstantiality to total loosening of associations, as in word salad.

Three-cornered therapy. *See* Co-therapy.

Three Essays on the Theory of Sexuality. Title of a book by Freud. Published in 1905, it applied the libido theory to the successive phases of sex instinct maturation in the infant, child, and adolescent. It made possible the integration of a vast diversity of clinical observations and promoted the direct observation of child development.

Tic. Involuntary, spasmodic, repetitive motor movement of a small segment of the body. Mainly psychogenic, it may be seen in certain cases of chronic encephalitis.

Timidity. Inability to assert oneself for fear of some fancied reprisal, even though there is no objective evidence of potential harm. In a therapy group, the timid person may make others fear the destructiveness of their normal aggression.

Tinnitus. Noises in one or both ears, such as ringing and whistling. It is an occasional side effect of some of the antidepressant drugs.

Tolerance. In group therapy, the willingness to put up with disordered behavior by co-patients in the group.

Too-tired-to-be-polite phenomenon. Phenomenon in a marathon group that stems from fatigue and results in the relaxation of the social facades of politeness. Some proponents of marathon groups have stressed the helpfulness of fatigue in breaking through the social games that participants play in the early stages of the group. *See also* Group marathon.

Totem and Taboo. Title of a book by Freud. Published in 1913, it applied his concepts to the data of anthropology. He was able to afford much insight into the meaning of tribal organizations and customs, especially by invoking the Oedipus complex and the characteristics of magical thought as he had discovered them from studies of the unconscious. *See also* Oedipus complex, Primal father.

Toucher. Someone who enjoys touching another person. When the touching is not of the clinging type, such a person in an encounter group usually helps inhibited people lose their anxiety about physical contact and closeness.

Traditional group therapy. Group therapy of a conventional type in which the role of the therapist is clearly delineated and the other participants are understood to be clients or patients who are attending the group meetings to overcome or resolve some definite emotional problems. *See also* Encounter group, Group psychotherapy, Sensitivity training.

Trainer. Professional leader or facilitator of a sensitivity training or T-group; teacher or supervisor of a person learning the science and practice of group therapy.

Training group. *See* T-group.

Tranquilizer. Psychotropic drug that induces tranquility by calming, soothing, quieting, or pacifying without clouding the conscious. The major tranquilizers are antipsychotic drugs, and the minor tranquilizers are antianxiety drugs.

Transaction. Interaction that arises when two or more persons have an encounter. In transactional analysis, it is considered the unit of social interaction. It involves a stimulus and a response. *See also* Complementarity of interaction, Forced interaction, Group stimulus, Structured interactional group psychotherapy, Therapeutic transaction.

Transactional analysis. A system introduced by Eric Berne that centers on the study of interactions going on in the treatment sessions. The system includes four components: (1) structural analysis of intrapsychic phenomena; (2) transactional analysis proper, the determination of the currently dominant ego state (Parent, Child, or Adult) of each participant; (3) game analysis, identification of the games played in their interactions and of the gratifications provided; and (4) script analysis, uncovering of the causes of the patient's emotional problems.

Transactional group psychotherapy. A system of therapy founded by Eric Berne. It is based on the analysis of interactions and on the understanding of patterns of transactions as they occur during treatment sessions. Social control is the main goal of therapy.

Transference. Unconscious phenomenon in which the feelings, attitudes, and wishes originally linked with important figures in one's early life are projected onto others who have come to represent them in current life. *See also* Countertransference, Lateral transference, Multiple transference, Rapport, Transference neurosis.

Transference neurosis. A phenomenon occurring in psychoanalysis in which the patient develops a strong emotional attachment to the therapist as a symbolized nuclear familial figure. The repetition and depth of this misperception or symbolization characterize it as a transference neurosis. In transference analysis, a major therapeutic technique in both individual and group therapy, the therapist uses transference to help the patient understand and gain insight into his behavior. *See also* Collective family transference neurosis, Dilution of transference.

Trend of thought. Thinking that centers on a particular idea associated with an affective tone.

Triad. Father, mother, and child relationship projectively experienced in group therapy. *See also* Nuclear family.

Trichotillomania. Morbid compulsion to pull out one's hair.

Tricyclic drug. Antidepressant drug believed by some to be more effective than monoamine oxidase inhibitors. The tricyclic drugs (imipramine and amitriptyline) are presently the most popular drugs in the treatment of pathological depression.

Tyramine. A sympathomimetic amine that is believed to influence the release of stored norepinephrine. Its degradation is inhibited by monoamine oxidase. The use of monoamine oxidase inhibitors in the treatment of depression prevents the degradation of tyramine. The ingestion of food containing tyramine, such as cheese, may cause a sympathomimetic effect, such as an increase in blood pressure, that could be fatal.

Unconscious. 1. (Noun) Structural division of the mind in which the psychic material—primitive drives, repressed desires, and memories—is not directly accessible to awareness. 2. (Adjective) In a state of insensibility, with absence of orientation and perception. *See also* Conscious, Preconscious.

Underachievement. Failure to reach a biopsychological, age-adequate level.

Underachiever. Person who manifestly does not function up to his capacity. The term usually refers to a bright child whose school test grades fall below expected levels.

Undeveloped potential. The behavior, feelings, and motivations of a person known neither to himself nor to others. It is the unknown quadrant of the Johari Window, a diagrammatic concept of human behavior. *See also* Blind self, Hidden self, Public self.

Undoing. An unconscious defense mechanism by which a person symbolically acts out in reverse something unacceptable that has already been done. A primitive defense mechanism, undoing is a form of magical expiatory action. Repetitive in nature, it is commonly observed in obsessive-compulsive neurosis.

Unisexual group. *See* Homogeneous group.

Universality. Total effect produced when all group members share specific symptoms or problems.

Up. The member who is the focus of discussion in group therapy, particularly in structured interactional group psychotherapy.

Up-tight. Slang term that describes defensive, rigid behavior on the part of a person whose values are threatened or who is afraid of becoming vulnerable and of experiencing painful emotions. Such a person frequently becomes a target for pressure in a therapy group.

Urine-testing. Thin-layer chromatography-testing for the presence of opiates, quinine, barbiturates, and amphetamines. Addict treatment programs use such testing to verify abstinence from illicit drug use.

Vector. An engineering term used to imply a pointed force being felt by the group. *See also* Hierarchical vector, Horizontal vector.

Verbal-deep approach. Procedure used in small groups in which communication is conducted exclusively through verbal means and is oriented to major goals. It is a technique used in analytical group therapy. *See also* Actional-deep approach, Actional-superficial approach, Verbal-superficial approach.

Verbal-superficial approach. Group therapy procedure in which language is the sole medium of communication and the therapeutic process is structured to attain limited objectives. It is a technique traditionally used in the treatment of large groups. *See also* Actional-deep approach, Actional-superficial approach, Verbal-deep approach.

Verbal technique. Any method of group or individual therapy in which words are used. The major part of most psychotherapy is verbal.

Verbigeration. Meaningless repetition of words or phrases. Also known as cataphasia, it is a morbid symptom seen in schizophrenia.

Verbomania. *See* Logorrhea.

Vertical vector. *See* Hierarchical vector.

Vienna Psychoanalytic Society. An outgrowth of the Wednesday Evening Society, an informal group of Freud's earliest followers. The new name was acquired and a reorganization took place in 1910, when the Society became a component of the newly formed International Psychoanalytical Society. Alfred Adler was president from 1910 to 1911, and Freud was president from 1911 until it was disbanded by the Nazis in 1938.

Visceral insight. *See* Insight.

Visitor. Guest who participates in discussions with patients in group therapy. In family therapy, members outside the nuclear family who are invited to the session are considered visitors. *See also* Extended family therapy, Social network therapy.

Visual hallucination. False visual perception.

Volubility. *See* Logorrhea.

Warming-up session. *See* Premeeting.

Waxy flexibility. *See* Cerea flexibilitas.

Wednesday Evening Society. A small group of Freud's followers who in 1902 started meeting with him informally on Wednesday evenings to receive instruction in psychoanalysis. As the society grew in numbers and importance, it evolved in 1910 into the Vienna Psychoanalytic Society.

West-Coast-style T-group. Sensitivity training or encounter group that is oriented toward the experience of union, intimacy, and personal awareness, with relative disregard for the study of group process. It is a style popular in California. *See also* East-Coast-style T-group.

Wild therapy. Group therapy conducted by a leader whose background may not be professional or whose theoretical formulations include widely deviant procedures when compared with conventional techniques.

Withdrawal. Act of retreating or going away from. Observed in schizophrenia and depression, it is characterized by a pathological retreat from interpersonal contact and social involvement, leading to self-preoccupation. In a group setting, this disorder creates a barrier for therapeutic progress.

Wittels, Fritz (1880–1950). Austrian psychoanalyst. One of Freud's early followers, he wrote a biography of him in 1924, during a period of estrangement, when he was under the influence of Wilhelm Stekel. Later, a reconciliation took place, and Freud conceded that some of Wittels' interpretations were probably correct.

Wolf-pack phenomenon. Group process in which a member or the therapist is the scapegoat.

Word salad. An incoherent mixture of words and phrases. This type of speech results from a disturbance in thinking. It is commonly observed in far-advanced states of schizophrenia.

Working alliance. Collaboration between the group as a whole and each patient who is willing to strive for health, growth, and maturation with the help of the therapist. *See also* Therapeutic alliance.

Working out. Stage in the treatment process in which the personal history and psychodynamics of a patient are discovered.

Working through. Process of obtaining more and more insight and personality changes through repeated and varied examination of a conflict or problem. The interactions between free association, resistance, interpretation, and working through constitute the fundamental facets of the analytic process.

Xenophobia. Fear of strangers.

Zoophobia. Fear of animals.

Contributors

Contributors

E. James Anthony, M.D.
Ittleson Professor of Child Psychiatry and Director, Division of Child Psychiatry, Washington University School of Medicine, St. Louis, Missouri; Training, Teaching and Supervising Psychoanalyst, Chicago Institute for Psychoanalysis; Professorial Lecturer, University of Chicago School of Medicine, Chicago, Illinois; Physician, Barnes and Allied Hospitals and The Jewish Hospital, St. Louis, Missouri.

George R. Bach, Ph.D.
Clinical Psychologist, Beverly Hills, California.

Robert S. Davidson, Ph.D.
Associate Clinical Professor of Medical Psychology, Department of Psychiatry and Human Behavior, University of California, Irvine California College of Medicine, Irvine, California.

Louis A. Gottschalk, M.D.
Professor of Psychiatry and Chairman of the Department of Psychiatry and Human Behavior, University of California, Irvine California College of Medicine, Ir-

vine, California; Program Director of Residency Training, Orange County Medical Center, Orange, California; Chief Consultant in Psychiatry, Veterans Administration Hospital, Long Beach, California.

Jacob L. Moreno, M.D.
Director, Moreno Institute; President, International Council of Group Psychotherapy, Beacon, New York; Founder of "Sociometry" and Group Psychotherapy, New York, New York.

Morris B. Parloff, Ph.D.
Chief, Section on Personality, Laboratory of Psychology, National Institute of Mental Health, Bethesda, Maryland.

Hyman Spotnitz, M.D., Med. Sc.D.
Author: The Couch and The Circle: A Story of Group Psychotherapy (Alfred A. Knopf, 1961); Modern Psychoanalysis of the Schizophrenic Patient (Grune & Stratton, 1969) New York, New York.

Frederick H. Stoller, Ph.D.
Senior Psychologist, Camarillo State Hospital, Camarillo, California.